SEASONS
of the HEART

SEASONS
of the HEART

*A Year of Devotions from One Generation
of Women to Another*

Compiled by
Donna Kelderman

Reformation Heritage Books
Grand Rapids, Michigan

Seasons of the Heart
© 2013 by Donna Kelderman

Reformation Heritage Books
2965 Leonard St. NE
Grand Rapids, MI 49525
616-977-0889 / Fax 616-285-3246
orders@heritagebooks.org
www.heritagebooks.org

Printed in the United States of America
19 20 21 22 23 24/10 9 8 7 6 5 4 3

ISBN: 978-1-60178-272-4

Library of Congress Control Number: 2013950316

For additional Reformed literature, request a free book list from Reformation Heritage Books at the above regular or e-mail address.

Dedicated to my mother-in-law,
Gertrude Kelderman,
who has been to me

a godly example,
a loving mother,
a bosom friend

Her children arise up, and call her blessed.
—PROVERBS 31:28

Preface

During a time of prolonged health problems, I read in Mary Winslow's *Heaven Opened*: "You belong not to yourself, but to Jesus. Say to Him, 'Lord, what wilt thou have me to do.'" After praying about this, the Lord wonderfully opened a door for me to embark on this project. Since I have often been fed with the writings of these dear sisters in the Lord who have gone before us, my prayer in compiling these devotional pieces is that their writings, such a rich treasury, would not be forgotten but that the Lord would use these devotionals to correct, admonish, comfort, cheer the downcast, and lead many to the foot of the cross.

This devotional has been drawn from the writings of twelve godly women from both Great Britain and America who lived from the sixteenth to the twentieth centuries. Several of these women never married and were faced with the challenges of singleness, while others were widowed at a young age and faced with raising a family alone. Like many today who suffer in various ways from bodily pain, several of these women suffered from chronic ailments. A few of them encountered severe persecution. Others among them suffered from various forms of depressions and trials. God used their trials to bring their strong wills into one with their Master's. In all these varied circumstances one truth remained constant: these women came to love the triune God and hate sin; they loved His Word and were daily immersed in it.

While several of the women whose writings are included here were published authors in their day, most of them recorded their thoughts in journals and letters, with a limited audience in mind. They often quoted Scripture, hymns, and other writers, probably from memory, but because they were not writing formally with publication in mind, they didn't provide Scripture references or other types of documentation. While we have lightly updated the language some of them used to make their writing more accessible to modern readers, we have not changed their informal tone by inserting Scripture references or footnotes to document their quotations of others.

I spent several months with these women through their writings, and have developed an even deeper appreciation for those who have taken care to preserve them for us. One of my hopes in compiling this devotional is that you, too, would be inspired by these daily excerpts, come to value these women's writings, and desire to read more of their work. With that in mind, I have provided brief biographical sketches of each of the twelve women at the end of the book with information about publications of their writing for those who would like to know more about them. May you be blessed, as I was, through these "teachers of good things" (Titus 2:3).

Acknowledgments

First and foremost I acknowledge the Lord, who not only planted the idea for this book but gave the daily strength and ability to complete it. I especially want to thank our dear children—Jeremy and Adriana, Rachael and Gerard, Micah, Nathan, Caleb, and Hannah—who were such a great encouragement to me. Each day they asked about the book's progress, always pressing me on, never complaining about my time being taken away from them. A special thanks to my sister, Linda den Hollander, who encouraged me to undertake this project and countless times gave me typesetting advice. Thanks to Jay Collier for overseeing this project through to completion. Thanks also to Amy Zevenbergen for the cover design and Annette Gysen, Gary den Hollander, and Dr. Joel Beeke, who spent hours editing and proofreading the manuscript. Lastly, my heartfelt thanks to my dear husband, Mark, who has constantly stood by my side and been a great support to me.

Christic the Physician of Souls

Deep are the wounds which sin hath made;
Where shall the sinner find a cure?
In vain, alas, is nature's aid,
The work exceeds all nature's pow'r.

Sin like a raging fever reigns,
With fatal strength in ev'ry part;
The dire contagion fills the veins,
And spreads its poison to the heart.

And can no sov'reign balm be found,
And is no kind physician nigh,
To ease the pain, and heal the wound,
Ere life and hope forever fly?

There is a great Physician near,
Look up, O fainting soul, and live;
See, in His heav'nly smiles, appear
Such ease as nature cannot give!

See, in the Savior's dying blood,
Life, health, and bliss, abundant flow.
'Tis only this dear, sacred flood
Can ease thy pain, and heal thy woe.

Sin throws in vain its pointed dart,
For here a sov'reign cure is found;
A cordial for the fainting heart,
A balm for ev'ry painful wound.

↲ ANNE STEELE

A New Year

LORD, make me to know mine end, and the measure of my days.
—PSALM 39:4

We are still journeying onward, but the question is *where.* Is it not a solemn thought? Should we not examine well our chart and the waymarks to see if we are going the right way? Would a wise person leave this an uncertainty? Again, I repeat the solemn truth: we are on an eventful journey, which must terminate in eternal life or eternal death. People who are blinded by the enemy will keep fully occupied with everything and anything but what would conduce to the soul's salvation. Beware of Satan's wiles! Turn in upon your own soul and ask yourself, "Am I ready to give my last account to the Judge of all the earth? Can I stand before His scrutinizing eye? Can He look upon me and see no spot, wrinkle, or any such thing? Can I appear in perfect holiness before the One who can only look upon sin with the greatest displeasure?"

Dear friend, let me entreat you to be honest with your own soul. Eternity—eternity with all its solemn realities—is before us. Flee at once to Jesus, the Savior of poor sinners, and do not leave Him until He speaks peace to your soul. Wrestle with Him for this mighty blessing; for I am sure that if you do, you will get it. Give no rest to your soul until you can say, "My soul is saved! Christ is my surety! Christ is mine, and I am Christ's!"

How busy is Satan when a poor sinner is securing a glorious inheritance! He will try every means to keep lost sinners from seeking Jesus, and they will never find Him until they do. Do not leave Jesus until He speaks peace to you and sends you away rejoicing in Him. Dear friend, give up your whole heart and soul to Jesus; He will accept you just as you are. He has said, "I will manifest myself unto you." Go and plead this promise.

≈ MARY WINSLOW

The Value of Time

The time is short. —1 CORINTHIANS 7:29

To the Christian, how valuable is time! God has given it to us only minute by minute, to show us how precious a thing it is that He grants in these small drops. How soon is time over! How short is the longest life! And yet time is given to prepare for eternity. As we spend our time, so shall we spend eternity. The question "Where shall *I* spend eternity?" must be decided in time. When eternity begins, it will be too late.

Time is given us to serve the Lord in. Time is given us to repent in and to believe the gospel. Time is given us to do our duty in our station. Time is given us to do good to others. How much time is wasted! Idle gossip from house to house, too much attention to dress rather than to neatness, foolish reading—so many things to waste precious time!

But there is one idea I should like you to have, one thought that I trust the Spirit may write in all our hearts, and I pray He may keep in them, too, for Satan and the world would wish us to think far otherwise. This is it: time is given us to prepare for eternity. I am answerable to God for my use or abuse of time.

Let us pray to God to give us grace to spend our time in His service, in doing our duty in our day and generation, and in preparing for the life to come. Then, when time shall be over, we shall enter upon a glorious eternity through Christ our Lord. The ungodly and the careless will then wish, when wishing will be vain, that they had in like manner devoted their time to God. What would sinners give at the last for one short day! Oh, then, be wise now. Be wise in time. Consider your ways, and prepare for a life that shall never end!

❧ ELIZABETH JULIA HASELL

Search the Scriptures

Search the scriptures. —JOHN 5:39

By the Word, we will grow in the knowledge of Christ. The mere surface of this is obvious. For how do we come to know more of anyone whom having not seen, we love? Is it not by reading and hearing what He has said and written and done? How are we to know more of Jesus Christ if we are not taking the trouble to know more of His Word? He has said, "Search the scriptures; for…they are they which testify of me." Are we really searching, or only superficially reading those Old Testament Scriptures of which He spoke? He says they testify of Him, meaning that they tell us all about Him. Are we acting as if we really believed that? "Beginning at Moses and all the prophets, he expounded unto them in all the scriptures the things concerning himself." Then there are things about Jesus in *all* the Scriptures—not only in the Psalms and Isaiah—but in every book! How very much there must be for us to find! Let us ask the Holy Spirit to take of *these* things of Jesus and show them unto us, that we may grow in "the knowledge of the Son of God."

"The words that I speak unto you, they are spirit, and they are life"—quickening and continually life-giving words. We want to be permeated with them; we want them to dwell in us richly, to be the inspiration of our whole lives, the very music of our spirits, whose melodious overflow may be glory to God and goodwill to man. Jesus Himself has given us this quick and powerful Word of God, and our responsibility is tremendous. He has told us distinctly what to do with it; He has said, "Search!" Now, are we substituting a word of our own and merely reading them? He did not say, "Read them," but "Search!" and it is a most serious thought for many comfortable daily readers of the Bible, that if they are only reading and not searching, they are distinctly living in disobedience to one of His plainest commands. What wonder if they do not grow!

› FRANCES RIDLEY HAVERGAL

The Patience of the Husbandman

*He which hath begun a good work in you will
perform it until the day of Jesus Christ.*

—PHILIPPIANS 1:6

The great Husbandman is watching over all, giving sun and rain as well as storms and frosts in due season. We like the showers and sunshine, but would rather go on without the cold and stormy weather, which is likewise needful and often very conducive to our spiritual growth. I have often said before the Lord, "Search me, O God, and know my heart: try me, and know my thoughts: and see if there be any wicked way in me, and lead me in the way everlasting." But when a cutting north wind has come, I have complained, little thinking that it was just an answer to my prayer.

Perhaps you may pass through some such experience, and in these wintry seasons you may think that growth is stopped and life will soon be gone—but no, it is "incorruptible seed" of which you are born, which lives and abides forever. Amid our many changes, how encouraging is the thought—and also the knowledge—that the great Husbandman has more interest in the seed than the seed has in itself. "Ye are not your own," but His who bought you with His blood. You are His portion, His inheritance, in whom He will be glorified.

Truly the gospel of the blessed God, while it is most strengthening, as showing all the work to be His, is most humbling, as showing all weakness and sin to be ours. Had it not been so, such mighty costs and pains would not have been needful for our redemption. I pray that the oil and wine of gospel grace may flow into your soul, for this makes us nothing and Jesus all. The Lord be with your spirit, strengthen your faith, and make all needed grace abound toward you.

* RUTH BRYAN

A Prisoner's Brave Faith

*Ah Lord GOD! Behold, thou hast made the heaven
and the earth by thy great power and stretched out
arm, and there is nothing too hard for thee.*

—JEREMIAH 32:17

Your difficulties and trials may not be comparable or similar to those of the Weeping Prophet, but they are very real and seemingly insurmountable to you. It is a fact that, of yourself, you can neither overcome nor endure them, so I want to remind you that the Lord's hand is not shortened, that what was true of His power in Jeremiah's time is as certainly true today, and that whatever present hardship may press upon you or whatever burden may be weighing you down, you—yes, *you*—may look up to Him with confident faith and say, "There is nothing too hard for Thee."

Oh, the blessed peace that such an assurance brings! I do not know what your particular sorrow or hardship may be, but I do know that, whatever its nature—cruel, bitter, or hopeless—it is as "nothing" to Him. He is able to deliver you as easily as you can call upon Him for succor. An old writer says, "Our God delights in what men deem extremities. He waits for extremes, He tarries for crises. And why? In order that He should be looked up to for wisdom, strength, and deliverance, and that, when deliverance comes, He should have all the glory."

Now, dear friend, think of all the hard things there are in your life—hard circumstances, difficult duties, grievous pains, sore struggles, bitter disappointments, hard words, hard thoughts, a hard heart of your own, a hard heart in others. Gather all these, and many more together, and pile them one on another till you have one great mountain of affliction. Your God still calmly asks the question, "Is there anything too hard for Me?"

ɚ SUSANNAH SPURGEON

Continual Praises

Let every thing that hath breath praise the LORD.
Praise ye the LORD.
—PSALM 150:6

Often, when I am in a pensive mood and the sun is for a time hidden behind some intervening cloud that unbelief has raised and I am just going to hang my harp on the willows, I with shame take it back again and begin some song of praise, and that sets all right. The Scriptures, and especially the Psalms, not only abound with praises to our God but assure us also that He is pleased with our praises.

I think scarcely any Christian seems to cultivate this temper of mind, this holy habit sufficiently; for it should not be an accidental, but a habitual frame of heart, not merely flowing from the sense of His mercies to us but from the contemplation of the glorious perfections and attributes of the triune Jehovah, as He is in Himself and in relation to us as poor, fallen creatures. What a theme does this open! Eternity alone can make us know and estimate it. Oh, for faith to look not at the things that are seen, which are temporal, tempestuous, contradictory, confused, and often heartsickening, but at those that are not seen, which are eternal, unchanging, certain, peaceful, and heart-cheering; not such a faith as generalizes, but realizes, and that makes the things of sense retreat and actually gives place to the things of faith, with as much certainty as if they were present and in possession.

This, my honored friend, is our high privilege and, I trust, our constant desire and aim, however we may fail in the attainment. And, as to our failings, we will mourn over them and fight against them, but give no place to despondency, even for a moment, while Christ our Savior ever lives to intercede for us at the right hand of the Majesty on high.

❧ SARAH HAWKES

Words in Company

Let no corrupt communication proceed out of your
mouth, but that which is good to the use of edifying,
that it may minister grace unto the hearers.

—EPHESIANS 4:29

L et us set the Lord always before us and behave in all company as in the presence of the holy God and His holy angels, who are always close by to hear our words and see our carriage. Let us watch and pray that we enter not into temptation, that we yield not to the suggestions of Satan or any of his instruments to draw us away from God. But let us stand as holy warriors, with our armor on, resisting the devil and opposing the powers of darkness to the utmost. For in all company they will oppose us and watch to get an advantage against us.

And if we are careless, we shall soon be worse off. "All company has in it," as a dear servant of Christ once said, "either the nature of fire or air; it either heats or cools." Let us watch both in spiritual company, to get and communicate more spiritually, and in carnal company, whenever for a time we are called to be in it, to restrain carnality and to kindle spiritual, heavenly fire in the carnal, earthly persons we converse with.

Let us always regard most strictly the rule that is given us, that "no corrupt communication proceed out of your mouth, but that which is good to the use of edifying, that it may minister grace unto the hearers" (Eph. 4:29). Oh, how much corruption does *one* corrupt word, many times, convey into and produce in the minds of the hearers! And so, on the contrary, how much grace is ministered to and produced in the hearts of hearers by *one* gracious word, when the Lord is pleased to work by it! And it is most certain that by our words—whether carnal or spiritual—carnality or spirituality will be increased in our own souls. And therefore we have need to watch our words. Oh, how much of the ungodliness of our time runs down through the channel of words!

&. ANNE DUTTON

The Hill Country of Perfect Trust

*Therefore I will look unto the LORD; I will wait for
the God of my salvation; my God will hear me.*

—MICAH 7:7

Heartrending griefs are often the forerunners of great spiritual blessing. It must be a heavy wave of affliction that casts some of us high and dry on the safe and sheltered shore of complete confidence in God. It was a most distressed acquaintance with earth's shame and sorrow that drew from the Lord's prophet the exalted utterance of the text, and we often have to learn the blessedness of turning to God and trusting Him by the sharp pain of finding out that He alone is a dependable and constant friend.

Come, my heart: God has set you a lesson to repeat that has stood you in good stead in many a time of sorrow! To say it over again will help you get it by heart. For you cannot remember too often the lovingkindness of the Lord and the many deliverances He has wrought for you. Though bruised and wearied by the roughness of the way, I have at last reached a safe shelter and resting place where I may wait till my Lord reveals Himself to me as my deliverer.

How blessed am I to know that one so mighty both in love and power watches over and directs my steps—one who is not only God, but the God of *my salvation!* He has a more tender and personal interest in me than the angels of heaven, for I am that marvel of marvels: a sinner saved by grace, a soul redeemed unto God by His most precious blood! For Him I will wait, confident and expectant. As someone lately said, "I know I am cared for; but just what His care may deem best for me, this I do not know." I can leave all with Him and wait with the unfolding of His will and purpose concerning me.

꙳ SUSANNAH SPURGEON

True Heart Knowledge

The LORD searcheth all hearts, and understandeth all the imaginations of the thoughts: if thou seek him, he will be found of thee; but if thou forsake him, he will cast thee off for ever.

—1 CHRONICLES 28:9

When I look into my own heart and behold those endless complaints against God that lurk there, and when I think what must be the fountain from which they spring, it would seem as if I should be filled with repentance, as if I should mourn, with deep and penitential sorrow, over my unspeakable, my amazing guilt. But still I am freezing with impenitence! The law is holy, and the commandment holy, just, and good; man is bound to comply with it. God must not relax His requirements. If He should, His law would not be strict enough to check the progress and influence of sin, and sin, unrestrained, would soon disorganize His whole moral system and banish happiness from the universe. This I know and believe—and yet I rebel! Yes, the worm lifts her unrighteous head and asks, "What doest Thou? And why doest Thou thus?" This is what troubles me.

I am afraid I have never been brought truly to submit all things to the disposal of God, especially to submit to His righteousness in the condemnation of sinners. I fear I have never yet seen aright the dreadful evil of sin, as to its just desert of eternal punishment, and this is the source of the misgivings I sometimes experience. But Jehovah is—I know He is—righteous in all His ways and holy in all His works, and He has said that "the wicked shall be turned into hell; where their worm dieth not, and the fire shall never be quenched." Hush, then, every murmuring, doubting thought, every rebellious, discontented feeling! Oh, for deeper views of the vileness—the exceeding vileness—of sin, for stronger and more abiding confidence in the rectitude and the goodness of God!

ॐ SUSAN HUNTINGTON

Who Can Tell?

Who can tell whether GOD will be gracious to me?
—2 SAMUEL 12:22

The day of grace has not passed you or any soul that has the least desire to find mercy. It is now, now, with you still. The voice of the gospel to you is, "Today, after so long a time;…today if ye will hear his voice, harden not your hearts" (Heb. 4:7). Oh, turn not away from the dear Savior, who most lovingly invites you to come unto Him, even you, as it were, by name, saying, "Come unto me, all ye that labour and are heavy laden, and I will give you rest" (Matt. 11:28). Oh come, dear soul, and tell the Lord Jesus all your griefs. For compassion, there is none like Him. Show before Him all your burdens; His own kind hand will take them off your shoulders. Oh, come and see how good, how gracious, how mighty to save the Lord the Savior is! And how faithful He is to His promise! I will give you rest. I will in no wise cast out. Oh, say not in unbelief, "There is no mercy for me," but come to Christ and see. Come, see what the Savior will say to you, if His mercy will not bid you live. Yea, come, though you have done as evil things as you could, though laden with innumerable sins, griefs, and fears.

For the Savior will abundantly pardon, abundantly comfort, abundantly deliver, and in all respects will do for you more exceeding abundantly than you can ask or think! Oh, return unto the Lord, with a "who can tell but He may be gracious?" Thousands of souls who came to the throne of grace have found mercy, only with a possibility that they might find it and even though they were attended with innumerable fears that they should not. Yea, let me say, *never* did any soul perish that cast itself down at the Savior's feet, in all its misery, to find mercy—nor ever shall, even to the world's end. Mercy reigns, mercy triumphs, mercy rejoices against judgment. "For I will be merciful to their unrighteousness, and their sins and their iniquities will I remember no more." This is God's new covenant of free grace in Christ. And He calls poor sinners to come unto Him and promises to make it with them.

&ProbablyOrnament; ANNE DUTTON

The Abiding Joy

These things have I spoken unto you, that my joy might
remain in you, and that your joy might be full.
—JOHN 15:11

Anyone who has known anything of joy in the Lord has asked, "But will it last?" And why has the question been so often the very beginning of its not lasting? Because we have either asked it of ourselves or of others, and not of the Lord only. His own answers to this continually recurring question are so different from the cautious, chilling, saddening ones His children so often give. They are absolute, full, reiterated. To the law and to the testimony, O happy Christian! There you will find true and abundant answer to your only shadow on the brightness of the joy. So long as you believe your Lord's word about it, so long only it *will* last. So soon as you ask of other counselors and believe their word instead, so soon shall it fail. Jesus meets your difficulty explicitly. He has provided against it by giving the very reason He spoke the gracious words of His last discourse: "That my joy might *remain* in you." Is not this exactly what we were afraid to hope, what seemed too good to be true— that it might remain? And lest we should think that this abiding joy only meant some moderate measure of qualified joy, He adds, "and that your joy may be *full.*"

Never in His Word are we told anything contradicting or explaining away this precious and reiterated promise. When it is suggested that we cannot expect to be always joyful, remember that it is written, "Rejoice in the Lord [not sometimes, but] *always.*" "As sorrowful, yet *always* rejoicing." The joy of the Lord is your strength. Perhaps in that word *of* lies the whole secret of lasting joy, for it is more than even "joy *in* the Lord." His own joy flowing into the soul that is joined to Him alone can remain in us, not even our joy in Him. Let us, then, seek not the stream, but the fountain; not primarily the joy, but that real and living union with Jesus by which His joy becomes ours.

     ❧ FRANCES RIDLEY HAVERGAL

Paul's Prayer for the Ephesians

Wherefore I also, after I heard of your faith in the Lord Jesus,
and love unto all the saints, cease not to give thanks
for you, making mention of you in my prayers.

—EPHESIANS 1:15–16

Happy are those who have praying friends! The Christian, however great her attainments may be, will never be *beyond* the prayers of her friends on this side of the grave. The Ephesians were "saints," and they were "faithful in Christ Jesus." Like Paul himself, they were "accepted in the beloved," having been chosen of God in Christ "before the foundation of the world." Moreover, they "were sealed with the Holy Spirit of promise, which is the *earnest* of our inheritance." Paul had heard of their "faith in the Lord Jesus, and love to all saints." We may say that the Ephesians were *advanced* Christians, and yet Paul does *not* therefore cease to pray for them.

What did Paul ask for the Ephesians when he prayed for them? First, he prayed that they might have the spirit of wisdom and revelation in the knowledge of God. They required this. We all need it now; we all need far more heavenly wisdom. The next expression is very striking: Paul desired that the eyes of their understanding be enlightened. Paul especially desired that the spiritual eyes of the Ephesians might be opened for one reason: he longed that they might "know what is the hope of his calling, and what the riches of the glory of his inheritance in the saints." This inheritance is promised equally to all believers in every age. May *our* eyes be enlightened to see its glory, and to desire it.

And last, Paul prayed that the Ephesians might know the greatness of God's power working in believers. Do *we* ever cease to need this, and can we dream of the extent of this power, unless, by God's mercy, we experience it ourselves? The little he knows makes the good man long for more, and hereafter he shall be satisfied in the presence of Eternal Wisdom and Perfect Light.

❧ ELIZABETH JULIA HASELL

Advancing in Divine Life

This is the way, walk ye in it. —ISAIAH 30:21

How is it at present with your soul? Christ is dear to every member of His mystical body. Are you still in the same position, or have you got further on the road? They who are running a race should not stand still. There are stages in the Christian's life when, in one sense, she is to stand still; that is, when Providence hedges up the way and she is at a loss what to do. She is then to place herself in a waiting position, listening to hear the well-known voice behind her saying, "This is the way, walk ye in it" (Isa. 30:21).

But, in another sense, she is to be always making headway, growing in grace and in the knowledge of her Savior-God. Beware of all hindrances. If you really have placed yourself under the guidance and guardianship of Christ, shelter beneath His outstretched, all-powerful wing. Have you surrendered to Him your *whole* heart? Then blessed are you. Fear not; He will watch over you day and night, for He cares for you.

Do not attempt to transfer your interest from His hands into your own. He knows the end from the beginning, and infinite wisdom, power, and love are all engaged on your behalf. If you have committed your soul to Him, cannot you trust Him to regulate and conduct your earthly concerns? A fretting against God's providence is very dishonoring to Him and causes Him to leave His perverse child to have, for the time, her own way. Then how bitter it is in the end! The Spirit is grieved, the sensible presence of Christ is withdrawn, and the soul is left in trouble and sorrow and darkness. Live upon Him as a loving Father. Lean upon Him, and He will support you under all trials of life, for He is a present help in every time of trouble. Give yourself up wholly to Him—body, soul, and spirit. Go and tell Him all. You need not shrink from opening your whole heart to Him. He will keep all your secrets and will do all things well. What He does withhold He sees would not be for our good. Learn early in life to trust Him with your all, and He will be all to you.

❧ MARY WINSLOW

Come into the Ark

Come thou and all thy house into the ark.

—GENESIS 7:1

We are either inside or outside the ark. There is no halfway in this. Outside is death; inside is life. Outside is certain, inevitable, utter destruction. Inside is certain and complete safety. Where are you at this moment? Perhaps you dare not say confidently and happily, "I am inside," and yet you do not like to look the alarming alternative in the face and say, "I am outside!" You prefer trying to persuade yourself that you do not exactly know and can't be expected to be able to answer such a question. You say, perhaps with a shade of annoyance, "How *am* I to know?" God's infallible Word tells you very plainly: "If any man be in Christ, he is a new creature; old things are passed away; behold, all things are become new." "A very severe test!" you say. I cannot help that; I can only tell you exactly what God says. So then, if old things have not passed away in your life, and if you are not a new creature, born again, altogether different in heart and life and love and aim, you are not in Christ. And if you are not *in* Christ, you are *out* of Christ, outside the place of safety.

Come into the ark! It is one of the devices of the destroyer to delude you into fancying that no very decided step is necessary. He is very fond of the word *gradually.* You are to become more earnest—gradually. You are to find salvation—gradually. You are to turn your mind to God—gradually. Did you ever think that God never once uses this word or anything like it? Neither the word nor the sense of it occurs in any way in the whole Bible with reference to salvation. You might have been gradually approaching the ark and gradually making up your mind to enter, but unless you took the one step *into* the ark, the one step from outside to inside, what would have been our fate when the door was shut? Come thou into the ark! I want the call to haunt you, to ring in your ears all day and all night, till you come.

∾ FRANCES RIDLEY HAVERGAL

All Directly from Father's Hand

My times are in thy hand.
—PSALM 31:15

Why need I trouble or tremble? That great, loving, powerful hand keeps all the events of my life sealed and secure within its almighty clasp, and only He, my Maker and Master, can permit them to pass from His keeping and be revealed to me one by one as His will for me. What a compassionate, gracious arrangement! How eminently fitted to fulfill that sweet promise of His Word, "Thou shalt keep him in perfect peace, whose mind is stayed on thee, because he trusteth in thee!" If we fully believed this, we should be absolutely devoid of the care that corrodes and chafes the daily life of so many professing Christians.

Not one or two important epochs of my history only, but everything that concerns me—joys that I had not expected; sorrows that must have crushed me if they could have been anticipated; sufferings that might have terrified me by their grimness had I looked upon them; surprises that infinite love had prepared for me; services of which I could not have imagined myself capable—all these lay in that mighty hand as the purposes of God's eternal will for me. But, as they have developed gradually and silently, how great has been the love that appeared, enwrapping and enfolding each one! Has not the grief been measured, while the gladness has far more abounded? Have not the comforts and consolations exceeded the crosses and complaints? Have not all things been so arranged, ordered, undertaken, and worked out on our behalf that we can but marvel at the goodness and wisdom of God in meting out from that dear hand of His all the times that have passed over us? You agree with me in all this, do you not, dear reader? Then, I pray you, apply it to your present circumstances, however dark or difficult they may be. They have come direct from your Father's hand to you, and they are His dear will.

&ereve; SUSANNAH SPURGEON

Pretense

Having a form of godliness, but denying the power.
—2 TIMOTHY 3:5

You who profess faith in Christ and hope for salvation by Him and yet live in sin, in a course of wickedness and open immorality: remember, the Savior did not come to save persons *in* their sins, but *from* them. And if you do not have that faith given you that purifies the heart, and that hope that makes him that has it to purify himself, even as Christ is pure, you are yet unbelievers, without hope and without God in the world. And if you abide in your present state, you will die in your sins and perish forever. Your hope will be as the spider's web at the giving up of the ghost. It will be swept away by the broom of destruction, and your naked souls will fall into eternal perdition. All whom Christ saves to glory hereafter, He saves to holiness here, for without it, no one shall see the Lord. And no true holiness can there be without true, living faith in Christ—without the special work of the Holy Spirit of God in regeneration, renewing the soul in holiness after the image of Christ, and the Holy Spirit's dwelling in the holy soul to enable it for holy actions.

Oh, poor souls, you who content yourselves with a bare profession of Christ without any experience of the power of His grace in your hearts, constraining you to live to Him, to deny yourself, to take up your cross and follow the Lamb, even wherever He goes, in the face of a thousand reproaches from wicked men: Christ will be ashamed of you, will not own you as Christians and His disciples, but will deny you as such before His Father and His holy angels when He comes in His glory. Never please yourselves, therefore, with bearing the Christian name without bearing the image of Christ in your hearts and lives. So necessary it is that everyone who names the name of Christ should depart from iniquity, that without it, he cannot be His disciple here nor glorified with Him as such hereafter. Consider then, dear souls, what a great thing it is to be a true Christian.

ॐ ANNE DUTTON

Think It Not Strange

*Think it not strange concerning the fiery trial which is to try
you, as though some strange thing happened unto you.*

—1 PETER 4:12

Wherefore, my beloved and longed-for, "think it not strange concerning the fiery trial which is to try you, as though some strange thing happened unto you." Whether that trial is inward exercises from indwelling sin, the fiery darts of the wicked one, outward affliction, or something in prospect that makes the heart tremble, for all these, and every other, we have the promise: "My grace is sufficient for thee, my strength is made perfect in weakness." What can be weaker than a worm? Yet the Lord says, "Fear not, thou worm Jacob, I will help thee, saith the LORD, and thy redeemer, the Holy One of Israel." "I will hold thy right hand, saying unto thee, Fear not." "When thou passest through the waters, I will be with thee, and through the rivers, they shall not overflow thee: when thou walkest through the fire, thou shalt not be burned; neither shall the flame kindle upon thee." These are sweet cordials for a time of weakness and trial. The Lord fulfill them in your experience and grant that your faith fail not. May you be kept instant in prayer, "watching thereunto with all perseverance" to learn the mind of the Lord respecting you. Times of trial are inquiring times.

There are those now living who can testify to the Lord's glory that they have found a great blessing in the close dealing with God to which they have been brought by afflictive dispensations under the divine exercising of the Holy Ghost. It is spoken of ancient Israel that "the more they were afflicted the more they multiplied and grew." Often, indeed, is it thus with the spiritual seed of Abraham; being "chastened of the Lord," there is growth out of self into Christ. The Lord grant you like experience, that with me you may have to say, "It is good for me that I have been afflicted."

࿔ RUTH BRYAN

The Two Natures in the Regenerate

Whosoever is born of God…cannot sin,
because he is born of God.

—1 JOHN 3:9

In the regenerate there are two natures, called in Scripture the old man and the new man. There is no mixture of the two natures. The old man remains sinful and desperately wicked until we leave it behind at death. The new man is of a divine nature and cannot sin because it is born of God, while the old man cannot cease to sin because it is not of God. Some explain the passage to mean that the believer cannot sin as formerly or that he cannot sin willfully. But why not take the Word of God just as He has given it? The apostle says: "Whosoever is born of God…cannot sin, because he is born of God." That is, the new man, or the new nature, cannot sin because it is divine: it is born of God. The old man, or the unrenewed nature, cannot cease from sin because it is of the flesh and remains flesh until it dies. Thus, there are two natures in the regenerate, warring the one against the other. Sin in every shape is hateful to the believer. It is his daily burden and grief. He would be holy as God is holy.

The old man, which God could in a moment destroy, is allowed to remain for wise purposes, even to increase the believer's diligence and quicken his activity and thus bring out every grace to perfection, especially the grace of faith, by which he overcomes the world, the flesh, and the devil. But if we feel the indwelling of the old man, we also feel the indwelling of the Spirit, and so we can exclaim, "Thanks be to God, who giveth us the victory." It is thus God who brings good out of evil. Who would suppose that this fountain of iniquity within us should bring glory to God? But so it is. It is more glorified by its remaining in us than had He chosen to empty us of it at once. He makes the very thing we hate and abhor conducive to advancement in the divine life and glorifying to Him.

 MARY WINSLOW

The Perpetual Presence

Lo, I am with you alway. —MATTHEW 28:20

Some of us think and say a good deal about a sense of Christ's presence—sometimes rejoicing in it, sometimes going mourning all the day long because we have it not; praying for it and not always seeming to receive what we ask; measuring our own position, and sometimes even that of others, by it; now on the heights, now in the depths about it. And all this April-like gleam and gloom instead of steady summer glow is because we are turning our attention upon the sense of His presence instead of the changeless reality of it!

It comes practically to this: Are you a disciple of the Lord Jesus at all? If so, He says to you, "I am with you alway." That overflows all the regrets of the past and all the possibilities of the future and most certainly includes the present. Therefore, at this very moment, as surely as your eyes rest on this page, so surely is the Lord Jesus with you. "I am" is neither "I was" nor "I will be." It is always abreast of our lives, always encompassing us with salvation. It is a splendid, perpetual now.

Is it not too bad to turn round upon that gracious presence, the Lord Jesus Christ's own personal presence here and now, and, without one note of faith or whisper of thanksgiving, say, "Yes, but I don't realize it!" Then it is, after all, not the presence but the realization that you are seeking—the shadow, not the substance! Honestly, it is so! For you have such an absolute assurance of the reality put into the very plainest words of promise that divine love could devise, that you dare not make Him a liar and say, "No! He is not with me!" All you can say is, "I don't feel a sense of His presence." Well then, be ashamed of doubting your beloved Master's faithfulness, and never open your mouth anymore in His presence about it. What shall we say to our Lord? He says, "I am with you alway." Shall we not put away all our imperfect and double-fettered experience and say to Him, lovingly and gratefully, "Thou art with me!"

❧ FRANCES RIDLEY HAVERGAL

Seeming Contradictions

Come, and let us return unto the LORD: for he hath torn, and
he will heal us; he hath smitten, and he will bind us up.

—HOSEA 6:1

The mind that is peculiarly susceptible of impressions—though I have sometimes thought it needs more grace to enable it to sustain afflictions than one of a different mold—has, perhaps, some peculiar advantages. In such a mind, if it is a sanctified one, the sense of dependence must be much stronger and, of course, application to Him whose grace is sufficient in every time of need more frequent. And whatever leads us to God for strength is a great blessing, for all that is obtained anywhere else but from the fullness that is in Christ is but weakness, however specious its appearance may be. Your feelings are acute, and, on this account, you have a harder struggle; but, for the same reason, you will have a more glorious victory. And He who has wounded will heal; He who has broken will bind up. He knows how much to inflict to accomplish His gracious designs concerning you, and He will lay no more upon you than He will enable you, if you look to Him, to bear.

Distrust is the sin against which we have more need to be on our guard—I had almost said, than any other. No sin is more offensive to God, none more distressing to us. How glorious, how triumphant would the Christian shine in sufferings, would she, at all times, exercise that unshaken faith that her religion enjoins! Hers would not be the lifeless calm of the cessation of feeling, but the divine union of those seeming contradictions: "sorrowful, yet rejoicing; having nothing, and yet possessing all things!" Let us, my dear friend, endeavor, whether in prosperity or adversity, to cling to the cross of Christ, which possesses a virtue that will render the one harmless and the other salutary or, rather, that will render both salutary.

≈ SUSAN HUNTINGTON

What Distresses You?

Come unto me, all ye that labour and are
heavy laden, and I will give you rest.
—MATTHEW 11:28

What is it, my beloved friend, that distresses you? Is it the absence of Jesus? Ah, that is a sorrowful condition! But He loves you just as much as when you leaned on His bosom, and He *will* come again and embrace you, making you ashamed of the jealousies you now feel, for surely it is not knowing a friend to trust him only so far as we can see him. Oh, then, may the Spirit enable you even in the dark to trust in the Lord and stay upon our God.

Is it sin that breaks your heart? The blood of Jesus cleanses from *all* sin (I am a living witness of it)—from indulged and repeated heart-and-life sin, sins of ingratitude and carelessness, sins against light and knowledge, and a thousand other. Do not, therefore, be cast down; since I have found mercy, none need despair. Venture with all your guilt upon Christ; you know He has borne the curse due to it, and He will restore peace to your conscience.

But, perhaps, you have been looking over your evidences of grace, and by reason of the mist that now envelops you, they appear so dim that you question whether they are genuine. I have found it sometimes well to give Satan a little ground here. Throw evidences away and suppose what he says is true—that we have been deceived—and then fly to Christ just as we are, without one plea, hanging simply upon His blood and righteousness as a helpless sinner, determined that if we perish it will be in venturing upon Him. Thus shall we prove whether it is true that He can and will save to the uttermost all who come unto God by Him. You cannot think what relief I have had in this way. But, whatever your case is, the remedy is in Christ. May it soon be feelingly applied.

&ernds; RUTH BRYAN

The Power of Prayer

*As a prince hast thou power with God and
with men, and hast prevailed.*
—GENESIS 32:28

What an unburdening of the heart is a holy, unconstrained, and loving interview with God, our best friend! He is so ready to do us good—and that from everlasting and unbounded love, sovereign in its character and independent of all deserts in ourselves. Is it not a high privilege to have such a one to whom we may go when oppressed? The special promise given to me from God Himself, in days of great trial, "I will be a father to thy fatherless children," still holds good.

Praise be to His holy name for the fulfillment of that most gracious promise, which I have yet to plead before Him. It has been to me like a note of hand, ever ready to be presented by faith, never yet rejected nor ever will be, by Him who has endorsed it with His own name. Here is my stronghold.

O the power of prayer with God! With men's hearts we can have nothing to do, but with the heart—the tender, loving heart—of the God-man, Christ Jesus, who has said, "Ask anything in my name, and I will do it," we have to do. Here is the privilege of the Christian, and a great and mighty one it is. Make the most of it. It is only to last for time, and then eternity will unfold to our astonished view the whole map of God's unchanging love, set forth in all the ever-varying, yet never-erring dispensations of His providence. Ask much at His hands. We cannot ask too much when we ask in the name of Jesus.

❧ MARY WINSLOW

Christ's Gracious Liberality

Whatsoever ye shall ask the Father in
my name, he will give it to you.
—JOHN 16:23

What makes me so bold and hardy to presume to come to the Lord with such audacity and boldness, being so great a sinner? Truly nothing but His own word. For He says, "Come unto me, all ye that labour and are heavy laden, and I will give you rest" (Matt. 11:28). What gentle, merciful, and comfortable words are these to all sinners! Is he not a frantic, mad, beastly, and foolish person who would run for aid, helps, or refuge to any other creature? What a most gracious, comfortable, and gentle saying was this, with such pleasant and sweet words, to allure His enemies to come unto Him! Is there any worldly prince or magistrate that would show such clemency and mercy to his disobedient and rebellious subjects, having offended them? I suppose worldly rulers would not with such words allure their enemies except to call those whom they cannot take and punish, being taken. But even as Christ is Prince of princes and Lord of lords, so His charity and mercy exceed and surmount all others.

It is no small or little gift that I now require, neither think I myself worthy to receive such a noble gift, being so ungrateful, unkind, and wicked a child. But when I behold the benignity, liberality, mercy, and goodness of the Lord, I am encouraged, boldened, and stirred to ask such a noble gift. The Lord is so bountiful and liberal that He will not have us satisfied and contented with one gift, neither to ask simple and small gifts. And therefore He promises and binds Himself by His Word to give good and beneficial gifts to all those who ask Him with true faith (John 16:23–24), without which nothing can be done acceptably or pleasing to God (Rom. 8:8). For faith is the foundation and ground of all other gifts, virtues, and graces, and therefore I will say, "Lord, increase my faith."

ɞ KATHERINE PARR

God's Love in Little Chastenings

*Now no chastening for the present seemeth
to be joyous, but grievous...*

—HEBREWS 12:11

There are some promises that we are apt to reserve for great occasions, and thus lose the continual comfort of them. Perhaps we read this one with a sigh and say, "How beautiful this is for those whom the Lord is really chastening! I almost think I should not mind that if such a promise might then be mine. But the things that try me are only little things that turn up every day to trouble and depress me." Well, now, does the Lord specify what degree of trouble, or what kind of trouble, is great enough to make up a claim to the promise? And if He does not, why should you? He only defines it as "not joyous, but grievous."

Perhaps there have been a dozen different things today that were not joyous, but grievous to you. And though you feel ashamed of feeling them so much, and hardly like to admit their having been so trying, and would not think of dignifying them as chastening, yet, if they come under the Lord's definition, He not only knows all about them, but they were, every one of them, chastenings from His hand—neither to be despised and called "just nothing" when all the while they did grieve you, nor to be wearied of, because they are working out blessing to you and glory to Him. Every one of them has been an unrecognized token of His love and interest in you, for "whom the Lord loveth he chasteneth."

*What shall Thine afterward be, O Lord?
I wonder, and wait to see
While to Thy chastening now I bow
What peaceable fruit may be ripening now,
Ripening fast for Thee!*

› FRANCES RIDLEY HAVERGAL

The Sure Afterward

...nevertheless afterward it yieldeth the peaceable fruit of righteousness unto them which are exercised thereby.

—HEBREWS 12:11

Hebrews 12:11 says that, "nevertheless afterward *it* yieldeth," not *they* yield. Does not this indicate that every separate chastening has its own special "afterward"? We think of trials as intended to do us good in the long run and in a general sort of way, but the Lord says of each one, "It yieldeth." Apply this to the present: the particular annoyance that befell you this morning, the vexatious words that met your ear and grieved your spirit, the disappointment that was His appointment for today, the slight but hindering ailment, the presence of someone who is a grief of mind to you. Whatever in this day seems not joyous, but grievous, is linked in the good pleasure of His goodness, with a corresponding afterward of peaceable fruit, the very seed from which, if you only do not choke it, this shall spring and ripen.

If we set ourselves to watch the Lord's dealings with us, we shall often be able to detect a most beautiful correspondence and proportion between each individual chastening and its own resulting "afterward." The habit of thus watching and expecting will be very comforting and a great help to quiet trust when some new chastening is sent, for then we shall consider it as the herald and earnest of a new "afterward." Do not let us reserve this promise for some far future time. The Lord did not say *"a long while* afterward," and do not let us gratuitously insert it. It rather implies that, as soon as the chastening is over, the peaceable fruit shall appear unto the glory and praise of God. So let us look out for the "afterward" as soon as the pressure is past. This immediate expectation will bring its own blessing if we can say, "My expectation is from him," and not from any fruit-bearing qualities of our own, for only "from me is thy fruit found," the Lord says. Fruit from Him will also be fruit unto Him.

❧ FRANCES RIDLEY HAVERGAL

Spiritual Slumbering

Watch ye, stand fast in the faith.
—1 CORINTHIANS 16:13

As in nature, when people go to sleep, they disband all cares and compose themselves to rest, so in grace, when people once grow careless and indulge in spiritual slumber and sleep, they are presently overcome therewith. And as in natural sleep the natural senses are bound up and restrained from their proper exercise, so in spiritual sleep the life of grace in believers is, as to its exercise, prevailed over by the death of sin that dwells and works in them, and their spiritual senses are rendered inactive toward those glorious objects about which they ought to be conversant. Natural sleep, indeed, in due measure, as to the present state of our frail bodies, is necessary and useful for the preservation of our natural life. But spiritual sleep directly tends to the destruction of our spiritual life; it preys upon our graces and comforts and eats up the vitals of Christianity. While we sleep spiritually, we lose our time, our precious opportunities of growing in grace and in the knowledge of Christ; of being useful to others, both saints and sinners, in our generation; of glorifying God in this world.

And, therefore, we have reason to dread spiritual slumber, and in the use of all appointed means, at our Lord's command, to watch: that our lights may be burning, our loins girded, and ourselves like women who wait upon their Lord. I well know that we can't hold our own souls in life. But by our neglect of frequent secret prayer unto God, reading of His Word, and meditation thereon, we doubtless may, and many times do, provoke the Lord to withhold from us the quickening influence of His grace. Let us beware of this great sin, this deadly evil of spiritual sleep. Let us not lie down, loving to slumber. On the other hand, when we find spiritual drowsiness begin to seize us, if we attempt our duty in the Lord's strength to stir ourselves and call upon our God, we shall find that, drawing nigh unto God with our frequent requests, He will draw nigh unto us with His quickening grace.

❧ ANNE DUTTON

Waiting at the Gate

I wait for the LORD, my soul doth wait,
and in his word do I hope.

—PSALM 130:5

I am a suppliant at the door of a palace, a beggar at the gate of a King, but with this gracious dissimilarity to usual petitioners: that the Lord of the palace is my personal friend, and, though I am waiting outside at present, I possess an invitation to enter and know that the door will be wide open to me some day. Nay, more than this, if I tell all that is in my heart, I am daily expecting that the King Himself will come and call me in and admit me to His presence as His own child.

Well, my soul, surely this is a blessed condition of favor and privilege! You may well afford to wait patiently for so glorious a hope as this. You know that waiting is far better than wandering, and that silently uplifted hands plead more eloquently than a torrent of words. Keep your tarrying, entreating posture, and if the summons does not come yet, it will be joy enough to wait and watch for *His* time and *His* will and to anticipate the coming glory in which He has promised that you shall share.

For what do you say you are waiting? Alms? Entrance? Welcome? You have the first even now, for His bounty reaches you as you stand watching daily at His gates, and the better blessings are certain when He has perfected what concerns you, for then you will know with glad surprise "what he hath prepared for him that waiteth for him." What is His Word to you, my soul? Have you already gathered your daily manna and tasted its sweetness? The heavenly food lies thick around you, for the Lord has strewn the pages of His Word with promises of blessedness to those who wait for Him. And remember, His slightest word stands fast and sure; it can never fail you.

&ngrave; SUSANNAH SPURGEON

Search and Meditate on God's Word

This book of the law shall not depart out of thy mouth;
but thou shalt meditate therein day and night.

—JOSHUA 1:8

Sometimes a few words, even on an important subject, arrest the attention. Sometimes people attend to a very short paper when a longer discourse would be cast aside. May it be so now! May a few imperfect observations cause those who read them to think for themselves! Far more people read the Bible than those who read and *also* think about it. It is well to read the Bible daily; it is a holy habit, and most needful. But it is not always the quantity that we read; far more is it how we read that benefits our souls.

In reading God's Word, we should especially seek the teaching of God's Spirit. My friends, there is no teacher and preacher like the Holy Ghost. Do you pray that the eyes of your spiritual understanding may be opened, to understand the Scriptures? Do you take God's own Book in your hands, feeling it is like no other book, and that it can make you truly wise and happy?

Sermons, instruction, and good books are all useful and blessed of God, but do not only be contented with what good men say or write about the Bible. Read it for and apply it to yourselves, seeking the help of the divine Spirit. Thus, draw water for yourselves out of the wells of salvation. Take each of you your own pitcher to the eternal fountain. Water is purer, clearer, and sweeter in the deep, rocky well, where it springs, than in its onward course, and so the "water of life," which we are invited to take so "freely," is far best also at its source. Search the Scriptures, therefore, for yourselves. Despise no helps to understand the Scriptures, but above all read God's Book quietly and with prayer, and think about it.

ॐ ELIZABETH JULIA HASELL

A Surrendered Will

That the trial of your faith, being much more precious than of gold that perisheth, though it be tried with fire, might be found unto praise and honour and glory at the appearing of Jesus Christ.
—1 PETER 1:7

In all trying circumstances there is love, such love as mortals cannot fathom, and we must arrive in glory before we can have even a glimpse of what its fullness is. Afflictions for the present are not joyous, but in process of time God works by them in our souls the peaceable fruits of righteousness. He sends them for this purpose, and there is no fruit clustering upon the branch so holy, so precious, and so God-glorifying as a surrendered will. I have noticed, not only in my own experience but in that of God's saints, that God, in His varying dispensations, will bring us to this point. The trial will last until we are brought to surrender our will to the divine will, with a firm conviction that His will is best, whether the trial be removed or not. And in numerous cases, when the believer is brought to this holy state of submission, the Lord then removes the trial.

Oh, to be like Christ in this! He was thus tried. As man (and He was truly man, as He was truly God) His faith was tried when He prayed that the cup might pass from Him: "Nevertheless not as I will, but as thou wilt" (Matt. 26:39). Thrice He prayed for this. He was tempted in like manner with His people, that He might be, as their high priest, able to succor them that are tempted. And yet there is no sin in praying when in trouble that it might be removed, although the best posture is childlike submission. How little do or can those enter into the deep things of God who are at ease in Zion! A mere profession will or may carry one in such a way as will please the flesh, but as Christ walked through the wilderness, so must His followers more or less take up the same cross. We are to be "followers [or, imitators] of God, as dear children" (Eph. 5:1).

≈ MARY WINSLOW

I Will in No Wise Cast Out

*All that the Father giveth me shall come to me; and
him that cometh to me I will in no wise cast out.*

—JOHN 6:37

Perhaps everyone who comes to Christ has this sense of utter helplessness about it. This is because the Holy Spirit must convince us that the whole thing is God's doing, and not ours, so that He may have all the glory of saving us from beginning to end. It is not at all because He is not willing to save us, but just because He is willing, that He lets us find out for ourselves that our own will is so numb that it cannot rouse and move without the fire of His love and grace.

Now just think of His promise, "thou shalt come into the ark"; in other words, believe that His power and love are even now being exerted upon you and that your sense of helplessness is only part of His wonderful way of drawing you to Jesus. God the Father is not willing that any should perish, but that all should come to repentance. Do not fear to take the "thou" to yourself. Jesus said, "All that the father giveth me shall come to me." And the Father says, "I will cause him to draw near, and he shall approach unto me: for who is this that engaged his heart to approach unto me?" Whose heart? Is it not yours? You would hardly be reading these pages if your heart were not at all engaged to approach unto Him. And if it is so engaged, who engaged it? Who but the God from whom alone all holy desires do proceed?

When the dove found no rest for the sole of her foot and returned to Noah because the waters were on the face of the whole earth, "then he put forth his hand, and took her, and pulled her in" (that is, "caused her to come") unto him into the ark. What a beautiful picture is this little, helpless, tired dove of our helplessness and weariness, and the kind hand, strong and tender, that does not leave us to flutter and beat against a closed window, but takes us and pulls us unto Him into the ark!

❧ FRANCES RIDLEY HAVERGAL

A Loving Physician

My groaning is not hid from thee.
—PSALM 38:9

One of the strongest and sweetest consolations God gives to His sick and afflicted ones is the assurance that He not only "knows their sorrows" and tenderly sympathizes with them in their griefs, but that the appointment of the trial proceeds from Him, and that its whole course and continuance are watched by Him with infinite love and care. As a physician keeps his finger on a suffering patient's pulse, that he may know just the limit to which pain may be safely endured, so does our God hold our right hand while we are passing through the furnaces of trial that lie on our road to heaven, that He may support us through them and bring us forth in due time to praise Him for His comforting and sustaining grace.

Do remember, dear friend, that the God you love, the master you serve, is never indifferent to your grief or unwilling to hear your cry. David said truly, "Thou hast considered my trouble," and David's God is your God, with the added blessedness of the revelation of Jesus Christ the Savior, whose divine compassion is as infinite as His power. In time of trouble, the soul is greatly helped by cherishing great thoughts of God; they are sure to induce great longings after Him, great faith in Him, and great love toward Him. Thus, being filled with His fullness, we soar above and beyond all earthly distractions and disturbances that surround us and seek to cast us down.

Pain, whether bodily, mental, or spiritual, is always unwelcome and at first sight wears an aspect that alarms and discomforts us. But it is often an angel in disguise, and many times we have found that, underneath its terrible exterior, there are hidden the tender smiles of God's love, the gentle discipline of His teaching, and the sweet pity of His marvelous forbearance.

❧ SUSANNAH SPURGEON

Refuge and Strength in the Mercy of God

My God, 'tis to Thy mercy-seat
My soul for shelter flies;
'Tis here, I find a safe retreat,
When storms and tempests rise.

'Tis here, my faith resolves to dwell,
Nor shall I be afraid
Of all the pow'rs of earth or hell,
If Thou vouchsafe Thy aid.

My cheerful hope can never die,
If Thou my God art near;
Thy grace can raise my comforts high,
And banish ev'ry fear.

Against Thy all-supporting grace
My foes can ne'er prevail;
But oh! If frowns becloud Thy face,
Faith, hope, and life will fail.

My great protector, and my Lord,
Thy constant aid impart,
And let Thy kind, Thy gracious word
Sustain my trembling heart.

O never let my soul remove,
From this divine retreat;
Still let me trust Thy pow'r and love,
And dwell beneath thy feet.

ñ ANNE STEELE

Form without the Power of Godliness

That old serpent, called the Devil, and Satan,
which deceiveth the whole world.

—REVELATION 12:9

This is the day of much lip profession without real heart work, and the "kingdom of God is not in word, but in power"; "it is within you." This is what Satan seems in this day to be most fighting against. He does not oppose a general profession of religion, which is now deemed respectable, nor does he mind great strictness in outward form, as that is often a means of lulling the conscience into false peace. He will not even disturb a sound creed and much zeal in contending for the truth of the Bible, so long as they rest only in the natural judgment, whereby they induce vain confidence and terrible self-deceiving. The great enemy of souls will endeavor to keep all in peace who have a name to live but are dead. And if one of his subjects passes over either from gross sins or from the more refined pleasures of this perishing world to an outward profession, he will not be alarmed. For he cares not whether souls perish under the title of worldling or Christian, so long as he gets them into his own fearful condemnation.

Oh the dreadful danger of such souls, soothed into carnal security but only blinded to their danger, not delivered from it! It would be better to endure years of anguish in weeping and seeking for mercy by Jesus Christ than to be turned to such "a refuge of lies" and to walk in such "sparks of their own kindling." Better to walk in sorrow all one's life than to lie down in sorrow at death to end in eternal woe. May the Lord deliver souls thus deceived from this snare of the great fowler, so that they may thankfully say, "The snare is broken, and we are escaped" by divine power into that kingdom of God that is not meat and drink (or outward things), but righteousness, peace, and joy in the Holy Ghost.

~ RUTH BRYAN

Diligent Keeping

Keep thy heart with all diligence;
for out of it are the issues of life.
—PROVERBS 4:23

Watch your hearts, and by faith in Christ's blood, kill sin—all sin—in its first motions. Call in help from above and labor to keep your hearts always in a praying frame. God is nigh to them that call upon Him, that call upon Him in truth. Keep a strict guard over your thoughts. When they press in upon your minds, ask them what they would have? Are they for Christ or against Him? And suffer none of His enemies to enter without calling in the help of your Captain to oppose their entrance into and lodging in a heart that ought to be wholly His, the spot of His possession.

And while the Lord teaches your hands to war and your fingers to fight, behave as good soldiers of Jesus Christ. Oh, how sadly do we drive Christ out of our hearts by letting in swarms of vain, foolish, sinful thoughts to dwell and ravage there!

Let us labor to set the Lord always before us, to walk in our inmost thoughts as under His eye and to meditate on His Word, to seek His face, to abide in His presence, and to be in the fear of the Lord all the day long. True religion, holiness of truth, begins at the heart, and from thence comes forth into the life. If we don't keep our hearts with all diligence, our heart-holiness will soon decay and, consequently, our life-holiness too. Oh, my dear sisters, let us look to our hearts, that we entertain not vain, carnal thoughts here, but whenever we find ourselves sink down to this earth, let us call for help from heaven and never rest till we regain a spiritual frame and are meet temples for a God glorious in holiness to dwell in. And so, leaning on divine wisdom and strength, let us come forth with God and for Him, from heart into life holiness.

ANNE DUTTON

Contentment through Trials

But godliness with contentment is great gain.
—1 TIMOTHY 6:6

You and I will always meet with fuel for our gloomy fire, as long as we live. We must, however, strive against depression, and melancholy is a growing evil because it is death to all exertion and to almost all comfort; and moreover, Satan takes great advantage of it, to injure and disturb our spirits and to hinder our progress in the best things.

The indulgence of melancholy and sadness is a cheat, even in a religious point of view. Though it may seem to favor spirituality, yet it does not do so in truth. It favors the feeling more than the principle. But you and I, in this tempestuous world, shall have more call for principle than feeling, though this too certainly has its place. Self-denial, submission of our will to adverse circumstances, taking up the most irksome cross, compliance with ten thousand arduous claims and demands—and all this in a spirit of kindness and cheerfulness—are lessons, only to be obtained in the combat, through the aid of divine grace.

Not only our faith must be tried, but our love, patience, submission, resignation, and humility—all these must be brought forth by the purifying fire. But one thing you must constantly bear in mind, or you will faint in the day of adversity: namely, that you are not called to undertake one single difficulty in your own strength. Good resolutions, the finest and most correct view, will all fail unless you go simply, as a child, to the Strong for strength and lean on all-sufficient grace. This is a secret which, I trust, you will understand more and more.

❧ SARAH HAWKES

The Fame-Excelling Reality

Thou exceedest the fame that I heard.
—2 CHRONICLES 9:6

Thou! Lord Jesus! For whom have I in heaven but Thee? And there is none upon earth that I desire beside Thee. Thou who hast loved me and washed me from my sins in Thine own blood. Thou who hast given Thyself for me. Thou who hast redeemed me, called me, drawn me, waited for me. Thou who hast given me Thy Holy Spirit to testify of Thee. Thou whose life is mine, and with whom my life is entwined, so that nothing shall separate or untwine it. "Thou exceedest the fame that I heard!"

Yet I heard a great fame of Thee. They told me Thou wert gracious. They told me as much as they could put into words. And they said, "Come and see." I tried to come, but I could not see. My eyes were prevented from recognizing Thee, though Thou wast not far. Then I heard what Thou wast to others, and I knew that Thou wast the same Lord.

For Thou exceedest the fame that I heard. I find in Thee more than I heard, more than I expected, more than all. The excellency of the knowledge of Thee, Christ Jesus my Lord, not only includes all other treasures of wisdom and knowledge, but outshines them all. Thou exceedest all that I heard in every respect. No one could tell me what Thy pardoning love, Thy patience, Thy longsuffering would be to me. No one could tell me how Thy strength, Thy grace, Thy marvelous help would fit into the least as well as the greatest of my continual needs. No one could tell me what grace was poured into Thy lips for me. Thou art all to each of Thy children—a complete and all-excelling Christ to everyone, as if it were only for each one. And if Thou exceedest all that I heard, now and here amid the shadows and the veils, how far more exceeding will be Thy unshadowed and unveiled glory!

↲ FRANCES RIDLEY HAVERGAL

Encouragements to Prayer

And all things, whatsoever ye shall ask
in prayer, believing, ye shall receive.
—MATTHEW 21:22

C hrist said, "All power is mine, in heaven and on earth." Oh, the mighty power of prayer with God our Father in the name of His beloved Son! We must get to heaven before we know what that power has been in its fullest sense. Oh, the luxury of prayer! We have communion truly, familiar communion with God—to talk with God. To go and shut the door and tell God all—all—that is in our heart! To feel that He is listening to hear what we have to say to Him, and then to wait and see what He will say to us!

Dear friend, such, as you know, is the privilege of all the saints. It may be long before you see your prayers answered, for faith must be brought into exercise. Often, when we are ready to give all up, then the Lord comes, and, although in a very different manner to what we expected, He answers our prayers and puts our unbelief to shame.

Oh, to have such a God to deal with, and to know that He is always dealing with us in His providence and by His Spirit! Glorious is our high calling in Christ Jesus. It is He who says, "Ask anything in my name, and I will do it. Is anything too hard for me?" says the Lord. Such is the power of the Most High, and such the fullness of Christ, and such the boundless love of God in Jesus, that I am greatly encouraged to make large demands upon Him, the dear and all-prevailing name of His own Son and of my Savior. So, you see, I would try to encourage you, too, to pray on, and to expect an answer when your faith is fully tried.

෨ MARY WINSLOW

Train Up a Child

Train up a child in the way he should go: and
when he is old, he will not depart from it.

—PROVERBS 22:6

There is scarcely any subject concerning which I feel more anxiety than the proper education of my children. It is a difficult and delicate subject, and the more I reflect on my duty to them, the more I feel how much is to be learned by myself. The person who undertakes to form the infant mind, to cut off the distorted shoots and direct and fashion those that may, in due time, become fruitful and lovely branches, ought to possess a deep and accurate knowledge of human nature. It is no easy task to ascertain not only the principles and habits of thinking, but also the causes that produce them. It is no easy task, not only to produce correct associations but to remove improper ones that may have found a place in the mind. But such is the task of every mother who superintends the education of her children. Add to this the difficulty of maintaining that uniform and consistent course of conduct that children ought always to observe in their parents.

Not only must the precept be given to love not the world, but the life must speak the same. Not only must we exhort our infant charges to patience under their little privations and sorrows, but we must also practice those higher exercises of submission that they will easily perceive are but the more vigorous branches of the same root whose feeble twigs they are required to cultivate. Not only must we entreat them to seek first the kingdom of God, but we must be careful to let them see that we are not as easily depressed by the frown or elated by the smiles of the world as others. In short, nothing but the most persevering industry in the acquisition of necessary knowledge, the most decisive adherence to a consistent course of piety, and, above all, the most unremitted supplications to Him who alone can enable us to resolve and act correctly, can qualify us to discharge properly the duties that devolve upon every mother.

 SUSAN HUNTINGTON

Becoming Mighty in the Scriptures

That their hearts might be comforted, being knit together in love, and unto all riches of the full assurance of understanding, to the acknowledgement of the mystery of God, and of the Father, and of Christ; in whom are hid all the treasures of wisdom and knowledge.

—COLOSSIANS 2:2–3

You have entered the school of Christ and have much to learn, far beyond what men or books can of themselves teach, and you have much to receive on divine credit, beyond what human reason can comprehend. I would recommend to you to read carefully, and pause as you read, and pray as you read for the teaching of the Spirit. A degree of mystery runs through the whole of God's revealed Word, but it is His, and to be received with reverence and believed with confidence, because it is His. It is to be searched with diligence and compared. By God's teaching and the assistance of His sent servants, the child of God becomes mighty in the Scriptures. Let not mystery stagger you. We are surrounded with mysteries; we, ourselves, are mysteries inexplicable. Nor let the doctrine of election stagger you. How small a part of God's ways do we know or comprehend! Rejoice that He has given you a heritage of His people—leave the rest to Him. "Shall not the Judge of all the earth do right?"

Jesus once took a little child and set him in the midst of the people, and said, "Except ye be converted, and become as little children, ye cannot enter the kingdom of heaven," intimating with what simplicity and docility men ought to receive the gospel. There are many promises made to the diligent searchers after the truth: "Then shall we know if we follow on to know the Lord." "The secret of the LORD is with them that fear him; and he will shew them his covenant."

☙ ISABELLA GRAHAM

The Lord's Oath

Wherein God…confirmed it by an oath.

—HEBREWS 6:17

As for your fears, and ten thousand more of like nature that may arise in the heart in time of darkness, they are altogether groundless, and though they may rob you of your comfort, they cannot rob you of your safety in Christ or of that inheritance reserved for you in heaven. No, blessed be God, you are still just where free grace set you: God has fixed you in His Son and laid you, by faith, upon Him, the Rock of Ages, and now your salvation stands as immovable as the rock on which it is founded. The rain may descend, the floods come, and the winds blow, all kinds of afflictions and temptations together may beat vehemently against your faith of safety in Christ, but your security in Him shall never fall, because it is founded upon a rock that is able to bear the greatest weights that are laid upon it and to secure the building from all danger in the greatest stress of weather that can possibly befall it.

The Lord well knew what mighty assaults would be made upon the faith and comfort of His children and therefore added His oath to His great word, "That by two immutable things, in which it was impossible for God to lie, we might have a strong consolation, who have fled for refuge to lay hold upon the hope set before us" (Heb. 6:18). And have not you, my dear sister, in times past, fled unto Christ for refuge? Yea, do you not even now? Dare you flee unto any other than the name of the Lord, the great Savior, as your strong tower for safety? And if you dare not, why should you question your safety, since God's Word assures you of it? God says that the soul that runneth into the name of the Lord is safe. Satan and unbelief say nay and produce ten thousand evidences against such a soul in its own heart and life. And thus there is strife. Well, God adds His oath because He can swear by no greater than Himself. That is, He engages all the perfections of His great being for the salvation of that poor sinner who flees to Jesus.

&ppp; ANNE DUTTON

Mutual Encouragement

*Exhort one another daily, while it is called To day;
lest any of you be hardened through the deceitfulness
of sin. For we are made partakers of Christ.*

—HEBREWS 3:13–14

The Lord's people should find time to encourage each other in the way of the kingdom. How hard it is, in the midst of the hurly-burly of time and sense, to keep a steady eye upon the end of the race. Satan is called the god of this world, and he certainly loses no opportunity of asserting his power over his infatuated subjects. But his great delight is so to encumber the minds and entangle the affections of God's own people that they can scarcely realize their heavenly origin. Now this should not be.

We must—not only the minister of the gospel, but every Christian—be on our watchtower. O to be ready, quite ready, having nothing to do the moment when we shall be called home. The world is but a dreary passage through which we pass to a glorious, lasting love. Let us not be ignorant of Satan's devices. I find, when caught in any way by his traps, the best plan is at once to lift up my heart to Jesus and cry for pardon and help. He will give both. We have not far to go to reach Him. Hold fast the conviction of your oneness with Christ. He took our nature, sin only excepted, and in conversion He gives us His own. Thus our bodies become the temple of God through the Spirit. Therefore, we are exhorted to grieve not the Holy Spirit by whom we are sealed unto the day of redemption.

The present is not worth a thought, save that it conducts us to the glory that awaits the tried believer. All is true. Many of the Lord's people are looking for His appearing now. I can truly say, "Come, Lord Jesus, come quickly." May He keep us in a state of readiness for His coming.

꙳ MARY WINSLOW

No Hurt

Nothing shall by any means hurt you.
—LUKE 10:19

Is not this one of those very strong promises we are apt to think are worded a little too strongly, and of which we take a great discount? "Nothing!" If He said "nothing," have we any right to add, "Yes, but except…"? Nothing can hurt those who are joined to Christ, "for with me thou shalt be in safeguard," unless anything could be found that should separate us from Him. And who shall separate us? Earthly tribulations, even the most terrible, shall not do it, for "in all these things we are more than conquerors through Him that loved us." Yet a farther-reaching and, indeed, entirely exhaustive list is given, none of which, "nor any other creature shall be able to separate us." Let us take everything that possibly could hurt us to that list and see for ourselves if it is not included, and then rejoice in the conclusion, based and built upon Christ's bare word, but buttressed and battlemented by this splendid utterance of His inspired apostle that it is indeed so.

But He who knows our little faith never gives an isolated promise. He leaves no chance of overlooking or misunderstanding anyone, except by willful neglect, because it is always confirmed in other parts of His Word. Is not all this enough? It might well be, but His wonderful love has yet more to say—not only that nothing shall hurt us, but that all things work together for our good—not merely shall work, but actually are working. "All things," if it means "all things," must include exactly those very things, whatever they may be, which you and I are tempted to think will hurt us, or, at least, may hurt us. Now will we this day trust our own ideas or God's Word? One or other must be mistaken. Which is it? Christ, my own Master, my Lord and my God, has given a promise that meets every fear; therefore, "I will both lay me down in peace and sleep: for thou, Lord, only makest me to dwell in safety," and nothing shall by any means hurt me.

&» FRANCES RIDLEY HAVERGAL

Looking Away from Our Trials

Unto thee lift I up mine eyes, O thou
that dwellest in the heavens.

—PSALM 123:1

My beloved friend in Jesus, "think it not strange concerning the fiery trial which is to try you, as though some strange thing happened unto you," but be comforted in knowing that the Lord's gold is always tried with fire, and that the trial often comes in a time and way least expected.

May I be allowed to say that whatever is the nature of your affliction, you will find it weakening to look at it; but, looking unto Jesus, you will have, moment by moment, incomings of strength and support—not a stock in hand, but just as you need it. When Peter looked at the waves, he soon began to fear and to sink, but while he looked at his Master, though they were still boisterous, yet all was well. So I find it, and so will you. When looking at this or that painful thing, it is quite too much for us, but when looking unto Jesus and leaving all to Him, we are borne through the trial, and the very mountains become a plain, and the floods we thought would overwhelm us are made to divide that we may pass safely through.

May the Lord increase our faith and cause us to live in the fullest privilege of those deep words, "Ye are not your own," and may He be pleased so to nourish your faith by His Word and Spirit that you shall find how sweet it is. Then you will say, "This is the Lord's doing, and it is marvelous in our eyes." Whatever your present state may be, my heart would say to you, "Is anything too hard for the Lord?" Nothing! He can support and deliver; He can make you joyful in the affliction and then bring you with joy out of it. If it be His holy will, may He soon command deliverance for you, saying, "I am the Lord that healeth thee."

&» RUTH BRYAN

The Breath of the Soul

The effectual fervent prayer of a righteous man availeth much.

—JAMES 5:16

Prayer and meditation help each other. The mind that is stored with heavenly treasure, drawn from God's Word, will not need words in which to pray. But there may indeed be real prayer with very few words. He whom we serve looks at our hearts. He needs not our eloquence, were we ever so gifted. How often in His agony did our example, our Lord, use the same words! May we gain more and more of the spirit of the same adorable Lord's own prayer! It is so short, so simple, and yet so full—in fact, so truly divine. In approaching God in prayer, those who can look to Him as a father are really happy, coming themselves to Him in the spirit of adoption, casting their cares upon Him, relying on His promise, and speaking to Him with all simplicity, but with holy reverence. Those who worship the Father must do so "in spirit and in truth," feeling what they say and really intending it.

It is very important to call to mind how we can approach the Father only through the Son, pleading continually His blood and making mention of His righteousness only. Nor are our prayers acceptable, unless inspired by the Spirit. Many and many a prayer is offered directly to the Savior and many a devout aspiration is addressed to the Holy Ghost, but the usual idea of prayer is that we seek the Father, through the mediation of the Son, and assisted by the Spirit. If we would walk with God, we must "pray without ceasing"; we must send up short prayers continually, besides our stated prayers of longer continuance. And how happy is the woman who truly prays! How blessed is she who knows something of the divine art of adoration! Happy indeed here, and to be blessed forever, where prayer will be turned into praise.

&amp；ELIZABETH JULIA HASELL

The Snare of Sin

Ye therefore, beloved, seeing ye know these things before,
beware lest ye also, being led away with the error
of the wicked, fall from your own stedfastness.

—2 PETER 3:17

Beware of the first enticement to sin! Deem no sin a trifle. May God implant His holy fear in your heart that you may not depart from Him! I would rather hear He had taken you to Himself than that you had dishonored His holy name and cause. You will have need of much prayer night and day, that God may guide and uphold you, preserving you from every snare that the wicked one might throw in your way, and that, sensible of your weakness, you might rely more upon His almighty strength to carry you safely through all the temptations that lie in your path.

The devil will tempt; the world will tempt; your own carnal nature will tempt—and all your own strength of resistance is perfect weakness. How can you stand against this threefold troop, but as your Savior puts strength in you?

Seek this in earnest prayer, and, with Christ strengthening you, you can do all things. May you be helped to live decidedly for eternity, with your eye upon that glorious crown that Christ has promised to them that overcome! But a short time you have to glorify Him; aim to do it in all things and at all times. Live to God! Live for God, and God will take care that you have all you need while you live. He will give grace and glory, and no good thing will He withhold if you walk uprightly.

᪣ MARY WINSLOW

True Satisfaction

If there be therefore any consolation in Christ,
if any comfort of love, if any fellowship of the Spirit,
if any bowels and mercies, fulfil ye my joy, that ye be likeminded,
having the same love, being of one accord, of one mind.

—PHILIPPIANS 2:1–2

What if our dealings on earth should cease? If we are the followers of the Lamb, our prayers will unitedly ascend to the same blessed throne while we live, and when our pilgrimage is ended, our friendship will exist and flourish forever. We are pilgrims; we are strangers in a barren land. This world is not our portion—it is incapable of satisfying our desires. The glittering toys of life are not calculated to afford real enjoyment. There is nothing in heaven or earth that can delight our hearts and ease us of the heavy load of sin but God.

Let us not be satisfied with the low and groveling pursuits of time, but let us look to the unchangeable Jehovah for a supply of His soul-refreshing grace. How much has God done for us individually! He has, as we humbly trust, made us partakers of His grace and redeemed us from eternal death. What shall we render to Him for this abundant mercy? O let our future lives evince gratitude and let our praises unceasingly flow to His throne.

Ȥ HARRIET NEWELL

The Light of Life

Make thy face to shine upon thy servant.

—PSALM 31:16

O my soul waiteth for the Lord, more than they that watch for the morning. Waiting soul, is He sure to come? Yea, verily—more surely than that tomorrow's sun will arise upon this world when the hours of darkness have fulfilled their mission will "the Dayspring from on high" visit those whose eyes are looking for Him and His glorious beams of grace.

But there was a time—dost thou not remember it, O my soul?—when "we hid, as it were, our faces from him"; nay, worse than that, for "He was despised, and we esteemed him not." What dense blindness was that which saw no beauty in one who is "altogether lovely"! Rather, far rather, would we be mourning over our distance from Him and languishing for the manifestation of His sweet presence than that He should ever again be to us only "as a root out of a dry ground," "without form or comeliness."

Let us thank God for opening our eyes as a necessary preparation for seeing the light. We should never have prayed, "Lord, make thy face to shine upon thy servant" if we had not seen the thick cloud of our transgressions that intervened between Him and our soul's vision of His splendor. I feel as if I were writing today for someone whose spiritual experience answers to my own, and I have the hope that such a one will be comforted by "the comfort wherewith we ourselves are comforted of God." Dear friend, there is no reason why you should remain in the darkness of the Lord's averted face if you truly long to be restored to His favor. Cry for and claim the incoming light that shines in a dark place; and, before you have finished reading these words, you may hear Him say, "In a little wrath, I hid my face from thee for a moment; but with everlasting kindness will I have mercy on thee."

☙ SUSANNAH SPURGEON

The Great Stronghold

Turn you to the strong hold.
—ZECHARIAH 9:12

Ah, my loved friend, it is this stronghold that Satan fights against, and fallen flesh is in league with him. Outward form and bodily exercise may be tolerated, but inward power is represented as contemptible, unreasonable, and is called fanaticism and enthusiasm, yet the world of glory is full of this, swelling broader and deeper the anthem of praise to the holy Lord God and the Lamb. Without this divine life within, no soul can be saved, as the great day shall declare. It is indeed fearful to think what that terrible day will reveal, and of all characters, I think those seem in the most fearful condition who have had Christ on the lips, but not in the heart, as in Matthew 7:21–23. My heart often says: "Search me, O God, and know my heart; try me, and know my thoughts: and see if there be any wicked way in me, and lead me in the way everlasting." True, it is our vigilant foe who does not mind a new creed, but he hates a new heart. He does not object to outward reformation, but hates inward regeneration and also the regenerated. He does not fear good words of prayer on the lips, but he well knows he shall suffer loss when it is said of a soul, "Behold, he prayeth," for

Satan trembles when he sees
The weakest saint upon his knees.

O you trembling souls, let not the subtle serpent drive you from this stronghold; your God will hear and help you. He has taught you to pray; He will answer your prayers. If He long delay, He is worth waiting for. If He shut His door against you, it is only to make you knock louder. It is better to wait on God for His salvation in sackcloth and ashes than to wait on the world and the flesh clothed in scarlet, "for the end of these things is death."

&ofcurrency; RUTH BRYAN

Infant Grace

Ye are of God, little children, and have overcome them: because
greater is he that is in you, than he that is in the world.

—1 JOHN 4:4

Fear not because you see so little grace in you that you have not
the truth of grace, and because you see so much sin that you are
all sin. For consider, grace is yet but in its infant state, and corruption that makes against it such great opposition is like an enraged,
mighty giant. And is it any wonder to see an infant knocked down
frequently and laid for dead sensibly by the wrathful hand of a
giant, and especially by a giant and irreconcilable enemy that dwells
with the infant and seeks its destruction continually? No, a marvelous wonder it is that the power of sin, influenced by Satan, has
not long since utterly slain the life of grace in you, in me, in all the
called of God unto fellowship with His Son Jesus Christ, and left it
neither root nor branch! And whence is this? Oh, it is because that
little spark of the life of grace in us is in an inseparable union to an
immense fullness of ever-flaming grace-life in Christ! So until sin
and Satan can pluck Christ down from His high throne in heaven
and get Him slain in His human nature again, and in that endless
life of the eternal Godhead that is in Him, they can never totally
destroy the life of grace that is His life in us! Attempt it they will,
and prevail against us in part, and for a time they may; but we,
like Gad, though overcome by a troop, will be overcomers at last
and made more than conquerors through the love and blood of our
incarnate God, our all-triumphant Head!

Therefore, in the Lord's name, let us set up our banner against
sin and Satan and go forth to the fight as those who are already
blessed with a complete victory in Christ. And to cheer our spirits, let us consider that stronger is the Lord that is in us than all
the force of the enemy that can possibly be against us; that infant
grace is and shall be maintained in life and raised to its perfection
by an almighty arm; and that by the omnipotence of an infinite
God, the giant sin shall have a full and eternal destruction!

❧ ANNE DUTTON

Seeking for His Commandments

Keep and seek for all the commandments
of the LORD your God.
—1 CHRONICLES 28:8

Is not this precept too often halved? We acknowledge our obligation to keep, but what about seeking for all the commands of the
Lord our God? Are we doing this? Even when, by His grace, we
have been led to take the beautiful steps in that path mentioned in
Psalm 119—believing them, learning them, longing for them, loving them, and not forgetting them—there remains yet this further
step, seeking for all of them. Perhaps we have even a little shrinking
from this. We are afraid of seeing something that might be peculiarly hard to keep; it seems as if it might be enough to try to keep
what commandments we have seen without seeking for still more,
and as if seeing more to keep would only involve us in heavier obligations and in more failures to keep them. And we almost wish we
had never seen this added command, forgetting that shedding of
blood was needed for sin through ignorance. But we have seen it,
even if we never noticed it before; it is shown to us today, and we
have no alternative but obedience or disobedience to it.

We need not fear being left to struggle with newly discovered
impossibilities, for with the light that reveals a command, the grace
to fulfill it will surely be given. It is very humbling when the Spirit's
light flashes upon some command of our God that we have never
observed, much less done, and yet it is a very gracious answer to
the prayer "Teach me to do thy will." In reading His Word, let us
steadily set ourselves to seek for all His yet unnoticed commandments, noting day by day what we find; thus, knowing more of His
will, will be a step toward doing more of it. Let us not be content
with vaguely praying, "Lord, what wilt Thou have me to do?" but
set to work to see what He has already said we are to do and then,
"whatsoever he saith unto you, do it."

❧ FRANCES RIDLEY HAVERGAL

Nothing Wavering

If any of you lack wisdom, let him ask of God, that giveth to all men liberally, and upbraideth not; and it shall be given him.

—JAMES 1:5

I have been thinking of those words of James, "If any of you lack wisdom, let him ask of God, that giveth to all men liberally, and upbraideth not; and it shall be given him. But let him ask in faith, nothing wavering." I believe Christians are often lean from day to day because, though they ask for grace, they do not ask in faith. I sometimes feel so little and so vile that I fear God will disdain to help me. But I am always unhappy when I am in such a frame. Surely the God who gave me a spirit capable of loving and serving Him cannot esteem it beneath Him to regard my cry when I plead that my soul may be fitted for His service.

I fear I indulge too much in a spirit of bondage, which generates gloom, terror, superstition, and despair. I am always happiest when I can view God as a merciful creator who is more ready to give spiritual than temporal blessings and has given us every encouragement we can desire to trust in Him.

The idea that God is not willing to help me, that He is a hard master, that I have not obtained and shall never obtain His grace, or any similar discouraging thought, paralyzes my exertions, throws a superstitious terror over my soul that drives me from prayer, and unfits me for every duty. I must believe that though the vision tarry, it is my duty to wait for it. Yes, my soul, wait at wisdom's gate, and you shall not be disappointed. Though your sins discourage you and your worldly attachments alarm you, wait upon that Jesus who was never called upon in vain. O my God, glory be to Thy name, that I can hope in mercy and believe that Thou wilt one day bruise Satan under Thy feet and give me a complete and final victory! I beseech Thee, let me not be deceived.

∾ SUSAN HUNTINGTON

True Conversion

For what shall it profit a man, if he shall gain the
whole world, and lose his own soul?

—MARK 8:36

The one object that is of more importance to you than were you the queen of the universe concerns that world which is to last through countless millions of years. This is all-important to you and me. The very thought of losing the future inheritance, and of the solemn results of such a loss, makes one shudder. I would not alarm you but would rather allure you to Christ. I would rather tell you of His love and willingness to save.

Will you not, then, make a full surrender of your heart to Christ? This you have not yet done. Conversion consists not of a mere change of sentiment or of head knowledge only; it is a change of heart. "A new heart also will I give you…and I will take away the stony heart out of your flesh, and I will give you an heart of flesh." It is a passing from death unto life—a translation out of Satan's kingdom into the kingdom of God's dear Son: out of the kingdom of darkness into the kingdom of life, light, and love. O that you but knew the real delight of sitting as a pardoned sinner at the feet of Jesus for five minutes. You would exclaim, "This is happiness such as I never tasted before!" When I reflect upon the fearful doom that awaits the unconverted, I feel intensely anxious that all dear to me should flee to the precious blood that cleanses from all sin.

It is not a little water in baptism nor an ocean of water that cleanses away sin and saves the soul; it is to be born again of the Spirit and to be washed in the blood of Christ, on the ground of which only can we enter heaven. Religion is a reality, a glorious reality. Go to Jesus; urge your pleas; take the position of Queen Esther, who stood between life and death, and Jesus will extend to you the golden scepter and your request shall be granted.

ও MARY WINSLOW

The Putting Forth of the Sheep

When he putteth forth his own sheep, he goeth before them,
and the sheep follow him: for they know his voice.

—JOHN 10:4

What gives the Alpine climber confidence in wild, lonely, difficult passes or ascents when he has not passed this way before? It is that his guide has been there before, and also that in every present step over unknown and possibly treacherous ice or snow, his guide goes before. It is to Christ's own sheep that this promise applies. It is when He puts them forth that it comes true—not when they put themselves forth or when they let a stranger lure them forth or such traitors as self-cowardice or impatience drive them forth. Sometimes it is a literal putting forth. We have been in a sheltered nook of the fold, and we are sent to live where it is windier and wilder. The home nest is stirred up, and we have to go. We do not put ourselves forth, as we would rather stay, but it has to be. But Jesus "goeth before." He prepares the earthly as well as the heavenly places for us. He will be there when we get to the new place. Sometimes it is putting forth into the rough places of suffering, whether from temptation, pain, or any adversity. Not one step here but Jesus has gone before us, and He still goes before us, often so very close before us, that even by the still waters we never seemed so near Him.

Sooner or later, perhaps again and again, He puts forth His own sheep into a position of greater separation—forth from an outer into an inner circle, always nearer and nearer to the great Center. Let us watch very sensitively for such leading. Every hesitation to yield to His gentle separation from the world results in heart separation from Him. When He thus goes before, shall we risk being left behind? He will put forth His own sheep at last into the path that none of them shall ever tread alone, because He trod it alone. Jesus knows every single step of that valley, and when His people enter it, they will surely find that their King shall pass before them, and the Comforter will say, "He it is that doth go before thee."

❧ FRANCES RIDLEY HAVERGAL

Precious Promises

And grieve not the holy Spirit of God.
—EPHESIANS 4:30

If, my dear sister, you would have increasing nearness to Christ, as to communion-love, don't grieve the Comforter by refusing to be comforted. Listen to and credit the testimony of the Holy Ghost in those sweet whispers of love to Christ that He is pleased to give to your heart at times by the application of particular promises. What, will you by your unbelief, in turning a deaf ear to the sweet voice of your Lord's love, obstruct that communion with Him therein that your soul so much desires? Will you grieve the Holy Ghost, your comforter, and dishonor Him who, in His witness of love of Christ to you through applied promises, is the truth, and by giving heed to the father of lies, who suggests to your mind that you have no right to those promises because they come not with so much power as you could wish?

Know and be assured that all the promises of God are yes and amen in Christ; to every soul that looks to Him for life, one and all the promises are yours, forever yours, as a looker unto Jesus. And the Holy Spirit as a comforter is given you from your own Lord Jesus, to apply to your heart, in your times of need, some of those many exceeding great and precious promises for your refreshment and consolation. And can you doubt, when any particular promise is from the Lord—when it suits your case, strengthens your faith, encourages your hope, and spreads abroad the savor and sweetness of Christ and of free grace of God in Him, throughout your heart, to your soul's refreshment and joy? O, my dear sister, there is not a promise brought to your mind that brings Christ and you, God and you, together, if it be but for a moment, but was from the Lord. That which comes from God leads to Him. Listen then, my dear sister, to the still, small voice of your Savior's love, when He doth but whisper, as it were. Say, "It is the voice of my Beloved!"

☙ ANNE DUTTON

The Idle Word

But I say unto you, That every idle word that men shall speak,
they shall give account thereof in the day of judgment.
—MATTHEW 12:36

The wise man said, "Pleasant words are as an honeycomb, sweet to the soul." And again King Solomon tells us that "a word fitly spoken is like apples of gold in pictures of silver." Wise, kind, and pleasant words are as highly praised in the Bible, as idle, wrong, and foolish words are condemned in the Book of books. When God gave man the gift of speech, He made Him to differ from all other animals. It was a noble gift, and one that may be used for the holiest, or abused for the basest purposes. As man uses speech, he honors, or else dishonors, his creator; he benefits or grievously injures his fellowmen; he advances the kingdom of God, or he impedes it. There can be no doubt that, at the last day, God will call us to account for our words.

How will the profane swearer account for his oaths and irreverent use of the sacred name of God? How will the liar and the slanderer account for their mischievous and wicked words? How will the idle busybody in other people's matters and the mischief maker account for their words? May they take warning while time is granted them, and, repenting of their sins, turning to God in Christ, may they amend their use of the noble gift of speech!

And what an account will they have to give who take pleasure in speaking of those things that should not even be named among Christians! Remember that the words we have been speaking of are far more than idle words; they are wicked words, a most grievous abuse of the use of speech and exceedingly sinful. If the future Judge of the world will condemn "every idle word," where will the swearer, the liar, the slanderer, and the man of unholy talk appear at the last great and terrible day?

ॐ ELIZABETH JULIA HASELL

God's Word the Believer's Rule

Thy word have I hid in mine heart,
that I might not sin against thee.
—PSALM 119:11

Let us aim to live more above the world and look alone to the Bible as our divine directory in all things and alone to our God for His approbation. Let us be ashamed of nothing but sinning against Him and grieving His Holy Spirit. Oh, if we did but this at all times, how much more should we adorn the doctrine of God our Savior in all things, and how much easier should we pass through a world lying in wickedness! The Lord is with His people at all times, and blessed is the man that trusts in Him. It is high time we awoke out of sleep, and, with the blessed Word of eternal truth in our hands, aim to live more for eternity, to live more for God and to God. With the world—its opinions and maxims—we, as believers, have nothing to do, for they are contrary to God's Word.

We have nothing to do with what other people do and say. We have got to do with God's Word and God only, and when we can bring all our poor concerns, little and great, and our poor hearts, too, to Him and lay them all before Him, I am persuaded we need fear nothing, for God will order all things for us, will bless us, make His love known to us more and more; and we shall see His dear hand held out to help and guide us through this wilderness safely and honorably, to that happy home His love has prepared for us above. Oh to love Jesus and to know that He loves us! To aim, although we constantly come short, to glorify Him in all we do and say, and to let that be our highest aim.

☙ MARY WINSLOW

The Call of the Spirit

For the Son of man is come to seek and to save that which was lost.

—LUKE 19:10

Have you thought about the love of the Spirit? Have you realized that God's loving Spirit says to you, "Come"? Are you conscious that if you refuse to listen to this gentlest call, you are grieving the Holy Spirit of God—vexing Him by the rebellion to which this refusal really amounts—resisting the Holy Ghost? Every "come" in the Bible is the call of the Spirit. And every time that a still, small voice in your heart says, "Come," it is the call of the Spirit. The last time those words "come unto Me" came into your mind, whether in some wakeful night hour or suddenly and unaccountably amid the stir of the day, did you think it was the very voice of the Holy Spirit speaking in your heart? Or did you let other voices drown it, not knowing that the goodness of God was leading you by it?

Every time an ambassador of Christ bids you come, and every time that anyone who loves Him tries to speak a word for Jesus to you, it is the call of the Spirit and the bride, for the bride is the church of Christ, and she is the privileged instrument through which music of the call is most often heard. What makes you take the trouble to read this book? Why is there any attraction at all for you in the subject? Is it not that the Holy Spirit is causing your heart to vibrate—it may be but very feebly as yet—at the thrill of His secret call? Your awakening wish to come is the echo of that call. If you stop and listen, it will be heard more distinctly and willingly. The call will grow fuller and stronger as you turn and yield and follow it. And the same blessed Spirit will give you power to do this. He will show you your need of Jesus, and He will testify of Jesus to you, so that you shall be very willing to come. But it is not a light thing to put away a holy desire, however feeble, because it sprang not from your own heart but is the voice of the Spirit saying, "Come!" It will not always speak if not obeyed. But He is striving now, and he is calling now: "To day, if ye will hear his voice, harden not your heart."

º FRANCES RIDLEY HAVERGAL

All Grace Abounding

And God is able to make all grace abound toward you;
that ye, always having all sufficiency in all things,
may abound to every good work.

—2 CORINTHIANS 9:8

What a treasure trove is here for poverty-stricken souls! If our faith were but strong and eager enough to gather up the riches stored in this chest of blessing, what millionaires in grace we might become! "But the chest is fast locked," you say. "How can we grasp what we cannot see?" True, yet faith is the key that not only unlocks these treasures but also gives us the right to claim them as our own and use them to the constant enrichment of our daily life.

I do not know how it is with you, but when I look upon such an exhibition of divine possibilities as is contained in this and similar portions of God's Word, I wonder, with sore amazement, at my own spiritual condition, which, far too often, is reduced to one of indigence and distress. The grand assurance, here given by the apostle, of our God's ability to supply all our need, is not a new thing to us. We know that He "is able to make all grace abound" toward us; we fully recognize the blessedness of "always having all sufficiency in all things"; we desire intensely to "abound to every good work"; but few of us have joyfully entered upon this inheritance.

O come, all you longing souls; come, poor, doubting reader; come, weak and trembling writer; gird up the loins of your mind and let your faith march boldly into this Promised Land, never again to leave it till it is exchanged for the heavenly Canaan! Think for a moment how wealthy we should be could we but thus believe in our God. What could we not be, and do, and suffer, if all grace abounded toward us? With what persistency and impressiveness does the apostle repeat the word *all*—that little word with so vast a meaning! Can we imagine the bliss of possessing all grace—always (or, all ways), and having all sufficiency—in all things?

☙ SUSANNAH SPURGEON

Like Christ

See then that ye walk circumspectly, not as fools, but as wise.

—EPHESIANS 5:15

If we would strive against sin and be holy women to God, let us labor to be and do this in the whole of our actions, toward all that we have to do with. If our actions do not agree with our words, our words will be of little weight with those that hear them. Oh dear Christians, let us use the most diligence in all of our stations, relations, and employments to behave as becomes saints: to be like Christ in all manner of conversation and to walk, even as He also walked. Let us love and increase in love and its labor, to and for all the saints of every denomination, as our dear brethren in Christ. And never let us open our mouths to speak one word against them, in anger, wrath, or malice. For we cannot do this without piercing Christ to the heart, as it were; we cannot touch the least of His, if it be but in their name, but we touch the apple of His eye. And if we bite and devour one another, we shall be devoured one of another. We shall provoke the Lord to let the fury of wolves upon us, to drive us nearer together in love.

Oh, let us love as brethren to Christ and to one another in Him, as children of our heavenly Father, as His dear children, and dearly let us love one another. Let us sympathize with each other in all our joys and sorrows, relieve each other's necessities, seek each other's good, bear each other's burdens, and so fulfill the law of Christ. Love one another even as He has loved us. How would the heart, lip, and life unity of the saints convince the unbelieving world of the truth of religion and of the excellency of the ways and people of God! And let us also abound in love, meekness, gentleness, and goodness toward all men. Let us every way seek their good, and, as we have opportunity, to do good to all. May the Lord incline all our hearts to follow the Lamb wherever He goes!

❧ ANNE DUTTON

Purge Us

Help us, O God of our salvation, for the glory of thy name:
and deliver us, and purge away our sins, for thy name's sake.

—PSALM 79:9

I earnestly desire to know the real state of my case and to have my soul laid open to the "sword of the Spirit, which is the word of God"; for whom He loveth He woundeth, and whom He woundeth He will heal. Faithful are the wounds of this friend, though painful, and I would rather covet them than hear Him say, "Let her alone. She hath loved idols; after idols let her go." Oh no, my precious Jesus; I could not bear that, even for a little while. I want to be continually with Thee in my own experience, to know much of Thy mind, enjoy much of Thy love, and daily to walk with Thee in endearing communion.

I want this also for the whole living family, and would especially plead for those zealous workers who are promoting every means to bring others to Thee, yet themselves rarely see Thy face or hear Thy voice and yet are not in mourning about it. Oh, grant them a revival, a requickening, a return, and a daily partaking of those fruits they are commending to others. Put in Thy pierced hand by the hole of the door of their heart and cause their affections to be moved for Thee, that with earnest longing they may say, "I will rise now" and go forth and "seek Him whom my soul loveth." Oh, precious Savior, we would seek Thee for them, and seek Thee with them, for our soul can never be satisfied with dwelling at Jerusalem without seeing the King's face. Shine on us, shine in us, shine through us—and in such light there will be living warmth. Bring us to sit at Thy dear feet and lean upon Thy bosom, and through much communion with Thee to be fragrant with Thy perfumes and thus to be refreshing to each other. Thus shall the Three-One Jehovah have glory, to whom Thy poor handmaid giveth heartfelt, though feeble praise: "Blessed be the God of Israel, from everlasting to everlasting. Amen and amen."

❧ RUTH BRYAN

Recognizing His Commandments

And this is his commandment.

—1 JOHN 3:23

We may be quite sure of three things: first, that whatever our Lord commands us, He really means us to do; second, that whatever He commands us is for our good always; and, third, that whatever He commands us, He is able and willing to enable us to do, for all God's biddings are enablings. But do we practically recognize all His commandments as commandments, and the breach of any one of them as sin? As we read each precept, let us solemnly say to ourselves, "This is his commandment," and oh, what a touchstone of guilt will it be! How we shall see that what we have been excusing as infirmity and natural weakness that we could not help, and shortcomings with regard to impossible standards, has been all sin, transgression, disobedience, needing to be bitterly repented of, needing nothing less than the precious blood of Christ for atonement and cleansing.

Perhaps this is the sad secret of many a mourning life among God's children. They are calling sin by other names. They think it is only natural temperament and infirmity, for which they are to claim sympathy, to go on doubting and distrusting their Savior and their God; yet this is His commandment, that we should believe on the name of His Son Jesus Christ, and this: trust in Him at all times. They think they are to be tenderly pitied for having such a burden to bear and such sadness of heart, yet this is His commandment: "Cast thy burden upon the Lord"; and this: "Rejoice in the Lord always." They do not think they can exactly help their hearts being so cold that they do not know whether they love Him or not, yet this is His commandment: "Thou shalt love the Lord thy God with all thy heart." Yet, oh, dear friend, if the Lord has indeed commanded these things, it is a state of disobedience. If He has said them, He means you to do them. Oh, come face to face with His Word; do not shrink from the terrible shock of seeing sin where you only thought of infirmity.

&. FRANCES RIDLEY HAVERGAL

The Redeemer's Sufferings

Recall, my heart, that dreadful hour,
When Jesus on the cursed tree
Infinite pains and sorrows bore—
Think, O my soul, was this for thee?

See, crowned with thorns that sacred head,
With beams of glory once adorned!
That voice, which heaven and earth obeyed,
Is now by traitors mocked and scorned.

And see those lovely melting eyes,
Whence kind compassion often flowed,
Now raised imploring to the skies,
For hardened souls athirst for blood!

Those healing hands with blessings fraught,
Nailed to the cross with pungent smart!
Inhuman deed! could no kind thought
To pity move the ruthless heart?

But oh! what agonies unknown,
His soul sustained beneath the load
Of mortal crimes! how deep the groan
Which calmed the vengeance of a God!

He groaned! He died! the awful scene
Of wonder, grief, surprising love,
Forever let my heart retain,
Nor from my Savior's feet remove.

Jesus, accept this wretched heart,
Which trembling, mourning, comes to Thee;
The blessing of Thy death impart,
And tell my soul, 'tis all for me.

≥ ANNE STEELE

A Lifting Up for the Downcast

In the LORD put I my trust.

—PSALM 11:1

The day will soon break and the shadows flee away; the dear Savior, whom you seek, will again comfort His returning prodigal. There is scarce a heaven-taught soul who has made any advances in spiritual warfare, but could sympathize with you from experience. What have you experienced more than the Scriptures tell us? That "the heart is deceitful above all things, and desperately wicked." Only the Lord can search it, and only He can cleanse it. You may strive and fight and resolve and vow—and all will not do; you lie at His mercy for holiness as well as pardon. He is exalted as a prince to give repentance, and He is the author and finisher of faith. He works all our works in us, and without Him we are not equal to one good thought. We are His workmanship, created anew in Christ Jesus. My dear friend, put the work into His hand and try to wait on Him in hope—hope in every situation; do more: trust.

None of us have our heaven here; no, sin dwells in us. The very best have their ups and downs. My safety depends not on my frames, but His promise. When tossed and tempted, dead and lifeless, emptied of every good, perhaps buffeted like you with abominable thoughts, the fiery darts of Satan—casting all on Him, I am as safe as when basking in the sunshine of His love and tasting what you have tasted; for you have tasted, and you shall yet taste the joys of His salvation.

All my advice may be summed up in this—trust in the Lord with all your heart; at least aim at this. I say aim at it, for this too must be given you. Roll yourself, your doubts, your fears, your sins, your duties, all on Him. Say "Lord I believe, help my unbelief." He is an almighty Savior to deliver sinners from sin as well as from punishment. I leave you on the Father of mercies.

→ ISABELLA GRAHAM

Our Light Affliction

For as the sufferings of Christ abound in us,
so our consolation also aboundeth by Christ.

—2 CORINTHIANS 1:5

It is the pleasure of our dear Father to exercise you in a very particular manner, and to continue it long upon you. But do not be cast down as if some strange thing happened, for as many as the Lord loves He rebukes and chastens. But perhaps you will say, "My affliction is very uncommon, has lasted a great while, and it is likely to endure so long as I am in this world." Well, be it so. Yet remember that God's special love to you ordained this particular trial, and His everlasting kindness keeps it still upon you. This was the means Infinite Wisdom pitched on for the display of boundless love to you. By this you are to be made conformable to Christ in sufferings and made fit for conformity to Him in glory. Since free grace has saved you, allow it to carry on your salvation in its own way. Though you pass through much tribulation, the kingdom is at the end. I doubt not but the Lord at times has opened much of His love to your soul in the present afflictions. The great opening of God's heart, in the gift of every trial, is reserved for us until we get over Jordan, on the other side of death, into the land of promise; then we shall remember all the way the Lord led us through the wilderness, and we see it was a right way to a city of habitation.

Meanwhile, we must live by faith strong enough to pierce the cloud of afflictive providences and discern the love of our Father's heart, which, as an infinite deep, coucheth beneath and is the spring of every dispensation. We should sing in sorrow, take pleasure in distresses, and glorify God in the fires. "Our light affliction," says the apostle, "which is but for a moment, worketh for us a far more exceeding and eternal weight of glory" (2 Cor. 4:17).

ॐ ANNE DUTTON

Showing Forth the Praises of God

*The heart is deceitful above all things, and desperately
wicked: who can know it? I the LORD search the heart, I try
the reins, even to give every man according to his ways,
and according to the fruit of his doings.*

—JEREMIAH 17:9–10

It is only by very slow degrees that the heart is taught to know its innate deceitfulness and total depravity, and it is only a gracious knowledge of this that can produce true penitence, deep humiliation, and self-despair. In proportion as this is learned, by the teaching of the Holy Spirit, the soul is brought to the foot of the cross and there casts itself upon the Savior and obtains a simpler and transforming view of His love, His suitableness, His beauty, His all-sufficiency to save. Then the work of the Redeemer begins to open in all its splendor, and the divine perfections of the glorious Trinity, in their different offices, shine forth with an effulgence of majesty and love.

Hereby the soul is gradually changed into the divine image and prepared for heaven. And now it begins to feel the importance of life. It is only the living who can show forth the praises of God—in suffering, in repentance for sin, in rejoicing in tribulation, in evidencing the truth of Scripture, in being an instructor and an example to others, and in manifesting that the life of God in the soul, with sweet communion and fellowship with the Father, Son, and Holy Ghost, is sufficient to keep the mind in peace and comfort, under the most severe and long-continued afflictions. If these blessed effects are in any measure produced, is there not sufficient cause to thank God for the preservation of life?

The greatest favor and honor that can be afforded to a believing sinner is to be permitted and enabled, if by any means, to glorify her Father in heaven. For this purpose Christ came from heaven, and this should be the business of believers on earth.

&- SARAH HAWKES

Our Only Strength

God is our refuge and strength, a very present help in trouble.

—PSALM 46:1

My dear friend, I am a perverse scholar, even in the school of affliction. I too often find that it is only the immediate pressure of trials that keeps me in anything of a suitable frame. Like those children who return to folly as soon as the chastening hand of the parent is withdrawn, I feel that I have an evil heart, continually inclining me to depart from the living God. Yet, great as has been my guilt in profiting no more by the rod, I would still humbly believe that these chastisements have afforded me some comforting views of God, which have strengthened and animated me to go on my way rejoicing, some manifestations of the state of my own soul, of the preciousness of the Word, and of the safety and sweetness of trusting in the Lord, which I should not otherwise have had.

My dear friend, why is it so difficult to confide in God in relation to what looks dark and doubtful before us, when we have so often found that He is a very present help in trouble and that He does make His severest dispensations work for our good? Why can we not cast all our cares upon Him that careth for us? It is a great dishonor to our compassionate God to doubt whether He will sustain us in our extremity or fear that He will lay more upon us than He will enable us to bear. No, no—it cannot be. Only let us entrust ourselves and all our interests unreservedly to Him who loved us unto death, and we must be safe. But ah, these vile hearts! Faith struggles and struggles and prevails; then we have comfort. Then unbelief, secretly but successfully, undermines our hopes, and we are in darkness. Yet let us not fear. God will, I trust, one day bruise Satan under our feet.

☙ SUSAN HUNTINGTON

The Reasonableness of Praise

While I live will I praise the LORD: I will sing praises unto my God while I have any being.

—PSALM 146:2

How seldom are our hearts tuned to praise, and yet every hour and each moment of our existence should be so. David says, "I will sing praises unto my God while I have any being." How sweetly and blessedly was he taught of God, and how experimental are all his writings. When I feel I want my heart incited to praise, I read the Psalms. And when I want my faith increased, I turn to some of God's dealings with the saints of old, knowing that He is the same now that He was then. What a mercy it is to have an almighty friend powerful and willing to help in every time of need.

I often think it requires more faith to go to Him with small things than in great trials. We are apt to think He will not take notice of our little difficulties and feel ashamed to call upon so great and mighty a being for every trifle. But this thought originates with Satan and the pride of our hearts, for in one sense, the universe itself and ten thousand such worlds are trifles in comparison to God. But when we read that every hair of our head is numbered, what encouragement we have to take all and everything to Him who alone can deliver us out of all our troubles.

I think carrying our little troubles and wants to God honors Him even more than when we go to Him with greater, and so with regard to faith. God always has honored little faith, however small. And this will ever be the case. Faith is His own peculiar and gracious gift, and He never fails to honor it.

◈ MARY WINSLOW

Rough Ways Made Smooth

The crooked shall be made straight, and the
rough ways shall be made smooth.

—LUKE 3:5

Let us refer wholly to the will and wisdom of our heavenly Father the little things we are apt to desire and to lay out for ourselves as a path to walk to heaven in. Alas! We will make a foolish choice if left to our own wisdom; we should soon be undone if left to our own conduct. Let us not affect it; there is a snake in the grass of those pleasing things that we desire to lie down in that the Lord denies us of, that we do not see, that would soon destroy the health and comfort of our souls. We naturally love smooth things, but, alas, we have so much roughness in us that we must have rough things to smooth us. It is good we have a Father who loves us infinitely, who is infinitely wise and well knows how to make us as glorious as He designs us; who will not spare for our crying but will remove our knots and blemishes and hew and carve us into stately pieces of His workmanship, whatever labor it costs Him, whatever sharp things are needful to be used about us, or whatever blows are requisite to be given us.

Come, let us give up ourselves into our all-wise, all-gracious, and almighty Father's hands. He will make us sons of God indeed! He will put upon us a glory that is every way answerable to our high relation; He will work us up into the image, the glorious image, of His firstborn Son! And what matter which way He does it? If this blessed work is done, we shall rejoice and praise Him forever. Oh, we shall admire and adore the Lord's ways with us, which are mercy and truth; we shall see and say, they were like God—worthy of God—of His great being—of His glorious art! Till then, let us live by faith, and in the obedience thereof shroud ourselves under the shadow of Jehovah's wings, and cry unto Him continually, under a deep sense of our utter insufficiency and of His all-sufficiency to guide us by a right way to the city of habitation.

э ANNE DUTTON

Our Great Adversary

Be sober, be vigilant; because your adversary the devil,
as a roaring lion, walketh about, seeking whom he may devour:
whom resist stedfast in the faith.

—1 PETER 5:8–9

If Christians could only know the awful strength and might of their archenemy, they would be more vigilant, more constant in prayer, more unceasingly intent on abiding in Christ. There are many instances in which God's Word recognizes the power and malignity of the devil, but they are sufficient to prove the necessity of stern watchfulness against so powerful and insidious a foe. If we are not ignorant of his devices, it behooves us to be prepared against his attacks.

Feeling somewhat downcast at the prospect of the ceaseless war that must be waged and the constant precautions that must be taken against the enemy; knowing, moreover, by sad experience, that the same dreadful power had a too willing ally within me and so could the more easily tempt and deceive my soul; with a cry to God for help, I turned to the following quotation: "Although we trust in the power of the death of Jesus to cancel the guilt of sin, we do not exercise a reliant and appropriating faith in the omnipotence of the living Savior to deliver us from the bondage of sin and the power of Satan in our daily life. We forget that Christ works in us mightily, and that, one with Him, we possess strength sufficient to overcome every temptation."

Here was just the word of gracious strengthening that I needed, and truly my heart did bless God for it. Yes, Satan is strong, but my Lord Jesus is stronger than he. The devil may hate me with all the vehemence of his malicious nature, but "love is strong as death," and the love of God in Christ is my everlasting safeguard.

❧ SUSANNAH SPURGEON

The Safe Venture

Bid me come unto thee on the water. And he said, Come.

—MATTHEW 14:28–29

If Jesus says "Come!" don't you think you may venture? Perhaps it is night in your soul—as dark as ever it can be. It would not be so bad if you could even distinctly see the waves of the troubled sea on which you are tossing. You do not know where you are. All seems vague, uncertain, wretched, and confused. And though the Lord Jesus is very near you, though He has come to you walking on the water and has said, "It is I, be not afraid," you cannot see Him, and you are not at all sure it is His voice, or if He is speaking to you. So of course you are troubled. And if, in this trouble, you go on trying to steer and row for yourself, these same waves will prove themselves to be awful realities, and you will be lost in the storm.

It does not matter in the least that you cannot see, feel, hear, or distinguish anything else at all. It does not matter in the least that you feel miserable and confused and that you don't know what will come next. It does not matter in the least that you cannot exactly understand how this simple coming can result in calm, peace, safety, and finding yourself at land. It does not matter in the least that the waters are casting up all the mire and dirt of all the sinfulness of heart and life, the old sins, and the besetting sins. It does not matter in the least that all the winds of doubt seem let loose upon you, boisterous and blowing from every point to which you turn. All this—and everything else that is contrary—is only so much the more reason for the simple venture. Just only you come! And even if in the very act of coming you are afraid and think you are beginning to sink, come on with the cry, "Lord, save me!" and immediately Jesus will save you; and with the strong grasp of His hand the unanswerable question will come, "Why did you doubt?" He will cause you to know His hand and His might; He will save.

❧ FRANCES RIDLEY HAVERGAL

The Value of Our Soul

*And the publican, standing afar off, would not lift up
so much as his eyes unto heaven, but smote upon his breast,
saying, God be merciful to me a sinner.*

—LUKE 18:13

How is it, more than everything else, with your soul—that better part that must live forever? And yet, though we know this, how much more are our thoughts engaged with this present evil world and our poor decaying bodies than concerned to know what awaits us in an endless eternity. Is not this one of Satan's devices? He will endeavor to engage our thoughts with often the veriest trifles that would shame a child in order to hide from us the eternal realities of the glory that awaits the believer. Oh, let us beware of Satan's devices! Many hard conflicts have I had with him through my long and checkered life, and, had I not been upheld by Jesus, the sinner's friend, I should have made shipwreck of my faith long since. But this dear friend stands ready to help you, too. Recollect, He is a present help in every time of need. You are not in a wilderness; rather, a wealthy land lies before you. Make your calling and election sure. Make sure your acceptance in Christ. Is there—or can there be—anything on earth of equal consequence to this? A soul saved or a soul lost!

Come, just as you are, to Jesus. The prayer "God be merciful to me a sinner," springing from a real sense of our need and breathed from a heart feeling its awful sinfulness and the utter impossibility of salvation in any other way, will, in due time, be responded to by the Holy Spirit. We cannot utter one real prayer but by the Holy Ghost. He it is who shows us our iniquity and helplessness, teaches us how to pray and what to ask for, and then responds to our prayer.

Oh, dear friend, pray over your Bible, that this same blessed Spirit may unfold to your mind the precious truths it contains. Never rest until you can say, "I have found Jesus, and my soul is saved!"

≈ MARY WINSLOW

Love for the Heathen

And the scripture, foreseeing that God would justify
the heathen through faith, preached before the gospel unto
Abraham, saying, In thee shall all nations be blessed.

—GALATIANS 3:8

How sweet is the gospel to the heart of the believer! How does the pure word of truth animate the desponding sinner and encourage him to apply to the Lamb of God for pardon and sanctification! But of this glorious gospel, which reveals to mortals the way of salvation, the far greater part of the inhabitants of the earth are deprived. "Where there is no vision, the people perish." Thousands of immortal souls are entering eternity and populating the dark realms of woe. If our souls are of greater importance than this world, with all its boasted treasures, how can we calculate the worth of these millions of souls which are equally as precious as our own?

We have had the Bible in our hands from our childhood, and we are instructed regularly from this precious volume every Sabbath. We have believing friends to associate with, and we enjoy the stated ordinances of the gospel. But the dear heathen have no such privileges. Have we any benevolence? Are we susceptible of feeling for the distresses of our fellow creatures?

As we value the salvation that a Savior offers, as we value His tears, His labors, and His death, let us now seriously ask what we will do for the salvation of the benighted heathen. If we are not permitted to visit them ourselves and declare to them the efficacy of a Savior's blood, yet we can ardently pray for them. Suffice it to say that when the whole universe shall stand collected at the bar of God, we shall meet them, and there render a solemn account for the manner in which we have conducted ourselves toward them in this world.

❧ HARRIET NEWELL

A Honeycomb of Delight

Because the LORD loved you.
—DEUTERONOMY 7:8

My gracious God, there is a honeycomb of delight and sweetness in these words: "because the Lord loved you." This is His great reason for all His dealings with His own. It is a full and convincing answer to all the doubts and questionings with which Satan can perplex and distress the Lord's timid ones. The enemy of souls has—alas!—a powerful confederate in the wicked unbelief that lurks within us, but they will both be vanquished when we have learned to use this weapon of war against them.

Come, my heart, try its blessed force and quality at this moment! The foe says, "Why does God send you affliction, sorrow, and suffering, when those who fear not His name have continual quietness and abounding prosperity?" If you can boldly answer, "It is because the Lord loves me," you will have given him such a sword thrust as will free you, for a time, at least, from his cunning devices and fierce onslaughts.

Or, look at the text as a shaft of sunlight piercing through a chink in the shuttered window of some dark experience. Bring your fears and forebodings out of the dusky corners and place them within the radiance of this light of love. You will be amazed to see them transformed into confident trusts; your doubts will vanish as if they had never been, and the evil and bitter things of life will all be changed to blessings in a moment. "Because the Lord loved you" is a master key that fits the wards of the hardest question and opens the mysteries of the deepest problem. It is a talisman of wondrous efficacy, and every believer in the Lord Jesus Christ may not only rejoice in its possession but also use it constantly to obtain all the desire of his heart in spiritual things.

~ SUSANNAH SPURGEON

The Sin of Pride

The pride of life, is not of the Father, but is of the world.

—1 JOHN 2:16

The sin of pride, as it springs from gospel unbelief, is directly opposite to the gospel of Christ in that it rejects the Savior, in whole or in part, and would rival it, in extreme vanity, with the Lord of glory. It would rob the Savior of His invaluable crown, who died in the place of sinners to raise them from death to that eternal life of a seat with Him on His high and everlasting throne; yes, it is directly contrary to the great design of God the Father, in and by the gospel of His Son, which is to make Himself an everlasting name, to display the exceeding riches of His free grace in the whole and in every part of a sinner's salvation and bliss, to the eternal praise of His own glory.

But pride—horrid pride—will not endure that the Lord should have the entire glory of His saving grace—of His free, rich, boundless grace—but sets up wretched self in Jehovah's place, to nullify, as much as in it lies, the sinner-saving, the God-glorifying, project of eternity. It sets up the creature as a co-partner with the Creator—a creature of time, a mere nothing, upon a level with the eternal I AM! Yes, it excludes God—the everlasting God—and takes to a human Jehovah's essential, eternal throne and in the height of insolence says, "I AM, and there is none besides me."

Pride renders the creature, man, though new-created in Christ, after the image of His purity and, as such, bearing upon him a fresh impress of divine glory, the most unlike to Jesus, who, by way of eminence and to an all-surpassing excellence, was meek and lowly!

Pride is such an abominable sin that no tongue or pen can express a thousandth part of its aggravated guilt. None but the Lord Jehovah, in His understanding infinity, can search the immense depth of this great iniquity.

☙ ANNE DUTTON

The Means of Growth

Grow in grace, and in the knowledge of our
Lord and Saviour Jesus Christ.

—2 PETER 3:18

Growing in grace and the knowledge of our Lord and Savior Jesus Christ is the thing we are longing to do, and perhaps mourning over not doing, and perhaps praying every day that we may do, and seeming to get no answer! But when God has annexed a means to the fulfillment of a command, we cannot expect Him to enable us to fulfill that command if we are not using His means. In this case the means are wrapped in another command: "Desire the sincere milk of the word that ye may grow thereby." Real desire must prove itself by action; it is no use desiring the milk and not drinking it.

By the Word, we shall "grow in grace." The beginning of grace in our souls was by the same, for it is written, "Of his own will begat he us with the word of truth," "being born again...by the word of God." At every step, it is the same Word that develops the spiritual life. The entrance of it gives light and understanding. The result of hiding it in our hearts is that we "might not sin against thee"; and how often by His Word has He "withheld thee from sinning against me!" Again and again we have said, "Thy word had quickened me." For it comes to us not in word only, but in power, in the Holy Ghost and in much assurance. It is "able to make thee wise unto salvation," and its intended effects of reproof, correction, and instruction in righteousness rise to what would seem a climax of growth, "that the man of God may be perfect, thoroughly furnished unto all good works." And yet there is still a more glorious result of this Word of God, "which effectually worketh also in you that believe," for by His divine power "are given unto us exceeding great and precious promises, that by these ye might be partakers of the divine nature." This is indeed the climax, for what can rise beyond this most marvelous effect of this blessed means of growth in grace! Oh, to use it as He would have us use it, so that every day we "may grow thereby"!

☙ FRANCES RIDLEY HAVERGAL

Encouragement to a Burdened Soul

He will guide you into all truth.

—JOHN 16:13

Grace, mercy, and peace be with you, from God our Father and the Lord Jesus Christ, by the anointing and teaching of the Holy Comforter. It is He who convinces of sin, who wounds and probes the wound and lays open the evil of our nature, causing us to know that we are corrupt within and without. But He not only thus discovers the malady, He also applies the remedy. He just abases the sinner to exalt the Savior and gives the deep sense of sin, that the great salvation may be more appreciated and enjoyed. We are as bad as we can be, and it is needful to know it, but our knowledge will not save us. It is, "Look unto me, and be ye saved, all the ends of the earth." Some seem to glory in their deep discoveries of depravity, but, rather, "Let him that glorieth, glory in the Lord.

The end of a thing is better than the beginning: the beginning of the Lord's teaching is to know ourselves; the end is to know Him, and to know Him is life eternal. Happy is it for those who tarry not in all the plain but, amid all the sense of sin and the loathing of self, are kept pressing on, crying, "That I may know Him"; "that I may find Him"; "that I may be found in Him"; "I press towards the mark"; "I long for the prize."

Yes, my precious Savior, with hand and heart do I subscribe thus. Thou hast power to save those whom none else could or would, for "Thou hast clothed such a vile sinner as I am" with the garments of salvation. Thou hast covered me with the robe of righteousness. Therefore my soul doth greatly rejoice in the Lord and is joyful in my God. Oh, those words, "My God," when lawfully and feelingly uttered, have in them a world of blessedness! Surely my heart's desire is that He may be enthroned in your affections, for "He is worthy," and the more unworthy you feel, the better He will suit you.

☙ RUTH BRYAN

Our Peculiar Religion

The LORD is nigh unto all them that call upon him.

—PSALM 145:18

It is the peculiar excellence of our religion that it enables its disciples to derive instruction even from those circumstances that, to human view, appear the most adverse. The promise of God stands sure that all things shall work together for good to them that love Him. All our religious privileges can be profitable only as God blesses them to us, and He is infinitely able to grant as great a blessing without them. We may receive as much religious improvement from being deprived of a means of grace we had anticipated with delight as from enjoying it.

In general, undoubtedly, God affords the blessing in the use of His established means, but when He sees a humble heart longing after the enjoyment of ordinances of which it has been deprived by His providence, He meets with such a soul and shows it that His presence and grace are not confined to particular places and circumstances. He is the Son, and all beams of light that illumine the Christian's heart in attending upon ordinances emanate from Him. He is the fountain from which all that is profitable in the faithful sermon, the most spiritual companion, the most useful connection, is derived. And to Him may every thirsty soul repair, without the intervention of any outward means, and receive an abundant supply for every want. What a source of comfort is this—that nothing can shut out the soul that longs after God from communion with Him! Bolts and bars may exclude the presence of man, sickness may prostrate the body and enfeeble the mind, persecutions may cut us off from all those outward privileges that usually are the means of sustaining the Christian's hope and joy, but all these combined cannot shut out God from the soul that desires His presence. "The Lord is nigh unto all that call upon him, to all that call upon him in truth."

❧ SUSAN HUNTINGTON

Christian Union

That they all may be one; as thou, Father,
art in me, and I in thee, that they also may be one in us:
that the world may believe that thou hast sent me.

—JOHN 17:21

It is time, when the enemy is coming upon the church like a flood, that the friends of Jesus should rally round His standard and, hand in hand and heart with heart, unite in brotherly love to withstand him, their common foe. This is no time to dwell and insist upon minor things. All who love Jesus and hold the doctrines of salvation as the Bible declares them should lay aside nonessential points and meet in union, obeying the last injunction of our risen Head, and love one another as He has loved us. It is one of the great mysteries of the religion of Jesus: the power of the Holy Ghost in the hearts of all His saints. This is a grand proof among thousands of others of the truth of our religion. "Know ye not that ye are the temples of the Holy Ghost?" How precious ought this to make Jesus to our souls. It was the price of His atoning blood that brought us sinners into such a close contact with a reconciled God and Father.

How much below our high calling we live, and one reason why we are so often tried is to bring us into a more experimental acquaintance with this great and holy mystery. I believe that the best of God's saints, in close view of a vast eternity, will have to mourn the distance of their walk from God: that they had Him not in all their thoughts, a present God, ever in view; their eye full upon Him, seeing and acknowledging Him in everything—for He is in everything, whether we see Him or not. To know that He is ours, and that we are His. To draw near in faith telling Him all that is in our hearts, conscious of having the ear and heart of Jehovah toward us. Is not this true substantial happiness?

☙ MARY WINSLOW

Cleaving to the King

The men of Judah clave unto their king.
—2 SAMUEL 20:2

It is not a matter of course that coming is followed by cleaving. Even when the King Himself, in His veiled royalty, walked and talked with His few faithful followers, "many of his disciples went back, and walked no more with him."

There was no word of indignation or reproach, only the appeal of infinite pathos from His gracious lips: "Will ye also go away?" Let this sound in our ears today, not only in moments of temptation to swerve from truest-hearted loyalty and service, but all through the business of the day, stirring our too-easy-going resting into active cleaving; quickening our following afar off into following hard after Him.

We cannot thus cleave without loosening from other interests. But what matter! Let us be noble for Jesus, like the men of might who "separated themselves unto David" and who "held strongly with him in his kingdom." Shall we be mean enough to aim at less, when it is our Lord Jesus who would have us entirely with Him?

The Bible never speaks of good resolutions, but again and again of purpose. And this is what we want, that "with purpose of heart" we should "cleave unto the Lord." Have we this distinct purpose today? Do we really mean, God helping us, to cleave to our King today? Do not let us dare to go forth to the certain conflicts and temptations of the day with this negative but real disloyalty of want of purpose in the matter. And if our hearts condemn us, let us at once turn to Him who says, "I have caused to cleave unto me the whole house of Israel." His grace shall enable us to cleave unto our King.

&ely; FRANCES RIDLEY HAVERGAL

No Time for Slothfulness

Be thou faithful unto death, and
I will give thee a crown of life.
—REVELATION 2:10

You have only a little time to serve Christ in the short space of your present life. We are not called to glorify God on the earth; we shall soon be glorified with Him in heaven. And how sad will it be if sin and Satan should hinder you in running the race set before you and so rob you of your crown! I mean not your eternal salvation—I trust that is in the hands of Christ—but of that reward He, of the freest grace, will give to those who have served Him fully and faithfully at the approaching day of His glorious kingdom. You know what our Lord says: "Hold that fast which thou hast, let no man take thy crown." There is a day hastening when "we must all appear before the judgment seat of Christ; that every one may receive the things done in his body, whether they be good or bad."

Oh, the awfulness of that day, when every one of our works must be tried by God's fire like the goldsmith seeks for his precious metal by casting it into the furnace and burning up the dross! Oh, how much dross will then appear to have been mixed with our purest religious performances! And oh, how many evil works are we daily guilty of, in thought, word, and deed, which that fierce day will burn up! How happy will those be, in that day, whose works will be found to have the least dross! Abiding in the fire, they shall receive a reward, even Christ's "Well done, good and faithful servant, thou hast been faithful in a few things, I will make thee ruler over many things; enter thou into the joy of thy Lord." Our great Lord will call that service which we think not worth the name and quite beneath His notice; not a thought, word, or deed, for Him or His, shall lose its reward. And oh, what heart can conceive the glory of the immortal crown that overcomers shall then wear, who have been enabled to fight it out on the side of Christ, against sin and Satan here!

ॐ ANNE DUTTON

God's Glory in the Wilderness

*And it came to pass, as Aaron spake unto the whole congregation
of the children of Israel, that they looked toward the wilderness,
and, behold, the glory of the LORD appeared in the cloud.*

—EXODUS 16:10

It is marvelous how full of blessed possibilities of unfolding and disclosure God's words are. However dark and indistinct a passage may at first sight appear to be, it will glow as with hidden fire when the Spirit of the Lord breathes upon it, and the eyes of faith and desire look closely into its depths. A text you may have read hundreds of times without noticing anything special about it suddenly becomes alive and speaks to your heart as the very voice of God Himself!

Cannot you make it your own? Look into your past life and see whether you cannot recall many times when you "looked toward" some wilderness of trial, sorrow, or affliction that lay directly in your pathway, but without the expectation of seeing "the glory of the Lord" there. Everything else you saw—the darkness, discomfort, and danger—and you feared exceedingly. Yet, has not it been true that where and when you most needed Him, your blessed God has come to you, and, before long, your dreary desert has "blossomed as the rose?"

Then, too, with what infinite compassion for our weakness does He manifest Himself! His unveiled glory would strike us with blindness, so He makes it appear "in a cloud." With tenderest condescension, He deigns to enwrap His splendor in a misty veil of light, that the brightness of His presence may shine through and yet not dazzle us.

Do not fear to look toward the wilderness, then, if your God has put you there, for here are the "goings forth" of the Lord from of old; even thus does He give "the light of the knowledge of the glory of God in the face of Jesus Christ."

∾ SUSANNAH SPURGEON

The Value of Confessing Our Sins (1)

If we confess our sins, he is faithful and just to forgive us our sins,
and to cleanse us from all unrighteousness.
—1 JOHN 1:9

I think confession of sin, even when the heart is glowing with holy joy, should make up one-half of our life. And when we reflect that we have to do with one so able and so ready to pardon, it is a pleasure blended with pain to unveil our whole heart in the acknowledgment of its iniquity before God. Thus it is we gather the strength of resistance and the skill that foils our arch foe; the conscience is kept tender, the heart sanctified, and the blood of Jesus becomes increasingly precious.

Let us, then, constantly resort to this cleansing fountain, that the sin, mental and heart sin cognizant to no eye but God's holy eye, may be cleansed. What a high privilege is this! Who can subdue our inbred sins but Jesus? As well might we attempt to upheave a mountain as to argue with and remove even a solitary corruption of our fallen nature. But if we carry it at once to Christ, He will do it all for us. This is one of the most difficult, though needed, lessons in the school of Christ.

Dear friend, keep close to Him. Let not the world and its cares come between you and Christ. If a cloud intervenes, rest not until it is withdrawn. Go, and go again, and should a shade still obscure the glorious vision, return not from His presence until even its shadow has dissolved unto full, unclouded light.

❧ MARY WINSLOW

The Value of Confessing Our Sins (2)

*If we confess our sins, he is faithful and just to forgive us our sins,
and to cleanse us from all unrighteousness.*
—1 JOHN 1:9

You will, perhaps, wonder why I should refer so pointedly to the subject of the confession of sin. The fact is, I had just returned from the throne of grace, and my soul had been sweetly refreshed and sealed anew with a sense of pardon, and I could not resist giving you my reflections upon this intensely interesting and deeply sanctifying theme. I think it is one of the most holy, as the most solemn, engagements of the Christian and should occupy a prominent place in our worship, both public and private. How clearly and indissolubly has God entwined the two—our confession and His forgiveness! "If we confess our sins, he is faithful and just to forgive us our sins, and to cleanse us from all unrighteousness."

What a marvelous spectacle is this—a poor sinner and a holy Lord God meeting together at the blood-sprinkled mercy seat! Is not this most blessed? I often go burdened and come away light as a feather, nestling beneath the very wing of the Savior and listening to His well-known, "Fear not!" I disclose to Him all that is in my heart, and He unveils His loving, tender, forgiving heart to me. Do not deal in general petitions and confessions, but descend to particulars. To know the Lord well, we must come, and come again, with all and the same, with the least and the greatest, wants, sorrows, and sins. One simple uplifting of the heart, even amid the crowd, is sufficient for Jesus. He knows all we want to say, and would say. A thought darting upward reaches God and meets His response. Lord Jesus, help us all so to live and so to die.

≈ MARY WINSLOW

Come Now!

To day if ye will hear his voice, harden not your hearts.

—HEBREWS 4:7

Come now! Nothing can be plainer. Therefore, if you postpone coming, you are calmly disobeying God. When we bid a child to come, we do not count it obedience unless he comes at once, then and there. It is not obedience if he stops to consider and coolly tells you he is really thinking about coming, and waits to see how long you will choose to go on calling. What right do we have to treat our holy Lord as we would not think of letting a naughty child treat us? He says, "Come now." And now does not mean tomorrow. "To day if ye will hear his voice, harden not your hearts."

Put it to yourself: What if this night God should require your soul of you, and you had not come? What if the summons finds you still far off, when the precious blood by which you might have been made nigh was ready? You do not know what a day may bring forth. There are plenty of things besides immediate death that may just as effectually prevent your ever coming at all if you do not come now. This might be your last free hour for coming. Tomorrow the call may seem rather less urgent, and the other things entering in may deaden it, and the grieved Spirit may withdraw and cease to give you even your present inclination to desire it, and so you may drift on and on, farther and farther from the haven of safety, until it is out of sight on the horizon. And then it may be too late to turn the helm, and the current may be too strong; and when the storm of mortal illness at last comes, you may find that you are too weak mentally or physically to rouse yourself even to hear, much less come. What can one do when fever or exhaustion is triumphing over mind and body? Do not risk it. Come now! And "though your sins be as scarlet, they shall be white as snow; though they be red like crimson, they shall be as wool."

⇒ FRANCES RIDLEY HAVERGAL

The Believer's Power

*I can do all things through Christ
which strengtheneth me.*
—PHILIPPIANS 4:13

A part from Christ, we have a power to do evil, but none to do good; yet after union with Him by the Spirit, and after He has been revealed in the soul through faith, it is our privilege to live by faith on His power, which works against our own evils and brings forth His good fruit in us. It is the privilege of faith to take hold of Him by the power of the Spirit for the continued exercise of faith and every other grace, that there may be strength and vigor in the soul.

But then it is asked, "Have we power to thus live in His strength? And have we power thus to take hold of Him?" Yes, we have, through the Spirit and by reason of our union with Him. He Himself says, "Come unto me." He says, "Labour for that meat which endureth unto everlasting life." He says further, "Abide in me," and that in so doing there shall be "much fruit." He does not say these things to mock us. His servant says, "Lay hold on eternal life," "fight the good fight of faith," "put ye on the Lord Jesus Christ," "walk in Him," and other similar exhortations. He does not say these things for nothing or only to make us feel we have no power, but to stir us up to prove wherein our strength lies.

So if I were asked, "Have you any spiritual power?" the most conclusive answer would be, "Christ is my power," and by faith I have the privilege and benefit thereof. I am all powerlessness, but He is power in me and for me, wherefore I rather "glory in my infirmity, that his power may rest upon me." I can do all things through Christ which strengtheneth me." May the Lord bring us more into union-privilege and union-power, which is blessed indeed.

≈ RUTH BRYAN

A Blessed Paradox

I have seen his ways, and will heal him.

—ISAIAH 57:18

Here is one of the blessedly incomprehensible paradoxes of God's love and mercy, which fairly startles us by its excess of compassionate grace: "I have seen his ways, and"—one would have thought the next sentence must be, "I will punish him," or, at least, "I will rebuke him"; but, instead of wrath, here is pardon. Pity makes room for love, and in the place of bitterness, the Lord gives a blessing! "I have seen his ways, and will heal him."

O wanderer, will not those tender words cause you to return to your Lord? O stony heart, will you not break at so loving a touch as this? O cold and half-dead soul, will not such a divine cordial revive you? "I have seen his ways." What ways has God seen in you? Have they not been "wicked, crooked, perverse, thine own ways—the ways of death"? Have you not turned aside from the path of life and refused to walk "in all His way" and chosen for yourself "a stubborn way"?

Our heart must give a sad assent to all these charges. As we bow humbly before Him and say, "Thou art acquainted with all my ways," we feel that such knowledge on His part intensifies our wonder and gratitude at the loving compassion with which He regards us. His love is divine, so He says, "I have seen his ways, and will heal him." O, sweet pitifulness of our God! O, tenderness inexplicable! O, love surpassing all earth's loveliest affection! Do not our hard hearts yield under the power of such compassion as this? God knows all our wickedness, and He has seen all our waywardness; yet His purpose toward us is one of healing and pardon, and not of anger and putting away. Lord, we lift up empty, beseeching hands to Thy full ones; lay upon them, we pray Thee, all that they can bear of Thy promised blessing!

&ᴑ SUSANNAH SPURGEON

Self-Love or God-Love

Then said Jesus unto his disciples, If any man will come after me,
let him deny himself, and take up his cross, and follow me.

—MATTHEW 16:24

Whether there is one besetting sin which attends the Christian, it has appeared to me, however, that our most distressing conflicts are not always with the same sins but with different ones that acquire strength and power by the change of our circumstances. As self-elevation may be our snare at one time, so a gloomy depreciation may be at another. It is our duty to rest satisfied that God has placed us in the situation best for us, and, instead of comparing its advantages and disadvantages with those of others, we should endeavor carefully to inquire, "What are the temptations to which I am now most exposed? What faculties does my situation afford me for doing good? How can I turn my present circumstances to the best account?" In our various situations in life, be what they may, self is the grand hindrance to our going on unto perfection. The world flatters, and we love its flatteries. Self-love, in us, is a perverted principle; it is selfishness. It seeks its own good too eagerly, and in a wrong way.

But let a soul be endued with the benevolent spirit of the gospel; let it feel something of that holy flame which animates the saints above; let it be filled and controlled by desires to serve God as they do, to do His will and promote His glory unceasingly, which is the true end of our being—and all the fascinations of the world would be poured upon it in vain. Nothing could promote the happiness of such a soul but what advanced the glory of the blessed God. And it would find ways to effect its object. It would be seeking the advancement of the kingdom of Christ, and, in seeking it, would seek to bring others into that kingdom. May the time come— speedily come—when you and I shall feel this blessed flame, as I trust we desire to, when we shall love God with all our hearts and serve Him without imperfections.

→ SUSAN HUNTINGTON

The Blessings of Affliction

He giveth power to the faint; and to them that
have no might he increaseth strength.

—ISAIAH 40:29

May this trial be as a lattice through which Jesus will show Himself to your soul. Trial is one that He often looks through, with much tenderness, upon His redeemed one. He looked through the pillar of fire and cloud to trouble His enemies and hinder their flight, but He was in the fire and cloud to preserve and guide His people safely through the deep, so that not even a little one was left behind. It might be that "little faith" looked at the walls of water and feared they would give way, but those fears did not make the promise of no effect, though they might rob the soul of comfort. Was it not wonderful that the same cloud that was light to Israel was darkness to the foe; and the same water that was as walls of salvation to one was death and destruction to the other? So it is with bodily afflictions and providential trials: to the worldling they are destroyers of his best enjoyments; to the child of God they are often the very high road to them. To the worldling they are only bitter; to the other it is a mingled portion, for

> *Though their cup seems mix'd with gall,*
> *There's something secret sweetens all.*

"I will sing of mercy and judgment; unto thee, O Lord, will I sing." And it is as of old: "Howbeit our God turned the curse into a blessing."

Oh, indeed! The love of God is a precious theme with those who feel it and can say, "We love him because he first loved us." What an amazing love to bestow such a gift! My soul does muse and marvel. May the Holy Spirit apply it, shed it abroad in our hearts, and encourage us to come unto the Father by Him. The Lord hath prepared of His goodness for the poor, so if you are learning your poverty, it is to prepare you for the feast prepared for you.

❧ RUTH BRYAN

Coming Boldly

*Let us therefore come boldly unto the throne of grace, that we
may obtain mercy, and find grace to help in time of need.*
—HEBREWS 4:16

B oldness and faith go together; fear and unbelief go together. It
is always lack of faith that is at the bottom of all fear. Why are
you fearful? is the question for those of little faith. So in order to
come boldly and therefore joyfully what we need is more faith in
the Great High Priest who sits upon the throne of grace. Now, do
not sigh, "Ah, I wish I had more faith!" It will not come to you by
languid lamentations about your lack of faith. It is the gift of God.
And if you knew this gift of God, and who it is that only waits to be
inquired of that He may give it to you, surely you would ask of Him!
For He gives to all men liberally, and upbraids not—not even with
all your neglect of Him and His gifts. Ask—and He says it will be
given you. You have not because you ask not.

People do not come for what they do not want. Until the Holy
Spirit shows us our need of mercy and puts reality into the prayer
"Have mercy upon us miserable sinners," we will never come to
the throne of grace to obtain mercy. So if you have never yet felt
that you could sincerely say, "God be merciful to me a sinner," and
have never yet felt particularly anxious to come to the throne of
grace to obtain it, I would urgently entreat you to pray, "Lord, show
me myself!" When the Holy Spirit answers that prayer, you will be
eager enough to come and obtain mercy. It will be the one thing
then that you will be particularly anxious about. Obtaining mercy
comes first, then finding grace to help in time of need. You cannot
reverse God's order. You will not find grace to help in time of need
till you have sought and found mercy to save. You have no right to
reckon on God's help, protection, guidance, and all the other splendid privileges He promises to the children of God by faith in Jesus
Christ until you have this first blessing, the mercy of God in Christ
Jesus; for it is in Jesus Christ that all the promises of God are yea
and amen.

꙳ FRANCES RIDLEY HAVERGAL

A Waiting Time, a Sowing Time

And yet I am not alone, because the Father is with me.

—JOHN 16:32

I feel for your loneliness, but I would have you live on such familiar terms with Jesus, your best friend—though out of sight now—that you can confidently repose in His hand and heart and see the way He would have you take. He, your guide and counselor, is all-sufficient for your difficult path. Perhaps He may keep you waiting to try your faith awhile. Be of good courage and walk closely with Him, and He will show you what He would have you to do. Our waiting time is often the Lord's sowing time. We must reap some good while we are kept waiting to know what His will is concerning us. The Lord will have His people near to Himself. Why does He send trials, but that we may be better acquainted with Him, our best friend on earth and in heaven. How much discipline we require to bring us to His feet and in childlike faith to look to Him to do all for us!

O, pray! Pray on! Jesus will listen to your petition, bowing His loving ear to hear all that you have to say to Him. But wait patiently and see what the Lord's designs are. Let Him make the first move in the way He would have you walk, in the thing He would have you do. This is a world of tribulation; it was so to God's dear Son. Will we seek that it will be anything else to us? Rest in His love, with all your doubts, conflicts, and fears, and no good thing will He withhold from you. There is a needs be for all the trials that we have. When He places us in the furnace, He enters into it with us. We can never be separated from Christ, in life, in death, or in eternity, for Christ and we are one.

☙ MARY WINSLOW

To Grow Better by Suffering

Be still, and know that I am God.

—PSALM 46:10

It is a great thing to grow better by suffering. God sends judgments upon His children to wean them from the world and sin and to make them more like Him. I hope you will find that God is an unfailing refuge in every time of trial. Do not be discouraged, but carry all your sorrows to Him by whose power all things are controlled. He will not suffer you to be tried above what He will enable you to bear. Trust in the Lord Jehovah, with whom is everlasting strength. Those who wait on Him shall renew their strength; they shall never faint. Though He may see that His children need the rod, and, if I may use the expression in reference to Him, to be constrained in faithfulness to visit them with it; yet, blessed be His name, to them He always tempers the stroke with mercy.

Keep near, I entreat you, to Him who is a sun and shield to His people. Wait upon Him by constant prayer and supplication. Some of David's psalms are exactly suited to your case. He was, more than once, afflicted and ready to die; he was chastened sore, yet he was not delivered over to spiritual death. The God he loved, in his heaviest hours, sanctified to him the overwhelming calamities, which sometimes seemed ready to swallow him up. He could say, "God is our refuge and strength, a very present help in trouble; therefore will we not fear, though the earth be removed"—that is, though the heaviest calamities befall us. Happy, happy man! What real evil can touch those who have such a confidence in their Maker? Strive to profit by the rod. Let sin be made more hateful to you by it, for this is the procuring cause of all sorrows. And try to glorify God in your tribulations. If His glory is near our hearts, our comfort and salvation are near His.

❧ SUSAN HUNTINGTON

Beneath the Shadow of the Cross

He humbled himself, and became obedient unto death,
even the death of the cross.

—PHILIPPIANS 2:8

Well may it be asked, "Who is this wondrous Beloved that would go to such depths for His spouse and on whom the weak, fair one is leaning as she comes up out of the wilderness?" It is He who, in the fullness of time, scorned not the lowly virgin's womb, but became a babe and was found in fashion of a man. He is a Holy One of the holy ones, and yet "a man of sorrows and acquainted with grief; holy, harmless, undefiled, and separate from sinners," and yet "numbered with the transgressors." Under the weight of sin and its punishment, Jesus agonized in the sacred garden of Gethsemane and sweat, as it were, great drops of blood falling down to the ground. Oh, those rich, rich drops from His precious veins, of more value than all the gold and gems His hands have made!

This is the matchless Bridegroom of whom we speak. His love has saved, and it does kindle the soul now trying to tell of His worth, who, on Calvary, was stretched on the accursed tree, and there finished the love scene of His mystic sufferings. Come, sit with me a moment beneath the shadow of His cross. It will not mar, but heighten the joys of our nuptial day. Look up, and remember it is as a husband He hangs bleeding there. It is the Bridegroom, in love for the bride, enduring those unknown pangs. See how His holy flesh is bruised with scourging and His precious hands and feet pierced with rugged nails. How is His heavenly brow torn with pricking thorns and His dear side with the cruel spear, each gaping wound proclaiming, "Man is guilty; God is love." But God is justice too! Oh, see His precious blood trickling down. It flowed forth for sinners like me—like you! Look and wonder; look and be comforted; look and adore.

Here look till love dissolve your heart,
And bid each slavish fear depart.

⇄ RUTH BRYAN

Thy Will Be Done

O my Father, if this cup may not pass away from me,
except I drink it, thy will be done.

—MATTHEW 26:42

Your observations respecting our inability to attain resignation of ourselves, so as to say unreservedly to our heavenly Father, "Thy will be done," are undoubtedly just. But let us not forget the nature of this inability. It is not such as furnishes any excuse or extenuation of our sins when we are not resigned, but is the very thing that constitutes our guilt, proceeding from the opposition of our hearts to the character and government of God. It should therefore produce in us deep humiliation and contrition and drive us to the foot of the cross. The lack of this resignation to this perfect acquiescence in the will of God is one of the principal sources of the unhappiness of which we constantly complain.

Could we acquiesce with cheerfulness in the dispensations of an unerring providence, we should at once feel a spark of celestial happiness enkindled in our hearts. But this is a state of which frail humanity comes far short, at the best. We wish to have this or that desire complied with and think that, could we but obtain the accomplishment of our wishes, we should be blessed indeed. But it is best they should not be granted; the wisdom and goodness of God assure us it is so. And yet, because they are denied, we sink into despondency and grief. My dear friend, I believe that if we could view things as they really are, we should find reason to say, "The Lord has done all things well; mercy and peace go before Him continually." Afflictions are sent for our profit, and if we do not profit by them, the fault is entirely our own. They are designed to convince us of the unsatisfying and fleeting nature of all things beneath the sun. We should not, therefore, when they are upon us, indulge the sorrow of the world, which works death, but pray that they may be made to work in us the peaceable fruit of righteousness and, in the future world, a far more exceeding and eternal weight of glory.

&ampsp; SUSAN HUNTINGTON

Desiring to Love Christ
without Wandering

Ye earthly vanities, depart,
Forever hence remove;
Jesus alone deserves my heart,
And every thought of love.

His heart, where love and pity dwelt
In all their softest forms,
Sustained the heavy load of guilt,
For lost rebellious worms.

His heart, whence love abundant flowed
To wash the stains of sin,
In precious streams of vital blood—
Here, all my hopes begin.

Can I my bleeding Savior view,
And yet ungrateful prove,
And pierce His wounded heart anew,
And grieve his injured love?

Forbid it, Lord, O bind this heart,
This rebel heart of mine,
So firm, that it may ne'er depart,
In chains of love divine.

              ❧ ANNE STEELE

Finished

It is finished. —JOHN 19:30

What agony of soul did our Beloved not endure when He had no answer from God! It is wonderful to see how "He was in all points tempted like as we are"—not only tempted with evil by Satan, but tried by His friends, tried by His Father, and tried in all the sensibilities of the nature that He had taken; yet, in all, He endured without sin.

His sorrowful utterances were to show that He had the tenderest susceptibility of feeling in all His sufferings. But there was not one murmur or rebellious feeling or one hard thought. He pitied His disciples—"the flesh is weak"—and though He knew they would all forsake Him through fear, He even made a way for that escape in His matchless love: "If ye seek me, let these go their way." This precious, spotless One gave Himself for us to the sorrows of death and the pains of hell, which bitter cup of trembling He drained, even to the very dregs, so that He could triumphantly say, "It is finished." The sufferings are past. He has entered into glory, but the full revelation of it, in and to His bride, is yet to come. Oh, wonderful Bridegroom, reveal to us more of Thy wonderful love in Thy humiliation and exaltation. Let us live in that undying flame, that in our joys and sorrows we may be a sweet savor of Thee to Thy loved ones. Only continually draw us out of self into Thee, and cause us to grow up in Thee in all things, while many winds and storms and heartaches cause us to root down in Thee also. Oh, do Thou shine more and more brightly in us, to the perfect day.

It is blessed, dear friend, to spend Good Friday under His shadow as the crucified One; there His fruits are sweet to our taste. It is precious to be led on by His Spirit to His joy as the glorified One, for then our joy is full.

→ RUTH BRYAN

Was It for Me?

For even hereunto were ye called: because Christ also suffered
for us, leaving us an example, that ye should follow his steps:…
who his own self bare our sins in his own body on the tree, that
we, being dead to sins, should live unto righteousness:
by whose stripes ye were healed.

—1 PETER 2:21, 24

L et us observe the infinite love of God to us in the wounding, bruising, and smiting of His own Son—His sinless, holy Son, the darling of His heart—in our place, that we might go free from the soul-killing pain, although we were rebels against Him. Let us observe the infinite love of our Lord Jesus Christ in thus putting Himself in our place to bear off the deadly blow from us. Let us observe the infinite wisdom of the great Jehovah in finding out this way of salvation for us that were righteously doomed for destruction, and must have sunk inevitably into eternal misery. And, let us observe the infinite virtue of Christ's sufferings for our healing.

And was it you, was it me, for whom our great Lord was thus wounded, bruised, and stricken? Oh! What a debt of love and praise in heart, lip, and life we owe to our all-wise, all-gracious God, and to the worthy Lamb, who loved us and bought us with His blood! And by His stripes are we healed in our own persons initially. Let us give Him glory, and firmly believe that we shall be healed perfectly and eternally.

And when we are wounded by sin, and the fiery law pierces our conscience, let us apply by faith to this healing remedy afresh. For we are healed in Him and shall be healed by Him, and the infinite virtue of His God-like blood can never, never be exhausted nor wasted. There are immense treasures in that open fountain for healing and cleansing from all sin.

* ANNE DUTTON

A Sight for Men and Angels

He shewed them his hands and his feet.

—LUKE 24:40

My soul, has your Savior showed you these indelible seals of His dying love for you? And, beholding them, have you realized the enormity of your guilt in God's sight, which could be pardoned only at such a price as this? Can you not hear Him say, "I suffered this for you," and can you, unmoved, see such a sight and hear such words? No, rather must your full heart follow the experience of those disciples to whom the amazing revelation was first made, for it is recorded that "they believed not for joy and wondered."

Those hands, which did so many sweet deeds of mercy; those feet, which made so many weary journeys to help, bless, and save others, are now bearing the marks of the cruel suffering endured for my sake. Lord Jesus, my heart melts with love and grief as I ponder on the unknown agonies of Thine atonement! For these scars on Thy hands, Thy feet, and Thy side are but the outer physical tokens of the inner spiritual anguish, bruising, and smiting of Thy soul for my sin.

O, Thou heavenly love, my faith, sees Thee as Thou didst stand that night in the veiled majesty of Thy resurrection life, pleading, by the eloquence for those "poor dumb mouths" on Thy sacred body, that those whom Thou hadst loved "even unto death" should believe in Thee and trust Thee for their soul's salvation!

My soul, come afresh to your risen Lord and ask Him to show you again something of what His love for you cost Him! Your pardon is in His passion, your healing in His stripes, your life in His death! The two Marys "came and held Him by the feet, and worshipped him." You do this also, and while, with penitent love and fully surrendered heart you adore Him, He will accept you and give you grace to say, "My Lord, and my God."

> SUSANNAH SPURGEON

Wounded for Our Transgressions

But he was wounded for our transgressions, he was bruised for our iniquities: the chastisement of our peace was upon him; and with his stripes we are healed.

—ISAIAH 53:5

The prophet explicitly declares the true cause of our Lord's sufferings, which was our sins. Our sins are the procuring cause of His sufferings; He was wounded, tormented, pierced through and through, in name, in circumstance, in His ministry, in soul, in body: wounded by men, by friends, by enemies, by the sins of both; by enraged devils let loose upon Him; by the law's curse, which took hold on Him; by the wrath of an incensed God, which like a sharp sword awaked against Him and smote Him in body, in soul, in life, in death, and in all this, by the righteous hand of strict, avenging justice. But oh, why was this innocent Lamb of God thus wounded? It was for our transgression. He was bruised—pounded as spices in a mortar—for our iniquities. The chastisement of our peace, the unmitigated punishment due to us, was upon Him. It must fall on Him or light on us; but bearing it for us, He thereby procured our peace.

No peace with God could have been had for us but through the wounds of a stricken, smitten, pierced Jesus. But peace being thus made, "with his stripes we are healed." With His stripes for our sin, infinitely strict and avenging justice is fully satisfied, the righteous law fulfilled and magnified; and from the infinite virtue of His peace-making stripes, our sin-wounded souls are healed and shall be fully and eternally saved. God's chosen, all the Lord's redeemed among Jew and Gentile, even as many of both as were ordained unto eternal life and bought with the Lamb's blood and as under the Holy Ghost's work, have believed, do, or shall believe on this wounded, bruised, stricken Jesus. By His stripes we are healed and shall be everlastingly saved by free, rich, sovereign grace.

⮞ ANNE DUTTON

God's Love for Humanity

For scarcely for a righteous man will one die: yet peradventure for a good man some would even dare to die. But God commendeth his love toward us, in that, while we were yet sinners, Christ died for us.

—ROMANS 5:7–8

Let us by faith behold and consider the great charity and goodness of God in sending His Son to suffer death for our redemption when we were His mortal enemies, and after what sort and manner He sent Him.

It is to be considered—yes, to be undoubtedly with a perfect faith believed—that God sent Him to us freely, for He did give Him and sold Him not. A more noble and rich gift He could not have given. He sent not a servant or a friend, but His only Son (John 3:16), so dearly beloved—not in delights, riches, and honors, but in crosses, poverties, and slanders; not as a lord, but as a servant (Phil. 2:7); yes, and in most vile and painful passions, to wash us not with water but with His precious blood, not from mire but from the puddle and filth of our iniquities. He has given Him not to make us poor, but to enrich us with His divine virtues, merits, and graces; yes, and in Him he has given us all good things, and finally Himself, and that with such great charity as cannot be expressed.

Was it not a most high and abundant charity of God to send Christ to shed His blood, to lose honor, life, and all for His enemies (Rom. 5:6–8)? Even in the time when we had done Him injury, He first showed His charity to us with such flames of love that greater could not be showed. God in Christ has opened unto us (although we are weak and blind of ourselves), that we may behold in this miserable estate the great wisdom, goodness, and truth, with all the other godly perfections that are in Christ. Therefore inwardly to behold Christ crucified upon the cross is the best and godliest meditation that can be.

&ear; KATHERINE PARR

Christ Suffering for Sinners

Surely he hath borne our griefs, and carried our sorrows: yet
we did esteem him stricken, smitten of God, and afflicted.

—ISAIAH 53:4

By the prophet, the Holy Ghost informs us what the cause of our Lord's sufferings was (that they were not for His own sins, but they were "our griefs," "our sorrows") that we deserved for our sins that He bore. He carried them as a porter does his load—to take away the curse, to remove them from us, to give us peace, joy, and rest, and to bring us unto God. "Yet we, (the unbelieving Jews), did esteem him stricken, smitten of God and afflicted." And we, the unbelieving Gentiles, notwithstanding our notion that He suffered for sinful men, are very far from thinking close upon His sufferings as caused by our sin, by our disobedience. Thus we all, while in unbelief, are far from fixing our eyes upon a suffering Jesus as bearing and carrying our sorrows and griefs.

Hence, the mighty love of our suffering Lord in bearing and carrying our deserved load; its intolerable weight that He bore would have sunk us forever out of the reach of the favor of God and plunged us into the bottomless gulf of infinite and eternal wrath.

And our Lord, in His great love, which was stronger than death—for you, for me—did bear all our sorrows and griefs; He has thereby taken away the penal evil of all our afflictions and will make the greatest natural evil to work for our good and turn to our salvation. And forever He has thereby secured us from the danger we were in of eternal damnation. O how light are our burdens, our heaviest cross, if compared with those ponderous weights our Jesus bore for us! How worthy is our condescending, suffering Lord of our highest love! And how greatly should we mourn and be in bitterness for Him for our stupidity in disregarding His mighty love and sufferings, in both of which, to and for us there was an infinity.

ANNE DUTTON

A Paradox of Providence

And he brought us out from thence,
that he might bring us in.
—DEUTERONOMY 6:23

The lesson set before us may be "He had torn, He hath smitten," "He maketh sore, he woundeth"; and in our own experience, we may feel how painful is the truth thus taught. But if the eye of faith can discern the precious postscripts that follow—"He will heal," "He will bind us up," "His hands make whole"—we are strengthened to endure patiently the trial that is so sure to end in triumph. And we say, "Ah, Lord! Thou dost but frown to make Thy smile the sweeter; Thou dost kill only that Thou mayest make alive!" Blessed wounding, gracious suffering, which places us under the Great Physician's love and care!

He must bring us out of self and sin and Satan's slavery before He can bring us in to holiness, pardon, and the liberty wherewith Christ makes us free. Many times the Lord has had to disturb our nest and bring us out of some earthly refuge that was becoming too easy and too dear to our soul. But, as music sounds the sweetest when heard across the waters, so do God's dealings make the purest harmony in our hearts when they reach us over the waves of affliction and trial. When a tried and tempted soul stays itself on God and sings in the midst of the flood or the fire, such praise must, methinks, be more glorious and glorifying to Him and His mighty grace than the hallelujahs of unfallen angels.

Mark the tenderness of our dear Lord and Shepherd; He does not drive us either way, in or out. No, for "when He putteth forth his own sheep, he goeth before them, and the sheep follow him." God grant that this may be true of you and me, dear reader! May we never hesitate to go where He leads or think any road too rough or dark when we hear His dear voice calling us to come!

ॐ SUSANNAH SPURGEON

Thine (1)

I am thine. —PSALM 119:94

This is a wonderful stone for the sling of faith. It will slay any
Goliath of temptation, if we only sling it out boldly and deter-
minately at him. When self tempts us (and we know how often that
is), let it be met with "not your own," and then look straight away
to Jesus with "I am Thine." If the world tries some lure, old or new,
remember the words of the Lord Jesus, how He said, "If ye were of
the world, the world would love his own…but I have chosen you
out of the world"; and lest the world should claim us as "his own,"
look away to Jesus and say, "I am Thine."

Is it sin, subtle and strong and secret, that claims our obedience?
Acknowledge that "ye were the servants of sin," but now, "being
made free from sin, ye became the servants of righteousness," and
conquer with the faith-shout, "I am Thine!"

Is it terrible hand-to-hand fight with Satan himself, making a
desperate effort to reassert his old power? Tell the prince of this
world that he has nothing in Jesus and that you are in Him that is
true, a member of His body, His very own; and see if he is not forced
to flee at the sound of your confident "I am Thine!"

But after all, "I am Thine" is only an echo, varying in clearness
according to faith's atmosphere and our nearness to the original
voice. Yes, it is only the echo of "thou art Mine," falling in its mighty
music on the responsive (because it is Spirit-prepared) heart. This
note of heavenly music never originated with any earthly rock. It is
only when God sends forth the Spirit of His Son in our hearts that
we cry, "Abba, Father." Therefore, do not overlook the voice in the
gladness of the echo. Listen, and you will hear it falling from the
mysterious heights of high-priestly intercession: "They are thine.
And all mine are thine, and thine are mine."

☙ FRANCES RIDLEY HAVERGAL

Thine (2)

I am thine. —PSALM 119:94

This is not a vague and general belonging to Christ, but it is full of specific realities of relationship. "I am Thine" means "Truly, I am thy servant." I am one of Thy dear children. I am Thy chosen soldier. I am Thy ransomed one. I am Thine own sheep.

In deeper humility and stronger faith, let us listen further to the voice of our Beloved as He breathes names of incomprehensible condescension and love. Shall we contradict Him here, in the tenderest outflow of His divine affection, and say, "Not so, Lord"? Shall we not rather adoringly listen and let Him say to us even in our depths of utter unworthiness, "My sister, my spouse," "My love, my dove, my undefiled," answering only with a wondering, yet unquestioning, "I am Thine," and "I am all that Thou choosest to say that I am"?

The echo may vary and falter (though it is nothing short of atrocious ingratitude and unbelief when it does), but the voice never varies or falters. He does not say, "Thou art mine" today, and reverse or weaken it tomorrow. We are a people unto Thee forever. Why grieve His love by doubting His word and giving way to a very fidget of faithlessness? Love that is everlasting cannot be ephemeral; it is everlasting, and what can we say more?

The more we by faith and experience realize that we are His own in life and death, the more willing we shall be that He should do what He will with His own, and the more sure we shall be that He will do the very best with it and make the very most of it. May we increasingly find the strength and rest of this our God-given claim upon God. "I am Thine; save me!" And He will save. He will rejoice over you with joy; He will rest in His love.

∾ FRANCES RIDLEY HAVERGAL

Following the Birds

Whoso offereth praise glorifieth me.
—PSALM 50:23

The time of the singing of birds is come, and from early morning until the sun sets, their sweet notes are a constant reminder of the duty and delight of thanksgiving. Out of the joy of their hearts they trill forth their gladness for the sunshine and the opening flowers and the unfolding leaves, and I have heard the same tender song when the rain has fallen and cold winds have blown and dark clouds have swept across the sky. Many a time have the birds in the garden sung a lesson in my listening ears and rebuked my dullness or my unbelief by their gleeful carolings.

Ah! Dear friends, some of us do not praise our God half enough. We "raise an Ebenezer" now and then, but we pitifully fail to obey the command "rejoice in the Lord always." Yet how much we have to bless Him for, and what sweet encouragement is given to our gratitude by His assurance, "Whoso offereth praise glorifieth me!" How often are we told, in His Word, that He takes delight in our thanksgiving and songs! The praise we render is dearer to Him than that of angels—for they cannot bless Him for redeeming love, for pardoned sin, and the blessed hope of resurrection glory.

Oh! Is it not to the eternal praise of a covenant-keeping God that poor pilgrims, wandering through a wilderness and having to wage constant war with the world, the flesh, and the devil, should yet be enabled to sing gloriously, as they put their enemies to flight, and overcome by the blood of the Lamb? It is the overcoming ones who learn to praise. The fingers that can most adroitly use the sword are the most skillful in touching the harp. Each time God gives us the victory over sin, we learn a new song with which to laud and bless His holy name. The feeble notes uttered on earth by a truly thankful and sanctified heart must, I think, swell into anthems of glorious melody as they rise to the throne of God!

∾ SUSANNAH SPURGEON

Our Great Strength-Giver

*Blessed is the man whose strength is in thee; in whose heart
are the ways of them. Who passing through the valley of Baca make
it a well; the rain also filleth the pools. They go from strength to
strength, every one of them in Zion appeareth before God.*

—PSALM 84:5–7

What a mercy, dear friend, that all our strength is in safe keeping; it is in Jesus and is given to us as we stand in need of it. All our own boasted strength is perfect weakness, but His strength will never fail us but will increase as we travel onward, upholding us, defending us, and enabling us to overcome all our enemies, and at last is engaged to bring us off more than conquerors.

Blessed be God for all the rich supplies afforded us in the wilderness! Such a friend is Christ to us—always ready to help us, strengthen us, comfort us when we are cast down, and lift us above the low cares of time and to speak sweet peace to our too-oft failing and doubting hearts. Oh, what a Savior we have, if we did but believe all we profess to believe! Unbelief—cruel unbelief—destroys more than half our comforts while we are on our short passage to glory. A little while and we will be put into possession of our glorious inheritance, and all our poor, short-lived trials, crosses, and disappointments are so many rich blessings in disguise to prepare us for it. What a hope we have of being shortly with Him. Oh that we might be kept disentangled from the rubbish of the fall. Look forward more! Are we not too much like children playing with toys, and when they are broken, sitting down mourning over them? Let us compare them with the happiness of being with God. Countless millions of years before us—pure, holy, perfect beings, capable of the full enjoyment of that heaven of heavens prepared for us in eternal, unchangeable love. Then let us take fresh courage and look up.

❧ MARY WINSLOW

Manifesting the Life of Jesus

*That the life also of Jesus might be made
manifest in our mortal flesh.*

—2 CORINTHIANS 4:11

Is not this a high, holy, and heavenly calling? Yet even hereunto you were called because Christ also suffered for us, leaving us an example that we should follow His steps. Hereunto you were called to do just as He would have done, sometimes even just as He did do in like circumstances—to show not our patience, but the patience of Jesus Christ; not mere human meekness and gentleness, but the meekness and gentleness of Christ; and so on with all the other beautiful holy qualities that shone in the life also of Jesus. While our life is hid with Christ in God, His life is to be manifest in our mortal flesh—yes, magnified in my body.

How shall this be? First, Jesus Himself must dwell in our hearts by faith, or His life cannot be manifest. We want Him to make us vessels meet for this great use—pure and transparent vessels through which His glorious life may shine: so transparent, that, like clear glass, they may be altogether lost sight of in the light that streams through them; so pure, that they may not dim the radiance of His indwelling.

The word "manifest" is more than mere showing; it implies a bringing to light, a shining forth, and comes from the idea of a torch or lantern. We can only shine as lights in the world by bearing the Light of the World within us. But it is a grand and solemn responsibility. Our Lord Jesus is hidden from the eyes of the world; they do not see Him. They see only us, and our lives are to show them what His life is. What a tremendous trust our Master has given us! Who is sufficient for this thing? It is very real. He, our precious Lord, will be held in more or less esteem this day; His power, His grace, and His sweetness will be judged of according to what the outsiders see in our lives.

✤ FRANCES RIDLEY HAVERGAL

Undoing Our Work

If any man will come after me, let him deny himself,
and take up his cross daily, and follow me.

—LUKE 9:23

Our Father has determined that Christ shall be all, and we nothing. To accomplish this experimentally, He undoes our work. When we have been washing with niter and soap, He plunges us in the ditch; when we seem to be getting on a little better than usual, He turns us upside down. This is hard work, and while the process is going on, we think it must be for destruction, for we appear to grow worse and worse. But in truth it is for salvation—to show ourselves to ourselves, to bring us to forsake ourselves, and to give us to Christ, instead of ourselves. Oh, what a blessed exchange! It is worth being spoiled in all the labor of our hands and marred in our very best things to possess such a treasure. There can be no drinking of the living waters while we have a price in our hand, be it much or little; no buying the gospel wine and milk while we have any money; no triumphing in "the Lord Our Righteousness" while we are hunting about for shreds of our own and sewing them together. All this is Christ-rejecting and God-dishonoring.

Therefore be not cast down at the Lord's ways toward you, for if we are anything or have anything, Jesus cannot be everything; and if He be not everything, He is nothing. He must be all—for holiness and happiness, for justification and sanctification, for acceptable appearing before God and suitable walking before men, for holy living and happy dying. Do we want good works? We are "created" unto them in Him. Do we desire "the fruits of righteousness"? We are filled with them by union with Him. In short, our Father has "blessed us with all spiritual blessings" in Him, and the reason we do not enjoy them more is because we seek them in ourselves. Oh to have the single eye that looks to Jesus only! Then would our whole body be "full of light."

↣ RUTH BRYAN

Grievous Inconsistency

Why call ye me, Lord, Lord, and
do not the things which I say?
—LUKE 6:46

In what pathetic tones He pleads with us to note the inconsistency of our words and actions! "Lord, Lord," we say, professing to be His happy and devoted servants. But, as a matter of fact, do we not constantly do our own will rather than His? We please ourselves in most of the matters that should be subject to His approval, and we constantly comport ourselves as if no vows of obedience and consecration had ever passed our lips. Is our money spent chiefly for His honor and glory, looked upon as absolutely His, and lent to us only for His service and kingdom? Do we ask counsel at the Lord's hands over everything that occurs in our daily life?

Of course there are occasions when, with a start, we wake up to a sense of our deep responsibility to our Master as His professed servants. But does our daily, hourly life show that we are striving in everything to do His commandments, and thus prove our love and loyalty to Him?

Dear friends, my sense of shortcoming in this respect is so painfully strong that I would fain write with tears, rather than with ink, if I could thereby bring you and myself to a practical realization of our duty to our Master if we have once taken His vows upon us and called Him Lord. I do not wish to judge you, but if, in judging and condemning myself, you should find your own experience described and repeated in mine, I earnestly pray that you will receive my words as a message from God to you personally and not rest till your sin has been confessed and pardoned.

* SUSANNAH SPURGEON

The Rock

And that Rock was Christ.
—1 CORINTHIANS 10:4

What do we think of when we stand underneath a massive, high, hoary-looking, time-stained rock? We think of strength; we think of age; we think of something very lasting and very strong. We look at houses and other works of man, which soon decay, but we know that the ancient rock has lasted for ages past and will last till the last convulsions, or burning up of this our world. Yes, a rock suggests the idea of age, of strength and majesty. And does this not make us think of the everlasting Rock of Ages—of the eternal Savior—of Jesus Christ, the same yesterday and today and forever; of Him on whom we are built; of the sure foundation on whom we depend? Are we reminded of His majesty, who is the Mighty God; of His age, who is Himself eternal; of His strength, who is strong and has strength to spare for us?

Let me ask you, my dear friends: What are your feelings with regard to this Rock, even the Rock of Ages? Have you fled to Christ as an all-sufficient Savior? Have you sought shelter in that refuge of eternal love? Do you believe on the Lord Jesus Christ? Can you say, from broken and contrite hearts,

Nothing in my hand I bring,
Simply to Thy cross I cling.

"Ho, every one that thirsteth, come ye to the waters." Come to that never failing stream of spiritual benefits (pardon, peace, holiness, everlasting salvation) that flowed for you on Calvary, when the Rock of Ages was smitten. "Yea, come, without money and without price." You bring nothing with you; you come to receive everything. This "pure river of water of life" is not exhausted; the Israelites' refreshing stream did once cease to flow for a time. Our Stream has always availed for penitent believers and is flowing still.

&ped; ELIZABETH JULIA HASELL

God's Design

Thou shalt increase my greatness, and comfort me on every side.

—PSALM 71:21

It is God's design, in the deepest dejection and humiliation of His children, to raise them thence to a higher exaltation and a more abundant consolation. The Lord's Christ, after His deepest dejection and humiliation, was raised by His Father to the highest exaltation. And thus the apostles, after their deepest deaths, were raised by God unto higher honor and glory in the church militant, and reserved for them, to their higher glory and joy, was a richer crown in the church triumphant. And as it is the Lord's design to advance all His favorites highly, to prepare them for the enjoyment of that advancement more safely, to show His grace more gloriously in its bestowment, and the more abundantly to sweeten their enjoyment of it, He suffers them, in His infinite wisdom, to sink into the deepest misery; that from thence, in His boundless grace, He might take occasion to exalt them more highly by His all-triumphant mercy and eternal truth and veracity.

Thus it is in all temptations from the world or Satan and in trying dispensations of providence with which the Lord Himself is pleased to exercise His dear children. Darkness and death must be first to set off even more that light and life with which they are to be blessed. So wondrous is the Lord in His working that He brings an increase of light and life out of the thickest darkness and deepest death; the greatest joy out of the utmost grief; the highest honor out of the deepest disgrace; the most plenteous fullness out of the most penurious circumstances; and eternal glory out of time misery. Who, then, of His children would not give up himself entirely, most humbly and cheerfully, into His all-wise, all-gracious hands in the most trying seasons? He sees a need for it, "that His children be in heaviness through manifold temptations, that their faith may be tried and thereby increased, and that it may be found unto praise and honor and glory at the appearing of Jesus Christ."

❧ ANNE DUTTON

Are You Prepared?

And I will say to my soul, Soul, thou hast much goods laid up for many years; take thine ease, eat, drink, and be merry. But God said unto him, Thou fool, this night thy soul shall be required of thee: then whose shall those things be, which thou hast provided? So is he that layeth up treasure for himself, and is not rich toward God.

—LUKE 12:19–21

How careful we ought to be that religion is our principle concern. Perhaps this night our souls may be required of us. We may end our existence here and enter the eternal world. Are we prepared to meet our Judge? Do we depend upon Christ's righteousness for acceptance? Are we convinced of our own sinfulness and inability to help ourselves? Is Christ's love esteemed more by us than the friendship of this world? Do we feel willing to take up our cross daily and follow Jesus?

As heirs of immortality, one would naturally imagine that we should strive to enter in at the strait gate and use all our endeavors to be heirs of future happiness. But alas! How infinitely short do we fall of the duty we owe to God and to our own souls.

Religion is worth our attention, and every moment of our lives ought to be devoted to its concerns. Time is short, but eternity is long, and when we have once plunged into that fathomless abyss, our situation will never be altered. If we have served God here and prepared for death, glorious will be our reward hereafter. But if we have not, our souls will be irrecoverably lost. Oh, then, let us press forward and seek and serve the Lord. May the Spirit guide you, and may an interest in the Savior be given you.

❧ HARRIET NEWELL

Most Blessed Forever

*For thou hast made him most blessed for ever: thou hast
made him exceeding glad with thy countenance.*

—PSALM 21:6

Probably everyone who reads this has at least one of those golden
links to heaven that God's own hand has forged from our
earthly treasures. It may be that the very nearest and dearest that
had been given are now taken away. And how often "no relation,
only a dear friend" is an "only" of heart-crushing emphasis! Human
comfort goes for very little in this; but let us lay our hearts open to
the comfort wherewith we are comforted of God Himself about it.

There is not much directly to ourselves; He knew that the truest
and sweetest comfort would come by looking not at our loss, but at
their gain. Whatever this gain is, it is all His own actual and immediate doing. "Thou hast made him" (read here the name of the very
one for whom we are mourning) "most blessed."

Most! How shall we reach that thought? Make a shining stair-
way of every bright beatitude in the Bible, blessed upon blessed,
within and also far beyond our own experience. And when we have
built them up till they reach unto heaven, still this "most blessed"
is beyond our sight, in the unapproachable glory of God Himself. It
will always be "most," for it is "forever"—everlasting light without a
shadow, everlasting songs without a minor.

No more death, neither sorrow nor crying, neither shall there be
any more pain. And the inhabitant shall not say, "I am sick." No more
sunsets, no more days of mourning. The troubling of the wicked
and the voice of the oppressor ceased forever. No more memory
of troubles; no more tears. No more anything that defiles! At this
moment they are exceeding glad, and the certainty of it stills every
quiver of our selfish love. The glory and joy of our Lord Christ are
revealed to them, and they are glad also with exceeding joy, rejoicing together with Jesus.

❧ FRANCES RIDLEY HAVERGAL

Unholy Jealousy

Jealousy is cruel as the grave.
—SONG OF SOLOMON 8:6

A suspicious, jealous spirit is one of the most corroding evils and uncomfortable states of mind an unhappy individual can be tormented with. It makes its subject, and all others, miserable. It impairs confidence, weakens friendships, separates the best of friends, and produces incalculable mischief far and wide. It was jealousy that hurled the sinning angels from heaven. It was jealousy that caused the fall of our first parents and drove them from Paradise. It was jealousy that led to the first murder. It was jealousy that produced hatred and revenge in Esau toward Jacob. It is marked in God's Word as a hateful, God-dishonoring, soul-destroying sin.

Let us beware of it, watch and pray against it, and the moment we detect its workings within us, crush it at once. It is the offspring of Satan and the destroyer of mankind. Let us also beware of engendering and encouraging dislike to anyone with whom we associate. This evil, unchecked, tends to corrode the whole inner man, sours the temper, and causes us to be an annoyance to everyone around us. The instant we discover that hateful feeling, let us go at once to Jesus, lay the heart open before Him, unveil the festering wound to His loving eye, and He will heal and give us the victory over ourselves.

❧ MARY WINSLOW

Mercy for the Chief of Sinners

Come now, and let us reason together, saith the LORD: though your sins be as scarlet, they shall be as white as snow.

—ISAIAH 1:18

Well, my dear friend, the Prince of life, the Lord of glory, did not come from heaven to save little sinners, but chief sinners: lost sinners, helpless sinners, the vilest of sinners, such sinners as poor Ruth and her trembling friend. He did not come to cleanse from only moderate guilt, but sins red as scarlet and crimson; yea, sins black as hell does His blood take away. Oh, do not dishonor Him by saying you are too bad or your case is too hard! There are before the throne, and on the way to it, those as bad, as hard, as unlikely as ever you can be. What can resist omnipotence? He who died for sinners has an omnipotent arm to pluck them from the burning and bring them up from the pit, however low they may be sunk in the mire. This I have proved many times. May the Holy Spirit testify of Jesus in your soul, and may that faith spring up which is the gift of God, so that with another unbelieving one you may cry out, "My Lord and my God!"

Is anything too hard for the Lord? No, truly, He is able to raise up Gentile sinners, as hard as stones, to be children of Abraham; the more unlikely the material, the greater glory to His name in forming thereof a vessel meet for His use. Oh, that your heart may be encouraged and that you may see what honor He will have in forgiving and saving you and me, who owe Him not fifty, or five hundred pence—but ten thousand talents! Oh, think what joy is in heaven over such sinners as we are when our repentings are kindled by Him who is exalted to give repentance unto His Israel, and remission of sins. Come, my friend, take courage; hate sin and loathe it as much as you will, but never magnify it above the efficacy and merits of the death and blood of Jesus. Forget not how great will be His glory in our salvation, in bringing those who were so far off "nigh by the blood" of His cross.

❧ RUTH BRYAN

Adversity the School of Love

*O my dove, that art in the clefts of the rock, in the secret places
of the stairs, let me see thy countenance, let me hear thy voice;
for sweet is thy voice, and thy countenance is comely.*

—SONG OF SOLOMON 2:14

I am sure that if we wish to know much of the reality and worth of God's love, we must experience and feel real adversity. How precious is Jesus at such times, when all other love fades into nothing. Then His love dissolves the heart, softens, and wins it. At such seasons we feel we can but weep our thanks to God for this "Brother for adversity"—born for my adversity, as if there were not another being in the world who needed and felt it but myself! Such is Jesus to the sorrowful soul. In this way the believer can rejoice in tribulation—yes, and does rejoice—not because of the tribulation, but because of the matchless love of Christ manifested at such seasons.

The Lord knows when to pay His loving visits. He knows how to time them—even when we need them. There are stolen visits from heaven to earth. No eye sees Him, or ear hears Him, or heart feels Him but the poor, tried, tempted soul. If ever sin appears most hateful, that is the time. Who can withstand the love of Christ? How it humbles, and yet exalts; casts down, and yet uplifts. How it weans from the earth and draws to heaven. Tears of joy and tears of sorrow flow together. Then does the believer feel that if she had a thousand hearts, she could give them all to Christ; and that if it were possible, she would never, no never, sin against one so full of love and so beloved again. There is a constant interchange of affection between the Lord and His people. The heart is opened, and all is told. Christ speaks, and the believer responds. All is love, nothing but love. No upbraidings from Him, and a full surrender of the whole heart to Him. This is the reason why we are often tried and cast down, even to show us what is in the heart of God toward us—how much He loves us.

ॐ MARY WINSLOW

The Royal Bounty

*And king Solomon gave unto the queen of Sheba
all her desire, whatsoever she asked, beside that which
Solomon gave her of his royal bounty.*

—1 KINGS 10:13

All God's goodness to us is humbling. The more He does for us, the more ready we are to say, "I am not worthy of the least of all the mercies and of all the truth which thou hast showed unto thy servant." The weight of a great answer to prayer seems almost too much for us. The grace of it is "too wonderful" for us. It throws up in such startling relief the disproportion between our little, poor, feeble cry and the great shining response of God's heart and hand, that we can only say: "Who am I, O Lord God, that thou hast brought me hitherto? Is this the manner of man, O Lord God?"

But it is more humbling still when we stand face-to-face with great things the Lord has done for us and given us, which we never asked at all, never even thought of asking—royal bounty, with which not even a prayer had to do. It is so humbling to get a view of these, that Satan tries to set up a false humility to hinder us from standing still and considering how great things the Lord has done for us; thus, he also contrives to defraud our generous God of the glory due unto His name. To begin at the beginning, we certainly did not ask Him to choose us in Christ Jesus before the world began and to predestinate us to be conformed to the image of His Son. Was not that royal bounty indeed? Then, we certainly did not ask Him to call us by His grace, for before that call, we could not have wished, much less asked for it. Then, who taught us to pray and put into our entirely corrupt and sinful hearts any thoughts of asking Him for anything at all? Was not all this royal bounty? Look back at our early prayers. Has He not more than granted them? Did we even know how much He could do for us? Did He not answer prayer by opening new vistas of prayer before us, giving us grace to ask for more grace, faith to plead for more faith? Why, it is all royal bounty from beginning to end!

❧ FRANCES RIDLEY HAVERGAL

Reasons the Saints Should
Love One Another

Love one another, as I have loved you.
—JOHN 15:12

The love of God to us is the great original ground for why we should love one another. The love of God to us, in all His persons, lays us under the highest obligation to love Him and one another for His sake. Are we, our individual persons, beloved of God the Father in election? Has He fixed His heart's love upon us, passed by others, and chosen us in His dear Son before the world was, unto endless glory with Him, although as considered sinners, we had deserved a place in eternal torment with the devils? Oh what obligation does this lay us under, to love Him and His! Has God the Father, of old, appointed us to obtain salvation through Jesus Christ and to be happy in time and to eternity in a love union with Himself and each other in His dear Son? And shall we be at variance among ourselves! Shall we, by want of love to each other, do all that in us lies to thwart this great end of electing love!

Are we redeemed by the Lamb's blood, out of every nation, kindred, tongue, and people, from endless misery to eternal glory? Oh, what obligation does this lay us under, to love the Redeemer and His redeemed! Has our dear Lord loved us and given Himself for us to make us one in love among ourselves, one in Him, and in the Father?

Are we the temples of the Holy Ghost? Has the Holy Spirit, sent from the Father and the Son, come down in His boundless love and taken possession of our souls to form Christ's image, His love-image there, and to bring us up to that love-unity with God and each other that was ordained and procured for us in electing and redeeming grace? How great is our obligation hence to love the Holy Ghost and those in whom He dwells! Oh may the love of God, of the three-one God to us, constrain us to love one another with a pure heart fervently!

ॐ ANNE DUTTON

The Kindness of God

My kindness shall not depart from thee.

—ISAIAH 54:10

Sometimes we like to think of the consolation that awaits us in heaven, when our warfare is accomplished and our iniquity is pardoned; but here, in this precious word, we have comfort and help for our daily life and strife of earth. The kindness of God is unutterable, illimitable, unchangeable! Every believer has experienced it, but the whole host of the redeemed, gathered from all lands, throughout all ages, could not tell the heights and depths and lengths and breadths of this great, everlasting, loving kindness that dwells in the heart of God.

God's negatives and affirmatives are like great rocks jutting out from the insecure and shifting sands of all earthly experiences. When a troubled, bewildered soul is enabled by faith to cling fast to one of these, all fear vanishes, all anxiety is gone, and nothing can move it from its confidence and peace. We have suffered, more or less, from the ever-changing influences around us; perhaps we ourselves have added somewhat to the sorrow that is in this world by reason of inconstancy and changeableness. But never, for one moment, has our God withdrawn the love with which He loved us from all eternity; never has He forsaken or forgotten those who have put their trust in Him. There is no such thing as departing kindness with Him: "no variableness, neither shadow of turning."

Oh, my loving Lord, let the stay and comfort of this precious "shall not" sink deep into my soul and strengthen me to face every difficulty and resist every evil and bear any trial with the courage such assurance gives!

இ SUSANNAH SPURGEON

Refreshment

Times of refreshing shall come from the presence of the Lord.
—ACTS 3:19

All our times of refreshing, my dear sister, come from the presence of the Lord. If God is present with our souls by the special gracious influence of His Holy Spirit, we are refreshed; if God is absent as to His sensible influence, we find no refreshment in reading, hearing, and praying. We are dry and barren if the Lord does not sensibly water us. We are cold and frozen if His sun-like face does not shine to thaw, warm, and comfort us. All the refreshment that newborn souls—the offspring of Christ, the new Adam—the heavenly man enjoy, does and must come down from heaven.

Nothing that this earth affords can refresh and solace the spiritual part of a heaven-born soul. No, such a soul is a creature of a high make and is prepared for a higher glory than any to be seen and enjoyed among the creatures and things of this lower world. Such a soul opens its mouth wide after God and His gracious influence to refresh and comfort it, as the earth in a time of drought opens its mouth for the natural influence of the heavens for the dew and the rain to descend for its refreshment. "Give me Christ, and God in Him," says the newborn soul, "or I die. God is my life, my exceeding joy, and without His gracious, comforting presence, my spirit dies, I sink in sorrow." Thus the psalmist: "O God, thou art my God; early will I seek thee: my soul thirsteth for thee in a dry and thirsty land, where no water is" (Ps. 63:1). And when God is enjoyed by the newborn soul, when the river of His grace, love, and mercy, which runs through a crucified Jesus, with its rich streams overflows the heart, right glad it makes a citizen of Zion. Wherefore, bless God for the refreshment from His presence you then have and take it as an earnest of more to come, through time and to eternity.

ANNE DUTTON

Our Works in God's Hand

Commit thy works unto the LORD.
—PROVERBS 16:3

S uppose an angel were sent down to tell us this morning that he was commissioned to take all our work under his charge today, that we might just be easy about it because he would undertake it, and his excellent strength and wisdom would make it all prosper a great deal more than ours. How extremely foolish it would be not to avail ourselves of such superhuman help! What a day of privilege and progress! And how we should thank God for the extraordinary relief His kindness had sent!

Far higher is our privilege this day—not merely permitted, but pressed upon us by royal command—"Commit thy works unto Jehovah!" Not an angel, but Jehovah bids us this day commit our works to Him. It is not approving the idea or thinking about it or even asking Him to take them that is here commanded, but committing them: a definite act of soul, a real transaction with our Lord. Will you not, before venturing away from your quiet early hour, commit your works to Him definitely, the special things you have today and the unforeseen work that He may add in the course of it?

And then leave it with Him! Leave details and results all and altogether with Him. You see, when you have committed it to Him, your works are in the hand of God. Really in His hand! And where else would you wish them to be? Would you like to have them back in your own? Do you think His grasp is not firm enough or the hollow of His hand not large enough to hold your little bits of work quite securely? Even if He tries your faith a little, and you seem to have labored in vain and spent your strength for naught, cannot you trust your own Master enough to add, "Yet surely my judgment is with the Lord, and my work with my God"? Especially as He says, "Thou art my servant, in whom I will be glorified," by which you know that your labor is not in vain in the Lord.

ॐ FRANCES RIDLEY HAVERGAL

Our All in All

Whom have I in heaven but thee? and there is
none upon earth that I desire beside thee.

—PSALM 73:25

When I enumerate our many mercies, it is with deep humility that I look back on my past life and discover so little gratitude and so much unworthiness. How much has sovereign grace done for me! Though I have solemnly professed to find consolation in religion, do I derive my hopes of happiness only from God? Yet how often have I roved in the world in quest of pleasure and dishonored the best of masters by an unholy life.

How ungrateful have I been for the common mercies of life and for the still more precious blessings of the Holy Spirit. May every temporal blessing that your heart can wish be yours. But whatever is the trial through which you may be called to pass, may that heaven-born religion attend you that can sweeten the bitter cup of life, afford you joy in this vale of tears, support you in nature's last extremity, and conduct you to the heavenly Canaan, where undisturbed happiness will ever reign. Life is but a vapor. Whether we spend it in tranquility and ease or in pain and suffering, time will soon land us on the shores of eternity to our destined home.

These things, my heart tells me, are solemn realities. They are not fictions. Though the language of my past life has been, "There is no future state," yet I now feel there is an eternity where I shall meet my earthly friends and stand accountable to the great tribunal for my conduct toward them. I regret the loss of those hours I have spent in vanity and in wounding the cause of that dear Redeemer, whom, I think, if I am not greatly deceived, I can now call mine. I think I can say with the psalmist, "Whom have I in heaven but thee? and there is none upon earth that I desire beside thee" (73:25). His religion comforts and supports my drooping spirits; His promises encourage and His glories warm my heart.

* HARRIET NEWELL

A Feast for the Fainting (1)

I will not send them away fasting,
lest they faint in the way.
—MATTHEW 15:32

Surely this tender care of the Lord Jesus for the bodily needs of the multitudes around him should comfort us greatly and strengthen our faith in the fact He unfolded to us when He said, "Your heavenly Father knoweth that ye have need of all these things."

I wonder why it is that we learn so slowly this sweet lesson of confidence in God and are sometimes so backward in trusting Him with the sole management and supply of our temporal necessities. We should always be as blithe as the birds of the air and as beautiful as the lilies of the field if we depended on Him as absolutely as they do.

And this is true in spiritual matters. Can you think—poor, longing, hungry hearts—that the Lord Jesus will be less pitiful to your soul's need than He was to the fasting multitude in the days of His flesh? Your hunger is keen for "the bread which came down from heaven"; your thirst is unquenchable till "the water of life" touches your lips. It matters not that the source of supply is not visible to you. "Whence should we have so much bread in the wilderness," said the full and undiscerning disciples, "as to fill so great a multitude?" They forgot, as we—alas!—too often forget, "what manner of man" this is and what He can accomplish by the power of His word. See, dear soul, if you have come to the Lord hungering and thirsting for His love and pardon, it is not possible that He should send you away empty. His heart is too tender, His hands are too full of blessing, His desire to feed and comfort you is too intense for there to be any failure on His part in supplying to you all that you crave.

◈ SUSANNAH SPURGEON

A Feast for the Fainting (2)

I will not send them away fasting,
lest they faint in the way.
—MATTHEW 15:32

I know there are some who say they are seeking Christ and yet cannot find Him. Dear hearts, do not be angry with me, for I write for myself as well as for you when I tell you that if you are not fed, it must be because you will not eat! Suppose you had been one of that favored company on the mountainside and that you had, at the Lord's command, sat down with the others, but when one of the disciples brought to you the basket of food, made ready by the Lord's own hand and blessed by His own lips, you had refused to take it from some foolish whim or caprice or doubt that possessed you. Would you have anyone to blame but yourself if you had fainted with exhaustion on your return journey over the hills of Judea to your home?

Ah! None at that wonderful feast were as foolish and unreasonable as you and I sometimes are, for it is recorded that "they did all eat, and were filled." Now, will not some poor sinful, suffering, starving one take heart of grace from the teaching of this miracle and come at once to the compassionate Savior to have all her needs supplied? The more hungry you are, the greater will be your joy in being filled; and He has said, "I will not send them away fasting." Trust Him, and be abundantly satisfied. Dear Mr. Spurgeon once happily said, "He may make us wait to awaken appetite, but He will not in the end dismiss us unfed." So let nothing discourage you. Sit on the ground before Him, as He bids you, till the basket comes round; or if the disciples pass you by, venture to His side and take the blessing straight from His loving hand. He will never chide you for trusting Him too much!

☙ SUSANNAH SPURGEON

Healing for a Desperate Disease

He feedeth on ashes: a deceived heart
hath turned him aside.
—ISAIAH 44:20

I must solemnly testify that Christ only is the rock upon which the soul can be safe and triumphant when the waves of death seem to be going over the body. At such a time the world stands afar off; friends can only look on or look up, and all that is to come appears a vast forever, either in the fiery wrath or the blissful presence of the Lord God and the Lamb. Nothing can be solid but "Christ in you, the hope of glory." To realize this is worth a thousand such worlds as this, and, indeed, whatever you may be called to give up is not worth a name in comparison of a precious Christ.

My heart glows with a desire to speak well of His dear name, His finished work, His glorious person, and, if it might be His will, to set other souls on fire or longing after Him. For what do I do away from my glory home but be a savor of Christ, telling poor, dead sinners that whatever is their profession, they are "feeding on ashes"; that "a deceived heart hath turned them aside" from the only way of salvation? I would also seek to encourage poor, trembling souls, who are already brought into judgment and feel the sentence of death in themselves, to put their case, bad as it is, into the hands of the "Wonderful Counselor," Prevailing Intercessor, and "Advocate with the Father," who is "Jesus Christ the Righteous."

May the Comforter reveal Christ as He convinces of sin and take of His precious things and set them against your vile ones, giving you heavenly skill and understanding to plead His precious blood against your sin, His perfect obedience against our constant disobedience, His power to heal against your desperate disease.

☙ RUTH BRYAN

The Intercession of Christ

He lives, the great Redeemer lives,
(What joy the blest assurance gives!)
And now before His Father God,
Pleads the full merits of His blood.

Repeated crimes awake our fears,
And justice armed with frowns, appears;
But in the Savior's lovely face
Sweet mercy smiles, and all is peace.

Hence then, ye black, despairing thoughts;
Above our fears, above our faults,
His powerful intercessions rise,
And guilt recedes, and terror dies.

In every dark distressful hour,
When sin and Satan join their power;
Let this dear hope repel the dart,
That Jesus bears us on His heart.

Great advocate, almighty friend—
On Him our humble hopes depend;
Our cause can never, never fail,
For Jesus pleads, and must prevail.

∾ ANNE STEELE

Do Thou for Me

Do thou for me.
—PSALM 109:21

The psalmist does not say what he wanted God to do for him. He leaves it open. So this most restful prayer is left open for all perplexed hearts to appropriate according to their several necessities. And so we leave it open for God to fill up in His own way. Only a trusting heart can pray this prayer at all; the very utterance of it is an act of faith. We could not ask anyone whom we did not know intimately and trust implicitly to do for us, without even suggesting what.

Only a self-emptied heart can pray it. It is when we have come to the end of our own resources or, rather, come to see that we never had any at all, that we are willing to accept the fact that we can do nothing and let God do everything for us. Only a loving heart can pray it. For no one likes another to take her and her affairs in hand and do for her, unless that other is cordially loved. We might submit to it, but we should not like it, and certainly should not seek it.

There is sure to be a preface to this prayer. Neither know we what to do. Perhaps we have been shrinking from being brought to this. Rather, let us give thanks for it. It is the step down from the drifting wreck onto the ladder still hanging at the side. Will another step be down into the dark water? Go on, a little lower still! Fear not! The next is that we know not what we should pray for. Now we have reached the lowest step. What next? Do Thou for me. This is the step into the captain's boat. Now He will cut loose from the wreck of our efforts, ladder and all will be left behind, and we have nothing to do but to sit still and let Him take us to our desired haven, probably steering quite a different course from anything we should have thought best.

≈ FRANCES RIDLEY HAVERGAL

Why Halt Ye?

*How long halt ye between two opinions? if the LORD
be God, follow him: but if Baal, then follow him.*

—1 KINGS 18:21

It matters not who may deride or scoff or how your own evil heart may shrink from contempt of the cross. "How long halt ye between two opinions? if the LORD be God, follow him: but if Baal, then follow him." You cannot serve them both. Oh, be wise. If the world and Satan and the flesh seem too strong for you, as they surely will, go into your closet and pour out your heart before the Lord; He will be a refuge for you. "He giveth power to the faint; and to them that have not might he increaseth strength." The sighs and groans of a broken heart are heard in the high court above, and the tears of a contrite spirit are audible there; for before the throne is Jesus, the Brother of the brokenhearted, the propitiation for sin, the advocate for sinners who loathe themselves for their iniquity. That blessed Savior understands all the broken utterances; He knows what each would say if he could, and "He ever liveth to make intercession for them."

It may be the law condemns you, O trembling one; conscience condemns you; thoughts, words, actions all condemn you. Be it so, and may it be your mercy, and the beginning of your salvation, for this is like the power with which the Holy Spirit begins in the soul, thereby translating it out of the kingdom of darkness "into the kingdom of God's dear Son." The religion of Jesus is a religion of power, and if, through the power of the Holy Spirit, there is a discovery of sin and condemnation, may Jesus say, "Thy sins (oh, the sweetness of personality!), which are many, are all forgiven thee"; then the burden is lawfully lost, and the soul has solid peace. Thus shall it be with every one quickened by the Spirit. May the Spirit enable you to come just as you are!

❧ RUTH BRYAN

The Opened Treasure

The LORD shall open unto thee his good treasure.
—DEUTERONOMY 28:12

W hat shall He "open unto thee"? In a word, "the unsearchable riches of Christ." In Him "are hid all the treasures of wisdom and knowledge," but the Lord shall open them unto you. Riches of goodness, forebearance, and long-suffering shall be meted out in infinitely gracious proportion to our sins, provocations, and repeated waywardness—exceeding riches of grace for all our poverty now, and riches in glory enough and to spare for all the needs of glorified capacities through all eternity. All are yours in Him.

Faith is the key to this infinite treasury, and in giving us faith He gives treasure for treasure. He is ready to make us rich in faith and then still to increase our faith unto all riches of the full assurance of understanding. He shall open unto us the good treasure not only of the living Word, but of the written Word. This is indeed treasure to be desired, more to be desired than gold; and when Jehovah the Spirit opens this to us, we shall, we do rejoice as one that finds great spoil. Christ, the true Wisdom, has said, "I will fill their treasures," and "The chambers shall be filled with all precious and pleasant riches." It is only with God-given treasure that we can enrich others. When we want to give a word to another, it generally seems to come with more power if, instead of casting about for what we think likely to suit them, we simply hand over to them any treasure word which He has freshly given to us. Also, let us not stand idly waiting for some further opening in the treasure, but let there be search made in the king's treasure house, in the house of the rolls where the treasures were laid up, where decrees and records of our King are to be found. It is only continual drawing from His good treasure that will profit us, even the light of the knowledge of the glory of God in the face of Jesus Christ.

❧ FRANCES RIDLEY HAVERGAL

Begotten to Love

Every one that loveth him that begat loveth
him also that is begotten of him.

—1 JOHN 5:1

That special interest God has in His saints is ground for why we should love them. They are the children of God's love, His dear children. God the Father has predestinated them into the adoption of children by Jesus Christ unto Himself. He has set them apart for Himself as His own children, in distinction from all the world beside. He has settled an inheritance upon them—no less than His great self! He has formed the image of His Son in them and given them the spirit of adoption, whereby they cry "Abba, Father." They are the brethren of Jesus Christ: heirs of God and joint-heirs with Him. They are the bride, the Lamb's wife, the spouse, the queen of the King of glory. They are the members of His body, the fullness of Him who fills all in all. They are the temples of the Holy Ghost! He has chosen them for His habitation and dwells in them as His rest forever.

They are the choice of the Father, the purchase of the Son, and the conquest of the Spirit. The Lord has chosen, bought, and possessed them for Himself as His own portion. He esteems them as His jewels, His peculiar treasure, and they are unspeakably precious and highly honorable in His sight. They are His honorable servants to do His glorious work, His faithful witnesses in the earth, and His shining light in a dark world. He calls them His joy below and will rejoice over them as His crown of glory above. How dearly then should we love one another! How highly should we esteem each other in love for the Lord's sake!

&ﾟ ANNE DUTTON

The Exceeding Greatness of God's Power

What is the exceeding greatness of his power
to us-ward who believe.

—EPHESIANS 1:19

If I have true faith in the Lord Jesus Christ, then the exceeding greatness of the power of the Most High God, "according to the working of his mighty power," is to me-ward, is on my side, or—I say it with deep reverence—at my service, always at hand to help, to guard, to defend, and to provide for me. Do I believe this? Do any Christians really hold this faith? Is it possible that there can be among the feeble, doubting, self-engrossed, and half-hearted people that I see and hear of, any who possess the assurance that the power of the living God dwells in them and that they can do all things through Christ, who strengthens them? If there are any such, why do they not walk worthy of the vocation wherewith they are called?

Look to yourself, my soul. Is the exceeding greatness of your Lord's power manifest in you as it should be? What do you possess of the details of His mighty working—the filling-up, as it were, of the great plan of His will and design concerning you? What does "the effectual working of his power" produce in your heart and life? Are you wholly consecrated to His service? Have you given yourself and all that you have into His loving hands? Are you filled with His Holy Spirit? Does He control every thought, word, and deed? And are all the powers of your being and all the possessions of both soul and body subject and surrendered to His absolute sway?

Put forth in me the mighty grace that will make my daily life a proof that Thou art working Thine own will in me.

❧ SUSANNAH SPURGEON

Close Walking with God

*But it is good for me to draw near to God: I have put my trust
in the Lord GOD, that I may declare all thy works.*

—PSALM 73:28

What an unsatisfying world this is to have our all in! How trifling does everything appear that is not in some way connected with God's glory! Look upon all you now see or admire as passing away, yourself passing away with it. Every hour—yes, each moment—is bringing us nearer and nearer to the place appointed for all living. And yet, how little we realize it as we ought to; therefore does our good and gracious God see it needful to try us by some painful dispensation to arouse us from our lethargy and stir us up to a closer walk with Him. Oh, let an aged Christian urge on your mind a closer walk with God. Realize your oneness with Jesus. Live upon, and live for, Him. Be much in communion with Him. He is not far from you. He is all around you. His eye is ever upon you, and His ear—His loving ear—ever open to hear what you have to say to Him. Who that knows the blessedness of close intimacy and communion with Jesus would ever be without it?

My soul is rejoicing in God my Savior! He is indeed the chief of ten thousand and the altogether lovely. Let your transactions be close with Him, and all will go right. Nothing grows so strong as exercised faith, and this is one reason our Lord tries us so often.

Dear, dear friend, our friendship is not to end here, in this poor world; it is destined to be continued and increased in another. Think what is prepared for us and the glory that shall be revealed in us and set loose to all the tinsel glory of an empty, unsatisfying world. It is not worth a straw when compared with what awaits us!

☙ MARY WINSLOW

Earthly Comforts Taken Away

I will not leave you comfortless.
—JOHN 14:18

You know our gracious Lord said to His disciples, "It is expedient for you that I go away; for if I go not away the Comforter will not come unto you." It seems to me that friend after friend, comfort after comfort, might also say to our foolish, clinging, sensitive hearts, "It is expedient for you that we go away; for if we go not away the Comforter will not come unto you!" In other words, "If we remain, you will build on us part of your comfort, and then you will be a loser, not learning the height, depth, length, and breadth of love, sweetness, and fullness which are in Christ Jesus." A pang may be felt as one by one is taken away; yet how blessed to be in the position of the poor sinner who was left alone with Jesus, when His gracious lips did drop as the honeycomb into her heart, saying, "Neither do I condemn thee: go, and sin no more." Oh, it is worth being stripped of all that is our own to hear this secret of divine love and to enjoy Jesus as our "all in all."

Now, I know you will assent to this in your judgment, but I want you to have the full benefit and blessing in being brought nearer to Jesus. For I well know what creatures we are for self-hewn cisterns, and how when one is broken we seek for another instead of turning to the Fountain. Look at your own heart and see whether it is not so—whether you are not often wanting a friend, letter, or anything to break the desolate feeling. I long to draw you to the full bliss of forsaking all for Christ. Then shall you abundantly find all in Him and praise Him for every stripping and emptying that prevented your resting in a lower source of enjoyment or enjoying even Him through the medium of others. It is most precious to commune directly with Him and receive lessons of wisdom from His own blessed mouth.

❧ RUTH BRYAN

Taking God at His Word

Believe in the LORD your God, so shall ye be established.
—2 CHRONICLES 20:20

Of course Paul could be calm, bright, and confident, with a heart at leisure from itself to cheer and counsel others. Yet could any circumstances have been more depressing? Traveling in a miserable and crowded ship, to which our most wretched steamer would be a palace, exceedingly tossed with tempest, not a gleam of sun or star for many days, all reckoning lost, driving wildly on to certain shipwreck.

Whatever this day may bring forth, there can be nothing like this for us. Glance at the needs of this day—our weakness, our openness to temptation, our liability to fall, our besetting sins, our ignorance, our present or possible troubles, our longing for Him, which includes all other holy longings—seven pressing realities. Now let us hush our hearts to listen to the reality of His corresponding replies: "I will strengthen thee." "Ye shall be able to quench all the fiery darts of the wicked." "Able to keep you from falling." "He shall save his people from their sins." "I will instruct thee and teach thee in the way which thou shalt go." "I will not leave you comfortless." "I will come to you." Can we read these words—His own words—and say, "I do not believe God?" Even the recoil from such an expression may help a trembling one to the joyful and only alternative: "I believe God, that it shall be even as it was told me." Not less, not almost as, but even as, with God's own fullness of meaning in each word of each promise.

The ground of Paul's belief was not something, but Someone. Simply, I believe God! This belief, of course, includes all His messages, written or spoken. "If you will not believe, surely you shall not be established" is a word of continual application to the trembling or wavering steps of our daily path. But this is His commandment: "Believe in the LORD your God, so shall ye be established; believe his prophets, so shall ye prosper."

☙ FRANCES RIDLEY HAVERGAL

Being Purified

*Every branch in me that beareth not fruit
he taketh away: and every branch that beareth fruit,
he purgeth it, that it may bring forth more fruit.*

—JOHN 15:2

I find it a solemn and awesome thing to be a Christian. It is indeed a holy calling! God will at times cause His candle to emit a clearer light in the dark recesses of the heart, and there discover and drag out every lurking, retiring evil. Nor will He permit any plea, though we may say, "Is it not a little one?"

The secret business between the soul and God, when He shows Himself as a holy and jealous God, can never be described by language. It is no light matter when He calls the understanding, the will, and the affections each to bring their favorite objects and deliver them up to the fire that must either purify or consume, but this He will do to everyone that He has formed for Himself. "Every branch that beareth fruit, he purgeth it, that it may bring forth more fruit."

Young Christians know little of this requirement: "My son, give me thine heart!" I have long desired to give mine, but grace alone can enable me to do this. O, let the sacred fire consume every corruption that keeps it back! But, O, support me, while Thou purifiest! If I am called to be a living martyr, as most truly I am, bestow the martyr's faith! Let me have communion with Thee, and then I shall have society enough. If this sickness be not unto death, O, let it be that Thy Son may be glorified! And let me come out of it as gold purified in the fire!

» SARAH HAWKES

My Redeemer Liveth

For I know that my redeemer liveth, and that he shall
stand at the latter day upon the earth.

—JOB 19:25

There is no real religion which is not personal religion. If I would be saved, I must believe in Christ for myself; I must seek the Spirit's help for myself. It is no use that I know the Lord Jesus to be a Savior unless I seek and find Him as my Savior. It is no good to me that the blessed Spirit "sanctifieth all the elect people of God," unless I obey His call and become one of the number.

"I know that my redeemer liveth." With the full light of the gospel to shine back on the book of Job, how beautiful and full of trust do these words appear! The believer adopts them. He has never seen the Savior, but he knows that He lives and rejoices in Him, even here, "with joy unspeakable and full of glory." The believer looks up, and with the eye of faith beholds his ascended Savior, "mighty to save," ever living to intercede for him—"Jesus Christ, the same yesterday, and today, and for ever."

Whatever else changes, there is no change in the Savior. No death affects Him or that deathless world where He is: "I know that my Redeemer liveth." And here I pause to say that it is of the utmost consequence for you and me to be able to say, "He is my Redeemer. I believe in Him. I trust in Him. He is my hope in life and my trust in death. 'I know whom I have believed.'" Oh, rest contented with nothing less than this: a personal application to the Savior—an appropriation, in humble faith, of His finished work. May you each say from your heart, "This is my beloved Savior, with whom I am well pleased."

❧ ELIZABETH JULIA HASELL

The Gift of Peace

My peace I give unto you.
—JOHN 14:27

Peace. "Peace I leave with you"; "my peace I give unto you" is more. The added word tells the fathomless marvel of the gift— "My peace." This is not merely peace with God; Christ has made that by the blood of His cross, and being justified by faith, we have it through Him. But after we are thus reconciled, the enmity and the separation being ended, Jesus has a gift for us from His own treasures, and this is its special and wonderful value, that it is His very own. How we value a gift that was the giver's own possession! What a special token of intimate friendship we feel it to be! To others we give what we have made or purchased; it is only to very near and dear ones that we give what has been our own personal enjoyment or use. And so Jesus gives us not only peace made and peace purchased, but also a share in His very own peace—divine, eternal, incomprehensible peace—which dwells in His own heart as God and which shone in splendor of calmness through His life as man. No wonder that it passes all understanding.

But how? Why does the sap flow from the vine to the branch? Simply because the branch is joined to the vine. Then the sap flows into it by the very law of its nature. So, being joined to our Lord Jesus by faith, that which is His becomes ours and flows into us by the very law of our spiritual life. If there were no hindrance, it would indeed flow as a river. Then how earnestly we should seek to have every barrier removed to the inflowing of such a gift! Let it be our prayer that He would clear the way for it, that He would take away all the unbelief, all the self, all the hidden clogging of the channel.

Then He will give a sevenfold blessing: My peace, My joy, My love, at once and always, now and forever; My grace and My strength for all the needs of our pilgrimage; My rest and My glory for all the grand sweet home life of eternity with Him.

        ❧ FRANCES RIDLEY HAVERGAL

By the Blood of the Lamb

Out of weakness were made strong,
waxed valiant in fight.
—HEBREWS 11:34

You know those before the throne overcame Satan "by the blood of the Lamb," and our victories must come in the same way. Yet this way we are so slow to learn, because it is completely out of and against that self which it is so hard to leave. However, the Holy Spirit will not forsake His own work; the least beginning shall have a sure ending, for He will perfect that which concerns us. David tells us how he became such a skillful warrior: "It is God that girdeth me with strength." "He teacheth my hands to war." "By thee I have run through a troop; by my God have I leaped over a wall." There is a very encouraging word in Hebrews 11:34—"out of weakness were made strong"—strong through faith. This faith leaves the creature and creature's works behind and fastens upon a precious Christ, determined to go through all trusting in Him and saying heartily, "God forbid that I should glory save in the cross of our Lord Jesus Christ, by whom the world is crucified unto me and I unto the world."

My soul earnestly desires that you may obtain "like precious faith" to venture wholly upon Jesus. Though that faith should seem small "like a grain of mustard seed," it will not prove a delusion, for "He knoweth them that put their trust in him," although sometimes they know not to whom they really belong. May it please our gracious Lord soon to reveal Himself, as you desire, and grant you that sealing of the Spirit for which you long. May the Lord bless you indeed, enlarge you out of self into Christ, and keep you from evil, that it may not grieve you.

≥ RUTH BRYAN

A New Creature

The Spirit itself beareth witness with our spirit,
that we are the children of God.

—ROMANS 8:16

There are two ways whereby a soul comes to know that it is new-born. The first is by the revelation of the Spirit bearing witness to the soul in some word or other where this truth is declared. The second is by His enabling the soul to discern its own acts in divine light. A living infant, you know, when first born into the world has life, but it does not know it. It cries, desires the breast, tastes the milk, and is satisfied and sees the light and feels the heat with pleasure, all of which are visible demonstrations of its life to bystanders, but the child knows nothing of it because it is not capable of self-reflection. And thus it is with a newborn soul; there is a secret work of God upon all the heart, a principle of life given, and from thence some secret motions and faint stirrings now and then, begun under convictions, before it is brought forth into the visible life of grace. This life discovers itself as soon as the soul is born again in the breath or cry of the new creature, in its desires, its discerning, and its enjoyments. When these are communicated to grown Christians, they know such a soul is one of Christ's newborn babes.

A living child sees. What have you seen? Have you seen yourself to be a sinner by nature as well as by practice, in heart as well as life, and that you are utterly undone and must perish forever without an interest in Jesus Christ, as being utterly unable to do anything to deliver yourself from the wrath to come? Have you seen an excellency in Christ, as a complete Savior, that is exceedingly suitable to your case as a lost sinner? And do you have any discerning of the glory of God's free grace and mercy in Christ? Have you been made to cry unto the Lord, to lament your sinfulness before Him, and to supplicate His throne for mercy, praying Him to give you Christ, despite what He denies you? Then you have the new creature's breath, which flows from none but those that have the new creature's life.

ॐ ANNE DUTTON

Marvelously Helped

For he was marvellously helped.
—2 CHRONICLES 26:15

Uzziah seems to have been a variously busy and successful man. His architecture and his agriculture and his war organizations and engineering spread his name far abroad. For "as long as he sought the Lord, God made him to prosper." Yet the end of his story is a strange contrast—a leper, dwelling in a separate house, and cut off from the house of the Lord. Where was the turning point? Probably in the words, "He strengthened himself exceedingly." It had been God's help and strength before, and he had risen very high. Then he thought he was strong, and he was brought fearfully low.

"Marvelously!" For is it not wonderful that God should help us at all? Have we not wondered hundreds of times at the singular help He has given? If we have not, what ungrateful blindness! He has been giving it ever since we were helpless babies. The very little things, the microscopic helpings, often seem most marvelous of all when we consider that it was Jehovah Himself who stooped to the tiny need of a moment. And the greater matters prove themselves to be the Lord's doing, just because they are so marvelous in our eyes. Why should we fear being brought to some depth of perplexity and trouble when we know He will be true to His name and be our help, so that we shall be "men wondered at" because we have been so marvelously helped!

Let us turn our special attention to it each day. We need help of all kinds all day long. Now just observe how He gives it! Even if nothing the least unusual happens, the opened and watching eye will see that the whole day is one sweet story of marvelous help. And perhaps the greatest marvel will be that He has helped us to see His help after much practical blindness to it. And then the marveling will rise in praising the name of the Lord your God who has dealt wondrously with you.

❧ FRANCES RIDLEY HAVERGAL

Our School of Learning

Teach me thy way, O LORD; I will walk in thy truth:
unite my heart to fear thy name.
—PSALM 86:11

How wonderful is God in all His great and gracious dealings! He places us, as soon as the spiritual eye is opened, in His school—first, the infant-school, and then onward and upward, from class to class, losing no opportunity of spiritual instruction. Many hard lessons have we to learn and relearn. But, oh, the unwearied patience and tenderness of our Teacher! Some of His children are slow learners, dull scholars, and require the discipline of the rod to stimulate them to more earnestness, attention, and submission. Some imagine they have arrived at the end of their education and sit down at their ease; but presently they are called upon to solve some hard problem, and they find that they know less than they thought, and for their boasting are sent back to a lower class and made to commence where they first began. Such is the school of Christ.

Lord, teach me more and more of Thyself and of my own poverty, misery, and weakness. And oh, unfold to my longing eyes and heart what there is in Thyself to supply all my need, and in Thy loving, willing heart to do all for me, and all in me, to fit me for Thy service here and for Thy presence hereafter! Sanctify abundantly all Thy varying dispensations to the welfare and prosperity of my soul, and increase in me every gift and grace of Thy Spirit, that I may show forth Thy praise and walk humbly and closely with Thee. Thou knowest what a poor, worthless worm I am and how utterly unworthy of the least mercy from Thy merciful hands; but Thou lovest to bestow Thy favors upon the poor and needy, such as me, Thou, most precious Lord. Thou hast been a good and gracious, sin-pardoning God to my soul, and a very present help in every time of trouble. Helpless as an infant I hang upon Thee, to do all for me and all in me. Oh, what a friend is Christ to me!

❧ MARY WINSLOW

The Doubting Christian (1)

O thou of little faith, wherefore didst thou doubt?

—MATTHEW 14:31

W e are subject to a thousand weaknesses, the natural attendants of frail humanity. It is not strange, therefore, that we should sometimes feel oppressed with doubts and fears. Indeed, a certain religious author says, "The soul that never doubted, hath never yet believed: for while flesh remains in the believer, it is unbelieving flesh; and it is the office of faith to subdue this unbelief in all its activities."

There are, it appears to me, two kinds of doubt respecting our spiritual state, to which we are subject. One is a distrust of God's omnipotence, mercy, and willingness to save—something like, we should suppose, the apostles felt when they exclaimed with astonishment, "Who then can be saved?" The other proceeds from a consciousness of weakness, sin, and want of faith in ourselves. I do not think that my doubts are occasioned by any distrust of the blessed God! Oh, no—God takes not pleasure in the death of the wicked. Otherwise, why did He give His Son to be a ransom for sinners? Why does He run to meet the returning prodigal, while yet a great way off? Why does He continue to hold out to us the scepter of His mercy when we are practically saying to Him, "We desire not the knowledge of Thy ways?"

That God is love is evinced by everything around us, as well as by the declarations of His Word. He is able and willing to save, to the uttermost, all who come unto Him with faith in the merits of His Son.

❧ SUSAN HUNTINGTON

The Doubting Christian (2)

O thou of little faith, wherefore didst thou doubt?
—MATTHEW 14:31

It is a great thing to be a Christian at any time, especially in these last days when iniquity abounds and the love of many waxes cold, when "the declensions of Christianity" may be produced as "a sad argument of its truth." But it is God who works in us to will and to do of His good pleasure, and to Him the work is as easy now as at any other period. Were the whole world around us faithful disciples of Christ, there would still be a law in our members over which God alone could give us the victory through Jesus Christ our Lord. In such circumstances, however, there would be fewer temptations, and it would be easier to maintain a close walk with God. Nothing short of omnipotence can, indeed, cause light to shine out of darkness.

But the greatness of the work should not cause our hearts to sink in despondency. No work is too great for God to perform, and He has promised to help those who trust in Him and to give them all that they ask, agreeable to His will. Despondency must then arise from lack of faith. It was this in Peter that impelled him to exclaim, "Lord, save me, I perish!" He did not fully trust in the power of his divine Master, but yielded to fear, excited by the rough appearance of the waves on which he stood, forgetting that He whom the winds and the sea obey was at his side. It is this in us—the lack of faith—that leads us to doubt whether we can ever be saved. The Lord increase our faith and give us unwavering confidence in His faithfulness and mercy.

≈ SUSAN HUNTINGTON

MAY 17

The Pain of Temptations

The Lord knoweth how to deliver the
godly out of temptations.

—2 PETER 2:9

The same afflictions that every child of God meets with, as to his particular temptations, are accomplished in other brethren that are in the world. And though every particular temptation is not felt by every particular saint, yet temptations of all kinds are cast among the members of Christ as a collective body, and from this all the members because of their own particular experience have a kindly sympathy with each other in their particular trials. Christ, the dear Head of the church, painfully felt a collection of all temptations to fit Him for the most intense sympathy with every one of His particular members in each of their particular temptations, since He felt the same, and from a sea of flowing compassions, an infinity of yearning bowels in His heart, He affords them suitable succor in every time of need. He was tempted in all points like as we are, and in that He Himself has thus suffered, being tempted, He is able thus to succor them that are tempted.

Be of good cheer! Your compassionate Jesus, who feels your sorrows and makes them His own by sympathy, will support you under, do you good by, and deliver you from your present distresses. Flee to Christ—your hiding place from the wind of temptation. Tell Him how hard it blows upon you, and in infinite grace He will open His bosom for your relief, cover you in Himself from the storm, and cause you to take deeper root through these shakings, by which Satan would tear you up from your standing in Christ and in the truth as it is in Jesus. Venture not to fight with Satan in your own strength nor with your own weapons, but flee to the Lord, your strength—your very present help in trouble—and ask for weapons out of His armory; and thus commit the keeping of your soul to Jesus, and your temptations shall end well for the glory of your Lord—the captain of your salvation—and for the special advantage of your saved soul.

&» ANNE DUTTON

Undeserved Grace

Who forgiveth all thine iniquities.

—PSALM 103:3

Why should I now lament, sigh, and weep for my life and time so evil spent? With how much humility and lowliness ought I to come and acknowledge my sins to God, giving Him thanks that it has pleased Him, of His abundant goodness, to give me time for repentance. For as I consider my sins, I know them to be so grievous and exceeding in number that I have deserved very often eternal damnation. And because I deserve God's wrath, so many times owed to me, I must incessantly give thanks to the mercy of God, beseeching also that the same delay of punishment does not cause His affliction to be more painful, since my own conscience condemns my former doings. But His mercy exceeds all iniquity (Ps. 103:3).

And if I should not hope for this, alas, what man has the power to help me (Ps. 108:12)? And for the multitude of my sins, I do not dare to lift up my eyes to heaven, where the seat of judgment is, because I have offended God so much. Shall I fall in desperation? No, I will call upon Christ, the light of the world (1 John 1:5–7), the fountain of life, the relief of all those filled with cares, the peacemaker between God and man (1 John 2:1–2), and the only health and comfort of all true repentant sinners (John 3:1–21).

By His almighty power, He can save me and deliver me out of this miserable state, and has willed by His mercy to save even the sin of the whole world (John 3:16). I have no hope or confidence in any creature, either in heaven or earth, but in Christ my whole and only Savior. He came into the world to save sinners (Matt. 1:21) and to heal those who are sick, for He said that the whole have no need of a physician. Behold, Lord, how I come to Thee, a sinner, sick and grievously wounded. I ask not bread, but the crumbs that fall from the children's table. Cast me not out of Thy sight, although I have deserved to be cast into hell fire.

&ra; KATHERINE PARR

The Blessedness of Separation from the World

Mortify therefore your members.
—COLOSSIANS 3:5

The carnal mind would like to mix with the world and to compromise a little, desiring not to seem peculiar, but to let religion appear pleasant and agreeable to all, enjoying innocent amusements and recreations, serving God in this way as well as by other means and letting both the old man and the new have their part.

How very many are now deluding themselves with such a profession as this, which is mere *ignis fatuus* ["foolish fire"; a deceptive light] leading them on to the pit of perdition. But we "have not so learned Christ." We know that if the old man feeds, the new man starves, and that they cannot both fatten and strengthen at the same time. Moreover, we solemnly fear that those who can willingly mix with the world and do not find painful effects from it, do not have the true life that feels where death is, or the true light that discovers darkness and evil deeds.

Do not be alarmed, my dear friend. It is most blessed to forsake all for Christ, and when He calls you to any new forsaking, He will command your strength for it. The more He circumcises your heart to love Him and your lips to witness of and for Him, the more you will find those who merely profess to believe to forsake you. The more we lose for him, the more we find in Him, and to get rid of anything that is between us and Him is a gainful loss. Fear not. "His reward is with him," and a rich one it is, even the unfolding and enjoyment of Himself. Hear Him say, "Hearken, O daughter, and consider; forget also thine own people and thy father's house; so shall the king greatly desire thy beauty; for he is thy Lord, and worship thou him." It seems as if cleaving to the first-Adam family is like a cloud or veil over the beauty of the Spouse. Forsake them; so shall the King desire—yes, greatly desire—your beauty. How encouraging are these things for you, though many may rise up against you.

– RUTH BRYAN

Good Works Flow from Salvation

Wherefore we labour, that, whether present or absent,
we may be accepted of him.

—2 CORINTHIANS 5:9

How many there are who for years have been trying to do good in every way to commend themselves to God, working for their salvation instead of coming to Jesus just as they are—poor, blind, and naked—and casting themselves, as totally unable to help themselves, wholly upon His mercy, as able to save them without their work. Then they will find peace and joy in believing. Good works are the after-fruits of salvation. The tree must be good before it can bear good fruit.

Would that all the world did but know the happiness of loving God and of being loved by Him! One moment spent in communion with Christ is worth a million years spent in the pursuit and pleasures of this poor, dying, disappointing world. Oh, to live for eternity—a glorious eternity! What madness not to be preparing for it. There is nothing under the heavens so important as to be ready for this. You may leave your home in health and in high spirits, in the anticipation of meeting dear friends, and in a few hours be ushered into the presence of the great Judge of heaven and earth, to be tried at His bar and acquitted or condemned.

But this is a subject ridiculed and slighted. Try to live on earth as you expect to live in heaven. Walk holy and uprightly, just as if the Lord were with you and in your midst. And is He not with us? "Lo, I am with you alway."

&» MARY WINSLOW

Allegiance to the King

Thou art my King.
—PSALM 44:4

C an I say it? Is Jesus in very deed and truth "my King"? Where is the proof of it? Am I living in His kingdom of "righteousness and peace and joy in the Holy Ghost" now? Am I speaking the language of that kingdom? Am I following the customs of the people who are not His people? Or do I diligently learn the ways of His people? Am I practically living under the rule of His laws? Have I done heart homage to Him? Am I bravely and honestly upholding His cause because it is His, not merely because those around me do so? Is my allegiance making any practical difference to my life today?

Do I say it? God has said to me, "He is thy Lord, and worship thou him." Do my lips say, "My Lord and my God"? Does my life say, "Christ Jesus, my Lord"—definitely and personally, "my Lord"? Can I share in His last, sweet commendation to His disciples, the more precious because of its divine dignity: "Ye call me Master and Lord, and ye say well, for so I am"? Have I said, "Thou art my King" to Jesus Himself, from the depth of my own heart in unreserved and unfeigned submission to His scepter? Am I ashamed or afraid to confess allegiance in plain English among His friends or before His foes? Is the seal upon my brow so unmistakable that always and everywhere I am known to be His subject? Is "Thou art my King" blazoned, as it ought to be, in shining letters on the whole scroll of my life, so that it may be "known and read of all men"?

Answer Thou for me, O my King! "Search me and try me," and show me the true state of my case, and then, for Thine own sake, pardon all my past disloyalty and make me, by Thy mighty grace, from this moment totally loyal, for "Thou art my King"!

☙ FRANCES RIDLEY HAVERGAL

Together in Suffering and Glory

Behold, how good and how pleasant it is for
brethren to dwell together in unity!

—PSALM 133:1

That community the saints have in sufferings and in glories is a great reason why they should love one another. The same common enemies—sin, Satan, and the world—are jointly engaged against them all. They all groan, being burdened with an indwelling body of sin and death—a law that they find in their members that wars against the law of their minds and brings them into captivity to the law of sin and death. Satan, their grand enemy, incessantly molests and fights against them all. He either sets traps and snares to take them by his subtilty and flattery or terrifies them with his rage as a roaring lion. One way or other, he is always seeking to devour them. These same afflictions are accomplished in the brethren throughout the whole world, and not one of them escapes sufferings from the policy and power of hell, from the legions of devils combined against them. Satan roars against them. And shall they not have compassion for each other?

Again, that community the saints have in glories should oblige them to love one another. They are all beloved of God—of Father, Son, and Spirit—chosen, redeemed, and called by the same grace. They are washed from their sins in the Lamb's blood, justified in His righteousness, and adorned with His Spirit and grace. They are all made kings and priests unto God. They are all honored to be the servants of God and of the Lord Jesus Christ. They are all jointly engaged in the Lord's work, as valiant solders under the captain of their salvation, in the same war against the powers of darkness, and concerned to promote one common interest, even the glorious cause of their royal Master. And since the saints have such a community in glories, oh, what unity of affection should there be among them!

❧ ANNE DUTTON

The Mourner's Comforter

The Lord GOD will wipe away tears from off all faces.

—ISAIAH 25:8

How often are we constrained to cry, "Mine eyes do fail with tears," for the sin which still rises up with terrible force in our heart, and how constantly we have to weep over the evil that is present with us! Such tears are mute but eloquent witnesses of our repentance toward God and faith in the Lord Jesus, and no jewels can be so comely and precious in His sight as the tears of a sinner for his sin. The salt drops that steal down our cheeks through physical suffering, wrung from our eyes by mortal pain and weakness, are all seen by our loving Lord; they are put into His bottle. His purpose concerning them shall be manifest when their mission is accomplished, and then the source from whence they sprang shall be forever dried up. God shall wipe all tears from their eyes.

And with what inconceivable tenderness shall the bitter tears caused by bereavement be wiped away when we get home! Here, the deep waters of our sorrow seem to be assuaged for a little while, only to burst forth again with greater power to deluge our hearts with the memory of past anguish. But how completely will all traces of grief vanish there! When we see for ourselves the glory of that land where our beloved ones have passed before us, our wonder will be that we could have sorrowed at all at sparing them from life's woes to enter into the "fullness of joy" at God's right hand.

Yes, the world is full of weeping; even Paul spoke of "serving the Lord with many tears." Every heart knows its own bitterness, and every heart has a bitterness to know. Sin must bring sorrow; tears are the inheritance of earth's children. But in the city where we are bound, "God shall wipe away all tears from their eyes; and there shall be no more death, neither sorrow; nor crying, neither shall there be any more pain: for the former things are passed away."

ॐ SUSANNAH SPURGEON

Telling the Hand of God

Then I told them of the hand of my God which
was good upon me; as also the king's words that he had
spoken unto me. And they said, Let us rise up and build.
So they strengthened their hands for this good work.

—NEHEMIAH 2:18

Those who fear the Lord speak of it often to one another. Yet many hold back from what they call talking about religion under the pretense that they fear it too often leads to talking about self. And yet what about the general conversation that is about other things, not the things that are Jesus Christ's? Are the "other things" free from self and wholly profitable? Is it with grace, seasoned with salt? Yet this is what we are commanded that our speech should always be.

Let us lay aside this unscriptural notion of talking about religion, which may only be controversy and criticism, and see what our Lord would have us talk about. The sum of our conversation should be, as recorded of Anna, "She...spake of him." Here is our keynote, and what wealth of melody and fullness of harmony spring from it! But there is the point. If we do not want to speak of Him, let us beware of plausibly persuading ourselves that it is because we do not want to speak about ourselves. Let us be honest and own that the vessel does not overflow because it is not very full of faith and love. Christ said, "Out of the abundance of the heart the mouth speaketh." Men say, "No such thing! One does not speak when one's heart is full!" Yet let God be true, but every man a liar, and let us see whether our unwillingness to speak of Him does not arise from our having nothing to say.

We must first know and consider how great things He has done for us, and then the voice of Jesus says not only show but tell how great things the Lord has done for you, that thus showing and telling, the communication of your faith may become effectual by the acknowledging of every good thing that is in you in Christ Jesus.

≈ FRANCES RIDLEY HAVERGAL

A Spotless Spouse

There is no spot in thee.

—SONG OF SOLOMON 4:7

Can our loving Lord really mean this—and mean it of you and me, dear reader? He does, indeed, if only we have believed on His name to the saving of our soul and trusted in His precious blood to wash away all our sin. But is it not a love passing knowledge that can cause such a statement to be absolute truth? "There is no spot in thee." Where, then, are all my spots, dear Lord, for they were legion? And sin must have rendered me vile and loathsome in Thy pure sight? The reply comes directly from the Lord's own Word: "When I passed by thee, and looked upon thee, behold, thy time was the time of love; and I spread my skirt over thee, and covered thy nakedness: yea I swore unto thee, and entered into a covenant with thee, saith the Lord God, and thou becamest mine."

All the uncleanness—past, present, and future—all the deformity and blackness is put aside by love, cleansed away by blood, covered by another's righteousness; and so completely is this done, that God Himself can find no remnant or stain of that which would have meant eternal death to an unwashed soul.

Now, my poor heart, will you not accept your Lord's own verdict concerning you, and rejoice in His assurance that you are comely with His comeliness that He has put upon you? That He who thinks you to be "all fair" will make you guard against any defilement and keep aloof from anything that could sully your purity; that He should say, "My love," will help you to listen more eagerly for His sweet voice, waiting upon His lips lest one love word should be lost; and that He should declare, "There is no spot in you," will make you so tenderly circumspect that you will be enabled to "walk worthy of God" and of love so unspeakable and divine.

∾ SUSANNAH SPURGEON

Seven Times in a Day

*And if he trespass against thee seven times in a day
and seven times in a day turn again to thee, saying,
I repent; thou shalt forgive him.*
—LUKE 17:4

How would a habit of bringing the faults of others, as a mirror in which to see my own, cure me of censuring and high-mindedness? Instead of doing this, the reverse is too often the case. The faults of others are dwelt upon—magnified—while my own, through self-love, are excused, palliated, passed lightly over. May I henceforth learn a better lesson! If a brother—that is, any human being—is commanded to extend, beyond all limits, forgiveness to a brother, what may I not infer as to the extension of the divine forgiveness? Why, then, does every fresh failure—repeated more often, alas, than seven times in a day—produce a timid backwardness to go to my Savior and say, in deep humiliation, "I repent"? And why do I not simply believe that He will forgive me in a way no brother could forgive a brother?

Does my heart, in the sight of God, honestly bear testimony that, after every sinful deviation and failure, I do truly repent and am heartily sorry for such misdoings; or, do I experience only a partial regret? Does every fresh application to Christ for pardon render sin more hateful and increase real contrition, self-abhorrence, and indignation? Does it excite a holy jealousy and produce a reverential fear of offending, or does the freeness of pardon and grace incline to carelessness or negligence? If I loved a friend as my own soul, would I, for all the world, grieve or offend her? And if I do offend, is there any sorrow so poignant and in proportion as my friend is ready to forgive me, but I am not able to forgive myself? Have I such feelings as these with respect to my Savior? If I dare answer in the affirmative, then I need not fear to go seven times a day and say "I repent" nor fear the freeness and fullness of pardoning mercy and strengthening, renewing grace. Lord, increase my faith!

☙ SARAH HAWKES

Resigned to Christ's Will

*But the God of all grace, who hath called us unto his
eternal glory by Christ Jesus, after that ye have suffered a while,
make you perfect, stablish, strengthen, settle you.*

—1 PETER 5:10

This is not our rest; through much tribulation all Christ's disciples must follow Him. There is a rest prepared for the people of God. As far as it is tasted in this world (and in this world it is tasted), it consists in a mind resigned to the will of God, in proportion as it can say, "Thy will be done on earth as it is done in heaven." Christ Himself was made perfect through suffering, and all His followers shall be so in their appointed measure.

What is our cup to His? O, my dear friend, we are ransomed, we are redeemed, and we are fitting and preparing for the purchased inheritance, that perfect rest prepared for the people of God when their warfare is finished. Let Him do all His pleasure with us here; let Him subdue our iniquities in His own way; let Him glorify His name by our sufferings. His glory is ever connected with His people's best interest. We shall one day acknowledge that He has done all things well and that not one word of all that He has promised failed.

I have asked but one thing with importunity, and by that I abide. I did not ask for temporal life, but the life which Christ died to purchase and lives to bestow. Let Him answer my petition by means of His own appointing: by health or by sickness, by riches or by poverty, by long life or early death. Only let all mine by the ties of nature be His by regeneration of His Spirit.

ॐ ISABELLA GRAHAM

A Friend Till Death

He hath said, I will never leave thee, nor forsake thee.
—HEBREWS 13:5

Do not grieve that you are left alone, as it were, and have few friends that you can open your heart to, for your dear Lord Jesus will never leave nor forsake you, and He is a friend that sticks closer than a brother. You have had the sweet experience of Christ's friendship ever since you were first acquainted with Him, and His love toward you, His care for you, and His power to save you are still as great as ever. Time has not altered Christ's heart, no, nor all the weaknesses and provocations He has seen in you; but having loved you freely and fully, He will love you eternally. Your Jesus, your best friend who has cared for you all along, will never cast you off. He has graven you upon the palms of His hands, and your walls are continually before Him. Creatures may forget, but your Jesus, in His boundless compassions, will not—cannot—forget you. He will know your soul in adversity, when refuge fails you, and no man cares for your soul.

The Lord well knew that His people would yet at times be subject to fears, from their own weakness and unworthiness and from the occurrence of new difficulties, that He should leave them; and that they would be concerned about how they should get the rest of their way through the wilderness. And therefore He says, "Hearken unto me, O house of Jacob, and all the remnant of the house of Israel, which are borne by me from the belly, which are carried from the womb: and even to your old age I am he; and even to hoar hairs will I carry you: I have made, and I will bear; even I will carry, and deliver you" (Isa. 46:3–4). The Lord is so far from waxing weary of doing for His people because He has already done so much for them, that He takes an argument from what He has already done to do still more for them. Oh, my dear sister, there is grace through all your remaining trials, even down to death and up to glory. Therefore, trust in the Lord forever, for in the Lord Jehovah is everlasting strength; and be free with Him, your ever-living and ever-loving friend.

☙ ANNE DUTTON

The Power of Faith

Who are kept by the power of God through faith unto
salvation ready to be revealed in the last time.

—1 PETER 1:5

I feel sure that the living church is, in the present day, much held in bondage by seeking to live more by feeling than by faith. The life of faith is not an unfeeling life, a cold life, a half-hearted life, a life of worldly conformity. It is faith that follows Christ fully and forsakes all for Him, as Joshua and Caleb did when all the people talked of stoning them. They well knew their own weakness and the strength of the enemy but rested all their trust in the love and faithfulness of the Lord, while those who walked by sight and sense looked only at the giant foes and at their own weakness. Thus it is with us spiritually. When poring only upon what we are, we grow more and more discouraged, and, seeking water from the creature cistern, our tongue fails for thirst, for there is none there; but it is in the fountain of living waters, even our precious Jesus, in whom all fullness dwells for poor and needy souls. And when we are brought to this extremity, He kindly says, "I the LORD will hear them: I the God of Israel will not forsake them." How feelingly can my heart renew the cry, "Lord, increase my faith," for, alas, I often stagger through unbelief, not upon the subject of personal interest in Christ, but upon many others of less importance.

"The life which I now live in the flesh, I live by the faith of the Son of God." Faith humbly presses on through the tribulation path, looking unto Jesus, and fully understands that excellent saying of Hewitson: "The soul will be staggered even by loose stones in the way if we look manward; if we look Godward faith will not be staggered even by inaccessible mountains stretching and obstructing apparently our outward progress." I wish you every blessing and all needful grace, for He is able to make all grace abound toward you.

❧ RUTH BRYAN

Lack of Will

Ye will not come to me, that ye might have life.
—JOHN 5:40

It is almost certain that some whose eyes glance over these pages will be conscious that they do not very much care to come to Christ, for this is at once the most common and most fatal hindrance. You cannot honestly say that you want to come. You perhaps go so far as to say, with momentary seriousness, "I wish that I wished!" but no further. In your inmost heart you would rather be let alone, not considering that that is the most terribly certain beginning of doom. You are not perfectly comfortable, but you are not so uncomfortable as to feel inclined to make an effort. As long as you can keep from thinking about it, you say you are very happy. Now, believe me, yours is a ten-times-worse and more dangerous state than if you were a condemned murderer, knowing his doom, realizing his sin, and therefore seeking the Savior and coming to Him with all the desire of his mind.

You will say, "I can't help it! I can't make myself care!" Exactly so; and just in this fact lies not your excuse, but your one hope and help. You cannot make yourself care to flee from the wrath to come. You cannot rouse yourself to be willing to come to Christ for salvation. But One can. And you may and can ask for the Holy Spirit to make you willing. You can say, "O God, give me Thy Holy Spirit to make me willing to come, for Jesus Christ's sake." God makes no condition whatever as to giving this. The blessed Spirit is promised most simply and unconditionally to them that ask Him.

Remember that one spirit or the other is now working in you. It is very awful to read of the "spirit that now worketh in the children of disobedience"; and what is more direct disobedience than not coming when Jesus calls? Therefore ask, and ask at once, for the other spirit, the Holy Spirit, who can make you willing in the day of His power.

ê FRANCES RIDLEY HAVERGAL

The Voice of the Creatures

There is a God, all nature speaks,
Through earth, and air, and seas, and skies:
See, from the clouds His glory breaks,
When the first beams of morning rise.

The rising sun, serenely bright,
O'er the wide world's extended frame,
Inscribes, in characters of light,
His mighty Maker's glorious name.

Almighty goodness, power divine,
The fields and verdant meads display;
And bless the hand which made them shine
With various charms profusely gay.

For man and beast, here daily food
In wide diffusive plenty grows;
And there, for drink, the crystal flood
In streams, sweet winding, gently flows.

By cooling streams, and soft'ning showers,
The vegetable race are fed,
And trees, and plants, and herbs, and flowers,
Their Maker's bounty smiling spread.

Ye curious minds, who roam abroad,
And trace creation's wonders o'er,
Confess the footsteps of Thy God,
And bow before Him, and adore.

                                   ❧ ANNE STEELE

Times of Refreshing

Oh that thou wouldest rend the heavens,
that thou wouldest come down.

—ISAIAH 64:1

Will you unite your prayers for the outpouring of the Holy Spirit upon us all? Oh, we are too slack concerning this thing—this great, promised boon. It is true, all true, that there are seasons of especial descent of the Holy Spirit—"times of refreshing from the presence of the Lord." At these times sinners are converted, slumbering saints are awakened, slow travelers are quickened in the Lord's way. Oh, for more wrestling prayer! For this gracious baptism I am now panting and praying and would be pleased to enlist all the Lord's praying people, the wrestling Jacobs of His one church.

Let us give the Lord no rest until He bows the heavens and comes down and makes bare His arm, and the glory of His work shall appear to us, to our children, and to our children's children. Only let us believe, and it shall be according to our faith in the promised descent of the Holy Ghost in these last days. For this pray, long, and weep. Surely He will hearken and arise and bless, and make Jerusalem a joy.

How slow of heart are we to believe all that the prophets and apostles wrote about the Holy Ghost! Everything around us, viewed in relation to eternity, is alarming. The unconverted are passing into the world of woe, the church is slumbering, error is prevailing, worldliness is abounding, and the love of many for the Lord and His truth is waxing cold. Do we so believe that there is a hell and a heaven as to rest not until we behold the power of God descending to give efficacy to His gospel? Alas! We do not half believe what He has promised in His Word. Oh, let us prove the Lord now herewith and see if He will not open the windows of heaven and pour down such a blessing as shall make this weary wilderness bloom and blossom as the rose. He is faithful that has promised, and He will do it.

≈ MARY WINSLOW

Praying to the Holy Spirit

*Howbeit when he, the Spirit of truth, is come, he will guide you
into all truth: for he shall not speak of himself; but whatsoever he
shall hear, that shall he speak: and he will shew you things to come.
He shall glorify me: for he shall receive of mine, and shall shew it
unto you. All things that the Father hath are mine: therefore
said I, that he shall take of mine, and shall shew it unto you.*

—JOHN 16:13–15

How seldom do we hear prayer offered up to the Holy Spirit
Himself! And yet, how much spiritual life in our souls
depends upon Him! I love to plead with the Holy Ghost, the life-
giving Spirit, to recognize His divine personality and official part
in the work of our salvation. He alone can take of the things of Jesus
and show them unto us. He it is who carries on the mighty work
in the kingdom of God, in the soul from first to last. I love, the first
thing in the morning, to commit myself—my thoughts, desires, and
whole heart—to His control, praying that He would suffer nothing
to dishonor or grieve Him; and that if I do, to make me quick in
discerning and as quick in confessing it.

We know how rapid thought is, and Satan is as rapid in trying
to take possession of our thoughts for himself, so that the best way
is to be beforehand with the Spirit and commit our thoughts to His
safe-keeping as soon as we open our eyes. May He help us to be
wiser and more watchful in these things, that Satan and the flesh
may be foiled and so not obtain the advantage of us!

&ban; MARY WINSLOW

The Snare of Discontentment

Not that I speak in respect of want: for I have learned,
in whatsoever state I am, therewith to be content.
—PHILIPPIANS 4:11

There is nothing upon which I look back with more real shame—and, I hope, real sorrow—than upon past seasons of murmuring, discontent, and fretfulness. I say "past seasons" because—though I am still too apt to feel the same evil spirit and am never at any time a thousandth part so thankful as I ought to be—that which I now, through great mercy, feel only occasionally, I in those seasons felt continually, and almost constantly. While robbers are in the house, we are often either in a sound sleep or do not hear them or are too much terrified to recollect what spoils they may make; but afterward, when our recollection returns, then we perceive the plunder. Thus it has been with me.

While I was under the dominion of discontent and unthankfulness, I did not consider the devastation. All this time I was being robbed of my faith, hope, peace, confidence, my innumerable comforts, my pleasant prospects. I was resigning the temple that was being prepared for the Holy Spirit's residence into the hands of evil spirits; for when once a discontented devil gets in, his name is Legion, and if he is not directly cast out by faith, watchfulness, prayer, and continual care to cultivate the opposite spirit, he will soon gain possession and destroy every holy, pleasant plant.

There are many of us who may, I trust, with safety be numbered among believers who would be shocked if we were under the dominion of open sins; yet they are not sufficiently aware that if the sin of discontent is not so scandalous in the eyes of man, it is as hateful in the sight of God, and perhaps more fatal because it is less marked. It "will eat as doth a canker"; it blights and withers all the Christian graces; it robs God of glory; it turns all the privileges and blessings we have into poison. Nothing can be more opposed to that exhortation of the apostle: "Let this mind be in you, which was also in Christ Jesus."

৯ SARAH HAWKES

The Drawing Bridegroom

I am the LORD that healeth thee.

—EXODUS 15:26

Wonder, O heavens, and be astonished, O earth! that this most glorious Immanuel, the Prince of Peace, whom angels worship and before whom the seraphim bow, should from all eternity engage to come and seek His bride from this poor world and claim her for His own. Yet so it is. But she is filthy and polluted! Then His own precious veins shall pour forth the rich crimson flood to cleanse her, and His Spirit shall open the fountain to her for her sin and uncleanness. But she is naked and bare. Then He will cast His skirt over her and will weave for her in the loom of the law fine linen—clean and white—a robe in which she shall be fit to appear at His court. Moreover, the Spirit shall bring near His righteousness, clothing her with "the garments of salvation" and covering her with the "robe of righteousness," as a bridegroom decks himself with ornaments and as a bride adorns herself with her jewels. But she is diseased; she is a leper, yet He will bring her health and cure, for He says, "I am the Lord that healeth thee." He is made to be sin for her, that she might be made "the righteousness of God in him."

But she has no personal charms—she is ugly. Then He will put His comeliness upon her, and through it her beauty shall be perfect. But she is poor, so He bestows Himself and His fullness upon her, and thus endows her with a good dowry. But she is unwilling and has no heart for the match, for she obeys a hostile prince; her delights, too, are in the world and the flesh. A new heart will He give her, and a right spirit will He put within her; the Spirit shall make her willing in the day of His power "and take away the names of Baalim out of her mouth," so that, prostrate at His feet, she will say, "Other lords beside Thee have had dominion over me, but by Thee only will I make mention of Thy name."

☙ RUTH BRYAN

God Understands

Thou knowest my downsitting and mine uprising,
thou understandest my thought afar off.
—PSALM 139:2

W ho does not know what it is to be misunderstood? Perhaps
no one ever is always and perfectly understood because so
few Christians are like their Master in having the spirit of quick
understanding. This does not make it the less trying to you. But this
precious Word, which meets every need, gives you a stepping-stone
that is quite enough to enable you to reach that brave position, if
you will only stand on it.

Even if others daily mistake your words, He understands your
thought, and is not this infinitely better? He Himself, your ever-
loving, ever-present Father, understands. He understands perfectly
just what and just when others do not. Not your actions merely, but
your thought—the central self that no words can reveal to others.
All my desire is before Thee. He understands how you desired to
do the right thing when others thought you did the wrong thing.
He understands how His poor, weak child wants to please Him and
secretly mourns over grieving Him. "Thou understandest" seems
to go even a step further than the great comfort of "Thou knowest."
His understanding is infinite. Perhaps you cannot even understand
yourself. He may show you that those who have, as you suppose,
misunderstood you, may have guessed right after all. He may show
you that your desire was not so honest, your motives not so single
as you fancied; that there was self-will where you recognized only
resolution, sin where you recognized only infirmity or mistake.

Let Him search; let Him declare it unto you. For then He will
declare another message to you: "The blood of Jesus Christ his Son
cleanseth us from all sin." Almighty God, unto whom all hearts
are open, all desires known, and from whom no secrets are hid:
Cleanse the thoughts of our hearts by the inspiration of Thy Holy
Spirit, that we may perfectly love Thee and worthily magnify Thy
holy name, through Christ our Lord.

☙ FRANCES RIDLEY HAVERGAL

The Cry of Faith

And the apostles said unto the Lord, increase our faith.

—LUKE 17:5

If the believer makes any attainment in the knowledge of God and of herself, or any advance in the divine life, she must have much to do with the varied and changing providences of God. In this way the Spirit chiefly and mainly works in her and grounds and settles her in the truth. There is not a single truth in God's Word that will be of any avail to us, but as it is wrought out in the experiences of the soul by the power of the Holy Ghost through the varying dispensations of divine providence. We are such obtuse scholars, and I often wonder, and wonder again, at the patience of a good, gracious, and unchanging God toward us. He varies His dealings that He might teach us our nothingness, weakness, and total helplessness.

Faith, too, is constantly brought into exercise and is increased in strength by an increasing knowledge of our God's veracity, power, and love. We often pray, "Lord, increase our faith." In answering this prayer, the Lord places us in such circumstances as call it forth. The little we have (and we often find we have much less than we thought we had) is set to work with God, with whom alone faith has to do. Providences, adverse and painful, stir up to cry mightily unto God. Then come in the promises. These become unspeakably precious. Faith takes them, as so many promissory notes, to the great Promisor for acceptance. Faith knocks and waits, knocks and waits again; thus it is exercised and increased. Presently the hand, the helping hand, is held out, and deliverance comes, and God, the mighty Deliverer, is seen. Then we say, "The Lord is my helper; I will not fear what man can do unto me." All our journey through, from first to last, the great work of preparation for the usefulness in His service here, and for the rich enjoyment of His presence in glory, is thus carrying on in the soul of the believer.

ॐ MARY WINSLOW

Christ's Precious Blood

Unto you therefore which believe he is precious.

—1 PETER 2:7

Salvation is not of merit but of mercy, so none need despair because of crimson sins; the rich blood of my precious Savior makes them white as snow. This I can well witness, for none could be worse. What a glorious company will there be on the Mount Zion above of blood-washed sinners—once so black, then so white; once so far off, then so near; once so full of fear and trembling, then so safe forever and ever. How shall we praise the worthy Lamb who brought us there at the cost of His own heart's blood! Oh, that poor, doubting souls had more conception of the virtue and efficacy of that blood that has cleansed and will cleanse millions and millions of black sinners and made them fit company for God and the Lamb. How it would encourage them to come to that fountain opened for sin and for uncleanness, which is free to every longing soul who is crying, "Wash me, Savior, or I die!" Would that I had more conceptions of the freeness and fullness of the finished salvation and that this contracted heart were enlarged to apprehend more the love of the Savior to poor, needy sinners.

What an amazing object our Father has given us to behold by faith, even His crucified Son, who was the brightness of His glory and the express image of His person. Yet for poor sinners was His visage marred more than any man's. His meat and drink was to do the will and work of His Father; yet "it pleased the Lord to bruise Him," and thus marred, bruised, and crucified, He says to bruised reeds, "Look unto me, and be ye saved"—unto Me, bleeding, agonizing, made a curse for your sin. Look unto Me on the cross to be healed of your diseases and forgiven your iniquity; none ever looked in vain. Oh, to live believing by the power of the blessed Spirit, who takes of the things of Christ and shows them to the soul, drawing it out toward this adorable Man, who is more precious than the gold of Ophir!

→ RUTH BRYAN

The Everlasting Arms

Underneath are the everlasting arms.
—DEUTERONOMY 33:27

It is a sweet thing to suffer with Christ—to have such a sweet companion in tribulation! Surely a believing thought of it must sweeten our bitterest portions. If Christ, the Tree of Life, is cast into the bitter waters of affliction, will He not sweeten them so well that our hearts will freely drink them? To suffer with Christ should make our hearts leap for joy! For if He is with us, we will not sink in sorrow; everlasting arms underneath us will raise us from deepest depressions. The Lord is risen; saints must rise. Sorrows will not hold us a moment beyond the appointed time, nor exceed their appointed degree. Soon our momentary light cross will be turned into a weighty eternal crown. If we suffer with Christ, we will reign with Him; we will be glorified together. O this sweet word—together! It puts a glory upon glory itself—a sweetness into those rivers of pleasure which are at God's right hand. The once-suffering Head and the once-suffering members glorified together! Oh, how will they enhance each other's joy in glory!

The sorrows both of Christ and Christians will then be turned into perfect joy, and their eternal joy and glory will be so much the greater for all the time-sorrows they endured and the deaths they survived, to reign in life together unto ages without end. Sorrows will not hurt us if we are enabled to live unto God under them. Nothing but sin will be bitter upon reflection, and the sorrows that we meet with, even from sin itself through God's forgiving and subduing grace, will be turned into the joy of victory, to His eternal praise. But oh, this killing thing—sin! It dishonors God our Father, wounds our Lord-Redeemer, and grieves our Lord our Comforter; it puts death into our comforts and a sting in our crosses. Let us beware of yielding to sin, and then we need not, with a slavish fear, dread sufferings; let us be humbled before God for all our unbelief and impatience under afflictions and press forward most earnestly with a greater measure of faith and love.

ANNE DUTTON

Frequent Self-Examination

Examine yourselves, whether ye be in the faith.
—2 CORINTHIANS 13:5

When we reflect that our happiness depends upon our possessing real religion, both for time and eternity; that the least mistake may be productive of evils, the nature and extent of which exceed our powers of conception; and that this religion must be diligently sought for before it can be obtained; we must surely, unless our hearts are totally blinded by sin and harder than a nether millstone, be excited to exclaim, with sincerity and earnestness, "What must I do to be saved?" It is a small thing to profess Christianity, to acquire a theoretical knowledge of its doctrines, to speak of its nature and excellence, and, in a pharisaical manner, to mold our external to its precepts. To do all this is but a small thing, but when done, if unaccompanied with that grace of God which is like a refiner's fire or the fuller's soap, it is but washing the outside of the cup and platter, while inwardly we are full of corruption.

The work of sanctification is a great work, which nothing but the mighty power of God can accomplish; for who but He can bring a clean thing out of an unclean and release the creature, sold under sin, from his bondage to Satan, when he is himself opposed to his deliverance, and bring him into the glorious liberty of the sons of God? But great as the work is, and diverse as it is from anything that man or devils can effect, it is nevertheless one that Satan and the corruptions of our own hearts use all their efforts to counterfeit. The adversary, we are told, can "transform himself into an angel of light," and "the heart is deceitful above all things and desperately wicked." On these two affecting and alarming truths is reared that strong delusion by which so many are led blindfold to eternal despair. How necessary, then, is it that we should, frequently and carefully, examine ourselves, whether we be in the faith.

❧ SUSAN HUNTINGTON

Assurance, a Sanctifying Attainment

Having therefore these promises, dearly beloved,
let us cleanse ourselves from all filthiness of the flesh
and spirit, perfecting holiness in the fear of God.

—2 CORINTHIANS 7:1

It is the opinion of some Christians that few attain to the real knowledge of their acceptance in Christ. But I must differ from them. The Word of God is full and powerful on this point. If we believe in Christ at all, we must believe in all that He says. We are not to believe one part and disbelieve another. "He that believeth on the Son of God hath the witness in himself." This witness is the Holy Spirit bearing witness with our spirit that we are the children of God. Yes, this assurance of our acceptance is attainable, and every believer who walks in an uncertainty in this respect must necessarily walk much below his privileges. Faith is the great grace of the Holy Spirit and the parent of all other graces. Without faith it is impossible to please God. Faith honors God, and He honors it, however small may be its degree.

If there is anything that will make a poor sinner lay low in self-abasement, abhorring her sin and repenting in dust and ashes, it is a sense of sin pardoned and blotted out forever from the book of God's remembrance. It never will, it never does, exalt a poor sinner. Will she not strive to be holy, aim to please Him who died and lives again for her? It is our high privilege, one no believer should fall short of, to know her oneness with the Lord.

I think that the confession of sin is a most holy, sanctifying exercise of the soul; it subdues pride, promotes humility, and by the sprinkling of the blood applied afresh by the Holy Ghost, purifies the conscience and sanctifies the heart. I believe that there are none who walk with God so closely and who aim so much to please Him as those who have the witness within that their sins are washed away in the blood of Jesus.

&~ MARY WINSLOW

The Loveliness of God's Will

Thy will be done in earth, as it is in heaven.
—MATTHEW 6:10

Resting in the will of God is one of the most comforting and blessed experiences of the Christian life. To say, "Thy will be done"—not in a reluctant or compulsory way, as if we were shrinking from some inevitable pain, but with a sincere and glad conviction that our dear Father is really doing for us what is best and most loving, although it may not look so to our dull eyes—is glorifying to Him and supremely consoling to us.

God's plans and purposes for me and you, dear reader, were all made and determined from the beginning, and, as they are worked out day-by-day in our lives, how wise we would be if, with joyful certainty, we accepted each unfolding of His will as a proof of His faithfulness and love! When once I, as a believer, can say from my heart, "This is the will of God concerning me," it matters not what the "this" is—whether it be a small domestic worry or the severance of the dearest earthly ties. The fact that it is His most blessed will takes all the fierce sting out of the trouble and leaves it powerless to hurt or hinder the peace of my soul. There is all the difference between the murderous blows of an enemy and the needful chastisement of a loving father's hand. The Lord may make us sore, but He will bind us up. He may wound, but His hands make whole. How often must the Lord break a heart before He can enter into it and fill it with His love! But how precious and fragrant is the balm which, thenceforward, flows out of that heart to others.

Doing the will of God from the heart must be at least the reflection, the copy, of the perfect obedience of the saints in light. Oh, to be thus beginning the service of heaven while yet on earth! Practicing here to be made perfect there! Learning the laws, manners, and customs of the land where our eternal inheritance awaits us!

ॐ SUSANNAH SPURGEON

The Candor of Christ (1)

*Come, see a man, which told me all things
that ever I did: is not this the Christ?*

—JOHN 4:29

It is not merely a vague, general belief in Christ as the teacher who will tell us all things that suffice for heart conviction of the reality of Jesus Christ, but the individual knowledge of Him as the searcher who told me all things that ever I did. This was what led the woman of Samaria to exclaim, "Is not this the Christ?" This was to her the irresistible proof of His Messiahship.

What about us? If we know anything of true interaction with the Lord Jesus, our experience will not be unlike hers. When He who searches Jerusalem with candles turns the keen flame of His eyes upon the dark corners of our hearts and flashes their far-reaching, all-revealing beam upon even the far-off and long-forgotten windings of our lives; when in His light we see the darkness and in His purity we see the sin that has been, or that is; when He declares unto man what is His thought, and then convinces that as he thinks in his heart, so is he, then we know for ourselves that He with whom we have to do is indeed the Christ.

He does not merely show us; it is something more than that. It is not merely an invisible hand drawing away a veil from hidden scenes and a light brought to bear upon them, so that we can see them if we will; it is more personal, more terrible, and yet more tender than that. He tells us what we have done, and, if we listen, the telling will be very clear, very thorough, very unmistakable.

☙ FRANCES RIDLEY HAVERGAL

The Candor of Christ (2)

Come, see a man, which told me all things
that ever I did: is not this the Christ?

—JOHN 4:29

At first we are tempted not to listen at all; we shrink from the still, small voice that tells us such startlingly unwelcome things. Many feel what one expressed: "Whenever I do think about it, I feel so horribly bad that I don't like to think anymore." Ah, if you had known, at least in this your day, that it was not mere thinking about it, but the voice of the Savior beginning to tell you what would have cleared the way for the things that belong to your peace, what blessing might not the patient and willing listening have brought! Oh, do not stifle the voice! Do not fancy it is only uncomfortable thoughts that you do not want to encourage because they might make you low-spirited! Instead of that, ask Him to let His voice sound louder and clearer and believe that the goodness of God leads you to repentance. Only listen, and He will tell you not only all things that ever you did, but all things that He has done for you. He never leaves off in the middle of all He has to tell, unless we willfully interrupt Him.

Perhaps we have gone through all this and know the humbling blessedness of being searched and told, and then pardoned and cleansed—and now again there is something not right. We hardly know what, only there is a misgiving, a dim, vague uneasiness. We really don't know of anything in particular, and yet there is something unsatisfied and unsatisfactory. There is nothing for it but to come to our Messiah afresh and ask Him to tell us what we have done, or are doing, that is not in accordance with His will.

Oh, never shrink from the probing of our beloved Physician. Dearer and dearer will the hand become as we yield to it. Sweeter and sweeter will be the proofs that He is our own faithful Friend, who only wounds that He may perfectly heal.

≈ FRANCES RIDLEY HAVERGAL

Forgiving Fellow Believers' Sin

How oft shall my brother sin against me, and I forgive him?
till seven times? Jesus saith unto him, I say not unto thee,
Until seven times: but, Until seventy times seven.

—MATTHEW 18:21–22

To be of a bitter, unforgiving spirit toward our brethren who are under the misery of their falls into sin, when the Lord gives them repentance, reflects the highest dishonor upon our merciful Father, our forgiving God, and is a piece of cruelty to His dear children. There is no circumstance the saints can be in while they are in the world wherein they need so much pity and tenderness to be shown them as when they are wounded by sin. If, therefore, we would love them at all, let us be sure to do it when they most want it.

The time of their misery ought, in an especial manner, to be the time of our mercy and compassion toward them. Then it is most needed and will be most welcome. When the dear saints are fallen into sin, all things within and without seem to be up in arms against them; their soul is, as it were, among lions, roaring upon them on every side to devour them. The guilt of sin wounds their souls exceedingly, even after forgiveness has been spoken to them, and Satan makes a hideous noise about it and pierces them with his fiery darts. And—it is sad to say—the dear saints are then so narrow-spirited that they often stand aloof from the sore of their wounded brethren. And, poor hearts, they are apt to be afraid that the Lord will in anger cast them off. Now, at such a time as this, to have a friend to love them, a sister to know their soul in adversity, to speak a word of comfort to them, to pour oil and wine into their wounds and bind up their sorrows—oh, what an ease, what a refreshment this affords them!

If, therefore, there be any love to Christ and fellowship of the Spirit, any bowels and mercies in our souls toward our poor brethren, let us with compassionate tenderness forgive and comfort them under all their sins and sufferings on this account!

≈ ANNE DUTTON

The Gospel

For I am not ashamed of the gospel of Christ: for it is the power
of God unto salvation to every one that believeth.

—ROMANS 1:16

What then, I ask, is this glorious gospel, this gospel of which Paul speaks so highly and of which he was "not ashamed." The gospel means "glad tidings," or "good news." These are the "good tidings of great joy" for all people, proclaimed by the angel at the birth of our Savior. These glad tidings excited the praise of the angelic host on that great occasion. "Every one that believeth" is a justified, or forgiven person. The gospel, then, proclaims a full and free salvation to all who will accept it in penitence and faith.

When the offer of God's mercy, through Christ, is simply and earnestly explained from the pulpit, the gospel is preached. But now comes another point. We must not stop here; we must remember that the gospel has its precepts, its rule of life, as well as its plain offers of mercy and pardon. Let no one think that because he has no goodness to bring God to obtain mercy that he is not to become holy—far from it. "Without holiness no man shall see the Lord."

The very purpose for which God offers pardon so freely to fallen man is to make him holy. Oh, that we put these questions to ourselves more often! Do I believe the glad news of the blessed God (or the gospel)? Do I rule my life by the precepts of the gospel? Do I know something of the excellence of that glorious gospel? Have I ever tried to promote its cause in the world? Or do I forget the solemn commands of my Savior, before His ascension? "Go ye into all the world and preach the gospel to every creature." How great is the goodness of our God and Savior in offering us, in the gospel, such marvelous mercies! May the eyes of our understanding be opened to know the great things so freely given to us of God!

ELIZABETH JULIA HASELL

Evil Speaking

Speak not evil one of another, brethren.

—JAMES 4:11

This is one of the most difficult of God's commandments, and yet one which is in peculiar degree for our good and personal happiness, as well as for those around us! The more difficult, the more need of grace; and the more need, the more fully the supply. Well might Paul say, "Put them in mind to speak evil of no man," for do we not easily fail to keep this in mind? The command is exceeding broad; let us not seek to narrow it, but humbly bow to our Master's distinct orders in all their exactness.

Do we really wish to know them fully, that we may obey fully? Then what are they? "Speak evil of no man." Shall we venture practically to say, "Yes, Lord, except of so-and-so?" "Laying aside all evil speakings." Does not this include the very least? "Let all bitterness...and evil speaking, be put away from you." Then does He give us leave to cherish even one little hidden root of that bitterness from which the evil speaking springs? "Put away" implies resolute action in the matter. Have we even tried to put away all?

But this great clause of the "royal law" is broader still: "Let none of you imagine evil in your hearts against his neighbor." And the characteristic of that charity, without which we are only sounding brass and nothing, is that it thinks no evil. Is not this the root from which the far-poisoning fruit springs? We have first disobeyed another order: "Whatsoever things are of good report...think on these things." Instead of that we think about the bad reports that we may have heard. We develop the unkind hint into suspicion—and perhaps in accusation—by thinking about it, instead of thinking on and thinking out the probable other side of the case. Oh, may He give us grace to keep our heart with all diligence, and Himself set a watch this day before our mouth and keep the door of our lips! May we cease to reason with unprofitable talk or with speeches wherewith we can do no good.

❧ FRANCES RIDLEY HAVERGAL

The Parent of All Graces

*If ye have faith as a grain of mustard seed, ye shall say
unto this mountain, Remove hence to yonder place; and it
shall remove; and nothing shall be impossible unto you.*

—MATTHEW 17:20

Dear friend, make much of your trials: they are treasures and blessings in disguise, and they quicken to prayer. Pray in the trial, pray over the trial, and pray after the trial, that you may not lose the good it is designed and calculated to import. It is through much tribulation we are to enter the kingdom; and it is our wisdom and our blessing diligently to watch His providence in all that befalls us in the smaller events of life as in the greater, and when we are tried, to go and ask the Lord to reveal to us the why and the wherefore. If He does not answer us at once, He will in due time make it plain to us, and it shall bring forth good to us and glory to Him.

We are passing through a world lying in the wicked one, and we have a body of sin and death to contend with within us. Faith, precious faith, and the parent of every other grace of the Spirit is given to enable us to overcome this host of enemies we have to combat with all our journey through; and God, even our own God, just places us in such positions as to draw it forth and bring it into exercise. He will honor it, however feeble it may be. Faith honors Jesus at such times, and He honors faith. And how precious is Jesus at such seasons! How blessedly He makes Himself known to us! He whispers sweet peace and rich consolation to our sorrowing hearts—lays us in His tender bosom, calms every rebellious thought, and quells every rising fear with His own gracious words: "It is I—I will never leave thee nor forsake thee." And then we are enabled to take a fresh view of our inheritance above and realize our title to its inalienable and eternal possession. Let us think more of it than we do. Let us view the world as passing away, and we ourselves as passing away with it.

❧ MARY WINSLOW

Soul Comfort

In the multitude of my thoughts within me
thy comforts delight my soul.

—PSALM 94:19

The first of Thy comforts, gracious God, is this—that Thou hast said unto my soul, "I am thy salvation." He saves us, not because of any merit in us or any of our own deserving, but because sovereign grace chose us and divine compassion redeemed us, and when we were far off, infinite pity brought us back and made us nigh by the precious blood of Christ. A saved and pardoned sinner can truly say, "Thy comforts delight my soul."

The next thought is that, having saved us, He keeps us. "We are kept by the power of God through faith unto salvation." Comparatively few Christians put God's keeping power fully to the test. If we would trust Him for the keeping, as we do for the saving, our lives would be far holier and happier than they are. "I will keep it every moment" is one of those grandly unlimited promises that most of us are afraid of, and we store them away in the background because we dare not believe them and bring them out into the light of our daily practice. O foolish and unbelieving hearts, how much soul-delighting comfort do we thus miss.

Dear friends, if you are His, you know the exceeding comfort of casting all your care upon Him and being quite sure that He will undertake for you. Have we not often come to Him oppressed and burdened, with an intolerable weight of anxiety and distress, and been enabled to roll the whole mass of it on Him, leaving it all at His feet, and returning to our work with a lightened and restful heart? Some of us have had burdens and sorrows that would have crushed the very life out of us if we had not been enabled to look up and say, "Thou, Lord, hast helped and comforted me." Yes, truly, God's care for us is one of the sweetest comforts of our mortal life.

❧ SUSANNAH SPURGEON

A Cup of Cold Water

*Inasmuch as ye have done it unto one of the least of these
my brethren, ye have done it unto me.*
—MATTHEW 25:40

I observe that it is not only with our purses we can serve our Lord.
You know all we have is His. By Him, are we graciously placed in
positions of influence? Let us use the influence so granted to us in
His service for the benefit of our poorer brethren, equally members
of His body with ourselves. The charity of one poor person toward
another is often shown most beautifully by the sacrifice of time,
sleep, and comfort, made in time of sickness for poor, sick neigh-
bors. If these sacrifices are made for Christ's sake, such charitable
poor persons will hear, at the last day, the Savior say to them, "I was
sick and ye visited me."

May we all bear in mind that the great thing is to make our
offerings of money, abilities, influence, time, and so forth, directly
to our Lord. By His grace may we seek to please Him. Our Savior
no longer sits at noon under an eastern sky, wearied with a journey,
to ask a draught of water; but even a "cup of water," given in His
name, shall be observed by Him and considered as done unto Him.
No ministering women now can attend the Lord of life on earth
and give Him of their substance; but those who attend His poor, His
sick, the destitute and the prisoners, from love to Him, shall hear at
last that it is in His sight as if done unto Himself. Truly noble, then,
may be the employments of all who work for Christ! How sure their
reward in heaven.

God grant that many who read this may so learn and do their
duty to Christ our Head, that, at the day of judgment, they may joyfully hear the words addressed to them: "Come, ye blessed of my
Father, inherit the kingdom prepared for you from the foundation
of the world."

&ed; ELIZABETH JULIA HASELL

The Making of a New Creature

But ye are not in the flesh, but in the Spirit,
if so be that the Spirit of God dwell in you. Now if any
man have not the Spirit of Christ, he is none of his.

—ROMANS 8:9

No man can make himself a new creature; he must be wholly beholden to the Holy Spirit for that work, in which the creature is wholly passive. It is the duty of every natural man to reform his life and abstain from every known sin, as by every sin he commits he brings more dishonor to God and treasures up for himself more wrath against the day of vengeance. But nothing that any natural man can do will make him a new creature. As he could not give himself a being in nature, neither can he give himself a being in grace. This is God's sole prerogative, to work by His Holy Spirit on whom He pleases; for those that are new creatures are said to be "God's workmanship, created in Christ Jesus unto good works," and be by Him "begotten again unto a lively hope by the resurrection of Christ from the dead."

And who can create a new and spiritual nature in the heart but God? What man can beget himself unto a lively hope? And yet, if he is not blessed with this work of God, he will not, cannot, be a partaker of the inheritance of the saints in light, having no fitness in himself for that glorious enjoyment. And as all enjoyment springs from the agreeableness of the object to the subject, and a natural man is an unholy man, what enjoyment can he have of an infinitely holy God? How can he that loves sin delight in a perfect conformity to God's holy image and an entire and eternal dedication to His sole praise, which are the felicities of saints in bliss while they behold Jehovah's face? And if these holy tempers are not wrought in our hearts here, in a begun-measure that shall be completed hereafter, our souls will be miserable forever, for no unclean person or thing shall enter into the New Jerusalem.

    ❧ ANNE DUTTON

Hope in Dark Times

I will build my church; and the gates of hell
shall not prevail against it.
—MATTHEW 16:18

How unhappy it is, my dear friend, that the little family of Christ should be so torn with internal animosities and feuds at a time when the state of the world seems to render it peculiarly necessary that all its members should be bound together in the unity of the Spirit and the bonds of peace. At no period in the history of the church can we discover so many and such powerful efforts of the prince of this world and his adherents to destroy its purity and its very existence as at the present time. What were the clamors of the ancient Jews, what were the distressing persecutions of the idolatrous Gentiles, and what were the contemptuous reproaches of the infidel philosophers of former days capable of effecting toward the overthrow of Christianity compared with that spirit of antichrist that has now gone forth into the world—a spirit that, while it professes to admire, directs all its energies to the destruction of the religion of Christ? The former gave the blow openly; the latter gives the deadly stab in secret. The former depressed but did not corrupt the truth; the latter infuses its poison into the very principles of our faith and leaves us nothing of Christianity but the form and the name. Surely these are "the last times" spoken of in the sure word of prophecy, when many shall be given up to strong delusions and left to believe a lie, and when faith shall hardly be found on the earth.

But thanks be to God—He is showing us, by the effusions of His Spirit on various places, that He still remembers His church and will not suffer the gates of hell to prevail against it. And blessed be His name for the assurance that none shall be able to pluck His children out of the Savior's hands or prevent His giving unto them eternal life! My friend, let us pray for each other. And may He, who is the believer's hope, finally present us faultless before the presence of His glory with exceeding joy!

❧ SUSAN HUNTINGTON

Faithful and Solemn Admonitions

I stand in doubt of you.
—GALATIANS 4:20

How solemn, if after all your profession you have yet to take the very first step in the divine life! Examine yourself by the revealed Word of God, and see how matters stand between Him and your own soul. This is a mighty concern, and one not to be trifled with. It is not a mere profession that will stand at a dying hour; you must have something essentially more. God has to do with the heart. "I, the Lord, search the heart."

If you have never yet felt yourself a lost sinner, then you have not sought Christ with your whole heart. "Ye shall find me when ye seek me with your whole heart." Trifle not with yourself; trifle not with an endless eternity, for God will not be trifled with. The world is still in your heart, and after your idol you will go. What will it profit you if you gain the whole world and at last lose your own soul? A little space is yet allowed you. Let me entreat you to make the best use of it to gain an interest in Christ. Why will you die?

Look fully at Christ; see what He suffered for sinners. Look at the wonderful goodness of God in giving His well-beloved Son, that sinners might be saved from the wrath to come. O flee to Christ just as you are. Lose not a moment in settling this great concern. Keep your eye upon the finished work of Jesus, and aim to get a close acquaintance with Him. The more you know of the desperate wickedness of your own heart, the more you will love Christ and see how suitable He is in every way to meet your lost condition. The more you hate yourself, the more you will love Jesus. Keep far from trifling religious professors, and be much in secret prayer.

꙳ MARY WINSLOW

Drooping Eyelids

Mine eyes fail with looking upward: O LORD,
I am oppressed; undertake for me.

—ISAIAH 38:14

Hezekiah had been sore sick when he wrote the psalm, or ode, from which these words are taken. A long and painful illness had brought him to "the gates of the grave," and he here expresses, in pathetic language, some of the groans, sighs, and cries that were wrung from his heart during the time when he feared that he might be deprived of the residue of his years.

Upon first reading these words, my heart felt envious of the poor, sick king's experience. What! To look up to God so constantly and continually that my eyes should be wearied with an upward glance? This surely would be a pleasant pain, a sweet sorrow, a most rare and blessed spiritual attainment. With me it is, alas, so different—my eyes mostly fail with looking inward!

But I look again carefully at the text and find that it should read thus: "Mine eyes fail upward." The two words "with looking" are interpolated; they are not in the original Hebrew. The meaning is, literally, "Mine eye-lids droop; mine eyes are too weak to look upward." Ah! Now I can understand, and Hezekiah's words touch my very soul. It is as if he had said (what I have so often had to say), "I am utter weakness, Lord; a weight of sin, sorrow, and sickness oppresses me. I am brought so low that I cannot even lift up mine eyes to Thee. But come Thou, sit by my bed, close to me, Lord, so that I need not look up, but can shut my weary eyes for very bliss that Thou art looking down in tenderest pity on me and saying, 'Fear not, for I am with thee.'" Oh, the blessed restfulness of putting everything—physical, mental, and spiritual—into my Father's hands and just leaving all there. When once faith can heartily make this transfer, all is well with the soul, and its peace is perfect.

☙ SUSANNAH SPURGEON

Mental Food

Eat ye that which is good.
—ISAIAH 55:2

Good, wholesome, delicious food set plentifully before us, and yet we have to be told to eat that which is good and to let rubbish and poison alone! Is it not humiliating? We know too much about feeding on that which is not good, and what profit had we in those things whereof we are now ashamed? The Lord has had to testify of us, "He feedeth on ashes," "feedeth on wind," "feedeth on foolishness." Most gracious was His decree that "they shall eat, and not have enough"; "thou shalt eat, but not be satisfied." He would not let us be satisfied. And now, if we have tasted that the Lord is gracious, we cannot be satisfied with the old ashes and wind. But what about our daily practical obedience to this command? How much are we going to eat today of that which is good, in proportion to that which does not satisfy? Will it be a question of minutes for the Word by which we live, and hours for books that are, at best, negative as to spiritual nutriment? What about our appetite for the strong meat, the deep things of God? If other books contain necessary food mentally, and we are called to use them, so that by study of His works—His providences natural, mental, moral—we may be more meet for the Master's use, do we practically and consciously esteem the words of His mouth more?

The devil is very fond of persuading us that we have no leisure so much as to eat when it is a question of Bible study. He never says that if we have a novel or a clever magazine on hand! He wants us not to let our souls delight themselves in fatness. Jesus, our Wisdom, says, "Come, eat of My bread; eat, friends." One is utterly ashamed that it should ever be an effort to obey this loving invitation. How weak we are! But His hand touches us, and He says, "Arise and eat." May He open our eyes to see and rejoice in the provision so close beside us, the feast that He has made for us.

❧ FRANCES RIDLEY HAVERGAL

Forbearance

Seeing ye have purified your souls in obeying the
truth through the Spirit unto unfeigned love of the brethren,
see that ye love one another with a pure heart fervently.

—1 PETER 1:22

This channel in which our love to the saints should run is for-bearance toward them in their present imperfect state. We don't all yet see eye to eye. There are different measures of faith and light distributed to the saints by the sovereign Lord of all, both with respect to the doctrine of the gospel and the discipline of the church. And through the corruption of our nature, there is an apt-ness to slight and despise—yes, to speak evil of our brethren that are not just of our length and breadth. This is contrary to love.

If we love our brethren as we ought, we shall love them for Christ's sake, because they belong to Christ, and not merely, first or principally, because they are of the same way of thinking with us. The way to heaven is indeed narrow, yet there is some latitude in it. The saints, as strangers and pilgrims on earth, are all traveling home to their Father's house in heaven in Christ, the narrow way. Yet some walk in Christ in one path of duty, and some in another, according to the proportion of faith given them. And though we don't all walk in the same path, yet shall we all meet at last. Christ the way will bring us all to the Father. And shall we not then love as brethren?

If we can't walk together in all things, as to externals, let us walk in love, even all that are Christ's, in the very inward affection of our souls to each other. So far as we can discern any to hold to the Head, Christ, of which we ourselves are members, let us be one in love with them.

❧ ANNE DUTTON

Faith Cometh by Hearing

Faith cometh by hearing, and hearing by the word of God.

—ROMANS 10:17

You want to know more of your sonship? "We are the children of God by faith in Christ Jesus." Faith is the manifestation of sonship, and by it we come to the enjoyment of family privileges. Living faith is the gift of God, and "faith cometh by hearing, and hearing by the Word of God." While Rebekah was listening to Abraham's servant, I believe there was a moving of her heart toward his master's son, for when she was asked if she would so quickly leave all for him, she said, "I will go." So perhaps, while you are hearing of the "things which are Jesus Christ's," the Holy Ghost will be kindling love and longing in your soul, bringing it to believe and venture. May the blessed Comforter speedily make you as willing as Rebekah and work in you the same obedience of faith. She went forth, and her faith was not in vain; she found her husband more than she forsook for him. So shall you, for eternity will never unfold all the love, loveliness, and glories of our wonderful Immanuel. Oh, I do want to know more of them here and thus have all the things of earth bedimmed!

Sweet Testifier of Jesus! Thou Wind Divine! "Awake" and "come" blow away the dust of the earth, and clouds of flesh and sense, which seem to come between us and our souls' Beloved, revealing Him in warmer love, more manifested union, and more endeared communion. Oh, make us walk in Him!

If for Jesus you pine, come join to beseech Him for more of His love. Come, O Thou Beloved, into the garden of our souls; breathe upon the graces of Thine own Spirit there, that the spices may flow forth for Thy regaling. Eat, O Beloved, Thy own pleasant fruits, and give us, Thy unworthy ones, to find Thy fruits sweet to our taste— the fruits of Thy love, of Thy doing, of Thy suffering; give us to feast on Thy rich fruits—to eat, by faith, Thy flesh and blood and thus live by Thee.

&❧ RUTH BRYAN

Seeking to Excel

Seek that ye may excel. —1 CORINTHIANS 14:12

This is an almost startling command; yet it is addressed to all that in every place call upon the name of Jesus Christ our Lord, therefore unmistakably to ourselves. Very likely our thoughts have been quite different from God's thoughts about it. We have been thinking it was useless to seek to excel, because we saw no likelihood of doing so; that it was presumptuous to think of such a thing; that it was even positively wrong to aim at it. Yet, all the time, there the commandment stood: "Seek that ye may excel!"

It is only when we are coveting earnestly the best gifts that the exercise and development of all others comes in its right place; that is, we must be eagerly desiring and heartily striving and using His own means to grow in grace, to receive always more and more of His fullness, more light and love, more faith and power, more, above all, of His Spirit. Even when this is the case, how often we set some human standard before us, and say, "Ah! If I had only half as much grace as so-and-so!" Comparing ourselves among ourselves, we are not wise; it is a fruitful source of limitation and hindrance. Let us give it up, once for all, and strike out into God's more excellent way, and seek to excel. Let us open our mouth wide that He may fill it, asking for such great gifts that His royal bounty may be magnified because of our very poverty; asking for such excellence of power that it may be seen to be of Him and not us; asking that He would so fulfill all the good pleasure of His goodness that the name of our Lord Jesus Christ may be glorified in us.

There are diversities of gifts, but none are without any. Every person has his or her proper gift of God, one after this manner, and another after that. If we think it humble to profess, or are humble enough really to believe, that we have but the one talent, that is the more reason why we should eagerly make the very most of it for our Lord; for if it is only one, it is not our own but our Lord's money.

• FRANCES RIDLEY HAVERGAL

Watchfulness

Pray without ceasing. —1 THESSALONIANS 5:17

What a mighty God we have to do with, and who has to do with us, every instant of our fleeting existence! It will be our wisdom and mercy to keep this in remembrance; so shall we see His loving hand in all the varying dispensations of His righteous providence. Let us aim to walk by faith in a poor world, through which we are traveling home to a better. Our ever-vigilant foe, the devil, seeks to entrap and wound us, while we have a yet greater enemy within, ever ready to listen to his subtle reasoning. How much need have we to cry to the Lord, "Hold thou me up, and I shall be safe!"

But the Lord is constantly on our side. Let us apply continually to Him and not fail to take our little matters as well as our greater ones. I often find that it requires stronger faith to carry minor concerns to Him than weightier ones. Our lives are made up of little things, like small links in a great chain, forming a complete whole. Oh, to believe all that God has said, taking Him at His word! Surely our Christian course is warfare. Let us cling to Jesus, for He will never fail us if we but go to Him for all we want within and without. If we meditated more upon the approach of eternity; the nearness of the glory that awaits us; the goodly company who surround Jesus, basking in the full sunshine of His countenance while His eye beams ineffably upon them, it would encourage and stimulate us on our way. May we be preserved from earthly entanglements and grasp less at worldly riches and honors. Contemplate a man, so aspiring, upon his dying bed. What comfort will it all give him then? None! But one believing, precious view of Jesus as his portion is worth more than a whole empire to him at this moment! May the Lord Jesus enable us to live more to Him—and upon Him and for Him! The more we try Him, the more we shall realize what He is to us. May the Lord favor you with His sensible presence and keep you in the hollow of His hand.

– MARY WINSLOW

Fear of Falling

What time I am afraid, I will trust in thee.
—PSALM 56:3

O h, my dear sister, are you afraid that you will not hold out because you feel so little strength in yourself? You have forgotten where your great strength lies. Not in yourself, but in the Lord—the Lord Jehovah, in whom there is everlasting strength even in Him who, as the creator of the end of the earth, faints not, neither is weary. Jehovah-Jesus is your strength. Can you draw the well of salvation dry with your thousands and ten thousands of wants? Millions of needy souls, with innumerable wants, have been supplied from that place, and still the well of life is as full as ever! Christ is as full for you as He was for the first needy soul that ever came unto Him. Oh, come, poor, weak thing, and lie down by faith in the bosom of your Lord Jesus, in the bosom of that infinite fullness, that everlasting strength that is in Him, and take a holy ease from all anxious thought and perplexing fear because of the little strength that is in you.

"Can you, by taking thought, add one cubit to your stature?" Why will you thus depart from the Lord, your rest, to launch forth into a sea of trouble? What! Fear because you have so little strength? Why, then, will you stand mourning over your little strength, since there is strength enough in Christ to make you stand? And all the strength of the omnipotent Jehovah in Him is held forth in the free promise as a bosom for your weak soul to rest in. Come, bow to the Savior. He accounts it an honor done to Him when a poor sinner in his utmost felt weakness says, by faith, "In the Lord have I strength"—when he says so by way of dependence upon His fullness and by way of persuasion that he shall be supplied from that source. Oh come, cast your care upon Christ! In well-doing, commit the keeping of your soul unto Him as unto a faithful creator who will not forsake the work of His own hands nor suffer the weakest soul that rests on Him to fail.

ও ANNE DUTTON

A Wide Open Gate

The LORD taketh pleasure in them that fear him,
in those that hope in his mercy.

—PSALM 147:11

Let us look well at the blessed, encouraging words, "The Lord taketh pleasure in them that fear him." Can you not come in there? Do you not fear Him—I mean, in a spiritual sense, not a slavish sense—fear to grieve Him, fear to go contrary to His will, fear to miss His approval or occasion the hiding of His face? Then, if this is true, He takes pleasure in you! Think of it quietly for a moment. Lay down this little book and let the precious hope steal into your heart that this is truly a message of comfort for you, and that it ought to be immediately received, believed, and rejoiced in. Do not put it from you and refuse to accept the blessing because it seems too good to be true, and you feel too sinful, too selfish, too half-hearted to be worthy of such tender love.

Besides, do you not see that, as if this gate were not open enough for such timid ones as you, the Shepherd of love has flung it even further back in the next clause of the verse, "The LORD taketh pleasure…in those that hope in his mercy." Surely the most desponding and fearful of the Lord's children can come as far as that and with a lightened heart thankfully say, "Dear Lord, that must mean me!"

My friend, if you do, indeed, fear the Lord and hope in His mercy, you know it is not a question of what you are but of what Christ is for you. Faith in the Lord Jesus strips the soul of its filthy rags and wraps around it the glorious and priceless robe of the Savior's righteousness; and thus arrayed, it is easy to see that all who believe must be pleasing in the Father's sight. Ah, dear souls, a far better way is to believe God's Word and joyfully think of Him as taking pleasure in you, rejoicing in your desire after Him and the hope in His mercy which He sees in your heart.

& SUSANNAH SPURGEON

Life and Safety in Christ Alone

Thou only sovereign of my heart,
My refuge, my almighty friend,—
And can my soul from Thee depart,
On whom alone my hopes depend?

Whither, ah! whither shall I go,
A wretched wand'rer from my Lord?
Can this dark world of sin and woe
One glimpse of happiness afford?

Eternal life Thy words impart,
On these my fainting spirit lives;
Here sweeter comforts cheer my heart,
Than all the round of nature gives.

Let earth's alluring joys combine,
While Thou art near, in vain they call;
One smile, one blissful smile of Thine,
My dearest Lord, outweighs them all.

Thy name my inmost pow'rs adore,
Thou art my life, my joy, my care:
Depart from Thee—'tis death,—'tis more,
'Tis endless ruin, deep despair.

Low at Thy feet my soul would lie,
Here safety dwells, and peace divine;
Still let me live beneath Thine eye,
For life, eternal life is Thine.

           ❧ ANNE STEELE

The Proof of His Purpose

No man can come unto me, except it were
given unto him of my Father.

—JOHN 6:65

If some of us were asked, "How do you know you have everlasting life?" we might say, "Because God has promised it." But how do you know He has promised it to you? And then if we answered, not conventionally or what we think we ought to say, but honestly what we think, we might say, "I know I have everlasting life because I have believed and come to Jesus." And this looks like resting our hope of salvation upon something that we have done, upon the fact of our having consciously believed and consciously come. And then, of course, any whirlwind of doubt will raise dust enough to obscure the fact and all the comfort of it.

Do not shrink from the words. Do not dare to explain them away. The faithful and true witness spoke them; the Holy Ghost has recorded them forever: "No man can come unto me, except it were given unto him of my Father." There it stands—reiterated and strengthened instead of softened, because many even of His disciples murmured at it. So our coming to Jesus was not of ourselves; it was the gift of God.

How did the gift operate? Not by driving, but by drawing. "No man can come to me, except the Father which hath sent me draw him." Here comes in the great "whosoever will." For unless and until the Father draws us, no mortal born of Adam ever will want to come to Jesus. There was nothing else for it. He had to draw us, or we never would have thought of wishing to come; no, we would have gone on distinctly willing not to come, remaining aliens and enemies. Oh, the terrible depth of depravity revealed by this keen sword-word: "Ye will not come to me that ye might have life." Settle it, then, that you never wanted to come till He drew you, and praise Him for thus beginning at the very beginning with you.

☙ FRANCES RIDLEY HAVERGAL

Conformity to the World

And be not conformed to this world: but be ye
transformed by the renewing of your mind, that ye may prove
what is that good, and acceptable, and perfect, will of God.

—ROMANS 12:2

What a difficult matter it is to be in the world, and yet not be of the world! Our Lord has said of His disciples, "They are not of the world, even as I am not of the world." Christ Himself carried out this principle. He passed through the world as one who was not of it. Oh, that we could but imitate His holy example and aim only, while in it, so to let our light shine that others may take knowledge of us that we have been with Jesus and have learned of Him. It should be our whole endeavor to do all the good we can in it and for it, and yet to set at nought its spirit, principles, and maxims.

"How can this be?" I think I hear you say. Go to Jesus, and ask of Him strength for any duty that devolves upon us. "Without me ye can do nothing." And yet, with Christ strengthening us, we can do all things. What a present helper is Jesus! When we are called to go among those who know not God, let it be from an absolute duty and with a desire only to do good to their souls, and after much prayer—honest, sincere prayer—to be preserved from evil. Oh, how much need we have to watch over our hearts and ask the Lord to purify our motives in all that we do! We need to keep close to our dearest, our best friend, and beseech Him to save us from ourselves.

How can a believer walk through this world safely and securely unless he is upheld by a strength that is omnipotent? I am a subject of the kingdom of Christ; hence, it is my duty and high privilege to obey and to serve. And oh, His service is not slavery; it is perfect freedom. Dear friend, see, then, our high calling! He has called you and me to come out of the world and to be separate, in principle, in practice, in heart.

• MARY WINSLOW

What of These Light Afflictions

*For our light affliction, which is but for a moment, worketh for us
a far more exceeding and eternal weight of glory.*
—2 CORINTHIANS 4:17

A sense of the greatness of our loss should never be allowed to produce feelings of dissatisfaction with the dispensations of providence. God has a right to visit us with greater, as well as with smaller judgments, and it is our duty to be proportionately humbled and improved. If they promote these ends, they are only mercies in a more unpleasant form, for, as has been well remarked, "Whatever draws us nearer to God cannot be real adversity, and whatever entices us from Him deserves not the name of prosperity." If we could view objects in their proper light, many of those things that now overwhelm us with sorrow would appear desirable.

How happy it is for us that our lot is not at our own disposal. If it were, I am certain we should be wretched; for the deficiency of our judgments, in connection with our love of present ease, would lead us to reject those afflictions that, like some unpleasant but salutary medicine, are bitter to the taste but necessary to existence and health. Our deficient judgments would also lead us to grasp too eagerly those enjoyments that, if unaccompanied with sanctifying grace, only corrupt and vitiate the mind and render the possession of them wearisome and the deprivation of them insupportable; they destroy both the means and the power of attaining true happiness by drawing us away from Him, without whom we can no more acquire it than animal life can be supported without breath. Let us always rejoice that God reigns and that we are entirely at His disposal. How consoling the thought; for the Judge of all the earth will do right. Let us, my dear sister, learn to esteem everything in this life according to its proper value. Whatever cannot be depended upon should never be trusted. Let us, therefore, cease to hope for happiness from the evanescent pleasures of life and fix our eyes and hearts upon those things that will survive when heaven and earth have passed away.

∗ SUSAN HUNTINGTON

If Pride...

*But let him that glorieth glory in this, that he
understandeth and knoweth me, that I am the LORD which exercise
lovingkindness, judgment, and righteousness, in the earth:
for in these things I delight, saith the LORD.*

—JEREMIAH 9:24

If pride is so great a sin and has in it such a fullness of malignity against God and man, no wonder that the people of God are tempted to it by Satan, who hates God and us. Hence, we may learn to admire the infinite wisdom and love of God, which devised and provided a way, by and through the death of His only Son, to save His people from this abominable sin—to save them from its dominion here, by grace, and from its very being hereafter in glory. Learn we hence the infinite mercy of the Redeemer's blood, which atoned for this sin of an infinite guilt and reconciled such children of pride to an infinitely holy God, and which cleanses us continually from the filthy stains of this deep-dyed iniquity.

If pride is such a great iniquity, let us bewail it bitterly; humble ourselves before God on account of it deeply; wash in the fountain set open instantly; and entreat forgiving and subduing grace constantly. And let us rejoice in Christ Jesus who, when we fall even into this sin, is our righteous advocate with the Father, who pleads righteously and for our salvation prevalently.

Again, if pride is such an abominable sin, let us set ourselves against it with all our might, or, rather, to oppose and destroy it, let us be strong in the Lord and in the power of His might. And since we cannot serve God as we would and should in the church militant while this subtle, potent sin works within, let us long for the church triumphant and the nobler joys and employs of the saints in glory, where by pride, or by any other sin, we shall dishonor, wound, or grieve our great and good God, the God of grace and love, no more forever.

ঌ ANNE DUTTON

Trust and Commit

*Trust in the LORD, and do good; so shalt thou dwell in the land,
and verily thou shalt be fed. Delight thyself also in the LORD; and he
shall give thee the desires of thine heart. Commit thy way unto
the LORD; trust also in him; and he shall bring it to pass.*
—PSALM 37:3–5

Commit your soul into His hand; He "came not to call the righteous, but sinners to repentance"; His errand to our world was to seek and to save the lost. Trusting in His mercy, through Christ, your soul is as safe as His word is true; for none perish that trust in Him.

"Trust in the Lord with all thine heart, and lean not to thine own understanding"; be not discouraged because of deadness, darkness, wandering, want of love, want of spirituality, want of any kind. Who told you of these evils and wants? The Sun of Righteousness shining into your soul has shown you many of the evils there—but the half you do not know yet. The more you learn of the holiness and purity of the divine nature and the spirituality of His law, the more you will be dissatisfied with everything yours. Even a holy apostle said, "In me, that is, in my flesh [or natural body] dwelleth no good thing."

If this was the case with the apostle, who sealed his testimony with his life, is it strange that you and I should have hearts full of all abominable things? These realities are cause of deep humility before God, but none of despair or doubt. All are alike guilty and vile—the whole head is sick, and the whole heart unsound; therefore, we need a whole Christ to atone for our sin, to cover our naked souls with His imputed righteousness and to be surety for us; to sanctify us by His Spirit and prepare us for the purchased inheritance. O try to rest in Him: believe it, you are complete in Him. Give over, my dear friend, poring and diving into your own heart and frames, and try to trust in an almighty Savior to save you from foes without and foes within. The promise runs, "As thy day so shall thy strength be."

≈ ISABELLA GRAHAM

Impediments to Spiritual Growth

Give me neither poverty nor riches;
feed me with food convenient for me: lest I be full,
and deny thee, and say, Who is the LORD?
—PROVERBS 30:8–9

How plainly I see that ease and prosperity do not serve the children of God. Covet it not, I beseech you! How the creature steals the heart's best affections from God! But oh, of this one thing I am assured—that when that is the case, our good and wise Father knows how to deal with His children. He breaks their cisterns and destroys their gourds. What a snare, too, to the believer is the society of the unregenerate. Our nature is so much more inclined to evil than to good that we insensibly imbibe the poison, and it contaminates our whole spiritual being. Who could be enclosed in a sepulcher with a putrid corpse and not feel his health and strength and life decline?

May the Lord in mercy preserve us! It does not require a large increase of earthly good to cause the heart to wander from God. Only let one who professes religion sit down at his ease and feel that he has need of nothing, and if he has never so little, that will do it. If Satan ever tempts one of these to covet riches, it is to help those who need it; and yet we have to mourn over this snare. But Jesus soon appears and gives faith to resist the wicked one, and then we see in a moment how we should mar the blessed work in the soul and defeat the good their best Friend designs should issue out of poverty and trial. None but God Himself is a satisfying portion. Earth, with all its promised comforts, cannot do it. Therefore the apostle exhorts, "Let your conversation be without covetousness; and be content with such things as ye have; for He hath said, I will never leave thee nor forsake thee." So that we may boldly say, "The Lord is my helper, and I will not fear what man shall do unto me."

☙ MARY WINSLOW

Strengthening Hands

Strengthen ye the weak hands, and confirm the feeble knees.
—ISAIAH 35:3

Christ said, "He that is not with me is against me: and he that gathereth not with me scattereth" (Luke 11:23). So it is not enough merely not to hinder. We must help, for not helping generally amounts to hindering. Perhaps we tried yesterday not to be hinderers; today, let us "go on to completeness" and try to be helpers.

How shall we set about it? First, by prayer, as Aaron and Hur held up the hands of Moses. Helping together by prayer reaches all. Who knows how much of the weakness of hands, which distresses us or even annoys us, may be laid at our door because we talked about it instead of praying about it? Very likely, names will occur to us now; then take those names at once to the Mighty One, and ask Him to strengthen those weak hands and confirm those feeble knees.

Second, by personal contact. I suppose we never come in contact with one who is really strong in the Lord without being strengthened, whether we feel it or not. But we should not be content with the unconscious influence which it is our singular privilege to radiate. Jonathan arose and went to David in the wood. How are we to do it? Speak to the heart of Jerusalem. What comes from the heart goes to the heart.

Before we can really lift up other hands, our own must have been lifted up by His Spirit, and our own feeble knees must have been confirmed by much bowing at His footstool. "When thou art converted, strengthen thy brethren" (Luke 22:32). "Uphold me with thy free Spirit. Then will I teach" (Ps. 51:12–13). It is the climax of the grand procession of promises in that magnificent close of the words of Eliphaz. May our record on high be, "Thou hast strengthened the weak hands. Thy words have upholden him that was falling, and thou hast strengthened the feeble knees" (Job 4:3–4).

≈ FRANCES RIDLEY HAVERGAL

Bearing One Another's Burdens

*Remember them that are in bonds, as bound
with them; and them which suffer adversity, as
being yourselves also in the body.*

—HEBREWS 13:3

And so likewise to fellow believers, in all their sufferings on whatever account, whether more private or public, let us bear a part with them. Let us in sympathizing love put our shoulder under their burden. For this we are commanded, that we "bear one another's burdens; and so fulfill the law of Christ"; that is, of loving each other even as He hath loved us (Gal. 6:2). There is not the least kind or degree of sufferings that affects the members of Christ, even the very least of them, but the Head feels it. "We have not an high-priest that cannot be touched with the feeling of our infirmities." And, "In all our affliction he is afflicted." In boundless compassion, He bears a part with us. Our afflictions are the afflictions of Christ. And if the Head is so full of sympathy with the members, and from thence helps them right early, shall not the members sympathize with each other and afford all the mutual succors they are capable of?

Oh, if we loved Christ and one another for His sake as we ought, there would not be an affliction that would touch a child of God in the world, but we should bear a part of it as soon as it came to our knowledge! And how great that part would be, I cannot say. Doubtless, if our hearts were full of love, we should be full of sympathy. Our souls would run into one another; we should have, as it were, but one soul. All our burdens would be but one, and all our strength one to bear it. Oh how easy is a heavy burden to many shoulders that would press only one to the ground! If we love Christ then, and love one another, let us run under each other's burdens, bear our part, and help away with the load.

❧ ANNE DUTTON

The Real Question

The Son of man is come to save that which was lost.
—MATTHEW 18:11

Perhaps you sometimes think, "If I am not chosen, it is of no use desiring and praying." So I once thought, and it lay like a stone on my heart, choking and chilling each little sigh for mercy when the cry would have risen, "Lord, save me." But I have found it was one of Satan's devices to keep me from prayer—and so it is with you, if such are your feelings. This is as it was with the young man whom Satan threw down and tore when they were bringing him to Jesus. But he could not hinder the blessing, and that is the comfort.

The question with you should not be whether you are chosen, but what are the characters whom Jesus came to save and invites to come to Him? "The Son of man is come to seek and to save that which was lost." "I am not come to call the righteous, but sinners to repentance." "This man receiveth sinners and eateth with them." "Come unto me all ye that labour and are heavy laden, and I will give you rest." Jesus is a great Savior, and you are a great sinner; therefore, you are the very case for Him. It is true that even with all your endeavors you cannot repent, but God has exalted Jesus Christ to give repentance and remission of sins. Neither can you pray, but He gives the spirit of grace and supplications. You cannot mourn for sin, but He makes the heart soft. "They shall come with weeping, and with supplications will I lead them." You cannot believe, but He is the author and finisher of faith.

So all these are things not to keep you away, but just to bring you to Him, even though you do not know assuredly that He has chosen you. He says, "Him that cometh to me I will in no wise cast out." The Spirit says, "Come." The bride says, "Come," and "Whosoever will, let him take the water of life freely."

~ RUTH BRYAN

The Foundation

*For other foundation can no man lay than
that is laid, which is Jesus Christ.*

—1 CORINTHIANS 3:11

If a man prepares to build a strong and stately castle, what does he think of first? If he is a skillful and wise architect, he first thinks of the foundation. So, if a man is a truly wise Christian, he considers well on what he is building for eternity.

That many have no good foundation is but too clear; that many build on sand, as it were, we cannot doubt. Not so the truly wise Christian: he wishes to build for eternity, without any mistake. He searches God's Word to learn the true and safe foundation for his hopes for this life and the next, and he discovers that foundation to be the Lord Jesus Christ Himself. By God's grace, the Christian builds on the Rock of Ages, which is firm and true, unchangeable, mighty, strong, and safe. This is a tried foundation, for it never gave way; a precious foundation, for many have built on it; an elect foundation, for God the Father chose it. Those who build on this foundation shall be safe when all others fail. The unconverted man builds his hopes on anyone, or on anything, rather than on Christ. As to the Jews of old, this tried foundation is a rock of offense and a stumbling block to the unbeliever. But to those who believe, Christ is precious. Is he precious to you? Do you build your hopes for eternity upon Him?

And now I would conclude as I began. Look well, each of you, to the foundation on which you are building for eternity. Otherwise, you will be disappointed of your hopes when there is no time to build afresh. Examine yourselves, I pray you, very seriously, and remember that no other foundation can be laid for eternity "than that is laid, which is Jesus Christ."

⮞ ELIZABETH JULIA HASELL

Confession of Sin

I acknowledge my sin unto thee, and mine iniquity
have I not hid. I said, I will confess my transgressions unto
the LORD; and thou forgavest the iniquity of my sin.

—PSALM 32:5

Confession of sin is one of the holiest and healthiest exercises of the renewed soul. To go to Jesus conscious of failure in thought, word, and deed; to confess to Him the moment we detect sin and are sensible of its guilt—be it in the company or in the street or elsewhere—is our precious privilege. The Lord can read the thought, interpret the sigh, understand the look, hear the whisper, and in one moment apply the blood that speaks pardon, peace, and love from the loving, faithful heart of Jesus. David says, "I acknowledge my sin unto thee, and mine iniquity have I not hid. I said, I will confess my transgressions unto the LORD; and thou forgavest the iniquity of my sin" (Ps. 32:5). The apostle John says, "If we confess our sins, He is faithful and just to forgive us our sins, and to cleanse us from all unrighteousness.... If any man sin, we have an advocate with the Father, Jesus Christ the righteous" (1 John 1:9; 2:1).

Now this is just what the Lord wants. The humble, penitential, minute confession of sin will keep the conscience tender, create a watchful spirit within, sanctify the heart, and draw us closer and closer to the cross and to the Christ of the cross. Thus, go to Jesus. Never lose sight of your oneness. He is with you in all your concerns—in all your trials and blessings, in all of your sorrows and joys. His dear eye is ever upon you for good. He loved you with an everlasting love, and with lovingkindness drew you to Himself. Veil no secrets from Him. Keep an open heart with Christ. If your love be cold, He will warm it. If your spirit is depressed, He will raise it. If your corruptions are strong, He will subdue them. The oftener you come, the more welcome you will be. You cannot weary nor wear Him out.

❧ MARY WINSLOW

Sanctifying Grace

And of his fulness have all we received, and grace for grace.

—JOHN 1:16

The sanctification of a sinner, by faith in the Savior, is indeed a glorious gospel mystery—a mystery hid from the natural man and that even by spiritual men is not well known, that is, practically understood. And yet it is a mystery of the greatest concern, both with respect to the glory of God and the good of His people. Without some degree of real acquaintance with it, a man cannot be a Christian, and the more fully and sensibly he is acquainted therewith, the more holy and happy a Christian he is, and the more the God of all grace in Christ is glorified thereby. Oh, the life of faith in the Son of God is the everyday work of a believer. Without it, we shall soon be backsliders in heart and ways. And, oh, the infinite love, the boundless grace of God, that though we are bent to backsliding from Him and are every day guilty of it more or less, He will still call us His people and, according to His promise, will heal our backslidings and love us freely—aye, freely indeed!

Oh, what an unspeakable privilege it is, that such poor, backsliding children as we have such a merciful Father who will not cause His anger to fall upon us, though we have done as evil things as we could! And how should this influence our souls into child-like ingenuity to our heavenly Father and spouse-like loyalty to our royal Bridegroom! Surely it is our wisdom, as believers, to come to the Savior daily, as being in ourselves poor sinners, and to abide in Him continually by faith, to receive of His fullness and grace for grace—even all supplies of grace for multiplied pardon, abundant peace, full joy, renewed strength, and increasing holiness. So shall we be filled with all the fruits of righteousness here, which are by Jesus Christ unto the glory and praise of God, and shall have an abundant entrance hereafter ministered unto us into the everlasting kingdom of our Lord and Savior Jesus Christ, to whom be glory and dominion forever and ever. Amen.

☙ ANNE DUTTON

The Royal Invitation

Incline your ear, and come unto me.

—ISAIAH 55:3

This is the royal invitation, for it is given by the King of kings. We are so familiar with the words that we fail to realize them. May the Holy Spirit open our ear that we may hear the voice of our King in them and that they may reach our souls with imperative power. Then "they shall know in that day that I am he that doth speak."

"Lord, to whom shall we go?"—not "to what shall we go?" For the human heart within us craves a personal, living rest and refuge. No doctrines, however true; no systems, however perfect; nothing mental, moral, or spiritual will do as the answer to this question of every soul that is not absolutely dead in trespasses and sins. And so the great word of invitation, royal and divine, is given to us: "Come unto me!" "Unto me." Just think what that one word means! Seek out all the great and wonderful titles of Christ for yourselves and write after each one: "And he says, come unto me"—the mighty God—nothing less than that! He is "mighty to save" and "ready to save me."

Is it nothing to you, all that pass by, that both from the depth of sorrow and the height of glory this royal invitation comes to you? For it is not only of Jesus crucified, but of Jesus reigning and Jesus coming. See that you refuse not Him who speaks, for He is coming to judge the quick and the dead. He is reigning now, and there are no neutrals in His kingdom. All are either willing and loyal subjects or actual rebels—those who have obeyed the King's call and come, and those who have made light of it and not come.

Which are you? Think of the day when the great white throne is set, and the Son of Man shall come in His glory; when all will be gathered before Him, and He shall separate them one from another. And know that "this same Jesus" now says to you, "Come unto me!"

☙ FRANCES RIDLEY HAVERGAL

Tables in the Wilderness

Can God furnish a table in the wilderness?
—PSALM 78:19

I would fain take you into the wilderness with me and bid you look back upon some of the "tables" that, in past days, the Lord has furnished for you there. Do you not remember that desert experience of sore afflictions, when you were laid very low, when heart and flesh failed and you were brought into the dust of death? Did not the Lord then come and strengthen you upon "the bed of languishing" and tenderly furnish your sickroom table with the rich cordials of His love and the life-giving elixir of His healing power? And, after that display of His mercy, can you not recollect how quickly the fever left you and what joy it was to rise and minister unto Him?

Or, have you forgotten that dread hour of spiritual darkness, a "waste-howling wilderness" of terror, when your soul was assailed by some horrible temptation, and Satan beset you so furiously that, for a moment, you almost despaired of deliverance? Was not that the very moment of time of the Lord's gracious relief and succor? Did He not appear on your behalf and lead you forth from the conflict to find the table of His love spread as for a banquet for your sake and the leaves of the Tree of Life ready plucked for the healing of all your wounds?

Can you not recall those other seasons of distress, when some sad bereavement or some great crisis of your life had brought you into a Sahara of desolation and grief? Almost broken in heart, your soul fainted within you, and you "wandered in the wilderness in a solitary way," believing yourself cut off from the land of the living. But you cried unto God, and how blessed did He answer you. He turned the dry ground into springs of water, and there He prepared "a table before you," and the desert yielded royal dainties. Ah, these tables in the wilderness! They are standing rebukes to our lack of faith and constant memorials of God's faithfulness and love!

☙ SUSANNAH SPURGEON

Quietness in the Face of Afflictions

Just and true are thy ways, thou King of saints.
—REVELATION 15:3

O ur faith is seldom, if ever, more tried than when we are called to give up those friends with whose existence our happiness is materially connected. Nor can we, perhaps, have conclusive evidence of its genuineness until we are called to pass through the furnace of affliction. The faith of the formalist or the hypocrite may appear to be sound as long as God sheds upon him the unclouded sun of prosperity. But if He causes clouds and darkness to overspread his horizon, then he exclaims, "The way of the Lord is not equal!"

It is a proof of true faith to be able, when all things are against us, to lift a tranquil eye to Him who sits upon the throne of the heavens, holding the reins of universal dominion in His hand, and say, "Just and true are thy ways, thou King of saints." This disposition, my dear friend, I trust you feel, though it may be imperfectly. And if so, you may be assured this affliction will work for your good. Nothing deserves the name of adversity that leads us to a more perfect knowledge of and dependence upon Him whose favor is life and whose lovingkindness is better than life. Therefore, to the Christian, afflictions are as truly mercies as those gifts to which we are apt to appropriate the term.

Perhaps you say, "I fear I am not a Christian." Nothing is so distressing as this. Anything can be borne if it is tempered and sweetened with the presence and blessing of God. "Examine yourselves, whether ye be in the faith." I dare not say, therefore, hope without examining; but, my beloved friend, I may say do not despond. Look not to yourself: look to Christ, the Lamb of God who takes away the sin of the world. None of us needs despair while we have such a mighty and merciful Savior to whom we may repair, who is the author and the finisher of faith and who never yet cast off or never will cast off any who come to Him.

❧ SUSAN HUNTINGTON

A View of Christ Dims Earthly Things

Thou art worthy, O Lord, to receive glory and honour.

—REVELATION 4:11

In the precious name that is above every name, I come to inquire: Is it well with you? Does the vine flourish, and the tender grape appear? And do you find the savor of the Beloved's ointments give a very good smell? Is Jesus increasingly precious, more than ever desirable? Is He, in your esteem, better than rubies, and all the things that may be lawfully desired not to be compared to Him? Is the Holy Ghost sharpening your appetite for the Bread of Life, so that with more ardent longings you are saying, "None but Jesus?" When He is in the right place, other things will be so; it is His rising in the soul that makes them sink to their proper level. And, oh, He is so worthy, so suitable, so altogether lovely; we cannot prize Him too much or hold Him too fast or lean on Him too heavily. All I can say of Him is nothing, so mean is it, so far below His worth; but through rich grace, I, a vile sinner, have tasted and handled of this precious Word of Life and found such blessed benefit, such soul-invigoration, that I want to set others longing for these royal dainties.

Perhaps I might think that the Lord will do His own work, and I am only meddling in vain, if I did not read in His Holy Word about "exhorting one another" and "stirring up pure minds by way of remembrance." If by many poor attempts I may be used to stir up but one warm, loving remembrance of Him, I shall be thankful. Satan is ever striving to divert the mind from this object. He will allure or alarm, he will use what is pleasing or painful, anything to keep the soul from closing with Christ, from looking unto Jesus and believing in Him for life and salvation. Nevertheless, all those who are ordained unto eternal life shall believe in spite of his efforts, and all those in eternal union with Christ shall close with Him by living faith. Cords of love shall entwine, the bands of a man will draw, till the poor soul is brought into conscious union with the Beloved and can say, "Who loved me, and gave himself for me."

&ppwing; RUTH BRYAN

Wakeful Hours

Thou holdest mine eyes waking.
—PSALM 77:4

If we could always say, night after night, "I will both lay me down in peace and sleep," receiving in full measure the Lord's quiet gift to His beloved, we should not learn the disguised sweetness of this special word for the wakeful ones. When the wearisome nights come, it is hushing to know that they are appointed. But this is something nearer and closer-bringing, something individual and personal—not only an appointment, but an act of our Father: "Thou holdest mine eyes waking." It is not that He is merely not giving us sleep; it is not a denial, but a different dealing. Every moment that the tired eyes are sleepless it is because our Father is holding them waking. It seems so natural to say, "How I wish I could go to sleep!" Yet even that restless wish may be soothed by the happy confidence in our Father's hand, which will not relax its "hold" upon the weary eyelids until the right moment has come to let them fall in slumber.

Ah! But we say, "It is not only wish; I really want sleep." Well, wanting is one thing, and needing is another. For He is pledged to supply all our need, not all our notions. And if He holds our eyes waking, we may rest assured that, so long as He does so, it is not sleep but wakefulness that is our true need. Let us remember that He does nothing without a purpose, and that no dealing is meant to be without result. So it is well to pray that we make the most of the wakeful hours, that they may be no more wasted ones than if we were up and dressed. They are His hours. It will cost no more mental effort to ask Him to let them be holy hours, filled with His calming presence, than to let the mind run upon the thousand other things which seem to find even busier entrance during the night. Can we say, "With my soul have I desired thee in the night"? and, "By night on my bed I sought him whom my soul loveth?" Then He will fulfill that desire; the very wakefulness should be recognized as His direct dealing, and we may say, "Thou hast visited me in the night."

☙ FRANCES RIDLEY HAVERGAL

Abide in Christ

And now, little children, abide in him.

—1 JOHN 2:28

To you who from a possession of Christ make a profession of Him; who have felt the power of His gospel in your hearts and from thence have begun to profess its glorious doctrines, and by a holy walk, to praise free grace in your lives—to you let me say, "Abide in Christ by faith, and see that you abound more and more in good works." Oh dear soul, you are called unto holiness; see that you make it your business, your everyday work, to deny ungodliness and worldly lusts and to live soberly, righteously, and godly in this present world. You are saved by grace, purified by Christ's blood and Spirit unto Himself, on purpose that you should be zealous of good works. And well has free grace provided for your holiness; you are not called to work without strength. You are under grace and, as such, have the promise that sin shall not have dominion over you. All the fullness of Christ is yours, to pardon and subdue your iniquities, to communicate grace and holiness and quicken you to live to God.

By nature, you were without strength to overcome sin. But since free grace has brought you into Christ the Lord, in Him you have not only righteousness to justify you, but strength to sanctify you. Be encouraged, therefore, to engage in the work you are called to, to answer the purpose of your being Christians, which is to glorify Christ with your bodies and spirits, which are His. Christ has bought you, and you are no more your own. But all you are and have is the Lord's. Deny Him not His right. Is not the dear Lamb that was slain for you well worthy of you and all that you have? Did Christ live and die, and does He live forevermore for you, and will you not live to Him here, who hope to live with Him hereafter? I know, dear souls, that in your judgments you think it just and equitable that you and all you have should be the Lord's, and that according to the new nature, this is your earnest desire.

❧ ANNE DUTTON

The Sealing of the Spirit

But the Comforter, which is the Holy Ghost, whom the Father
will send in my name, he shall teach you all things.
—JOHN 14:26

Do not stop short of the best blessing God can give you, next to
Jesus—the sealing of the Holy Ghost, which is the earnest of
our glorious inheritance above. If you could come just as you are,
without trying to bring some price in your hand, you would soon
attain what I believe you are longing for. You say you do not feel sin
to be such a burden as you ought to feel it, and that that withholds
the blessing. Well, even this darkness and dimness of the understanding you are to take to Jesus, since it is part of your sin, and
must be brought to Him as such.

Tell Him all you feel, and all you ought to feel but do not feel.
Come poor, lacking everything to recommend you to God, and
you will soon see the golden scepter held out to you and a hearty
welcome to the very heart of Christ. It is good to come empty, that
we might be filled; and to come, too, that we might be emptied of
everything but Christ. "The LORD is my shepherd, I shall not want."

How He cares for us, and yet tries our little faith. He writes
death first upon the blessing He designs to give, and then when
submission to His will is realized, the blessing is bestowed in a way
and at a time we never expected. Such is God in all His dealings
with the ones He is training for heaven. I am encouraged to make
large drafts upon His goodness, and at times I feel that I cannot
ask or expect too much, because it is for Jesus' sake He gives and
in Jesus' name I ask. "Ask anything in my name, and I will do it."
What more could He say to encourage us to come to Him in any
circumstances and obtain in Christ all that is truly for our good and
His glory? May God in mercy reveal these things to us, causing us
to rejoice with joy unspeakable and full of glory.

❧ MARY WINSLOW

Submission under Bereavement

And Aaron held his peace.
—LEVITICUS 10:3

I know that sometimes anguish is too deep to bear the touch of human sympathy, and that there are cases which only He who gave to the heart its sensibilities can reach, and who can quell its most violent throbbing or speak peace to its most agitated and distracted emotions. Of whatever nature be the circumstances of our trial, nothing is so truly quieting as being enabled to bow to our Father's will and take the cup immediately from His hand. No events take Him by surprise. "Shall there be evil in a city, and the Lord hath not done it?" When useful, amiable, and valued lives are unexpectedly cut off, we marvel; but though deep the mysteries of Jehovah's permissive will, far too deep for us to fathom, yet these things do not happen by chance.

We see this in the case of Job, whose children were all cut off by Satan's agency, but not without divine permission. He, recognizing as in a father's hand the sword which had slain his earthly comforts, said, "The LORD gave, and the LORD hath taken away; blessed be the name of the LORD." While most puzzled by the Lord's providential movements and writhing under the smart of bereavement, it is most soothing and blessed to be enabled by the Spirit to feel, "Father, Thy will be done." "Father, glorify Thy name." Oh that our precious Jesus may draw near and bind up your bleeding heart, yea, all your hearts; and may He administer His strong consolations and cordials, as He is wont to do in times of special need!

To yourself, my loved friend, may He be very gracious, giving you even this "valley of Achor for a door of hope." May He keep Satan from gaining advantage, and you from giving place to him. He will provoke to fretfulness, but may the Lord rebuke him and give you to feel and say, "I know, O LORD, that thy judgments are right and that thou in faithfulness hast afflicted me."

&ᴥ RUTH BRYAN

Visiting the Saints

Be ye all of one mind, having compassion one of another,
love as brethren, be pitiful, be courteous.
—1 PETER 3:8

V isiting the saints is one of the duties of love we owe them. They that fear the Lord should speak often one to another. And I have experienced very great blessing to attend it, unto mutual edification in love. 'Tis a part of the communion of saints.

It is the glory of a Christian to be like Christ, and the more likeness to Him we attain, the more room will there be in our hearts for the cases of His children. If we loved them with a "pure heart fervently," we should have an ear open to all their complaints, and a bosom large enough to receive all their griefs, sorrows, and joys; and be sensibly touched with both, as we got knowledge thereof in visiting them. Oh, were such visits mutually, frequently, and conscientiously kept up among the saints—how much would they promote heart unity and brotherly love among them! And how directly would they tend to each other's happiness and glory!

Are any of the saints dejected? Let us do all we can to comfort them. Are they feebleminded? Let us support them. Are they tempted? Let us succor them. Are they dark and cold? Let us warm and enlighten them. Are they ready to faint? Let us bring them cordials. Are they in prison? Let us seek their liberty. And in a word, let us do all we can, in all manner of ways, to nourish and cherish them and encourage them in the way and work of the Lord in the closet, family, and church—that their holiness may increase and their usefulness be abundant, and that their happiness may be great in this world, and their glory in that to come.

&ANNE DUTTON

Among the Furnaces

Everything that may abide the fire, ye shall make it go
through the fire, and it shall be clean.

—NUMBERS 31:23

If we are God's gold, we must be subjected to constant purifying by fire. If He claims us as His silver, we shall be refined again and again, that our pollution may be purged, and all that is true and precious may shine forth with fresh luster to His glory. It is not the actual separation of the ore from its original dross that is here referred to, but the necessary cleansing of fashioned vessels and shapely treasures that have contracted any defilement or suffered some dishonor. Alas! Our inmost hearts tell us what abundant need there is that "the fire shall try every man's work of what sort it is."

The true work of grace in a human heart can abide the fire of any trial to which the Lord may be pleased to expose it. We can sing of His love when the heat is most vehement, and glorify Him by proving that promise true: "When thou walkest through the fire, thou shalt not be burned, neither shall the flame kindle upon thee." This is why the command is so frequently heard, thrilling through heart and life, "Ye shall make it go through the fire."

Because our faith is precious and our love golden, and our hope "maketh not ashamed," they must ever be subject to the Refiner's fire. Does the flesh sometimes shrink from such an assaying as this? Yes, doubtless it does. "The spirit indeed is willing, but the flesh is weak," yet need we not fear. The purpose of our great Refiner is to discipline, not to destroy us. He makes the sighs of the furnace to strike the keynotes of the new and everlasting song, and the coming forth of His "tried gold" will be found "unto praise, and honor, and glory at his appearing."

᠃ SUSANNAH SPURGEON

Christ, the Glory of Heaven

*For the Lamb which is in the midst of the throne shall
feed them, and shall lead them unto living fountains of waters:
and God shall wipe away all tears from their eyes.*

—REVELATION 7:17

D o you not almost envy those who have escaped from sin and sorrow and suffering, and are so signally honored as to see Jesus, to bask in the full sunshine of His glory and to sit forever at His feet? See the loved ones enter the gates of heaven—angels their attendants! See the glorified, loving Savior holding out the golden scepter and saying, "Come, ye blessed of my Father!" Could we be so selfish as to wish them back? Oh no! No more pain, no more sighing, no more sorrow, no more sin. "And God shall wipe away all tears from their eyes; and there shall be no more death, neither sorrow, nor crying, neither shall there be any more pain: for the former things are passed away." Heaven encircles the believer.

You are surrounded by the invisible world. Alas! We live so far below our high and heavenly calling, our glorious and eternal destiny. We have Christ within us, the hope of glory. Every soul will be filled with glory on entering the abode of the blessed, and as long as the existence of God, that soul, I believe, will be increasing in its capacity to receive its ever-increasing joy. Oh what a thought this is to comfort us in the departure of friends and to encourage us to have as much of Christ in our souls now as we can, that we may, in the same proportion, have of glory when we arrive there! This subject is with me inexhaustible. Follow on to know the Lord. Have much to do with Him day by day, hour by hour. Our knowledge of God grows by constant interaction with Him, and we should allow nothing, however lawful, to interrupt that interaction that a loving child would wish to have with a beloved parent. Christ is the glory of heaven, so let us live as to have much of Him in our souls now, that we may be filled with all the fullness of God.

❧ MARY WINSLOW

What Is "Coming"?

Him that cometh to me I will in no wise cast out.

—JOHN 6:37

What is "coming"? A person's very familiarity with the terms used to express spiritual things seems to have a tendency to make him feel mystified about them. And their very simplicity makes the person suspicious, as it were, that there must be some mysterious and mystical meaning behind them, because they sound too easy and plain to have such great import. "Come" means come—just that! And not some secret process of mental effort.

What would you understand by it if you heard it today for the first time, never having had any doubts or suppositions or previous notions whatever about it? What does a little child understand by it? It is positively too simple to be made plainer by any amount of explanation. If you could see the Lord Jesus standing there, right before you, and you heard Him say, "Come!" would you say, "What does 'come' mean?" And if the room were dark, so that you could only hear and not see, would it make any difference? Would you not turn instantly toward the glorious voice? Would you not—in heart, will, and intention—instantaneously obey it? That is, if you believed it to be Himself. For he that cometh to God must believe that He is. The coming so hinges on that as to be really the same thing. The moment you really believed, you would really come; and the moment you really come, you really believe. Now the Lord Jesus is as truly and actually near you as if you could see Him. And He as truly and actually says "come" to you, as if you heard Him. Fear not, only believe, and let yourself come to Him straight away! Take with you words and turn to the Lord. Say unto Him, "Take away all iniquity, and receive us graciously." And know that His answer is, "Him that cometh to me I will in no wise cast out."

≈ FRANCES RIDLEY HAVERGAL

Are You Bankrupt?

But I am poor and needy;
yet the Lord thinketh upon me:
thou art my help and my deliverer;
make no tarrying, O my God.

—PSALM 40:17

How is it with you, my beloved? Are you stripped of your own righteousness, emptied, and bankrupt? If so, I hail you blessed, for "the poor have the gospel preached to them." And it is written, "When they had nothing to pay, he frankly forgave them both." Nothing to pay! How our proud flesh does murmur and complain and only wish that it had something to bring! But why? "He hath magnified the law and made it honorable." He has endured every stripe that justice required, paying every farthing the creditor demanded, and that in heaven's own coin, for "without the shedding of blood is no remission." His pure blood was freely shed that sin might be honorably remitted. "The soul that sinneth it shall die." He dies, the just for the unjust, to bring us to God," and when, at the close of His work, He cried aloud, "It is finished," there was not a voice heard in heaven, earth, or hell to contradict Him.

Take courage, then, my beloved: we can afford to be poor with such "unsearchable riches in Christ," and all He is and has is ours, for "my Beloved is mine, and I am his." "All things are yours, for ye are Christ's, and Christ is God's." He is "head over all things to his body the church."

"Ah! but," say you, "I want to know more clearly that He is mine. I want personal application and appropriation." Well, this is not unlawful coveting; go on longing, for this very same Jesus "satisfieth the longing soul, and filleth the hungry soul with goodness."

❦ RUTH BRYAN

The Way to Glory

But as it is written, Eye hath not seen, nor ear heard,
neither have entered into the heart of man, the things which
God hath prepared for them that love him.

—1 CORINTHIANS 2:9

My dear friend, the way to glory in all the appointed paths of duty is uphill. To be religious in truth and sincerity and unto any growth and maturity, we are called to striving, running, fighting, wrestling—to strive against sin, to run with patience the race that is set before us, to fight the good fight of faith, and to wrestle, not only against flesh and blood (against wicked men and all their wicked ways to draw us off from God), but also against principalities and powers, against the powers of darkness, the armies of hell, who with all their might will oppose us in every step we take heavenward, in all our approaches to God and appearances for Him. And therefore, we had need to take unto us the whole armor of God, and especially the shield of faith, wherewith we shall be able to quench all the fiery darts of the wicked—of Satan, that wicked one, on whatever side he casts them at us. And a very necessary piece of a Christian's armor is that of all-prayer.

Thus, dear friend, be strong in the grace that is in Christ Jesus, and labor to walk by faith in Him and love to Him, every day, as if it were your last duty. You have no time given you to misspend. The Lord's redeemed are to glorify the Redeemer in the whole of their time, until they are glorified with Him in blessed eternity. Those happy souls who are the Lord's ought not to live unto themselves, but unto Him. And whatever we do in civil or religious things, in the common affairs of natural life, or in things that concern our spiritual life, we are to do all to the glory of God, as under His eye, His forgiving love and abundant goodness, to show forth the praises of Him who has called us out of darkness into His marvelous light and in the view of that blessed day when our Lord of the freest grace will give rewards unto His servants according to their works.

᠀ ANNE DUTTON

Making Sure Work of Heaven

Ask, and it shall be given you; seek, and ye shall find;
knock, and it shall be opened unto you.
—MATTHEW 7:7

Make sure work of heaven! Knock, and knock, and knock again, and let Jesus have no rest, nor allow you to rest, until He opens and reveals Himself to your soul. Oh, hear Him say, "Thy sins are forgiven thee." But, perhaps, at this point you will reply, "We have not committed so much sin; we have always said our prayers and have done all the good we could." To this I reply that, with all this, you must pass from death unto life. This, beloved, is what you want. Wrestle with Jesus by day and night until you are able to say, "Now I know the Lord; and my sins which are many, are all forgiven. He has spoken peace to my soul." Depend upon it, you will then see the vast difference between your present state and the new spiritual existence of the regenerate soul. Ask the Lord to show you to yourselves just as you are; ask honestly, perseveringly.

The Lord knows I would not discourage you for the world, but I want to see you rejoicing in the Lord, quite sure that you are converted. Go to Jesus as a poor, lost, undone sinner, and give Him no rest until He says, "Go in peace; thy sins are forgiven thee." You will know His voice when He speaks these words. Have you not been living all these years without God—for yourselves, and not for Him? Because you are engrossed with earthly things, God has not had His right place in your affections. You have been living for yourselves and to yourselves. Is not this a great sin? God created you for Himself, and He requires your hands and your heart, your whole, undivided heart. He is a jealous God. But go to your room, close and fasten your door, and call upon God until He opens His loving, sin-forgiving heart to you. Then will you know the essential difference between a sin-pardoned, accepted heir of heaven and a mere formalist, having the form of godliness and denying the power thereof!

&❧ MARY WINSLOW

Foolish Unbelief

And he did not many mighty works there
because of their unbelief.

—MATTHEW 13:58

God does not work wonders for us if we mistrust Him. His miracles of grace and power are wrought on behalf of those whose faith is strong enough to claim the performance of His word. How very few of us who call ourselves Christians ever live up to our high privileges as "heirs of God, and joint heirs with Christ!" Did we but realize our true position as sons and daughters of the Lord God Almighty, there would be nothing impossible to us. A recent writer on this subject says: "If there be a discrepancy between our life and the fulfillment and enjoyment of all God's promises, the fault is ours. If our experience be not what God wants it to be, it is because of our unbelief in the love of God, in the power of God, and in the reality of His promises."

Is not this the reason why so many of God's own children are living at such a miserably low level of spiritual existence? It is a positive fact that they do not believe what God has said; they are as distrustful as if He had never given them the blessed assurance, "I am the Lord, I change not"; as poor as though He had never made the promise, "Whatsoever ye shall ask in my name, that will I do"; and as unhappy and full of care as if His own lips had not spoken those other sweet words, "Let not your heart be troubled: ye believe in God, believe also in me."

❧ SUSANNAH SPURGEON

Cheerful Suffering

Yet if any man suffer as a Christian, let him not be ashamed;
but let him glorify God on this behalf.
—1 PETER 4:16

Why am I disposed to faint, or to complain under many various afflictions? Because my mind is not yet cast into the mold of the gospel. Does the Scripture mean anything or does it not, when, from beginning to end, it clearly and fully speaks not only of the trials, temptations, and sufferings of God's people but of the blessedness of such as are thus tried? Nay, I know, from happy experience, that "it is good for me that I have been afflicted." And yet I am often ready to say, "It is enough," as if I were wiser than God, or as if I would be treated differently from the rest of His children, or as if the things I read of in the Bible were written as a mere history rather than as what must be wrought into my own experience.

It is I, myself, that must "count it all joy" when I "fall into divers temptations." It is I that must "reckon the sufferings of the present time as not worthy to be compared with the glory that shall follow." It is I, as well as Moses, that must "endure, as seeing Him who is invisible" and with the very same faith as he did—substantially—actually—steadily.

"Lord, increase my faith!" Enable me to honor Thee by adding to the too few who suffer cheerfully, glorifying my Father which is in heaven. But this I can only do by the constant influences of Thy Holy Spirit.

☙ SARAH HAWKES

Captive Thoughts

Bringing into captivity every thought
to the obedience of Christ.
—2 CORINTHIANS 10:5

Are there any tyrants more harassing than our own thoughts? Control of deeds and words seems a small thing in comparison, but have we not been apt to fancy that we really can't help our thoughts? Instead of dominating them, they have dominated us, and we have not expected, nor even thought it possible, to be set free from the manifold tyranny of vain thoughts—and still less of wandering thoughts. Yet, all the time, here has been God's Word about this hopeless, helpless matter. Only where has been our faith?

It is very strong language that the inspiring Spirit uses here—not "thoughts" in general, but definitely, and with no room for distressing exceptions—"every thought." Must it not be glorious rest to have every thought of day and night brought into sweet, quiet, complete captivity to Jesus, entirely obedient to the faith, to His holy and loving influence, to His beautiful and perfect law?

But there is an order in their effectual working, and we must not begin at the wrong end. Before this triumph-leading of every thought can take place, there is the casting down of imaginations, or, more correctly, reasonings. As long as we are reasoning about a promise, we never know its reality. It is not God's way. It is the humble who hear thereof and are glad. Have we not found it so? Did we ever receive the powerful fulfillment of any promise so long as we argued and reasoned, whether with our own hearts or with others, and said, "How can these things be?" Has it not always been that we had to lay down our arms and accept God's thought and God's way instead of our own ideas, and be willing that He should speak the word only, and believe it as little children believe our promises? It is the old way and the only way: "Who through faith... obtained promises."

            ❧ FRANCES RIDLEY HAVERGAL

Soul Searching

For the LORD seeth not as man seeth; for man looketh on the
outward appearance, but the LORD looketh on the heart.

—1 SAMUEL 16:7

Oh, my dear friend, how infinitely vile and abominable must we appear in the eyes of Him who can fully realize what our feelings in relation to Him, to ourselves, and to sin should be, and knows exactly what they are! Surely we must be stupid if the thought does not cause us to exclaim, "It is of the Lord's mercies that we are not consumed!" I know nothing in which I am so deficient as in my apprehensions of sin. God grant it may be more and more opened to my view in all its odiousness, and more and more embittered to my soul! I believe the lack of clear views of this, the nature and vileness of sin, is the rock on which thousands split. It is the lack of this that makes the Arminian think he can save himself; the Unitarian deny the necessity of an atonement and the divinity of the Savior; the universalist, the eternity and perhaps the reality of future punishment.

It is the lack of this that produces those restless complaints against God, which are ever found upon the lips of the unregenerate. And may I not add that it is the lack of this that sometimes clouds, distresses, and agonizes the Christian, when contemplating the tremendous wrath, denounced in Scripture, against the finally impenitent? Oh, how much should professing Christians pray for each other! And when we reflect that there was an unhumbled Judas even among the Twelve, how should it excite us to seek, with anxious solicitude, to make our calling and election sure.

&ra; SUSAN HUNTINGTON

The Goodness of God

Ye humble souls, approach your God
With songs of sacred praise;
For He is good, immensely good,
And kind are all His ways.

All nature owns His guardian care.
In Him we live and move;
But nobler benefits declare
The wonders of His love.

He gave His Son, His only Son,
To ransom rebel worms;
'Tis here He makes His goodness known
In its divinest forms.

To this dear refuge, Lord, we come,
'Tis here our hope relies;
A safe defense, a peaceful home,
When storms of trouble rise.

Thy eye beholds, with kind regard,
The souls who trust in Thee;
Their humble hope Thou wilt reward,
With bliss divinely free.

Great God, to Thy almighty love,
What honors shall we raise?
Not all the raptured songs above
Can render equal praise.

&ounce; ANNE STEELE

Sinful Self

For I know that in me (that is, in my flesh,)
dwelleth no good thing.
—ROMANS 7:18

If I should look upon my sin and not upon Thy mercy, I should despair; for in myself I find nothing to save me, but a dunghill of wickedness to condemn me. If I should hope by my own strength and power to come out of this maze of iniquity and wickedness wherein I have walked so long, I should be deceived. For I am so ignorant, blind, weak, and feeble that I cannot bring myself out of this entangled and wayward maze; but the more I seek means and ways to wind myself out, the more I am wrapped and tangled therein.

So I perceive my striving therein to be hindrance, my travail to be labor spent in going back. It is the hand of the Lord that can and will bring me out of this endless maze of death. For unless I am made ready by the grace of the Lord, I cannot ask forgiveness or be repentant or sorry for my sins. There is no man can avow that Christ is the only Savior of the world, but by the Holy Ghost; yea, as Paul says, no man can say "the Lord Jesus" but by the Holy Ghost. The Spirit helps our infirmity and makes continual intercession for us, with such sorrowful groaning as cannot be expressed.

For I am most certain and sure that no creature in heaven or earth is of power or can, by any means, help me except God, who is omnipotent, almighty, beneficial, merciful, well-willing, and loving to all those who call and put their whole confidence and trust in Him. And, therefore, I will seek no means or advocate other than Christ's Holy Spirit, who is the only advocate and mediator between God and man, to help and relieve me.

&❧ KATHERINE PARR

Rejoicing with the Saints in Their Joys

Rejoice with them that do rejoice.
—ROMANS 12:15

L et us rejoice with the saints in all their joy, for this is a channel in which our love toward them should flow. As we should weep with them that weep, so, likewise, we should rejoice with them that rejoice. If one member is honored, the rest should rejoice with him (Rom. 12:15; 1 Cor. 12:26). If our brethren increase in grace, gifts, honor, and usefulness, we love them not if we don't rejoice with them. And in this duty of love, in rejoicing with them, as all envy and evil-speaking against them is forbidden, so all joy in the inward affection and outward expressions is therefore commanded.

We ought in no wise to grudge at and envy our brethren when they rise in grace, gifts, and usefulness, in honor and esteem—not even though they are near us and we may imagine that our own is somewhat eclipsed thereby. Oh, what wretched selfishness it is when we are afraid our brethren should outshine us, and therefore we slight them in our hearts and speak lightly, or perhaps reproachfully, of them to others and tell their faults to eclipse their virtues, that we might rise by their ruin!

What are we that our brethren must be nothing that we may subsist—that we may be something! Is not this murder of the highest kind? Is it not like the sin of devils? Is it not saying in our hearts, "I will ascend above the stars of God: I will be like the most high"? Yea, is it not saying "I AM, and there is none beside me"? And oh, what a hell does this sin deserve! And what a death did it cost our dear Lord to save us from it! Oh that it might not live and reign in our mortal bodies, that we should obey it in the lusts thereof! That there might not be just ground for any to say that we speak well of none but ourselves! Hence, then, if we love God and His glory, our brethren and their happiness—yea, ourselves and our own bliss— let us rejoice with the saints in all their joy.

☙ ANNE DUTTON

Testing Times, the Proof of Love

Fear not: for God is come to prove you.
—EXODUS 20:20

Whatever may be the grievous circumstances in which I am placed or the injustice of others from which I am suffering, if my God says, "Fear not," I ought surely to be brave and strong. If we can only get firmly fixed in our hearts the truth that the Lord's hand is in everything that happens to us, we have found a balm for all our woes, a remedy for all our ills. When friends fail us and grow cold, when enemies triumph and grow confident, when the smooth pathway upon which we have been traveling suddenly becomes rough, stony, and steep, we are apt to look askance at the visible second causes and to forget that our God has foreseen every trial, permitted every annoyance, and authorized each item of discipline with this set purpose: "The LORD your God proveth you, to know whether ye love the LORD your God with all your heart and with all your soul." Oh heart of mine, what is your response to this demand? Do you not love Him enough to endure any test to prove it?

I remember once reading words to this effect: that the moment we come into any trial or difficulty, our first thought should be not how soon we can escape from it or how we may lessen the pain we shall suffer from it, but how we can best glorify God in it and most quickly learn the lesson that He desires to teach us by it. Had we grace and faith enough to do this, our trials and troubles would be but as so many steps by which we should climb to the mountaintop of continual fellowship and peace with God. The soul that has learned the blessed secret of seeing God's hand in all that concerns it cannot be a prey to fear; it looks beyond all second causes straight into the heart and will of God and rests content because He rules.

∂ SUSANNAH SPURGEON

Gratitude

And Jesus answering said, Were there not ten cleansed?
but where are the nine? There are not found that returned
to give glory to God, save this stranger.

—LUKE 17:17–18

E ven the men of this world regard ingratitude to a benefactor as something mean and base. So far they are perfectly right in their judgment. But do they consider how grievously common a sin ingratitude to God is? Do they give a thought to the crime those commit who receive the blessings of this life as a mere matter of course? Still worse—do worldly men know their own ingratitude to a despised and neglected Savior? That "unspeakable Gift" is little cared for, and though God spared not His dear Son, yet man, in his natural state, sets little value on Christ or on His work for man. Ingratitude to an earthly benefactor is mean and despicable, but it is a thousand times more sinful when displayed toward the Father of mercies, the Fountain of blessing, the Author of every good and perfect gift.

I have chosen two verses to remark upon from the account of a most gracious miracle worked by our blessed Lord. He did indeed confer an unspeakable mercy on the ten men healed by Him on this occasion, for they were lepers. Out of the ten thus healed, cleansed, and restored to daily life by the Son of God, only one came back to thank the adorable Jesus. Only one returned, glorified God for His mercy, and gave thanks! This man was a Samaritan, and so despised by the Jews; the Samaritan was grateful, but where, indeed, were the nine? Alas! We are all too apt to forget the blessings and benefits of redeeming love. May the Holy Ghost revive His work in the hearts of those who have long loved their Savior, making them more grateful, and may He teach those to love and praise Christ so that we may all unite in blessing our God for the mercies of this life, but above all for "the hope of glory" through our Lord Jesus Christ!

ELIZABETH JULIA HASELL

Tarry Not

How shall we escape, if we neglect so great salvation?
—HEBREWS 2:3

Why do you tarry? Have you any reason whatever to give Him? What will you say? Do not flatter yourself that all this delay and putting off is any preparation for coming, much less any part of coming to Him. There are no steps in coming to Jesus. Either you come, or you do not come. There is only the one step—out of self, into Christ. There are no gradations of approach marked out in His Word. If you think there are, search and see. Do not take my word for it. Look for yourself, and see what the Lord's Word is about. You have nothing to gain, but very much—perhaps everything—to lose by tarrying. You are accumulating the guilt of disobedience. You are, it may be very unconsciously, hardening your heart and making the great step more and more difficult. Instead of being in a better position for coming tomorrow, you will be in a worse one.

While you are doing nothing, the enemy is very busy strengthening his toils around you, and they will be stronger tomorrow than today. While you are, as you fancy, only lying still, you are drifting fast down the stream into the stronger current, nearing the rapids, nearing the fatal fall. It is a question of life and death. Escape for your life; don't look behind you, neither stay in all the plain.

I do not know any one promise in all the Bible for the lingerers. And if you put yourself out of the sphere of God's promise, what have you to found any hope at all upon? Tarry not! Oh, if I could but reach you and rouse you! For one who perishes through straightforward refusal, there are probably thousands who perish through putting off. How shall we escape if we refuse—no, if we merely neglect—so great salvation?

&⊶ FRANCES RIDLEY HAVERGAL

Kept in the Furnace

For thou hast been a strength to the poor,
a strength to the needy in his distress, a refuge from the storm,
a shadow from the heat, when the blast of the terrible
ones is as a storm against the wall.

—ISAIAH 25:4

B eloved in the Lord, when anything tries me and my heart sinks, the moment I think of God, the burden is either lightened or removed. The name—the very name—of Jesus soothes and comforts, and I feel that nothing is wrong, but all is right that He permits.

Oh, it is sweet to repose in His bosom and shelter there until the storm is past. How is it that the Lord places His people so frequently, and keeps them so long, in the furnace? When one trial is over another comes, scarcely, sometimes, allowing breathing time between! Wave resounding to wave! Oh, it is because He loves us and will have us know it. And when trouble comes, small or great, we then shelter beneath His wings or nestle within His bosom and feel the very throbbing of His heart.

Who can sound the depth or measure the dimensions of the love of God toward His people—its depth, its height? Eternity alone can unfold it. It passes knowledge. We sometimes have such a taste of it here as makes us long to depart and be with Christ, which is far better. May the presence of the Lord be with you, may His love comfort you, and may His arms encircle you to preserve you from all evil!

෴ MARY WINSLOW

Divine Strengthening

I will strengthen thee; yea, I will help thee.

—ISAIAH 41:10

Who will come with me to the King, to lay at His feet a petition for the fulfillment of this word of His grace upon which He has caused us to hope? We shall be a company of Feeble-Minds, Much-Afraids, Fearings, and Ready-to-Halts, and we may make but a sorry appearance in His courts. But our necessities admit of no delay, and this King is so gracious and has so much love and pity for weak and needy ones that He is sure to grant us not an audience merely, but according to the desire of our heart. My own condition is such that I must have His help or utterly fail, and I know there are many in like stress of need who will seek the King's face with me.

Blessed be His name! We may come into His presence with holy boldness and confidence, bringing with us the warrant of our faith in His own precious promise, fairly and legibly written on the pages of His Word without blot or erasure, and with no "ifs" and "buts" to mar its sublime simplicity: "I will strengthen thee; yea, I will help thee." Does He not love to be trusted? Does He not honor faith? Can one word of His good promise fail, or shall not the thing which He has said surely come to pass?

And, as to our present need of succor, some of us can say, with tear-filled eyes, "O Lord, if weakness be a plea for Thy promised strength, then are we truly fit objects of Thy mercy, for we are at the lowest ebb of helplessness. We have scarcely strength enough left to feel that we are feeble." We are "brought into the dust of death." God has "weakened our strength in the way" to teach us our dependence upon Himself; He has humbled us that He may lift us up. He has shown us our own nothingness that He may be our all-in-all.

&ofSUSANNAH SPURGEON

His Grace Is Sufficient

And he said unto me, My grace is sufficient for thee:
for my strength is made perfect in weakness. Most gladly
therefore will I rather glory in my infirmities, that
the power of Christ may rest upon me.

—2 CORINTHIANS 12:9

When I sink under the contemplated difficulties of a missionary life, how consoling has been the beloved promise, "My grace is sufficient for thee." Have I anything but an unfaithful, depraved heart to discourage me in this great undertaking? Here the almighty God, the maker of all worlds, the infinite disposer of all events, has pledged His word for the safety of His believing children. Sooner will the universe sink into nothing than God will fail in performing His promises. The cause is good; the foundation is sure. If the Savior has promised a sufficiency of His almighty grace, what have I to fear? O that I had a stronger confidence in God—a heart to rely on Him for grace to help in every time of need. Be the difficulties ever so many, the trials ever so great, the employment ever so arduous, He has assured me that His grace will be sufficient to support, to comfort, and to carry me safely through. And when I reach my journey's end, how trifling will earthly sorrows appear!

This is indeed a wretched world! How few the joys! How many the various sorrows of life! Well, if this world is unsatisfying, "if cares and woes promiscuous grow," how great the consolation that I shall soon leave it! "Loose, then, from earth, the grasp of fond desire, weigh anchor, and the happier climes explore."

In the paradise of God, every rising wish that swells the heart of the celestial inhabitant is immediately gratified. O to be dismissed from this earthly tabernacle! O for an entrance into those lovely mansions! My soul pants for the full enjoyment of God.

❧ HARRIET NEWELL

From Death unto Life

*He that heareth my word, and believeth on him
that sent me, hath everlasting life, and shall not come into
condemnation; but is passed from death unto life.*

—JOHN 5:24

Two distinct states with nothing between. No broad space between the two where we may stand, leading to the one or the other; only a boundary line too fine to balance upon. Not many steps—not even two or three from one to the other, but one step from death unto life; the foot lifted from hollow crust over the volcanic fire and set upon the Rock of salvation. How tremendously important to know whether this step is taken, but how clear and simple the test: "He that heareth my word, and believeth on him that sent me, hath everlasting life, and shall not come into condemnation; but is passed from death unto life." Are you trembling and downhearted, wanting some very strong consolation for your very weak faith? Lay hold of this. See how the rope is let down low enough to meet the hand that you can scarcely lift.

"He that heareth my word." Can you say you have not heard? You have heard His word as His word, recognizing it as such, receiving it not as the word of men but as it is in truth, the word of God. It is come unto you because it is sent unto you. The word of Jesus is heard by your innermost self, and you would not be hearing and recognizing it if you were still dead. A marble statue hears not. "And believeth on him that sent me." "But that is the very question," you say. "If I were sure I believed, I should know I had everlasting life." Why should you know? Because He says so, and you could not but believe what He says.

This is your position now—made nigh instead of far off; reconciled to God instead of "enemies in your mind"; found instead of lost; passed from death unto life. And all because Jesus passed from life unto death, even the cross, for you; because it was the Father's will that He should come as the only required sacrifice for sin, and He, our Lord Jesus Christ, was content to do it.

☙ FRANCES RIDLEY HAVERGAL

Triumph of Faith over Difficulties

Let us hold fast the profession of our faith without
wavering; (for he is faithful that promised).
—HEBREWS 10:23

When a promise is given, it certainly will be fulfilled, but we are sure to come into circumstances to try it and try our faith in it. The Lord promised a son to Abraham and Sarah, but what years elapsed for the trial of faith before his birth; and when the son was given, what a fiery trial to take him up to Mount Moriah for a burnt offering. Could faith live upon its prospects through such a trial? And could the promise stand sure amid such apparent contradictions? Yes, indeed! "He was faithful who promised," and He enabled faith to rest in the promise. We know that faith was not disappointed.

Again, David was anointed king, and the kingdom was promised to him. But see how faith was tried when he was hunted by Saul like a partridge upon the mountains, when he was a stranger in Gath, and when, like a homeless wanderer, he was sheltered with his men in the cave of Adullam. Yet he was still a king in the divine purpose, and at the set time he possessed the kingdom. And thus throughout the Word and in our own experience, we find how faith and the promise have been sharply tried, providentially and spiritually. The Lord may seem to have given us a promise, faith and hope may have been drawn out to expect it, and the Word may quite warrant it, but it has to go into the fire before fulfillment, as it was with our fathers.

The soul looks for light but beholds darkness; for peace but beholds evil. This is a hard lesson, but it is the way of faith, and leads to the city which has foundations. See what apparent contradictions the worthies of old had to endure, how contrary to flesh and sense were the Lord's dealings with them. But as surely as the promised seed was born unto Abraham, and as surely as David sat upon the throne of Israel, so surely shall the soul which the Holy Spirit is exercising with the hard things of its nature's evils find the end better than the beginning.

≈ RUTH BRYAN

Faint Not

For which cause we faint not; but though our outward man
perish, yet the inward man is renewed day by day.
—2 CORINTHIANS 4:16

Oh the blessedness of having God for our helper! But we must keep near to Him. If His children transgress and forsake Him, He removes that light in which they live, and they are overwhelmed with sorrow. How much comfort do we lose by slackening our diligence in duty and neglecting to watch against sin? How oft have sin and Satan striven to draw my heart from Him I love? And alas! "How successfully," is the mournful language of every Christian.

But, there is a world where sin shall assault us no more, where the song of victory shall never be interrupted by regrets and lamentations, where progress in knowledge and bliss shall be rapid, unceasing, and endless. Blessed world! Does not the hope of it make the trials, sufferings, conflicts—the wrestling of this—comparatively easy? Oh! Keep heaven much in view. It will strengthen you to overcome those legions of corruptions against which every Christian must fight till he dies. Be daily and hourly committing yourself to Him who is mighty to save—who, if you look to Him, certainly will strengthen you to resist every sin, endure every pain, and bear every trial to His glory. What a blessed thing to glorify God in any way He appoints! It is better to glorify God than to possess worlds! And this you may do. This you will do if you go out of yourself and seek all your supplies of grace and strength immediately from Christ, for He will then enable you to do it.

May the God of mercy bless you. May the Savior of sinners wash and justify you. May the Holy Ghost sanctify you wholly, in soul, body, and spirit.

ॐ SUSAN HUNTINGTON

Counsels How to Meet Daily Cares

For his God doth instruct him to discretion, and doth teach him.

—ISAIAH 28:26

My heart has just been much drawn out toward you in Isaiah 28:26, desiring that you may have the experience of it in those domestic and secular cares that must necessarily devolve upon you, that you may not set them as a "wall between" your soul and your God. May each anxiety and perplexity, which seems to have more of Martha than of Mary, be to you just an errand to Him who is head over all things, that you may commune with Him in them and by them and thus walk with God while you walk in the duties of your family and station. How beautiful to read from verse 23 of the same chapter and to see that the Lord so minutely instructs the laborer how to prepare the ground and sow the seed, as also how to prepare the corn for food.

How touching also to read of David going to inquire of the Lord about everything with such sweet simplicity, asking whether he should go against his enemies and pursue those who had robbed him, even telling the Lord of a report he had heard about Saul and asking if it were true. Satan and the carnal mind would say, "It is not right to approach the Lord in such inward confusion; wait till the mind is more calm and spiritual." But David came in the midst of all, bringing his doubts and uncertainties with him, and in all the Lord answered him.

I cannot tell you how precious these thoughts have been to me or how often I have resorted to them to encourage my heart to trust in the Lord in secular things and to expect His teaching in daily cares great and small. I know the enemy will fight hard to keep you out of this privilege, trying to make it appear that in different circumstances you could walk more closely with the Lord. This is one of his devices to separate us from our God. Oh, for the Spirit's light to discover his snares of darkness! We each are in the best place to glorify the Lord; and present events, whether pleasing or painful, are those in which to be seeking Him.

☙ RUTH BRYAN

Christ's Glorious Victory

For as by one man's disobedience many were made sinners,
so by the obedience of one shall many be made righteous.
—ROMANS 5:19

If the victory and glory of worldly princes were great because they did overcome great hosts of men, how much more was Christ's greater, which vanquished not only the prince of this world but all the enemies of God: triumphing over persecution, injuries, villainies, slanders—yea death, the world, sin, and the devil—and brought to confusion all carnal prudence.

The princes of the world never did fight without the strength of the world. Christ contrarily went to war even against all the strength of the world. He would fight as David did with Goliath (1 Sam. 17), unarmed of all human wisdom and policy and without all worldly power and strength. Nevertheless, He was fully replenished and armed with the whole armor of the Spirit. And in this one battle He overcame forever all His enemies.

There was never so glorious a spoil, neither a more rich and noble, than Christ was upon the cross, who delivered all His elect from such a sharp, miserable captivity. He had in this battle many stripes, yea, and lost His life, but His victory was so much the greater. Therefore, when I look upon the Son of God with a supernatural faith and sight, so unarmed, naked, given up, and lone with humility, patience, liberality, modesty, gentleness, and with all other His divine virtues, beating down to the ground all God's enemies and making the soul of man so fair and beautiful, I am forced to say that His victory and triumph was marvelous. And therefore Christ deserved to have this noble title: Jesus of Nazareth, King of the Jews (Matt. 27:37).

❧ KATHERINE PARR

Faith's Sufficiency

*But the LORD thy God turned the curse into a blessing
unto thee, because the LORD thy God loved thee.*

—DEUTERONOMY 23:5

Here, my soul, in this most sweet assurance you will find the Lord's one reason for all His dealings with you, whether tender or severe. In this earthly pilgrimage, you do meet with so many experiences and providences that are inexplicable and mysterious, that you are apt to say, "Why this trial, Lord? Why this affliction? Why this disappointment of all my hopes and plans?"

My heart, until you have learned the lesson of perfect trust, doubts and misgivings are sure to arise and cloud your fairest prospects. The darkness looks impenetrable when you try to peer into it, the rough places seem impassable when your weary feet stumble over the big stones in the pathway, the mountains of difficulty appear inaccessible when the mists of unbelief veil their true proportions. Verily, the Lord is a God that hides Himself, and, oftentimes, His purposes are carried out on our behalf under cover of the thick clouds in which He enwraps Himself.

"Because the Lord thy God loved thee." It completely solves all doubts and wipes away all tears; it is a specific for every fear, a refuge from every distress. No sweeter assurance could fill my trembling heart with joy, no softer resting place could be found for a weary, heavy-laden sinner.

To know, of a surety, that all God's dealings with me are those of a loving Father toward a dear and well-beloved; to be absolutely certain that every sorrow conceals a blessing because He has appointed it; to look upon pain, trial, and bitter experiences as the outcome of a love that is so infinite that I cannot fathom it; this is to live in "the secret place of the Most High" and to "abide under the shadow of the Almighty."

స SUSANNAH SPURGEON

Our Compassionate High Priest

For in that he himself hath suffered being tempted,
he is able to succour them that are tempted.

—HEBREWS 2:18

It may be you will say, "Alas, I am so confused and dark, so weak and wounded, that I can neither stand my ground for Christ nor run to Him." If this is your case, then know for your comfort that the Captain of your salvation stands for you and will come to you when you cannot come to Him. Your compassionate High Priest has affections for you, every way proportionate to the measure of your distress. He is a man of affections—yea, the God of affections. The compassions of our gospel High Priest are infinite! And having Himself suffered, being tempted in all points like unto us, He is able also, from an inward, experimental feeling of the power of temptations, to succor us when tempted.

And as He has an ability of affections to pity us, and an ability of strength to help us, so He has also authority from His Father, the broad seal of heaven, to be our physician to heal us; and He is "faithful to him that appointed him," so that our Jesus is just such a Savior as we need. "The Spirit of the Lord," says He "hath sent me to bind up the brokenhearted, to proclaim liberty to the captives, and the opening of the prison to them that are bound…to give unto them…the oil of joy for mourning, the garment of praise for the spirit of heaviness; that they might be called trees of righteousness, the planting of the LORD, that he might be glorified" (Isa. 61:1–3). This was the work the God of all grace sent Him about, and, oh, with what amazing tenderness does He perform it. "He healeth the broken in heart, and bindeth up their wounds" (Ps. 147:3). And thus the Lord Jesus would deal with you, my dear sister; therefore, be strong, and fear not.

Into His arms I commit you, earnestly desiring that happy morning of divine favor shall arise upon your soul when the short night of your present weeping is over. Christ will see you again, and your heart shall rejoice, and "your joy shall no man take from you."

&ANNE DUTTON

Mine Eyes Shall See

And though after my skin worms destroy this body,
yet in my flesh shall I see God.
—JOB 19:26

Only the true servant of God can look forward, with holy joy, to seeing the Savior "stand at the latter day upon the earth." To all others His appearing will cause alarm and a just dread. But even the true believer must look forward to this event with awe and feel that if it were not for the blood of Christ to wash and purify him, and the merits and righteousness of Christ to dress him, he could never meet the Judge in peace. The best among us must be saved by mercy.

The next words refer to the well-known and sad fact that our bodies, after death, must see corruption, but true as this is, the astonishing truth comes next to comfort us: "Yet in my flesh shall I see God." Yes, my dear friends, we "believe in the resurrection of the body." After death and corruption—nay, in many cases after our dust cannot be distinguished from the ground around it—shall every body arise at that last day and every body be joined to its own soul and shall live forever. May you remember that your bodies will live again, and therefore may they now be temples of the Holy Ghost! So shall you attain unto a glorious resurrection through Jesus Christ our Lord.

Yes, "every eye shall see Him"—the bad and the good, the sinner and the saint. But how differently will the saint and the sinner view His appearing! My dear friends, however little some of you may have thought of these great things, yet begin to attend to them now. Your eyes must behold the Lord Jesus. May you meet Him in peace! My dear friends who do believe in the Lord and who do look for His appearing, I pray you be diligent, and make your calling and election sure.

❧ ELIZABETH JULIA HASELL

God in Our Small Events

But seek ye first the kingdom of God, and his righteousness;
and all these things shall be added unto you. Take
therefore no thought for the morrow: for the morrow
shall take thought for the things of itself.

—MATTHEW 6:33–34

How unspeakably precious and sweet it is when we can believe that God our Father in heaven is absolutely directing the most minute circumstances of our short sojourn in this wilderness world! That nothing, however trivial, takes place, whether it relates to the body or the soul, but is under His control—in fact, is ordered by Himself! But how hard it is to believe this, particularly when things look dark and we cannot discern the way we should take. It is, then, the providence of faith to wait upon the Lord, keeping a steadfast eye upon Him only, looking for light, help, and deliverance not from the creature, but from Jehovah Himself. This is conflict—for the flesh, the world, and Satan are in opposition to it. Well may it be called precious faith!

But how happy do those travel on whose faith can discern God's hand in everything, but I fear the number is very small who do so live. I cannot imagine how those who deny God's particular providence can get comfortably on, for they must perpetually be confronted with minute events in their history as mysterious and baffling to them as greater ones. And if, too, they really believe in a general providence extending over all events—ruling, governing, and shaping them at His will—they must believe that a universal necessity involves a particular government. I think, in the main, this is one reason God chooses poverty and affliction and want as the chief lot of His people here, that through the teaching of the Holy Ghost, this precious grace of faith might be worked out in their souls' experience.

❧ MARY WINSLOW

Coming after Jesus

Whosoever will come after me, let him deny himself,
and take up his cross, and follow me.
—MARK 8:34

Following is the only proof of coming. There is hardly a commoner lamentation than this: "I do not know whether I have come or not!" And nobody ever says that with a happy smile. When so much hinges upon it—poverty or riches, safety or danger, life or death—uncertainty must and will be miserable. Now, do you really want to know whether you have come or not? Our Lord gives you the test: "Come and follow me!" If you are willing for that, willing with the will that issues in act and deed, then the coming is real. If you are not willing to follow, then you may dismiss at once any idea that perhaps you have come or are coming. There is no reality in it, and there is nothing for you but to go away sorrowful, as the rich young man did, who came but would not follow.

The following will be just as real and definite as the coming, if there is any reality in you at all and if you are not deluding yourself with a deceitful cloud-land of sentimental religion, without foundation and substance, which is but a refuge of lies that the hail shall sweep away. Do not sit down in the most serious state of uncertainty, but give diligence to make your calling and election sure. But you say, "How am I to know whether I am following?" Well, following is not standing still. Clearly it is not staying just where you always were. You cannot follow one thing without coming away from something else. Apply this test. What have you left for Jesus? What have you left off doing for His sake? If you are moving onward, some things must be left behind. What are the things that are behind in your life? If the supposed coming has made no difference in your practical daily life, do not flatter yourself that you have ever yet really come at all. Jesus says, "If any man will come after me, let him deny himself, and take up his cross, and follow me." What light does that saying throw upon your case?

&- FRANCES RIDLEY HAVERGAL

Fathomless Ocean of Love

And to know the love of Christ, which passeth knowledge,
that ye might be filled with all the fulness of God.
—EPHESIANS 3:19

Though we have had so many feasts upon a precious Jesus, we find each time as much freshness as though we had never partaken before. This has been very striking to me; things of earth often repeated grow stale, but the same view of a precious Jesus a thousand times over is ever new. How often has the Divine Spirit testified in our souls "of the sufferings of Christ—and the glory that would follow." How often have we, by faith, beheld His bloody sweat in the garden and spent sweet, solemn moments at the foot of the cross. Yet, when Jesus shows Himself again to us in either of those sacred positions, is He not as a lamb newly slain? And is not His sacrifice a sweet-smelling aroma—as fragrant as though but just offered, without spot unto God? Oh yes, He is ever the same, without sameness, and will be to all eternity. The glories, beauties, and excellences of His person are infinite. And from these boundless sources our finite minds will be feasted forever and ever. We "shall be abundantly satisfied with the fatness of thy house; and thou shalt make [us] drink of the river of thy pleasures."

Oh that my poor, contracted heart were more enlarged into this our fathomless ocean of love and loveliness! Oh to abide in Him forever! "One thing have I desired of the Lord, that will I seek after; that I may dwell in the house of the Lord all the days of my life, to behold the beauty of the Lord, and to inquire in his temple." Christ is our true temple; in Him we may inquire of the Lord concerning all our hard cases and have an answer of peace. In Him we see the beauty of the Lord, even all His divine attributes harmonizing and glorified in saving poor sinners. This is seeing the King in His beauty, and beauty indeed it is in the eye of a sin-sick soul to see the holy Jehovah "a just God, and a Savior" too.

&. RUTH BRYAN

Out of the Dust

I was brought low, and he helped me.
—PSALM 116:6

Most of us have need of this discipline of complete failure in ourselves to convince us that our strength is in God alone. He has had to humble and prove us to know what is in our heart. And, alas! With some of us, it has taken as long a time to do this as in the days of old, when the Lord's people wandered in the wilderness for forty years before they learned the lesson. Ah! What trouble our God takes with us! What ungrateful, perverse, rebellious children we have been! He has had to empty us of so much that is abominable in His sight—our pride, our self-sufficiency, our carnal security, our own righteousness—before He could fill us with His Spirit and take pleasure in us, that it is no wonder the process has been a painful one and has cost us many a cry and groan. We have been cast headlong from the heights of our pride and self-exaltation, and then, as we lay bruised and bleeding on the ground of self-abasement, crushed under a sense of our own utter weakness, the Lord has drawn near and given this gracious assurance: "I will strengthen thee; yea, I will help thee. I, the Lord thy God, will hold thy right hand, saying unto thee, fear not."

But how shall I describe the joy with which we caught the first soft whisper of His tender voice and recognized the strength-giving touch of His mighty hand? "I was brought low," we said (the words were scarcely audible, we were so weak), but faith touched our lips with a cordial, and then, loud and clear from our unloosened tongue, rang out the triumphant testimony, "and he helped me."

Is it not wonderful, the incoming of divine strength into an empty heart? Now we know by experience what the apostle meant when he wrote, "He said unto me, My grace is sufficient for thee; for my strength is make perfect in weakness." Here we have the same Promiser and the same promise, but in other words.

❧ SUSANNAH SPURGEON

Only a Moment

*But he knoweth the way that I take: when he hath
tried me, I shall come forth as gold.*

—JOB 23:10

The shortness of the saints' affliction is matter of great consolation; it is but for a moment. A moment is but a short space—the smallest division of time—and unto a moment are our longest afflictions compared. Suppose they should last as long as we are in this world. Even our whole life if compared with a vast eternity is but like a moment, and as Mr. Dod well says, "What can be great to him that counts the world nothing? Or long to him that counts his life but a span?" Oh! Were we more frequent in our converse with eternity, it would make the afflictions of this present time appear short. Did we live more in the views of approaching glory, we should remember our afflictions as waters that pass away, that are here one moment and gone the next. But, alas, such is our folly, that we are taking thought for a great while to come and so make our apprehended future trials present distresses; whereas, were we under the most pressing weights and did take thought for no more than the day (and sufficient is the evil thereof), living by faith on the borders of glory, as just entering into the mansions of rest, it would alleviate our sorrows and make the longest trial appear short.

Could we thus reason with ourselves every day, "Well, I have got one day nearer home; the afflictions of the past day I shall never go through any more, and perhaps because I see another day in this world I may see glory's day—a morning that will have no clouds nor evening to succeed it, no sorrow, sin, nor death to darken its luster! Oh what a means would this be to increase our patience and make us of an enduring spirit! And what matter of comfort is it that while our short-lived afflictions last, Christ will be with us in them! So our dear Lord Jesus will stand among the distresses. His presence with us in affliction will make it light, and His delivering-kindness out of it will make it short.

&. ANNE DUTTON

Ongoing Speech

He being dead yet speaketh.
—HEBREWS 11:4

My dear friends, I would not speak to you today much of righteous Abel, of whom these touching words were actually spoken in Hebrews 11 in that memorable list of Old Testament worthies. His God accepted and commended him, for his sacrifice was of faith.

It is a very awful thought that wicked people, long after they have passed away from this world, yet speak. The bad and infidel writer, when his body is laid in the grave and when his unhappy soul too late discovers the truth of God's despised Word, yet speaks by the poisonous books he left behind him. The wicked parent who brought up his children in sin, "being dead," by his example "yet speaketh."

The words of the Christian, and still more the remembrance of his good example, may speak long after his death. The godly parent whose righteous example and good words were little heeded by a careless child during that parent's life "still speaketh" when the spirit of the parent is "with Christ," and the heedless son or daughter remembers the good example and conversation of the departed and turns unto God. The preacher whose voice warned the sinner, instructed the ignorant, comforted the afflicted, and edified the saint from the pulpit "still speaketh" after death! His words are not forgotten by his hearers, and his holy example is remembered.

All men, women, and children who have done their "duty in that state of life to which it hath pleased God to call them" (and no one can really do his duty who is not a Christian) "still speak," though far away from this world. Some speak to a larger circle, others to a lesser one. Are there any who have no influence and are voiceless after death? No, my friends, there never lived a person who had positively no influence whatever!

❧ ELIZABETH JULIA HASELL

The Bosom of Jesus

The righteous cry, and the LORD heareth.
—PSALM 34:17

There is no nest below without a thorn; this you well know and therefore will not expect it. But there is a bosom without a thorn, even where John leaned, and where, by faith, unworthy I often lean and find sweet rest and refreshing; in that dear bosom and in that dear heart "yet there is room," room even for you, O weary one! There you shall find no rebuke, no spurning, no upbraiding. The invitation to the laboring and the weary is, "Come unto me, and I will give you rest." Nor did those precious lips ever utter one unmeaning word. He means it all, and His ear and heart are open to all the sorrowful complaint of those poor and needy ones whom He invited to His rest.

How many a long, sad tale has He privileged me to breathe out to Him such as none else would have had patience to listen to or cared to redress. Others would have called it fancy or imaginary trouble, but He bore with it all and either delivered out of it or in it—either made a way of escape or gave strength to endure through finding in Him enough to fill and satisfy under it all. Then at other times He has discovered the illusion of the enemy, kindly shown me that I really was fretting under imaginary evil and, without upbraiding, has set me on high from him that was puffing at me. When under deep and sore trials, His heart and arm and counsel have been for my support all-sufficient. Oh, what a friend is Christ to me! And not less to you, my beloved. Oh! Come then and magnify the Lord with me, and let us exalt His name together. Do not let us be murmuring in these tents of flesh, but by faith going forth to Jesus. Our Father has not appointed us any portion in self, but He has given Christ, the true manna, to be our portion for time and eternity; and the more we are brought to feed upon Him by faith, the less we shall need or desire aught beside. Oh, may the blessed Spirit bring us to this dear privilege, so that we may grow up into Him, our living Head, in all things!

☙ RUTH BRYAN

The Conflict

There hath no temptation taken you but such as is common
to man: but God is faithful, who will not suffer you to be tempted
above that ye are able; but will with the temptation also make
a way to escape, that ye may be able to bear it.

—1 CORINTHIANS 10:13

These are sweet promises to a trembling soul that feels it cannot stand a moment alone and yet longs to walk in the Lord's way without stumbling—yea, to "run the way of his commandments" with an enlarged heart. Such may be overtaken in a fault, but they will not trifle with sin. They feel it an evil and bitter thing, and if they are sure that they are delivered from its final consequences, they want deliverance also from its present power. This is the breathing and panting of a regenerated heart; the new creature, or new man, is "created in righteousness and true holiness," though it dwells in a leprous house. I wish every act of conformity to the world may sting like an adder and bite like a serpent. How cruel! But it is what I wish for myself. Truly, we owe a hearty thanks to the convincing Spirit for all His sharp rebukes. He is that faithful friend who will not suffer us to sin without a reproof, but smiting is welcome from this Righteous One.

When the Lord is on our side, we will put the foot of faith upon the necks of our enemies, and He will subdue them. Fear not! The battle is the Lord's, and though you may often feel foiled, it is to teach you where your strength and victory lie—not in any conquests of your own but in the achievements of your Captain upon Mount Calvary. There see him bruise the head of Satan. There see your sin pierce Him. There see His Father bruise Him and put Him to grief for your iniquities and in your stead. Would you know what sin is, what justice is, what pardon is, what love is, what victory is? You must learn all at Calvary and in Gethsemane. I know the Holy Spirit keeps the key of those sacred places, but it is well to wait prayerfully at the gate till it shall be said, in experience, "Unto you it is given to know the mysteries of the kingdom of heaven."

෴ RUTH BRYAN

Looking from Self to Christ

*And I will bring the blind by a way that they knew not;
I will lead them in paths that they have not known: I will make
darkness light before them, and crooked things straight. These
things will I do unto them, and not forsake them.*

—ISAIAH 42:16

The Lord is leading you more and more into your own heart by nature, and when He empties you of all you are so prone to cling to, which is so hard to let go, then He will show you His own sufficient and all-glorious righteousness and the abundance of love treasured up for you, as if there were not another poor sinner upon the face of the earth to receive it but yourself. This will repay you for all the roughness of the path you are now treading. You must feel your lost and undone condition before you will ever come and cast yourself at the feet of Jesus. You may fancy you do come as such, but He who knows the windings and deceitfulness of the human heart can tell far better than you can. The whole need not a physician, but the sick; and if you would only dwell more upon Christ and recollect why He came into the world, and if it were fully settled in your mind as a matter of fact that He did come for no other purpose than to save sinners, you would soon feel your burden gone, succeeded by a heart full of joy.

Look off yourself, and look into the loving heart of Jesus, and be assured, the more you see of His loveliness, the more you will see your own nothingness. Lie low at the foot of the cross. Do not look within for comfort; look out of yourself, and you will find it all in Christ. The Lord is doing great things for your soul. It is the right way. The law is a schoolmaster to bring you to Christ. The law is not convincing you that you are a sinner; this the pride of nature resists. But the same blessed Spirit who is showing you the vileness of your own heart will in due time show you also the heart of Christ. Be of good courage; Jesus makes you whole. But do not stop until you are able to say with Thomas, "My Lord and my God."

ॐ MARY WINSLOW

The Warfare

Fight the good fight of faith, lay hold on eternal life.

—1 TIMOTHY 6:12

I now wish to say, hold fast the beginning of your confidence. Your experience is that of God's people. To rejoice in the Lord at all times is your privilege, but will not be always your attainment. The Lord has done great things for you, whereof I am glad. But, my dear friend, the warfare is not over: you must endure trials as others; engage with "principalities and powers, and spiritual wickedness in high places"; and, worst of all, a treacherous heart within, which, for all that it has seen and tasted, is yet corrupt and deceitful. The new life that Christ gives to the soul evidences itself in the desires of the heart and affections. As certainly as the newborn babe desires the breast, as certainly and as evidently does the newborn soul desire union to God, communion with Him, and conformity to Him in heart, life, and conversation. This principle is in its own nature perfectly pure, but the old nature, the law in the spiritual members, is perfectly corrupt: "In my flesh dwelleth no good thing."

In the order of God's covenant it has not pleased Him to deliver even believers, all at once, from sinful inclinations and passions. He has provided for their final complete deliverance, and sin shall not have dominion over them even here, but it is still in them while in the body, and a dying body. The remains of sin in the soul make the believer's life warfare, and this world a wilderness. Soul and body are diseased; both are redeemed, and provision made for the entire deliverance of both—for the soul at death, for the body at the resurrection. I write not to dishearten you, but as a friend I warn you, lest you fall again into unbelief. Look not within for comfort, for consolation, for confidence. Christ is the end of the law for righteousness, His blood the atonement, and you are complete in Him. His grace is sufficient for you, His strength shall be perfected in your weakness, and you shall go on.

☙ ISABELLE GRAHAM

The Proof of Christ's Ability to Save

Wherefore he is able also to save them to the
uttermost that come unto God by him, seeing he
ever liveth to make intercession for them.

—HEBREWS 7:25

See what proof that the Lord Jesus Christ is able to save you thus to the uttermost. It is that "he ever liveth to make intercession." For whom? For them "that come unto God by him." Or, as He Himself said in that wonderful prayer when He lifted the veil from His own divine communing with the Father—let us hear His mighty intercession—"Neither pray I for these alone, but for them also which shall believe on me through their word."

Only think what security there must be in it! If the Lord Jesus is praying for you, can you perish? If He is praying for you, will not the Father's answer of blessing be beyond anything you would ask for yourself? Is this not enough to answer all your misgivings as to what you will find and how you will get on when you have come?

There is a solemn side to it. He not only says nothing about making intercession for those who do not come, but He plainly and positively says, "I pray not for the world, but for them which thou hast given me," the proof of having been given to Christ being the coming to Him, for "all that the Father giveth me shall come to me." Then face the terrible position which is yours if you will not come. Christ will not pray for you. You shut yourself out from the prayer of Him whom the Father hears always. He prays not for all alike but only for those who receive His words. He says, "I pray for them; I pray not for the world." You dare not and cannot explain this away. It is no mere inference, no question of differing views, but spoken by Him whose words can never pass away.

&» FRANCES RIDLEY HAVERGAL

Under the Shadow

Because thou hast been my help, therefore
in the shadow of thy wings will I rejoice.

—PSALM 63:7

I should have no intermission from sinking fears and forebodings were it not for the measure of faith, small as it is, that my Savior graciously bestows; it enables me to flee to Him, as my strong tower and my constant hiding place. Every event and every possible occurrence of every day I commit to Him. Satan, with all his designs against my soul; sin, in all its secret workings; the want of my spiritual graces; my daily bread; my bodily pains and infirmities and the fearful apprehension of still greater; and with whatever else adds to my burdens, I gather up and to my Savior go with them and beg Him to enable me to roll them on Him—to leave them with Him—and to make me to abide under the shadow of His wings. And in proportion, as He enables me thus to do, what should proceed from my heart but praise and humiliation?

When I have the comfort of this experience, I say, "Ah, this is the fruit of redeeming love and of sanctified affliction!" Thanks be to God for His secret and sacred teaching! It is true, the east wind has blighted and stripped away those earthly fruits and flowers which I see many of my friends enjoying, but these might have been briars and snares in my carnal heart. Instead of such inferior things, He leads me into the green pastures of His love and by still and refreshing waters, where no deadly poison or envenomed sting lies concealed. I hope, therefore, I can and do say, "Bless the Lord, O my soul!" And oh, may He pity and pardon me whenever faith so fails as that I should for a moment cease to trust in Him or cease to magnify His holy name!

꙳ SARAH HAWKES

In Darkness without Jesus

It was now dark, and Jesus was not come to them.
—JOHN 6:17

I think I can hear some sorrowful soul say, "That exactly expresses my condition: I am sorely troubled and depressed; I see no light; and the dear Lord, who used to be so near, has withdrawn Himself from me." Shall we talk the matter over, dear reader, and try to find out why you are in the dark and why Jesus does not come? The first question is, "How came you there?" Did darkness fall upon you from natural causes, as the night overtook these disciples in the boat? Or, did the Lord bid you enter into the cloud? Is your gloom brought about by the deep shadows of bodily infirmity? Or, have you willfully closed your eyes and thus shut out the light of heaven? Give us now Thy wondrous "searchlight," O Spirit of God, that we may see our own true position!

Sometimes, God sends His children into the dark. The dispensations of darkness, which try the Lord's people, are often His appointment and purpose. An old writer says: "The uses of darkness are manifold: to humble us; to convince us of our absolute helplessness; to prove to us our monetary need of divine sustaining; to make Christ alone the ground of our hope and the object of our boasting by bringing the soul off from everything else, that it may look only to Him."

What must you do if God is thus dealing with you? You must "trust, and not be afraid." "Rest in the Lord, and wait patiently for him." His hand will lead you through the darkness into the light, and all the more quickly if you constantly tell Him how sorely your heart aches with the longing to see again the sunshine of His love. Be assured that He will not leave you comfortless. He will come to you.

꙳ SUSANNAH SPURGEON

Great Promotions

In all these things we are more than conquerors
through him that loved us.

—ROMANS 8:37

It has truly been said that "sanctified afflictions are great promotions." And those promotions come neither from the east nor from the west—but from the Lord alone, by whose power

> *Trials make the promise sweet,*
> *Trials give new life to prayer,*
> *Trials bring me to His feet,*
> *Lay me low and keep me there.*

Many a visit of love has the Lord paid, and many a secret of love has the Lord revealed in the time of affliction, and some of the sweetest communings in the wilderness have been with the thorn in the flesh or the cross on the back. Does not your soul respond to the truth of this? Is not Jesus a precious companion in tribulation? Are not His sympathies most tender? Has He not drawn near in the day when we cried unto Him and said unto us, "Fear not"? Oh yes, the fruits of the valley are very choice, but yet we fear to go down thither, forgetting who has said, "I will go down with thee, and will also surely bring thee up again." "As a beast goeth down into the valley, the Spirit of the LORD caused him to rest: so didst thou lead thy people, to make thyself a glorious name." Are we not brought down into the valley of trouble or humiliation to cause us to rest only in Jesus?

"These things [these afflictive things] I have spoken unto you, that in me ye might have peace. In the world ye shall have tribulation: but be of good cheer; I have overcome the world." At times trials seem to overcome us, yet "in all these we are more than conquerors through him that loved us." The rock of His faithfulness is a blessed retreat when our heart is overwhelmed within us. The honey of His love dropping from that rock does sweetly revive our fainting souls and makes us joyful in tribulation, so that we can sing even in the trial, "He has done all things well."

ૐ RUTH BRYAN

The Recall

O Israel, return unto the LORD thy God;
for thou hast fallen by thine iniquity.
—HOSEA 14:1

Have we not known a wretched mental nausea, a sense of discomfort and restlessness, a misgiving that something is wrong, though we can't say what? No actual pain, no acute attack of anything, but a nameless discomfort most easily described by a negative—that we are not as in months past. If this is the present state of any reader, do let me most earnestly and affectionately entreat you not to remain one day—no, not one hour—in this most dangerous state, the beginning of backsliding, and already a fall from your own steadfastness and your first love. Remember from where you are fallen; look unflinchingly at your position and recognize frankly the difference between today and the past days of closer walking and happy abiding. Do not let yourself drift on, or you will revolt more and more till the whole head is sick and the whole heart faint. Every day's delay will make your case worse.

Do not shrink from asking Him to show you how and why it is that you have fallen. The beautiful crown that He put upon our heads in the time of love would not have fallen from our heads but that we have sinned. It is by "thine iniquity" that thou art fallen— iniquity personal and real, though very likely unguessed by anyone and hidden from thine own eyes.

Perhaps the knowledge of this is already sent. If so, listen! "And I said after she had done all these things, Turn thou unto me." And again, "Though you may have gone after other lovers, yet return again to me," saith the Lord. Oh, forsake the thoughts as well as the way, and return unto the Lord, and He will abundantly pardon. For when He shows them their work and their transgressions, He also commands that they return from iniquity. For He has said, "I will heal their backsliding, I will love them freely."

~ FRANCES RIDLEY HAVERGAL

The Christian's Noblest Resolution

Ah, wretched souls, who strive in vain,
Slaves to the world, and slaves to sin!
A nobler toil may I sustain,
A nobler satisfaction win.

May I resolve with all my heart,
With all my pow'rs, to serve the Lord,
Nor from His precepts e'er depart,
Whose service is a rich reward.

O be His service all my joy,
Around let my example shine,
Till others love the blest employ,
And join in labors so divine.

Be this the purpose of my soul,
My solemn, my determined choice,
To yield to His supreme control,
And in His kind commands rejoice.

O may I never faint nor tire,
Nor wandering leave His sacred ways ;
Great God, accept my soul's desire,
And give me strength to live Thy praise.

                                   ❧ ANNE STEELE

Our Merciful Lord God

*And the L*ORD *passed by before him, and proclaimed, The L*ORD,
*The L*ORD *God, merciful and gracious, longsuffering, and
abundant in goodness and truth, keeping mercy for thousands,
forgiving iniquity and transgression and sin.*

—EXODUS 34:6–7

When was it that the Lord proclaimed this and took unto Himself a name? After Israel, His chosen, had been guilty of that awful sin in the wilderness of making the golden calf and proclaiming, "These be thy gods, O Israel." David takes it up in Psalm 103, "The Lord is merciful and gracious, slow to anger and plenteous in mercy." Read on, then turn to Psalm 130. This God is your God and has been long your God; His work was upon your heart even though you could not discern it. You have long been in bondage, but you were not a willing captive. Unbelief kept you in bondage long, long after your eyes were opened to see your bondage and even to discern, in some feeble measure, your remedy.

If not now, you shall in some after-time know and consider all the way by which He has led you, to prove you, try you, and show you what was in your heart, that He might do you good in your latter end. My friend has been a great unbeliever, yet has the Lord, the sovereign Lord brought you out of a "fearful pit, and out of the miry clay; set your feet upon a rock, and established your goings; put a new song into your mouth, even praise unto our God." Now you sing Psalm 34. Let us exalt His name together.

The Lord Himself is your shepherd. My Bible lies on my lap, and I had turned to Psalm 34 to know if it contained what I would point out to you; on finishing the last verse, I unconsciously turned my eye on the Bible. The words that met it were Psalm 32:8, "I will instruct thee and teach thee in the way which thou shalt go: I will guide thee with mine eye." And so it shall be. Amen, my God, amen. Do as Thou hast said.

                                                ❧ ISABELLA GRAHAM

The Cross before the Crown

If we suffer, we shall also reign with him.

—2 TIMOTHY 2:12

Is there a candidate for the crown of glory that is not tried? Jesus was a tried stone. He passed through deep, overwhelming tribulation and sorrow to save us from eternal woe. And shall we shrink to taste a little of the bitter waters while we pass to the glory that awaits us? He has placed you for a while in the furnace, but not a hair of your head shall be hurt. Only trust Him. This is all that He requests of you. He wants you to prove that He is all He has promised and that He is all that He says He is. Allow no enemy just now to harass you with the thought that you are not the Lord's because all this evil has befallen you. This very chastening is proof of your adoption, without which we should be bastards, and not sons. The Savior loves you too dearly to lay upon you one stroke more than is needful for your soul's best interests.

A life of faith in God is the happiest and holiest life on earth. It brings us into an acquaintance with the real character of God, from whom we walk at too great a distance. There is no part of God's truth that will be of any practical value to us but as it is wrought in our hearts by the Holy Spirit and brought out in our lives by God's providence. Our God knows what dull scholars we are and takes such means as will secure our greatest knowledge and promote our greatest usefulness. If we pause to think what steps we had best take in such-and-such circumstances and then go to the Lord, it is most likely we shall be left to take our own way. But let us go to Him first, with the prayer, "Lord, now direct; Lord, now give me wisdom; Lord, now lead me!" These simple, heaven-sent breathings God will hear and answer; and so shall the life of God in our soul be invigorated, and we shall in this school of trial and faith learn lessons taught us nowhere else.

❧ MARY WINSLOW

Midnight Rememberings

When I remember thee upon my bed, and
meditate on thee in the night watches.

—PSALM 63:6

Memory is never so busy as in the quiet time while we are waiting for sleep, and never, perhaps, are we more tempted to
useless recollections and idle reveries than in the night watches.
Perhaps we have regretfully struggled against them; perhaps
yielded to effortless indulgence in them and thought we could not
help it, and were hardly responsible for vain thoughts at such times.
But here is full help and bright hope. This night let us remember
Thee. We can only remember what we already know; oh praise
Him, then, that we have material for memory! There is enough for
all the wakeful nights of a lifetime in the one word "thee."

Perhaps we know what it is to feel peculiarly weary-hearted
and dispirited on our beds. But when we say, "Oh my God, my
soul is cast down within me," let us add at once, "therefore will I
remember thee." And what then? What comes of thus remembering
Him? "My soul [yes, your soul] shall be satisfied as with marrow
and fatness; and my mouth shall praise thee with joyful lips:
when I remember thee upon my bed, and meditate on thee in the
night watches."

What can be a sweeter, fuller promise than this—our heart's
desire fulfilled in abundant satisfaction and joyful power of praise!
Yet there is a promise sweeter and more thrilling still to the loving, longing heart. "Thou meetest…those that remember thee in
thy ways." And so, this very night, as you put away the profitless
musings and memories and remember Him upon your bed, He
will keep His word and meet you. The darkness shall be verily the
shadow of His wing, for your feeble, yet Spirit-given remembrance
shall be met by His real and actual presence, for "hath he said and
shall he not do it?" Let us pray that this night the desire of our soul
may be to Thy name and to the remembrance of Thee.

&ho; FRANCES RIDLEY HAVERGAL

For His Sheep

All we like sheep have gone astray, we have turned every one to his own way; and the LORD hath laid on him the iniquity of us all.

—ISAIAH 53:6

The Lord, by the prophet, informs us how it came to pass that the great Messiah was wounded for our transgressions and who they were for whom He suffered. The allusion here is to sheep in nature, as that creature has a natural inclination to stray from the fold, and none to return. The straying sheep acts as though it were set up for itself, rejects the government and guidance of its shepherd, puts itself from under his care for sustenance, and chooses to seek pastures at large. And thus indeed all mankind did, in their father, Adam, their federal head: they rejected the government of their God and did not choose to be under His care for sustenance, but chose to have their pastures at large; and they thereby, rejecting the government of their God, set up for themselves.

They cast a slight upon His munificent bounty, who had so well provided for their felicity, and set up for themselves as their own governors, and chose what they liked best to enhance their joy. And they did this, notwithstanding God's strict prohibition and severe threatening. And thereby, instead of gaining greater felicity, they were all plunged most righteously into all present infelicity and the desert and sentence of eternal misery, and all the sheep of Christ among the rest.

But the design of the Holy Ghost, in this text, is not to set forth the state of all men by Adam's sin, but of those sheep which were given to Christ in the everlasting covenant, to be redeemed by Him in the fullness of time, they being equally involved in the same guilt and misery with the rest of Adam's posterity, and for whom Christ was to be the sacrificed lamb. They here are called sheep, as being given from everlasting by the Father to Christ as their great shepherd. And His blood is hence called "the blood of the everlasting covenant," that being the condition of their salvation. And for His sheep, said the Good Shepherd, "I lay down my life."

☙ ANNE DUTTON

The Shadow of God's Wings

In the shadow of thy wings will I make my refuge.
—PSALM 57:1

It is very gracious of the Lord to use the homely illustration of wings and feathers in His Word, for the comfort of His people. The most simple, as well as the most sorrowful, can understand the beauty of it. Many a time have I profitably watched the feathered folk of the farmyard and been taught by them that, in every time of trouble, be it little or great, the safest place in all the world is "under the wings." How well the wee chickens know this! When the least thing alarms them, or the drops of rain come pattering down, they fly quickly to their mother's wings for shelter and safety, and you can see nothing of them but a collection of legs, tiptoeing in the eagerness to press very close to the warm breast that covers them.

Sometimes, I have dared to claim even such an experience! Not content with the blessed fact that I was hidden "beneath His wings," my faith nestled up, as it were, to the loving heart that brooded over me and found such a glow of everlasting love there that all outside ills and evils were as if they were not. Oh, that such times were less rare!

But if any timid, afflicted souls read these few lines, let me whisper to them to run at once to their God "when troubles assail, and dangers affright." We are so safe when "covered with His feathers," so cared for, and comforted, and welcomed, so defended from everything that could harm us.

The hen effectually conceals her brood from any passing enemy, and God is an impenetrable hiding place for His people. Surely this is the meaning of the psalmist when he says, "I will trust in the covert of thy wings."

&~ SUSANNAH SPURGEON

The Power of Sin Put to Death

Knowing that Christ being raised from the dead dieth no more; death hath no more dominion over him. For in that he died, he died unto sin once: but in that he liveth, he liveth unto God. Likewise reckon ye also yourselves to be dead indeed unto sin, but alive unto God through Jesus Christ our Lord. Let not sin therefore reign in your mortal body.

—ROMANS 6:9–12

Christ has not simply overcome sin, but rather He has killed it, inasmuch as He has satisfied for it Himself with the most holy sacrifice and oblation of His precious body in suffering a most bitter and cruel death. Also, He gives all those who love Him so much spirit, grace, virtue, and strength, that they may resist, impugn, and overcome sin, and not consent, neither suffer it to reign in them (Rom. 6–7).

He has also vanquished sin because He has taken away the force of it; that is, He has canceled the law, which was in evil men the occasion of sin (Col. 2:11–14). Therefore, sin has no power against those who are, with the Holy Ghost, united to Christ. In them there is nothing worthy of damnation. And although the dregs of Adam do remain—that is, our strong desires, which indeed are sin, nevertheless they are not imputed for sins if we are truly planted in Christ (Rom. 8:1–2). It is true that Christ might have taken away all our immoderate affections, but He has left them for the greater glory of His Father and for His own greater triumph. And although the children of God sometimes do fall by frailty into some sin, yet that falling makes them humble themselves and acknowledge the goodness of God, and come to Him for refuge and help.

&ev KATHERINE PARR

Our Compassionate Father

Like as a father pitieth his children, so the LORD pitieth
them that fear him. For he knoweth our frame;
he remembereth that we are dust.

—PSALM 103:13–14

I would especially speak today of the comfortable thought that the believer in Christ has a father in the almighty ruler of the universe. In one sense, as our creator, God is the father of all mankind, but not in the tender and endearing sense in which, for Christ's sake, the believer is encouraged to call God his father. In the apostle's words: "As many as are led by the Spirit of God, they are the sons of God." They "have received the Spirit of adoption, whereby we cry, Abba Father." These are "heirs of God, and joint-heirs with Christ."

The believer in Christ may take very great comfort from our short passage. It assures him that God has a very tender, gracious feeling toward him—a fatherly feeling—and that far beyond the strongest parental feeling any human creature could have. It assures the Christian that the Almighty has a perfect knowledge of him in every respect: soul and body are alike known and understood, so to speak, by their maker. We learn, from this passage, that God has a most tender and compassionate feeling for those that fear Him, and that His perfect knowledge of their frames, remembering they are but dust, will never suffer Him to lay upon any of His servants more than they can bear. How should this firm persuasion move us to trust more and more in Him, who is indeed a father to His people! And how delightful is it to observe the mercies—countless, welcome, acceptable, and appropriate—that daily come to the believer! How precious in our sight are daily exemptions from trial, relief from anxiety, and all other mercies when we thank God for them! All minor mercies and comforts are the more acceptable when received as drops from the Eternal Fountain of love.

๛ ELIZABETH JULIA HASELL

With Jesus, Yet Afraid

Where is your faith?
—LUKE 8:25

Ah! Dear friends, does not this teaching come home to our own hearts? Do not we behave in precisely similar fashion [as Jesus' disciples on the ship in the tempest] when we are placed in the same alarming circumstances? Some great trial or temptation bursts like a tempest into the serenity of our life and overwhelms us with a sense of danger and distress. We are terrified and trembling; we see nothing but the peril that surrounds us; we struggle against the storm as best we can till there is no more endurance in us; and then we go to the Master with the bitter cry of those about to perish!

Yet, as a matter of fact, He has been with us all the time. Has He not promised to never leave us? Is there not always access by faith to His gracious presence? He may be in the hinder part of the ship, asleep, and apparently oblivious of all that is passing around Him, but the pillow beneath His head is His own omniscience, and as surely as He ruled those winds and waves on Galilee's lake and reined in the tempest with a word, so certainly does He manage all the affairs of His children and appoint or permit all that concerns them. A sincere and steadfast faith in this blessed fact would keep our minds in perfect peace, whatever might befall us; it would lift us above all fear of the perils and storms of life and hide us in "the secret of his tabernacle."

O beloved, let us cast away from us, with shame and loathing, the bonds of this cruel sin of doubting, which grieves our Savior's tender heart and so shamefully dishonors His love! His pathetic question "Where is your faith?" plainly shows that He expects our absolute trust at all times and that He is disappointed when He fails to find the faith He so much values in His chosen.

࣋ SUSANNAH SPURGEON

Fellowship and Cleansing

Come ye, and let us walk in the light of the LORD.

—ISAIAH 2:5

It is not only the Spirit but the bride who says, "Come." And it is remarkable that the bride is never found saying "come" without including herself: "Come with us." "Come, and let us join ourselves unto the Lord." "Come and let us return unto the Lord." "Let us come boldly." It is always "us," expressed or implied, though the speaker be patriarch, prophet, or apostle. And you may be very sure that those who venture to say "come" to you are truly and deeply feeling the need of continual coming for themselves. If the Master's call were not sounding very fresh and sweet in their own hearts, they would not be constrained to sound it out to you.

"Come ye," then, "and let us walk in the light of the LORD." This is one of the blessed results and tests of true following, as following is of coming. For the Lord says, "He that followeth me shall not walk in darkness, but shall have the light of life." And the results of this walking in the light are fellowship and cleansing, and these, when fully accepted, are all that we can need for the brightest, happiest pilgrim course. "If we walk in the light, as he is in the light, we have fellowship one with another; and the blood of Jesus Christ his Son cleanseth us from all sin."

This is not merely fellowship with other Christians, though that, with all its warmth and pleasantness, is no doubt included. But scholars tell us that the true meaning is that we and the Lord have fellowship with each other—a marvelous mutual interchange of sympathy, interest, and love. "Truly our fellowship is with the Father and with his Son, Jesus Christ." It is the present fact, which yet we cannot fully apprehend, till "at that day ye shall know that I am in my Father, and ye in me, and I in you." "Come ye, and let us walk in the light of the LORD," that this glorious fellowship may be ours.

☙ FRANCES RIDLEY HAVERGAL

Trusting though Tempted

Though he slay me, yet will I trust in him.

—JOB 13:15

Wherefore, my beloved, "grieve not the Spirit"; "resist the devil and he will flee from you." It is he who tries to choke prayer, hinder faith, and feed unbelief. Your only successful resistance is by the "blood of the Lamb"; against that, Satan cannot stand, for it cleanses from all sin. He can bring plenty of accusations against us, and just ones; but when faith can venture them on blood divine, each fiery dart is quenched by that blood; and the self-condemned, hell-deserving sinner is "more than conqueror through him that loved us." No wonder, then, that subtle foe strives so hard against the first buddings of faith and will, if possible, nip the least putting-forth thereof to affright the poor soul from the only Stronghold when he cannot reach it. He shall not prevail ultimately; he shall not rob Emmanuel of one blood-bought jewel.

He has said to law and justice long ago, "If she has wronged you or owes you anything, put that on Mine account: I have written it with Mine own hand; I will repay it." Having bought you and paid for you, He will not lose you. And yet, though Satan shall not rob God of His right to you, he may rob your soul of present comfort, and by giving place to him, you will suffer loss experimentally.

Therefore write I thus, that by the divine blessing your weak hands that hang down may be lifted up, your feeble knees strengthened, and you, though so lame, may not be turned out of the way of faith, but rather have the sore of unbelief healed and be enabled to say, "Though he slay me, yet will I trust in him." "What time I am afraid, I will trust in thee." May you be encouraged to look toward Jesus; if you cannot look at Him, to hope in His salvation if at present you cannot enjoy or triumph in it. And though your sins rise mountains high, presenting a new mountain every day, seek faith, more faith, in that precious blood, which, as a mighty ocean, will overtop them all.

❧ RUTH BRYAN

Putting to Death the Deeds of the Flesh

For if ye live after the flesh, ye shall die: but if ye through the
Spirit do mortify the deeds of the body, ye shall live.
—ROMANS 8:13

It is not difficult to know and believe theoretically that the heart is deceitful and desperately wicked. But to feel it, to trace really its secret winding, to detect how sin insinuates itself into our motives, designs, objects, thoughts, prayers, and every action, sleeping and waking—and, on that account, truly and sincerely to be afraid and ashamed to lift our mouths out of the dust because we are vile and because we cannot open them without danger—these are lessons gradually learned under the teaching of the Holy Spirit in the various means He is pleased to use, and from continual occasions and circumstantial occurrences, by which, as in a glass, an enlightened, observant eye obtains important discoveries of what is hidden within.

You say you abhor yourself because you are proud; and so do I, yet I am proud still. But we must sentence this archfiend to die the death of crucifixion and every day drive in a fresh nail and pray to be made willing that nails should be driven in from every quarter, till it bleeds, if not to death (which it never will in this world), yet till it is enfeebled and overcome by the contrary feelings of self-abasement. The very discipline and subjugation of your natural abilities to the humility and simplicity of a little child will constitute one part of that obedience of faith which is so essential to the Christian character.

᠅ SARAH HAWKES

The Privilege of Intercession

Pray one for another. —JAMES 5:16

Here our divine Master takes up an impulse of natural affection, raising it to the dignity of a royal commandment, and
broadening it to the measure of His own perpetual intercession. For
unless a heart has reached the terrible hardening of being without
natural affection as well as without God, it must want to pray for
those it loves. Intercession should be definite and detailed. Vague-
ness is lifelessness. Paul besought the Romans to pray for him and
then told them exactly what he wanted, four definite petitions to be
presented for him.

We must not yield to the idea that, because we are feeble members doing no great work, our prayers won't make much difference.
It may be that this is the very reason the Lord keeps us in the shade,
because He has need of us for the work of intercession. Many of us
only learn to realize the privilege of being called to this by being
called apart from all other work. When this is the case, let us simply
and faithfully do it, lifting up holy hands without wrath and doubting, blessing His name who provides this holy and beautiful service
for those who by night stand in the house of the Lord.

See how wonderfully Paul valued the prayers of others. He distinctly expresses this to every church but one to whom he wrote.
Would he have asked their prayers so fervently if he thought it
would not make much difference?

Intercession is a wonderful help to forgive of injuries. See how
the personal unkindness of brother and sister stirred up Moses to
pray for each, and how repeatedly the wrong feeling, speaking,
and acting of the people against himself was made the occasion of
prayer for them. Let us avail ourselves of this secret of his meekness. Also, it is an immense help to love. Do we not find that the
more we pray for anyone, the more we love? Let us intercede while
we have time. The night cometh, when no man can work.

&~ FRANCES RIDLEY HAVERGAL

Blessed Rest

*I have fought a good fight, I have finished
my course, I have kept the faith.*
—2 TIMOTHY 4:7

There are two kinds of rest awaiting you: the one in this life, the other not to be attained till the mortal shall put on immortality. When was it that Paul, the great apostle, could say he had fought the good fight? Not till he could also say he had finished his course and was ready to be offered up; till then, he, like others, had to continue the warfare between grace and corruption; like others, found a law in his members warring against the law of his mind so that the thing that he would, he did not, and that which he would not, that he did.

Notwithstanding this, there is a blessed rest attainable here—rest from the fear of wrath and hell; a rest in Christ as our atonement, our surety, our complete righteousness, our title to eternal life, and all the grace necessary to fit us for it. This is the work of faith; or, rather, this is faith itself. The soul established in this can rest in all possible circumstances. It depends not on its frames: in darkness; when it is tossed, tempted, wandering, conscious of unhallowed tempers; perhaps of the actual commission of sin, though at such times the warfare between grace and corruption is so strong as to make the Christian exclaim, "O wretched man that I am! Who shall deliver me from this body of sin and death?"

He can still say, "The Lord lives; blessed be my Rock." The Christian can still say, "My Lord and my God." He is sure the conflict will end and that his God will bring good out of it. He enjoys hope. He feels his state as safe as in the most enlarged frame of mind when he can pray, praise, love, rejoice. This is a riddle that only Christians can understand, and even they require many lessons to comprehend it, many more to practice. Be comforted, fight on, aim at trusting; and you shall, in the Lord's time, also cease from your own works and rest, with more advanced Christians, on the faithfulness of your own God in Christ.

≈ ISABELLA GRAHAM

Planting by Example (1)

Come, ye children, hearken unto me:
I will teach you the fear of the LORD.

—PSALM 34:11

The question of what a religious education is becomes one of deepest interest. Is it to have our children baptized and initiated into knowledge of the general principals of Christianity? Is it to make them attend the regular administration of the Word, to catechize them, to remind them of the greatness of their obligations to become holy and set before them the terrors of the Lord, that we may persuade them to flee from the wrath to come? All this we undoubtedly ought to do. But all this we may do, and yet be found wanting. For we can never too earnestly press upon ourselves the conviction that education is not what we teach our children in detached periods of time, when we are giving them special instruction or explaining to them revealed truths, but rather what we teach them by the silent, but ever-influencing language of our general example.

The mother who recommends religion, in her formal instructions to her children, as a thing of the first importance, while, in her own case, it is habitually driven into a corner; who urges on her children the supreme desirableness of laying up treasures in heaven, while her dearest ones are evinced, by her conduct, to be on earth; who insists on the excellence and importance of meekness, patience, and charity, while she is no way remarkable for the exercise of these graces herself; who descants on the vanity of the world, while she is seen to be a slave to its opinions and fashions; can hardly expect much success from her labors.

But while we must all weep over our shortcomings; while we have occasion to confess to our God and, perhaps, sometimes to acknowledge to our children that the evil which we would not, that we do; it should inspire us with courage that we have a High Priest who is touched with the feelings of our infirmities and who is able to prevent the influences of unallowed miscarriages on the minds and hearts of our little ones.

❧ SUSAN HUNTINGTON

Planting by Example (2)

Come, ye children, hearken unto me:
I will teach you the fear of the LORD.
—PSALM 34:11

If there is a prevailing desire, and a settled purpose and endeavor, to walk before our house with a perfect heart, may we not indulge the humble hope that our accidental mistakes, or occasional deviations, from the path of duty shall not separate His mercy from us and our children?

"The kingdom of God is as if a man should cast seed into the ground; and should sleep, and rise night and day; and the seed should spring and grow up, he knoweth not how." The husbandman, who casts his seed into the bosom of the earth, waits in quiet expectation of the harvest. He plants, he waters, he removes carefully the young weeds that appear and endanger the growth of the grain; and, usually, he does not labor in vain. So is the kingdom of God, or His word in the heart. And, in due season, we may expect to reap if we faint not.

We must, however, prepare ourselves to meet with many hindrances, to resist many discouragements, to overcome many difficulties. The evils resulting from a nature altogether corrupt are too potent to be leveled at one blow. Nor must the recurrence of the manifestation of dispositions, which we had hoped were annihilated, or the relapse into sins that we believed were forsaken, disarm us of resolution and strength to apply, with a steady hand, the proper remedies for these disorders. We are apt to be impatient to enjoy now the fruit of our prayers and tears. And to desire that our little ones may be early brought into God's covenant is certainly proper. But we must remember that now is the time for working. This is our part; to give the blessing is the Lord's. Let us then strive to do our part faithfully and perseveringly. And may we not, safely, leave all that remains with Him?

                                   ❧ SUSAN HUNTINGTON

Encouragements to Venture on Christ

The Lord is very pitiful, and of tender mercy.

—JAMES 5:11

I desire to speak to you in love of our glorious Christ, who "hath been mindful of us, and will bless us." He will be with us through life in six troubles, and in death, the seventh, He will not forsake us. He is very pitiful and of tender mercy to everyone who knows and feels the plague of plagues—that of his own heart. "Go, shew thyself to the priest," however bad it is, for "Him hath God exalted to be a Prince and a Savior, for to give repentance to Israel, and forgiveness of sins." He sweetly invites all that labor and are heavy laden to come to Him and says, "I will give you rest." Are you weary of self and heavy laden with your sins, and are you coming to Jesus? "Come just as you are"; come to Jesus, who says, "Him that cometh to me I will in no wise cast out."

Not for hardness, coldness, darkness, wandering, past sin, present sin, the guilt that presses at this very moment, or for any other will Jesus cast out a coming sinner. The Spirit convinces of sin, the Father draws the sinner, and the Son "receiveth sinners." So the holy Three-in-One are engaged in this great work of bringing souls to Jesus, and who or what shall prevent their coming? Shall the world, or Satan without, or sin within? Nay, verily, "all that the Father giveth me shall come to me."

But, say you, am I given by the Father? Coming to Jesus is a proof of it. Desiring after Jesus is a proof of it. Hungering and thirsting for Jesus is a proof of it. Listen not to unbelief and Satan, who would keep you away from the only place of victory. Fall down at His dear feet and tell Him all the truth—the very worst of it—and it may be your heart will melt and your spirit soften into contrition in the doing of it. And it may be He will hold out the scepter and say, "Return unto me, O backsliding daughter; for I am married unto you."

❧ RUTH BRYAN

Temporal Things
Contrasted with Spiritual

While we look not at the things which are seen, but at the
things which are not seen: for the things which are seen are temporal;
but the things which are not seen are eternal.

—2 CORINTHIANS 4:18

How poor and contemptible are the riches, distinctions, and glory of this world when compared with the rich and enduring blessings of the "glorious gospel of the blessed God" and the prospect that awaits the Christian. Even at its longest periods life is but a dream, a vapor that appears for a little while and then passes away. The continuous voice of Jesus to us is, "Rise up my love, my fair one, and come away." How unwise, then, so to encircle ourselves with earth as to permit our hearts to be entangled with the trifles of time, thus keeping us from the sweet and holy enjoyment of eternal realities.

Our only help is prayer, much prayer, for the Holy Spirit to keep you near to Jesus, that we may put our hand, as it were, in His hand and thus travel through the wilderness, kept from the beasts of prey we meet with in our path. To walk with God here is our highest privilege, and one sweet faith's view of our personal interest in Christ of more value than the crown of the universe. While thus seeking to live above the world, we must remember that we have all our individual and relative duties to perform, but the greatest and holiest is to commend the gospel by our upright, holy walk and in entreating all around us to come with us that we may do them good. Let us be earnest with God for much of the Spirit's power in our souls, for "the diligent soul shall be made fat."

❧ MARY WINSLOW

Fighting Yet Victorious

And we know that all things work together
for good to them that love God.

—ROMANS 8:28

It has pleased God that our infirmities and adversities do remain to the sight of the world, but the children of God are, by Christ, made so strong, righteous, whole, and sound that the troubles of the world are comforts of the spirit (Phil. 4:6–9); the passions of the flesh are medicines of the soul. For all manner of things work to their commodity and profit (Rom. 8:28). For they in spirit feel that God, their Father, does govern them and disposes all things for their benefit; therefore, they feel themselves sure. In persecution they are quiet and peaceful; in time of trouble, they are without weariness, fears, anxieties, suspicions, and miseries. And finally, all the good and evil of the world works to their commodity.

Moreover, they see that the triumph of Christ has been so great, that not only has He subdued and vanquished all our enemies and the power of them, but He has also overthrown and vanquished them after such a sort, that all things serve to our health. He might and could have taken them all away, but where then should have been our victory, palm, and crown? For we daily have fights in the flesh, and, by the succor of grace, have continual victories over sin, whereby we have cause to glorify God who, by His Son, has weakened our enemy the devil, and by His Spirit gives us strength to vanquish His offsprings.

So do we acknowledge daily the great triumph of our Savior and rejoice in our own fights, the which we can no wise impute to any wisdom of this world, seeing sin to increase by it. And where worldly wisdom most governs, there sin most rules; for as the world is enemy to God, so also the wisdom thereof is adverse to God. And although He could have taken away all worldly wisdom, yet He has left it for His greater glory and triumph of His chosen vessel.

☙ KATHERINE PARR

The Everlasting Service

And he shall serve him for ever.

—EXODUS 21:6

The Hebrew servant had trial of his master's service for six years, and in the seventh he might go out free if he would. But then, "if the servant shall plainly say [plainly, avowedly, no mistake about it] 'I love my master,...I will not go out free,' then, publicly and legally, he was sealed to his service "forever." It all depended on the love. He would say, "I will not go away from thee," because he loved his master and his house because he was well off with him. How this meets our case, dear fellow servants! We do not want to go away from Jesus because we love Him, and we love His house, too—not only the house of God with which so much of our sevice is connected, but also His own house, the spiritual house, the blessed company of all faithful people. And are we not well off with Him? Where else so well? Where else anything but ill? Has he not dealt well with His servants? Why don't we speak out and let people know what a master He is, and what a happy service His is? Who will speak out if we have not a word to say about it? Let us stand up for Jesus and His service, every one of us!

Perhaps, when we do speak out, we shall realize the joy of this promise as never before. It was not till the servant had owned his love and given up "the rest of his time in the flesh" and had his ear bored that the word was spoken, "He shall serve him for ever"; and it is only the loving and consecrated heart that leaps up for joy at the heavenly prospect: "And his servants shall serve him."

Think about it a little. What will it be to be able to go on serving Him day and night, without any weariness in it, and never a hateful shadow of weariness of it; without any interruptions; without any mistakes at all; without any thinking how much better someone else could have done it or how much better we ought to have done it; above all, without the least mixture of sin in motive or deed—pure, perfect service of Him whom we love and see face to face! What can be more joyful?

❧ FRANCES RIDLEY HAVERGAL

What Sin Is to God

The way of the wicked is an abomination unto the LORD.
—PROVERBS 15:9

Sin is the worst of evils, the most abominable thing to God, and the most hurtful to His people. Sin must needs be the greatest evil because of its direct and entire contrariety to God, who is the chiefest good. And that which is contrary to God and separates from Him must needs be the worst of evils in itself and the most pernicious and destructive to the creature where it is—and this is sin! Sin is contrary to God, as darkness is to light. It is contrary to the goodness of His nature, to the goodness of His works, and the goodness of His law. It is entirely and eternally contrary. And though a believer, by Christ's bearing of his sin and satisfying divine justice for the same, is forever delivered from the penal hurt of sin, yet is he still exposed to the real hurt of sin in many ways, which God—for wise, holy, great, and gracious ends—suffers to befall him.

The Lord could have, had it been His pleasure, delivered His people at once from the being as well as from the curse of sin. But He suffers this monster to abide in their souls to show them their own vileness, to make His strength perfect in their weakness, and the more to commend His infinite grace, in its glorious super-aboundings, over all their abounding sinfulness. Our all-wise and gracious God suffers the monster sin to abide in the souls of His people to prove their love and obedience to Him, to keep them in constant exercise against the powers of darkness, as good soldiers under the Captain of their salvation, and thus to teach them the wars of the Lord, to the magnifying of His almighty power, in confounding the devil and destroying of his works by such weak worms. Thus our all-wise, almighty, and all-gracious God brings light out of darkness and life out of death while He effectually overrules all things, even the being and working of sin, for His own glory in the salvation of His people.

❧ ANNE DUTTON

The Night Watcher

I...will watch to see what he will say unto me.

—HABAKKUK 2:1

Do you notice, dear reader, the singular form of expression here used? "I will watch to see what he will say unto me." Watch to see what God says!

Those olden days of open vision and prophecy are gone by, but does not our loving Father, even now, though in gentler fashion, sometimes speak to His children by what they see, as certainly and truly as if a voice had reached their outward ears? Are any of my readers in such deep trouble that all around them looks black and thick and threatening, as did that notable midnight sky? If you watch with real desire to hear and obey, you will certainly see the light of His love parting the densest gloom, and the tokens of His mighty power appearing to reassure your fainting spirit. There are no clouds so thick that they can obscure His glorious light if He bids it shine; there are no troubles so black and appalling that they can fright the soul from beholding the brightness of His grace and truth when He reveals them; and the feeblest of His children may always trust Him to fulfill that blessed promise in His Word, "I will make darkness light before them."

And, oh, how small and light our greatest griefs and losses and afflictions seem when illumined by the bright beams of the glory-land! Away up there, where we are soon going, there are no clouds, no darkness, no nights of pain, no days of sorrow; and it is after all but a thin, dark veil that separates us from the "beautiful home on high." So cheer up your heart, poor, timid child of God. You may not be able to see your way on earth, but turn your eyes to heaven, and gaze long and lovingly there. You do not need to see the path down below, because He has said He will guide you, and you know the darkness and light are both alike to Him. Put your hand in His and trust Him, for "by His light you shall walk through darkness."

                                          ❧ SUSANNAH SPURGEON

A Father's Love

For the Father himself loveth you,
because ye have loved me.

—JOHN 16:27

God is the "Father of mercies," "the God of all consolation." We read that "God is love"; happy are those who not only read but, in their own experience, also know this. If we oftener looked up to heaven to our Father, we should receive more help than we do. God honors a loving and trusting spirit. Fear not to trust Him with your trifling concerns; none are beneath His gracious notice if they really affect you. "The LORD is good; a stronghold in the day of trouble: and he knoweth them that trust in him." Again, "The LORD is very pitiful, and full of tender mercy."

"All things work together for good to them that love God." He appoints all for His people, not to discourage them from doing their best but to do far better for them than they could have planned for themselves. A good man well says, "There is many a thing which the world calls a disappointment; but there is no such word in the dictionary of faith. What to others are disappointments are to believers intimations of the will of God."

I cannot but be aware how impossible it is to find words to express the delightful feeling that the "High and Lofty One," the glorious Jehovah, is gracious enough to feel for the trials and sufferings of His believing people. But if these unworthy observations should lead any to meditate more on the fatherly character of God, they will not have been written in vain.

& ELIZABETH JULIA HASELL

The Value of One Soul

*And let us not be weary in well doing: for in due
season we shall reap, if we faint not.*

—GALATIANS 6:9

How little do we think that one soul saved is worth more than a world of earthly glory! "What will it profit a man if he gain the whole world and lose his own soul?" Do we in our hearts really believe this? Or do we merely assent to it with our judgment? I think that the best of God's saints think too lightly of the conversion of sinners, and I take shame to myself that it has not had the influence upon my own mind that it ought to have had. Oh, how much and how deeply have I had cause to mourn over my lack of faithfulness to an immortal soul I knew was traveling the downward road that leads to eternal death; and yet, from fear of offending, have withheld the truth or have merely satisfied myself with some general hints, unsatisfactory and unconvincing!

Did we really believe that every unconverted person we met with, dying so, would be lost forever, should we not be in earnest to warn that soul to flee from the wrath to come? Should we not avail ourselves of every favorable opportunity of praying for them, expostulating with them, and beseeching them to consider their latter end and turn to the Lord that they might be saved? I know there is much wisdom to be exercised to know how and when to speak, all of which the Lord will give to those who are earnest in asking for it. May the Lord make us faithful—myself in particular! Lord, what wouldest Thou have me to do? Eternity, with all its solemnities, is before us; then, how necessary to be up and doing the work of the Lord from the heart! Every believer has a peculiar gift or talent, and the Lord says to him or her, "Occupy till I come." When we consider how short our time is here, and how much is gone to waste, surely we ought to be up and doing the will of the Lord.

&. MARY WINSLOW

The Perpetual Covenant

Come, and let us join ourselves to the LORD in a
perpetual covenant that shall not be forgotten.

—JEREMIAH 50:5

Paul said, "He that is joined unto the Lord is one spirit." To this we were invited—to be so joined that nothing shall separate; to be made one with Christ in blessed and eternal union. The instrument, so to speak, of the joining is our consent in faith and obedience to the perpetual covenant that shall not be forgotten. Herein lies the answer to all distressing doubts about persevering in which we "err, not knowing the Scriptures, nor the power of God." For see what the terms of the new covenant are! "I will put my laws into their mind, and write them in their hearts: and I will be to them a God, and they shall be to me a people." This seems all one-sided. It is all what God undertakes to do. Not a word about what we undertake to do! How different from any human covenant!

Ah, the Lord tried us with the other way, and we failed, and so the old covenant of works came to naught. It was not only the children of Israel who continued not in God's covenant; we have done just the same. We have proved in our own experience that we cannot keep any one condition of it, let alone the whole! And so the Lord makes a new covenant in which the marvelous terms are that He undertakes our part as well as His own by promising to put His laws into our minds and write them upon our hearts, so that we may keep and obey them. And when He says He will be to us a God, He has promised in that one word more than mortal thought or mortal desire can reach. And when He says we shall be to Him a people, He guarantees us all the safety and happiness and all the privileges and blessings, in all certainty and perpetuity which He promises to His people. He knows our total weakness and our utter inability to persevere, and so He stoops to undertake the whole thing for us, if we will only come and join ourselves to the Lord in simple faith.

☙ FRANCES RIDLEY HAVERGAL

Christ's Love for His Church

And we know that the Son of God is come, and hath
given us an understanding, that we may know him that is true,
and we are in him that is true, even in his Son Jesus Christ.
This is the true God, and eternal life.
—1 JOHN 5:20

The New Testament! O, who can tell the blessings and benefits contained in this testament, this dying legacy of our dear
Emmanuel, purchased and sealed with His blood! What is the
amount of it? What is the sum of blessings contained in it? Behold,
God is become our salvation. This is the amount. God Himself, God
in Christ reconciling us unto Himself by His mighty power subduing the enmity that is in us; melting our flinty hearts; drawing us
with cords of love; creating us anew after His own image, which we
had totally lost; uniting us to Himself, even us, who were enmity
itself, but now are become one with God, who is love.

This is the work we have this day been celebrating: a given, born,
living, suffering, dying, risen, ascended, glorified, reigning Savior!
The Lord of hosts, the King of kings, the almighty God dwelling
with men, dwelling in men, and feeding them with His own body
and blood. Behold, God is become our salvation; therefore with joy
will we draw water out of the wells of salvation. His attributes are
the never failing source; His ordinances the wells of salvation. God
Himself is ours; all that He is is ours to bless and make us happy. Ten
thousand springs issue from this blessed source, specified and par-
ticularized in His Bible, experienced and celebrated by His saints.

Let us drink and be refreshed, rejoice and praise, for, O, who
can tell the amount of our riches in having God for our portion! All
things are ours, we are Christ's, and Christ is God's.

❧ ISABELLA GRAHAM

Trusting in Darkness

Who is among you that feareth the LORD, that obeyeth the voice
of his servant, that walketh in darkness, and hath no light? let him
trust in the name of the LORD, and stay upon his God.

—ISAIAH 50:10

Before we take this peace- and strength-giving precept, with its enfolded promise, to ourselves, let us examine ourselves as to the conditions: fear of the Lord and obedience to the voice of His servant. They are very clear. If we are not casting off fear; if we have this beginning of wisdom, this perhaps not sufficiently recognized treasure, the fear of the Lord; and if we have sincerity of purpose about obeying the voice of His servant and are not persisting in some known and willful disobedience, which causes a different kind of darkness, the darkness that blinds our eyes, then we are called to listen to all the comfort of this commandment.

Let him trust in the name of the Lord. What name? "The Lord, the Lord God, merciful and gracious, longsuffering, and abundant in goodness and truth, keeping mercy for thousands, forgiving iniquity and transgression and sin." Is it dark now, dear friend? Will you, as a little child, simply do what I ask you this morning? Take this name of the Lord, in all its varied fullness, shut your door, and kneel down without hurry. Then, asking first the Spirit's promised help, pray over every separate part of it so beautifully revealed for our comfort. And as you take up each word in petition, tell the Lord that you will, you do trust that, even though you cannot see or feel the preciousness of it. Trusting in the name of the Lord, the triune Jehovah—Father, Savior, Comforter—will lead you on, not perhaps to any great radiance of light as yet, but to staying upon your God: for mark the added pronoun—first only the Lord, then his God. Both the trusting and staying may be at first in the dark, but they will not be always in the dark. He that believes on Him shall not abide in darkness. Unto him "there ariseth light in the darkness." But the promises are progressive: we must follow the Light as soon as we see it, for "he that followeth me shall not walk in darkness."

❧ FRANCES RIDLEY HAVERGAL

Proof of Sonship

Behold, I have refined thee, but not with silver;
I have chosen thee in the furnace of affliction.

—ISAIAH 48:10

D o we not find that those Christians who appear to be left almost to themselves, who pass along the path of life with few changes and trials, usually make but small advances toward a state of spiritual manhood? And, if our blessed God sees that the disciple, like his Master, must be made perfect through sufferings, ought we not to welcome every means which will conduce to this blessed end? Can we desire to be babes in Christ all our days? If it is a proof of sonship to be chastised, may it not prove a special favor to be greatly chastised? Putting myself entirely out of the question (and I feel that I ought to go with my face in the dust all the days of my life, that I have profited no more by my trials), I do believe, judging from the observation I have been able to make, that those persons who have become what we call eminent for piety have generally been made so, under God, by sufferings. This seems reasonable, for how will, how can depraved, idolatrous human nature ever rise heavenward when it can be satisfied with earthly objects? "Every branch that beareth not fruit, the Father taketh away; and every branch that beareth fruit, he purgeth it, that it may bring forth more fruit."

If we were asked what the greatest good is, should we not answer that it is conformity to God? If we were asked what the best circumstances are for the Christian to be placed in, should we not answer that they are those that will, most constantly and most effectually, promote his conformity to God? Shall we then pray for afflictions? By no means. We are weak, and are crushed before the moth. We should not pray for what we do not know that we could bear. We should habitually pray for conformity to God, and quietly leave it to Him to determine by what means He will effect this blessed end.

∾ SUSAN HUNTINGTON

Christ the Only Physician

*In the end of the world hath he appeared to put
away sin by the sacrifice of himself.*
—HEBREWS 9:26

Dearly beloved friend, these words still follow me: He had "appeared to put away sin by the sacrifice of himself." That word "sin" feels weighty to a sensible sinner, but, oh, that word "Himself" seems a million times more weighty. "Himself!" The mighty God, the precious man Christ Jesus. "Himself!" By whom all things were created and for whom they consist. "Himself!" Whose smile is heaven, whose frown is hell; whom all angels worship and all devils obey. "Himself!" The sacrifice. Such another could not be found. Sins deep as hell and high as heaven cannot overmatch it, for it is infinite. Sins of scarlet and crimson dye cannot resist its power, for it makes them whiter than snow. See as much as you can of the vileness of self and the demerit of sin. "Himself," a bleeding sacrifice, exceeds it all. Here is the sweet-smelling savor, or savor of rest, both to the Lawgiver and the lawbreaker. The Lawgiver is honored; the lawbreaker is saved.

See how He stands most lovingly, as with open arms, saying to every laboring, weary, heavy-laden sinner, "Come." "Come unto me, and I will give you rest." "I still receive sinners. To the uttermost I save them and never am weary of healing their backslidings, forgiving all their iniquities, and multiplying pardons as they multiply transgressions against Me; I blot out with blood and love them freely and forever."

"Sinner, will not this suffice?" It will, if the Spirit apply and open in a little measure Himself and His sacrifice in contrast to you and your sins. It will take an eternity to know it fully, but that your heart may find rest and refreshing in it now is the affectionate prayer of His gleaner.

೪ RUTH BRYAN

The Widow's God

Leave thy fatherless children, I will preserve them alive;
and let thy widows trust in me.
—JEREMIAH 49:11

In an ancient church, now restored and beautified, not far from the seacoast and in a remote part of the southwest of England, I observed a memorial window placed there by a noble lady in remembrance to her only son. And under this window were inscribed the simple and touching words of Luke: "the only son of his mother, and she was a widow." Afflictions are the common lot of the children of men. The evangelist's words, in all their beautiful simplicity, have been applicable to many in all stations of life and in every age of the world.

James instructs that it is an important part of "pure religion" "to visit the fatherless and widows in their affliction." God, speaking by Jeremiah, says, "Leave thy fatherless children, I will preserve them alive, and let thy widows trust in me." And the compassionate Savior, when on earth, took pity on the forlorn condition of the widow of Nain and raised her son to life again.

We may therefore conclude that a woman who has lost her husband and natural protector, and especially one who has also lost her son, the support of her advancing years, is especially the object of the compassion of God and that He would have His servants show sympathy with the widow in her desolation. And, should anyone thus afflicted ever take up this book, may she find a friend in her Savior, who can and will supply all her need! There is no friend like Him, "the same yesterday, and today, and forever," powerful, tender, full of compassion—with balm for every wound, with comfort for every sorrow! He who shed tears at the grave of Lazarus (for "Jesus wept") is still observant of the sufferings and trials of His poor servants and regards them with sympathy from the throne of His glory.

          ❧ ELIZABETH JULIA HASELL

Sin Hurts Believers

I will surely hide my face in that day for all the evils which they
shall have wrought, in that they are turned unto other gods.

—DEUTERONOMY 31:18

Sin hurts believers, in that it separates them from God, and therefore from all that life, happiness, and glory which is to be enjoyed in Him. By sin, a believer breaks Christ's commandment and the Father's commandment. He despises divine authority. He slights Christ as the sent one of God. He refuses to hear and obey Him, as the prophet and king of His church. And thus, by sin, in breaking Christ's commandments, a believer slights and despises the boundless grace of the Savior and the infinite love of the Father that sent Him. Yes, and is equally guilty of slighting and despising the infinite love of the Spirit.

By every act of sin, a believer does say, as it were, "I care not whether I have communion with God or not. Communion with God in love is of no value in my esteem." How great then is the guilt of a believer's sin! How greatly does he thereby dishonor the Father and the Son and grieve the Holy Spirit! The Holy Spirit, sent from the Father and the Son, comes in their name to manifest their love and grace and to manage all their great designs in and upon us! And how greatly do we, by sin, provoke the Lord to depart from us! And lo, our great and glorious God, to show us our folly and ingratitude and to teach us better obedience, withdraws from us. "I will go and return to my place," says He, "till they acknowledge their offence." He forsakes us for a while, hides His face in fatherly anger, covers Himself with a thick cloud, that we can't see Him, and withdraws the sanctifying and comforting influences of His Holy Spirit from us. How great, then, is the hurt that sin does to believers, as by it they despise divine authority, slight divine kindness, provoke the Lord to depart from them, and are thereby separated from God, from communion with Him who is their life, their joy, their glory, their all!

ANNE DUTTON

Watchfulness and Prayer

Alas, what hourly dangers rise!
What snares beset my way!
To heav'n O let me lift my eyes,
And hourly watch and pray.

How oft my mournful thoughts complain,
And melt in flowing tears!
My weak resistance, ah, how vain!
How strong my foes and fears?

O gracious God, in whom I live,
My feeble efforts aid,
Help me to watch, and pray, and strive,
Tho' trembling and afraid.

Increase my faith, increase my hope,
When foes and fears prevail;
And bear my fainting spirit up,
Or soon my strength will fail.

Whene'er temptations fright my heart,
Or lure my feet aside,
My God, Thy pow'rful aid impart,
My guardian and my guide.

O keep me in Thy heav'nly way,
And bid the tempter flee;
And let me never, never stray
From happiness and Thee.

&ewsp; ANNE STEELE

Good Trees

Every good tree bringeth forth good fruit.
—MATTHEW 7:17

Have you ever seen your miserable, wretched state by nature, that you were lost, undone sinners, helpless and hopeless in and from yourselves? Have you seen an absolute necessity of Christ's blood and righteousness to cleanse, to clothe your souls? And of His fullness of the Spirit and all grace to sanctify your nature and supply all your wants, to give you faith and every grace, to maintain and increase the same, and to land you safe in glory? Has Christ, so far as revealed in you, been made precious to your souls, altogether lovely in your view and the chief among ten thousand in your esteem?

And though you may have brought forth much evil fruit in your conversation, yet still there is help for you in God. The blood of Jesus cleanses us from all sin. The grace of Christ is sufficient to help you against sin. And know, oh you good trees, that you have no root of your own. The grace that is in your hearts is not sufficient to uphold itself or to make you holy in your lives. Christ, the root that bears you, your root of influence, must continually supply you, as branches in Him, with sap and nourishment, or all your graces will die and your holiness wither.

And if you would receive out of His fullness and grace for grace, abide in Him continually by repeated acts of faith for continual pardon of sin, and strength against it. Oh, for the Lord's sake, for His gospel's sake, for His people's sake, and for your own soul's sake, continue no longer in a carnal, sluggish, careless frame, about a growing conformity to Christ, in dying unto sin, and living unto God. But set about the work in good earnest.

ANNE DUTTON

Even Our Thoughts

Then they that feared the LORD spake often one to another:
and the LORD hearkened, and heard it, and a book of remembrance
was written before him for them that feared the LORD,
and that thought upon his name.

—MALACHI 3:16

Only think for one moment of the Lord's taking notice of even a thought in the heart of a poor sinner of Himself. What condescension this is in our God! Oh, how our hearts should flow out to Him in fervent love and holy ardor! Dear friend, let us live more in sweet fellowship with Jesus, and when we pray in secret—no ear hearing and no eye seeing us but His—let us never be satisfied without sensible communion with Him. If we conversed with a friend, and he looked at us but appeared to hear us not, and there was no response, should we be satisfied? Now, this is the way the Lord wishes us to deal with Him—never to retire from the throne of grace without His lifting up the light of His countenance upon us in gracious response. This is blessedly encouraging. We go away rejoicing in God, feeling our prayers are heard and in due time will be answered.

And rest not satisfied, dear friend, without being assured that your sins are forgiven, washed forever away in the blood of God's dear Son, and that your soul stands complete in the Beloved. This will strengthen your confidence in laboring for others, and sinners shall be converted to God. In a little while we shall pass away, and the place that knows us now will know us no more forever; but all that we now do will tell upon eternity.

                                      ❧ MARY WINSLOW

The Business of the King

The king's business required haste.

—1 SAMUEL 21:8

The King's business requires haste. It is always pressing and may never be put off. Much of it has to do with souls that may be in eternity tomorrow and opportunities that are gone forever if not used then and there. There is no "convenient season" for it but today. Often it is not really done at all, because it is not done in the spirit of holy haste. We meet an unconverted friend again and again, and beat about the bush, and think to gain quiet influence and make way gradually, and call it judicious not to be in a hurry, when the real reason is that we are wanting in holy eagerness and courage to do the King's true business with that soul, and in nine such cases out of ten nothing ever comes out of it. Have we not found it so?

Delay in the Lord's errands is next to disobedience and generally springs out of it or issues in it. "God commanded me to make haste." Let us see to it that we can say, "I made haste, and delayed not to keep thy commandments."

We never know what regret and punishment delay in the King's business may bring upon ourselves. Amasa "tarried longer than the set time which he [the king] had appointed him," and the result was death to himself. Contrast the result in Abigail's case, where, except she had hasted, her household would have perished. We find four rules for doing the King's business in His Word. We are to do it first, "heartily"; second, "diligently"; third, "faithfully"; fourth, "speedily." Let us ask Him to give us the grace of energy to apply them this day to whatever He indicates as our part of His business, remembering that He said, "I must be about my Father's business."

☙ FRANCES RIDLEY HAVERGAL

The Cause of Our Afflictions

Search me, O God, and know my heart:
try me, and know my thoughts.

—PSALM 139:23

I do not think that either you or I have far to seek as to the cause of our afflictions. We may find an answer in our own deceitful hearts and depraved nature, and especially if we enter deeply into the examination of what sin is. Many persons are apt to consider sin in the act only, whereas, this is to have but a very slight and superficial view of it. Nay, we must go deeper than even to our own inward feelings of its motions and risings: we must consider it in its original poison and mischief—as it contaminates our nature—as it flows in our veins and grows in our growth; and it must be in the business of our lives to enter into the design of God and to be coworkers with Him in its utter destruction.

The main effect of the discovery of sin, when attended by the teaching of the Holy Spirit, is that of deep penitence, humiliation, and resignation; hence proceed love, patience, and tenderness toward the failings of others. And what can produce fruits so contrary to our proud hearts but that culture of the divine Husbandman, who uses the best means for the best ends? Among other means, that of affliction seems to be the one by which He frequently chooses to operate. Did you ever read, hear, or know of any eminent saint who was not trained in the school of affliction? Then, is not your question answered as to what is the cause? It assuredly ought to be, and will be, the prayer of every honest heart: "Search me, O God, and try me: and see if there be any wicked way in me"—any secret reserves, any sins of ignorance, any lodgments of self-deceit. My question is not, "Wherefore am I so greatly afflicted?" but "Why am I not afflicted more?" The answer is because He is rich in mercy and considers we are dust, and will not correct us so as that the spirit should fail. You and I have every encouragement to hope that God "will perfect that which concerneth us."

❦ SARAH HAWKES

Reasoning with the Unsaved

Ye must be born again. —JOHN 3:7

It is in His name and for His sake I wrote to you, and for your soul's sake also. I feel constrained to write to you to remind you that He is "the friend of sinners." He only can give true happiness. He is the one thing which is needful to put all else into the right place. If you did but know His preciousness, you would think it worth forsaking all to find Him. He gives just what you need—a heart to love Him, His ways, and His people, for He says, "A new heart will I give you, and a new spirit will I put within you." He also gives true repentance and free pardon, for He is exalted "to give repentance to Israel, and forgiveness of sins." He gives deliverance from the power and love of sin. He washes crimson sins white as snow in His own precious blood. He puts the best robe on prodigals who have been vainly trying to find satisfaction in the husks of this world's pleasures. By His Spirit He brings them to their right mind, cleanses them in His blood, and clothes them in His righteousness.

Perhaps you will say, "And what is all this to me?" Why, it is this to you, beloved without these things you must perish forever. But you may object, "The things you have spoken of are for God's chosen people, and I do not know that I am one." You do not know that you are not one and should rather say, "Why not, my soul? Why not for thee?" And though they are a free gift not to be obtained by any creature power, yet ask God to give them to you. Ask Him to give you the Holy Spirit to make you feel your need of them. Oh, may that Holy Spirit

> *Convince you of your sin*
> *Then lead to Jesus' blood;*
> *And to your wondering soul reveal*
> *The secret love of God.*

❧ RUTH BRYAN

Fear Not

Fear not. —LUKE 12:32

There need be no difficulty in distinguishing between the holy and blessed fear of the Lord, which is our treasure and is only as the sacred shadow cast by the brightest light of love and joy, and the fear which has torment and is cast out by perfect love and simple trust. But it is a very solemn thought how very guilty we are as to this most absolute command of our King, reiterated by messengers angelic and human, and by His own personal voice, perhaps more often than any other. No wonder that we are left to suffer the fruit of our own thoughts when we do not even see our disobedience, much less cease from it. "Fear not." There is no qualification, no exception, no modification; it is as plain a command as "Thou shalt not steal." What excuse have we for daring to regard it as a lesser transgression, or even no transgression at all? If the heinousness of a crime might, to human judgment, be measured by its penalty, what must the true heinousness of this everyday sin be when God has said, "The fearful…shall have their part in the lake which burneth with fire and brimstone" (Rev. 21:8)?

Why should what seems only a natural infirmity be catalogued with the blackest sins? Because, if we honestly examine it, it is always and only the fruit of not really believing God's words, not really trusting His love and wisdom and power. It is a bold, "Yea, hath God said?" to His abundant and infinitely gracious promises. It is a tacit denial that He is what He is! Only let us sincerely and thoroughly trace down every fear to its root, and we shall (if the Holy Spirit guide our search) be convinced of its sinfulness, and by the commandment it will become exceeding sinful. Let Thy judgments help us, O Lord, in this matter.

❧ FRANCES RIDLEY HAVERGAL

The Lord Hath Done It

Precious in the sight of the LORD is the death of his saints.

—PSALM 116:15

Under the first overwhelming pressure of your present sorrows, I feel a strong desire to comfort you by the comfort wherewith I myself have been comforted of God. I want to tell you that the precious promise "My grace is sufficient for thee" is sure and steadfast. With respect to the removal of our dear husbands, there is one consideration that lies at the foundation of all our other motives for resignation: the Lord has done it. "Precious in the sight of the Lord is the death of his saints." He will not call one of them home till his work below is finished. So long as the blessed God is possessed of infinite wisdom to understand perfectly what is best for His children, of infinite mercy to will all that He sees to be best for them, and of infinite power to execute all the purposes of His will, shall we not choose to have Him do what He pleases?

If we were unwilling that He should take our beloved friends when He thinks proper, the question at issue would be this: What shall govern—the all-perfect Jehovah or ourselves? In this view of the subject (and it is unquestionably a correct view of it), who would not say, "Let the will of the Lord be done"? Oh, we may be assured that the reasons that have led Him to afflict us so deeply are satisfactory to Himself, and will be so to us, if we are so happy as to reach heaven at last. And can we dare to wish to change what God sees necessary for us? Can we dare to wish our beloved husbands to stay here when, like their Master, they have finished their work on earth and God has immediate employment for them in heaven? We suffer indeed, but we suffer alone. Those whose trials we used to feel as painfully as our own are far beyond the influence of the vicissitudes of this trouble. They are happy. Let us rejoice for them.

❧ SUSAN HUNTINGTON

Sin Weakens Faith

For whatsoever is not of faith is sin.
—ROMANS 14:23

Sin hurts believers, in that it weakens their faith and every grace. Faith is, as it were, the root grace from whence all others flow and are nourished. And, therefore, as this is weakened, all the rest are weakened proportionally. Unbelief is, as it were, the root sin from whence all sin flows and into which it resolves. Unbelief is the direct opposite of faith. And having all sins in itself, it makes head against faith, and so against every grace, against all grace and holiness at once, in every one of its actings. And therefore the brethren are exhorted to take heed, lest there be in any of them an evil heart of unbelief. Because unbelief, so far as it works, carries the whole soul off from God at once. Faith works by love and thereby cleaves unto God in the exercise of every grace. Unbelief works by fear, which, productive of every sin, makes the soul fly from God, as if there were nothing desirable in Him nor anything but what was dreadful to the sinner. And every act of unbelief strengthens the habit of it in the soul. And therefore when a believer yields to unbelief, and so far as he yields to it, his faith and every grace must needs be exceedingly weakened thereby.

If our heart condemns us for unholiness, if our souls are filled with the guilt of our sin, our confidence is wounded hereby. By every fresh act of sin, how is faith slain, as it were, and lies half dead, weltering in its blood! "Where's your faith in the promise now?" says unbelief. "What evidence have you of an interest therein? Where are the effects of the promise, the fruits of faith, in heart and life?" And with these faith-killing queries, the soul would utterly faint if everlasting arms were not underneath, if the God of all grace did not strengthen the soul afresh to lay hold on the promise by a direct act of faith, fighting its way through an army of unbelieving fears just as it did at first, as a poor miserable sinner.

❧ ANNE DUTTON

A Foretaste of Glory

As for me, I will behold thy face in righteousness:
I shall be satisfied, when I awake, with thy likeness.

—PSALM 17:15

O my glorious Christ, what will it be to see Thee, face to face in Thine own light! To see "the King in his beauty" and be absorbed in His love! This is the climax of love's anticipations; these are the mountains of myrrh and hills of frankincense—even His perfections, His glory, and His transporting charms. Oh, how riveted shall I be! Eternal ages will roll on, but still my eyes and heart will have room for no other object but for Him, who was dead for my sake but is alive again—my Lord, my life, my all!

Those love-prints in His hands, feet, and side; that precious body broken for you and for me—we shall behold, we shall gaze upon them. And from the scars of those once bleeding wounds, unutterable radiations of glory will beam forth forever. There we shall eternally see that He was crucified for us—"the Lamb as it had been slain." Truly, I feel that mortality could not bear it; such "new wine" would burst the "old bottle." But mortality shall be swallowed up of life, and then shall I be satisfied when I awake with Thy likeness.

Modern believers rebuke my deep longings to be "away in the land of praises"; yet in the works of the dear old writers I find warmhearted companions who step on, far beyond me, in foretasting the glory which is to be revealed. I am not afraid of walking in such company, because it is God, the eternal Spirit, who enlarges my heart with desire for this land of Beulah and gives me a sip of the ocean of love, which none can have without longing for the full draught—yea, to launch out into the ocean itself and be ever filled.

≈ RUTH BRYAN

The Only Son of His Mother

The only son of his mother, and she was a widow.

—LUKE 7:12

L et us pause a moment over the history of this miracle. First, let us not forget that we only three times read in the Gospels of the Lord raising the dead. The objects of His divine power were chosen with supreme compassion: an only son (the present instance), an only daughter, and an only brother. Next, let us call to mind that the divine power of Jesus over death was shown, as it were, in three different degrees. He raised the ruler's daughter from the bed on which she had just died; He called back the widow's son to life from the bier on which he was being carried to his burial; but Jesus actually raised Lazarus from the grave itself, in which the departed had been already four days, when he obeyed the voice of the Son of God!

He who "went about doing good" could not see the grief of the poor widow, following an only son to the grave, without compassion. He said to her, "Weep not." And when the Savior raised the young man to life, He "delivered him to his mother."

The Lord Jesus no longer treads this earth to work miracles of love and power; the mourner can no longer hope for Jesus passing by to restore the dead. How often, in reading this gospel story, must afflicted persons have wished they had lived in the days when the Lord was on earth and could have brought their dead back to life again! But let us remember that the compassion and sympathy of Jesus are just the same in heaven. He says to every mourner who comes to Him for comfort, "Weep not." He is not an unmoved spectator of the troubles of His poor members here below. Suppose a poor and pious widow now lost her son. If that son died in the Lord, shall they not meet again in a world where partings are unknown? And in the meantime, she will find a "brother born for adversity" in the Lord Jesus—for "none of them that trust in him shall be desolate."

≥ ELIZABETH JULIA HASELL

God's Word, Our Guide

Thy word is a lamp unto my feet, and a light unto my path.

Enrich your minds with a full acquaintance with the Word of God! Lay it up in your memories when you can do nothing more. Be assured, if ever you are made wise unto salvation, it must be by this Word. If ever you are taught of God, He will teach you by the words contained in the Bible. "Search the Scriptures, for they are they which testify of me; search the Scriptures, for in them are contained the words of eternal life." "Be followers of them, who, through faith and patience now inherit the promises."

David went forward, heavenward, improving in the knowledge of God, of himself, and of God's plan of salvation for ruined sinners, by studying the Word, the works, and the providences of God, but chiefly the Word of God. He was a king and had the cares of the nation to occupy his mind; he was a man of war and had that art to study. But, O, the privilege of the Christian! He goes through every part, even of his earthly way, leaning upon his God.

How comfortably might Christians go through life if they did walk with God in their daily business and occupations, carefully observing the leadings of providence, cautiously avoiding either running before or lagging behind—but in all things making their requests known to God; at all times committing their way to Him, being careful about nothing, but to use with diligence the means of grace and also the means of acquiring the good things of life, leaving the issues of both to God, in the full assurance that what is good the Lord will give. "Trust in the LORD, and do good; so shalt thou dwell in the land, and verily thou shalt be fed" (Ps. 37:3).

☙ ISABELLA GRAHAM

The Readiness of the King's Servants

Behold, thy servants are ready to do whatsoever
my lord the king shall appoint.

—2 SAMUEL 15:15

This is the secret of steady and unruffled gladness in "the business of the Lord, and the service of the King." It makes all the difference! If we are really, always, equally ready to do whatsoever the King appoints, all the trials and vexations arising from any change in His appointments, great or small, simply do not exist. If He appoints me to work there, shall I lament that I am not to work here? If He appoints me to wait indoors today, am I to be annoyed because I am not to work out-of-doors? If I meant to write His messages this morning, shall I grumble because He sends interrupting visitors, rich or poor, to whom I am to speak or show kindness for His sake? If all my members are really at His disposal, why should I be put out if today's appointment is some simple work for my hands or errands for my feet instead of some seemingly more important doing for my head or tongue?

Does it seem a merely ideal life? Try it! Begin at once. Before you venture away from this quiet moment, ask your King to take you wholly into His service and place all the hours of this day quite simply at His disposal, and ask Him to make and keep you ready to do just exactly what He appoints. Never mind about tomorrow; one day at a time is enough. Try it today, and see if it is not a day of strange, almost curious peace, so sweet that you will be only too thankful, when tomorrow comes, to ask Him to take it also—till it will become a blessed habit to hold yourself simply and "wholly at thy commandment" for any manner of service.

Then will come, too, an indescribable and unexpected sense of freedom and a total relief from the self-imposed bondage of "having to get through" what we think lies before us. By thus being ready, moment by moment, for whatsoever He shall appoint, we realize very much more that we are not left alone, but that we are dwelling with the King for His work.

           ❧ FRANCES RIDLEY HAVERGAL

Our Great Responsibility

Work out your own salvation with fear and trembling.
—PHILIPPIANS 2:12

Let me entreat you to be earnest in religion. Remember that no great object is likely to be obtained without persevering diligence and a courageous determination not to be defeated by difficulties. If this is the case in reference to temporal objects, surely it is the case with spiritual things. Difficult, indeed, impossible, would it be for us to obtain this best of all knowledge, the knowledge of ourselves and of the Lord Jesus Christ, were not the grace and strength of Him, who is able to save to the uttermost, promised to all who really seek them. "It is God which worketh in us both to will and to do of his good pleasure," and on this account, we are exhorted to "work out our own salvation with fear and trembling."

Remember, you have a part to perform in this great work. In reading the blessed Word of God, carefully distinguish between what He has engaged to do and what He requires you to do. I do not mean that you can do anything that will serve you as a ground of justification, anything to lay the Most High under any obligation to bestow His mercy upon you. One thing we do know—that it is the duty of every subject of God's moral government to observe all the statutes of the Lord, to do them. You are called upon to seek first the kingdom of God, to strive to enter in at the strait gate, to ask that you may receive, to repent and believe the gospel, to enroll yourself on the Lord's side, to renounce the world and take up your cross and follow the Savior. Do you say, "I cannot do this"? I answer, has not God commanded you to do it? And does He command us to do what we are unable to do? Is there unrighteousness with God? Do not encourage, on slight grounds, the hope that you are a Christian. Remember, you are laying your foundation for eternity. Solemn thought! Do not rest satisfied so long as the all-important question "Am I a Christian or not?" is undecided.

℆ SUSAN HUNTINGTON

Alive, but Not Lively

Continue ye in my love.
—JOHN 15:9

Our dear Lord says, "Continue ye in my love," not thereby implying that His love can be turned away from its objects, but exhorting us to a continued realization or apprehending of His love by the lively acting of a Spirit-wrought faith. Thus will our little spark be increasing into a flame by constant communication with the fire from whence it springs. Of this communication, faith seems to be the medium, and if this precious grace be not kept in healthy exercise upon the person and work, the suffering and death, the blood and righteousness of our dear Redeemer, the soul will be sure to be languid and drooping in its spiritual condition. Prayer, praise, love, joy, peace, and all other graces will be at a low watermark, and whatever external appearances of profession there may be, the heart will be conscious of distance and shyness with its Lord.

I am speaking of one who has been quickened by the Spirit and is a living soul, for we may be alive but not lively; we may be active in our Lord's cause but not spiritual in our own souls; we may be earnest for the salvation of others but not living in the joys of salvation ourselves; we may be instrumentally distributing the bread and water of life but not be enjoying daily refreshment therefrom in our own experience. The reason I thus judge is from finding persons so lively in conversing upon what they are doing for the Lord, yet so slow to speak of what He is doing for them. They seem delighted to tell of the great things which are doing all around, but immediately shrink back if any heart-subject is brought home to them. This is a day of great profession, but yet real, vital godliness is at a low ebb, and close walking with God in sweet communion is too little sought after. Solemn, indeed, are these facts; we may well say with David, "Search me, O God, and know my heart; try me and know my thoughts; and see if there be any wicked way in me: and lead me in the way everlasting."

❧ RUTH BRYAN

Grateful Giving

*For whosoever shall give you a cup of water to drink
in my name, because ye belong to Christ, verily I
say unto you, he shall not lose his reward.*

—MARK 9:41

He who commended the mites of that poor widow we read of in the gospel is no longer seated here on earth to scan the gifts bestowed on His poor and on His church, for He has ascended into heaven. But, from His throne of glory, the Savior takes notice of every gift and still more of the motive of the giver. He sets a very different price on these gifts from what mortal man would put upon them: many a shilling—nay, many a penny—is more in His sight than many a pound. It is not only the value of the gift that the Savior considers; He knows why a gift is given, and, far from despising the poor man's offering, we have every reason to believe it to be especially pleasing in His sight. And when a richer disciple makes an offering suitable to his larger means, it is also graciously accepted by Him who has given that servant a more extended stewardship.

Whatever you give, be it in your power to bestow little or much, try to remember, to think, "I am giving this to Christ my Savior"; or, "I am permitted to serve my Great Head by this act of charity to His poor member"; or, "I offer this to my Lord, for the use of His church on earth"; or, "I give this to Christ, to forward the spread of the gospel among the heathen." These are Christian motives. When we give because others do or to give more than others, we act from low, earthly motives. Remember that the important point is the motive, and that even every sincere Christian must mourn over his own too often very mixed motives.

෨ ELIZABETH JULIA HASELL

Sin Unfits Believers for Divine Service

Cleanse me from my sin.
—PSALM 51:2

Sin hurts believers, in that it unfits them for divine service. As sin prepares a believer for every evil work, so it unfits him for every good work. When a believer has sinned, he is all in pain, all out of tune, without strength, as unfit to go about any piece of service for God as a person is to engage in worldly employment that has his bones dislocated or broken. When David had sinned, he complained of broken bones in Psalm 51:8: "Make me to hear joy and gladness; that the bones which thou hast broken may rejoice." David, by falling into sin, broke his own bones. And though he here says God did it ("the bones which thou hast broken"), it is only to set forth, as I humbly conceive, the suffering and chastening hand of God therein, that the Lord righteously suffered, permitted him to fall into sin, and thereupon withdrew the sanctifying and comforting influences of His Holy Spirit from him, setting on the guilt of sin upon his conscience, to his pain and grief. This made him as unfit for divine service as a person is for worldly business when his bones are broken.

And therefore he says in verses 9–13, "Hide thy face from my sins, and blot out all mine iniquities. Create in me a clean heart, O God; and renew a right spirit within me. Cast me not away from thy presence; and take not thy holy spirit from me. Restore unto me the joy of thy salvation; and uphold me with thy free spirit. Then will I teach transgressors thy ways; and sinners shall be converted unto thee."

It is as if he should say, "Lord, I can do nothing in Thy service while my bones are thus broken, but if Thou wilt set my bones, restore, strengthen, comfort, and uphold my soul, I will again go forth into Thy service and particularly tell of the wonders of Thy free love in healing my backslidings, that other poor sinners, under the like misery of broken bones, may put their trust in Thee."

⮞ ANNE DUTTON

Seeing Self in Light of the Cross

*By the which will we are sanctified through the offering
of the body of Jesus Christ once for all.*

—HEBREWS 10:10

Truly it may be most justly verified that to behold Christ crucified, in spirit, is the best meditation that can be. I certainly never knew my own miseries and wretchedness so well by book, admonition, or learning, as I have done by looking into the spiritual book of the crucifix. I never knew my own wickedness, neither lamented for my sins truly, until the time God inspired me with His grace, that I looked in this book. Then I began to see perfectly that my own power and strength could not help me, and that I was in the Lord's hand, even as the clay is in the potter's hand (Jer. 18:6; Rom. 9:21–23).

For except this great benefit of Christ crucified be felt and fixed surely in man's heart, there can be no good work done acceptable before God. For in Christ is all fullness of the Godhead (Col. 2:9), and in Him are hid all the treasures of wisdom and knowledge. Even He is the water of life, whereof whosoever shall drink, he shall never more thirst, but it shall be in him a well of water, springing up into everlasting life (John 4:14). Paul says, "There is therefore now no condemnation to them which are in Christ Jesus, who walk not after the flesh, but after the Spirit."

It is no little or small benefit we have received by Christ if we consider what He has done for us, as I have perfectly declared heretofore. Wherefore I pray the Lord that this great benefit of Christ crucified may be steadfastly fixed and printed in all Christian hearts, that they may be true lovers of God and work, as children, for love—not as servants, compelled with threatenings or provoked with hire.

❧ KATHERINE PARR

Walking in the Spirit

If we live in the Spirit, let us also walk in the Spirit.
—GALATIANS 5:25

If we pray in the Spirit, we must walk in the Spirit, and "the exceeding greatness of his power to us who believe" is more than equal to any strain that our cares or circumstances can bring to bear upon it.

Surely, could we but realize the close presence of the Lord Jesus, hour by hour and minute by minute, heaven would be begun on earth. But sometimes even work for Him so entirely engrosses thought and heart that He Himself seems forgotten. Sweet "frames and feelings" vanish when the burden and heat of the day oppress both soul and body.

Yet I am sure this should not be. Christ says, "Abide in me," and He would not tell me to do an impossible thing. Blessed Jesus, put forth Thy hand and take Thy poor, silly, fluttering dove into the ark of Thy love!

What a revolution there would be in all our Christian circles if each one of us carried into every thought and word and action of the day the fragrance and freshness of our seasons of sweet communion with our Master! It is good to talk with God; it is far better to walk with Him. About the former, we may be self-deceived, but about the latter—never!

Well, dear friends, we cannot set the world right. We have not the power to persuade or convince multitudes of their errors of doctrine or practice, but we can see to it that we ourselves are walking "worthy of God" and letting our light shine so brightly that all may see more plainly the pathway to the Celestial City because we are passing along it.

❧ SUSANNAH SPURGEON

A Delightful Day

Call the sabbath a delight.
—ISAIAH 58:13

It has been justly said that while most people will attend church on the Lord's Day, the private observance of Sunday is but too little considered. Now the believer desires, above all things, to be "in the Spirit on the Lord's Day," to keep that day in a really spiritual manner. When the true Christian says he does not travel on Sunday or read ordinary books and that, in fact, he devotes the day, as much as possible, to holy employments, it is not so much that he feels he ought not to do this or that; it is that, with his tastes for prayer, praise, holy reading and thinking, and God's service in the sanctuary, he has no desire to waste the time otherwise. And when we consider what the employments of heaven will be, as far as we know anything about them, it ought to seriously alarm us if now we have no spiritual tastes, no preparation of heart and soul, so as to be ready for it.

I am certain that if an ungodly person could enter heaven and could stand among its holy inhabitants, whom we all hope to join after death, such a person would be miserable and would wish himself away. If then eternity be a certainty—if it will be passed either in heaven or in the wretched abode of lost souls—how unwise are we not to be preparing for the society and the employments of that heaven, where all hope to go at last! The Lord's Day affords us a quiet pause every week in which to "hear of heaven and learn the way." I would say to all my readers that these verses from Isaiah are most remarkable and full of instruction. The spiritual blessing promised to those who, by God's assisting grace, keep His day, not doing their own ways nor finding their own pleasure nor speaking their own words, is that they shall delight themselves in the Lord. They will not find the Sabbath "a wearisome day," for God Himself will teach them to love it and prepare them for the rest remaining for the people of God, even the eternal Sabbath in heaven.

❧ ELIZABETH JULIA HASELL

The Friendship of the King

He that loveth pureness of heart, for the grace of
his lips the king shall be his friend.

—PROVERBS 22:11

Who can say, "I have made my heart clean; I am pure"? Who must not despair of the friendship of the King if this were the condition? But His condescension in promising His friendship bends yet lower in its tenderly devised condition. Not to the absolutely pure in heart, but to the perhaps very sorrowful longing lover of that pureness come the gracious words, "The king shall be his friend."

Who has not longed for an ideal and yet a real friend—one who should exactly understand us, to whom we could tell everything and in whom we could altogether confide; one who should be very wise and very true; one of whose love and unfailing interest we could be certain? There are other points for which we could not hope—that this friend should be very far above us and yet the very nearest and dearest, always with us, always thinking of us, always doing kind and wonderful things for us; undertaking and managing everything; forgetting nothing; failing in nothing; quite certain never to change and never to die—so that this one grand friendship should fill our lives and that we really never need trouble about anything for ourselves any more at all.

Such is our royal friend, and more, for no human possibilities of friendship can illustrate what He is to those to whom He says, "Ye are my friends." We, even we, may look up to our glorious King, our Lord and our God, and say, "This is my beloved, and this is my friend!" And then we, even we, may claim the privilege of being "the King's companion" and the "King's friend."

❧ FRANCES RIDLEY HAVERGAL

Lessons in the School of Grace

But grow in grace. —2 PETER 3:18

The Christian, in this world, is an unapt scholar. God has undertaken to prepare him for heaven. He has determined that this shall be done. But there is almost everything in the way to hinder and oppose the accomplishment of this benevolent purpose of the blessed God. Within, a nature wholly and inveterately inclined to evil, and without, everything calculated to operate powerfully and successfully on the depravity of his nature. Alas! How could he get forward if the promise of God did not secure to him his sanctification, as well as his justification? This, blessed be God, it does! "The LORD thy God will circumcise thine heart, to love the LORD thy God with all thine heart, and with all thy soul, that thou mayest live." But this promise must be fulfilled by the instrumentality of means. And oh, how kindly, how mercifully, how patiently does our almighty Redeemer chasten, reprove, refine, and purify His children.

Sometimes He pours upon them the temporal blessings of His providence. But if this turns away their affections from Himself, He visits their transgressions with the rod and their iniquity with stripes; nevertheless, His lovingkindness He does not utterly take from them nor suffer His faithfulness to fail. Every stripe is intended to embitter to them that sin which He hates, that sin which cleaves to His children while they live, and that sin which He is determined to destroy. And shall we not trust our whole souls with this blessed being? Shall we not be willing that He should manage our concerns in His own way, if He will but make us like Himself and prepare us for Himself? Oh, yes, yes!

Two things we ought to especially be anxious to learn under our trials: a humble, penitent, brokenhearted conviction of our own sinfulness and unworthiness; and a filial, practical, quickening sense of the unspeakable goodness and love of God and of our obligations to be entirely and eternally His.

⁊ SUSAN HUNTINGTON

Coming to Christ

*For God so loved the world, that he gave his
only begotten Son, that whosoever believeth in him
should not perish, but have everlasting life.*

—JOHN 3:16

The same Scripture that testifies of the misery of man reveals also his remedy—a remedy of God's own providing, by which man may be restored to the image and favor of God and to that communion with Him which is life and bliss. "God so loved the world, that he gave his only begotten Son, that whosoever believeth on him should not perish, but have everlasting life. For God sent not his Son into the world to condemn the world; but that the world through him might be saved" (John 3:16–17). "And this is life eternal, that ye believe on him whom he hath sent" (John 17:3). When man becomes convinced that he is lost, helpless, wretched, lying at mercy, and submits to the method of God's own providing; casts himself on the mercy of God in Christ, and, coming to Him, rests on His free promise, "Him that cometh to me, I will in no wise cast out." Disclaiming all confidence in himself or in his own works, he accepts of God's offered grace, in God's own way, a free and finished salvation.

Believing this, according to his faith it shall be. Christ shall be in him "a well of water springing up to eternal life." He will shed abroad His love in his heart and, according to His promise, give him "power to become a child of God." The Holy Ghost, the Comforter, shall be given unto him to teach him the knowledge of the Scriptures and to become a principle of holiness in his heart. Then shall he find that wisdom's ways are ways of pleasantness, and all her paths peace. Then shall he experience the blessedness of "that man whose God is the Lord." Then is the way open for communion and converse with God the Father, Son, and Holy Ghost.

᠍ ISABELLA GRAHAM

Unbroken Communication

Keep yourselves in the love of God.
—JUDE 21

I feel more and more the deep importance of being kept in a freshness of experience by the anointings of the Spirit, so that whatever engagements we may have for the good of others, and however abundantly we may be laboring for their salvation, there should still be a constant communication kept up with our dear Lord, and our souls should never rest satisfied without freedom at court.

To be constantly employed in errands for the King and never to see His face, hear His voice, or receive a token from Him—oh, how chilling to one who has enjoyed His love, has sat under His shadow with great delight, and has found His fruit sweet to the taste. How unsatisfying to one truly longing to taste that the Lord is gracious. The former may well say, "Restore unto me the joy of thy salvation," and the latter, "Remember me, O LORD, with the favor that thou bearest unto thy people! Oh visit me with thy salvation!" When we are enjoying personal communion with the King, and by faith walking in Him and living on Him, then will His messages be most warmly delivered, being fresh from Himself. Then will there be evidently a sweet savor of Him, as well as a good word for Him.

I cannot tell you how sad it is to my heart when I find this savor wanting in some who have been long in the Lord's ways and active in serving Him too. They are cumbered with many things and too little alone with Jesus, without which we shall become like salt which has lost its savor. It matters not what great works there be if the spice of love be wanting. Oh, may our gracious Lord bring us closer and closer to Himself and cause us to dwell in love and "to comprehend with all saints what is the breadth and length, and depth and height, and to know the love of Christ which passeth knowledge."

ॐ RUTH BRYAN

Sin Stumbles the Weak

Through thy knowledge shall the weak brother perish,
for whom Christ died? But when ye sin so against the brethren,
and wound their weak conscience, ye sin against Christ.

—1 CORINTHIANS 8:11–12

Sin hurts believers, in that thereby they become a means of offending and grieving their brethren. Oh, how the sins of believers stumble the weak! They don't know what to make of religion when believers act contrary to the holiness of that pure religion which they profess. And they are tempted to question the work of God in the souls of those which they see fall into sin, the truth of grace in their own hearts, and also their final perseverance. Yes, by the sins of some believers, others may be drawn into the same evils.

Examples are very powerful and have an attracting force in them. When a believer obeys Christ's commandments, he not only keeps them himself but practically teaches others obedience; so on the contrary, when he disobeys the same, he not only breaks them himself but thereby does many times draw others into sin.

Thus, by sin, a believer weakens the faith, joy, and holiness of others and in this sense causes his weak brother, for whom Christ died, to perish. The apostle speaks concerning those who only eat things sacrificed to idols from a persuasion of the lawfulness thereof in the presence of those who doubted of the same and thereby drew them into the same practice, which to them was sin (1 Cor. 8:11). And our Lord says, "Whosoever therefore shall break one of these least commandments, and shall teach men so, he shall be called the least in the kingdom of heaven." And when the children of God are not stumbled at and drawn into evil by the sin of others, yet the sins of their brethren are a great grief to them. As 2 Corinthians 2:5 says, "But if any have caused grief." How great then is the hurt that sin does to believers, in that it makes them an offense and grief to their brethren.

&ANNE DUTTON

The World's Last Days

Stablish your hearts: for the coming
of the Lord draweth nigh.
—JAMES 5:8

The man who is eagerly watching for the dawn of morning sees the first faint light in the east long before the actual rising of the sun. The Christian, expecting his Lord's second advent, discerns the tokens of His coming and hopes he sees signs of the return to earth of the glorious "Sun of Righteousness." We know the event is certain. We know that we ought to be preparing for it. We know it will come upon many "as a snare," utterly surprising them. Now our Lord tells us that, in the latter days, up to the very last indeed, people will be going on just as usual, eating, drinking, marrying, and giving in marriage. Then will the second advent break in, most awfully, upon their careless security.

It is not enough to make anyone safe for Christ's coming, to be just going on like other people. No, the person who has no thought for anything above and beyond this world, till Christ shall come, will perish with this world. And, at the advent of the Lord, two people may have been very near together in life who will then be parted for all eternity. Two women may have occupied the same pew in church who will be together again no more forever.

How comforting to the Christian is the thought of his Lord's speedy return! How anxious should he be to be ready! His aim should be so to live that his Lord may find him watching; then, if he is called away by death before the advent, he would be equally prepared for that. He would never cease to be the Lord's. Not neglecting the duties of our calling, let us be anxious to live above them, to live for eternity, to be ready for the second advent. So when the number of the elect is accomplished and Christ has come to reign, may we enter into the joy of the Lord, and hear Him say, "Come ye blessed!"

⇛ ELIZABETH JULIA HASELL

The Omniscience of the King

There is no matter hid from the king.
—2 SAMUEL 18:13

The very attributes that are full of terror to the King's enemies are full of comfort to the King's friends. Thus, His omniscience is like the pillar, which was "a cloud of darkness" to the Egyptians but "gave light by night" to the Israelites. All things are naked and opened unto the eyes of Him with whom we have to do, and the more we have to do with Him, the more glad and thankful we shall be that there is not anything hid from the King.

In perplexities—when we cannot understand what is going on around us; cannot tell whither events are tending; cannot tell what to do because we cannot see into or through the matter before us—let us be calmed and steadied and made patient by the thought that what is hidden from us is not hidden from Him. If He chooses to guide us blindfold, let Him do it! It will not make the least difference to the reality and righteousness of the guidance.

In mysteries—when we see no clue; when we cannot at all understand God's partial revelation; when we cannot lift the veil that hangs before His secret counsel; when we cannot pierce the holy darkness that enshrouds His ways or tread the great deep of His judgments where His footsteps are not known—is it not enough that even these matters are not hid from our King?

Our King could so easily reveal everything to us and make everything so clear! It would be nothing to Him to tell us all our questions. When He does not, cannot we trust Him and just be satisfied that He knows and would tell us if it were best? He has many things to say unto us, but He waits till we can bear them. May we be glad that even our sins are not hid from Him? Yes, surely, for He who knows all can and will cleanse all. He has searched us and known us, as we should shrink from knowing ourselves, and yet He has pardoned, and yet He loves!

                                   ✒ FRANCES RIDLEY HAVERGAL

Making Our Calling and Election Sure

Let no man deceive himself.
—1 CORINTHIANS 3:18

A Christian should never say his time is his own, for all he is and all he has is the Lord's, who has bought him at a great price, even His own precious blood. Therefore we are not our own, but the Lord's. May we never forget this!

What a vast eternity awaits us, and how brief the space of time is left us to prepare for it! Should not this be our constant inquiry: "Lord, what wilt Thou have me to do? I am Thine; employ me for Thyself, and use me for Thy glory." What if we should be found unprofitable servants at last! How often this reflection causes me deep searching of heart! How awful it is to see God's creatures living as if there were no eternity before them! I have just heard of a gentleman, now upon his dying bed, feeling himself a lost sinner but without one ray of hope. The Lord has suddenly called him to give an account of his stewardship, and he is not ready! The Lord Jesus is full of compassion for poor sinners, but it is dangerous to trifle with convictions, for the day of grace may pass away and the soul not be saved. Religion composed of mere desires will not do for a dying bed.

You may be happily situated and all pleasant as respects to temporal things, but the soul—the soul—is the concern that demands your chief thoughts! Are you in Christ? Have you found Jesus? If you have, you are happy indeed, though you dwell in a mud-wall cottage. Oh that men would be wise and consider their latter end! Life here without Christ is misery indeed. But oh, to know Him, to love Him, to be borne in His tender bosom through this wilderness of sin and sorrow, is a happiness indeed which cannot be described and can only be known by experience!

≈ MARY WINSLOW

God's Revelation of Himself

All scripture is given by inspiration of God,
and is profitable for doctrine, for reproof, for correction,
for instruction in righteousness: that the man of God may
be perfect, thoroughly furnished unto all good works.

—2 TIMOTHY 3:16–17

I have not time to say all I intended on the subject of reading the Bible. The best description of my views which I can give at present is that we should not only read in order to know what we should be and do, as real Christians, nor only to know what God has done and will do in the relation in which He stands to us as His creatures, and particularly as His children. But the Scripture is a glass where He has, in a most glorious manner, given us a revelation of Himself—of His perfections and His infinite eternity of being; we should therefore, at seasons, delight ourselves with tracing out the different features of His glorious majesty.

In thus reverently studying the divine character, our minds will obtain larger apprehensions of the various perfections of God, and the discoveries that the Holy Spirit will help us make will cause our hearts to burn within us; our faith, love, and confidence will be increased; and a fresh interest will be given to everything we see because we shall trace everything upward and say, "Here I see the touch of His hand." The more we behold of deity, the lower we shall sink in humility and self-abasement, and selfishness—hateful, narrow selfishness—will be lost.

❧ SARAH HAWKES

Sweet Words to the Oft Afflicted

*For I reckon that the sufferings of this present time are not worthy
to be compared with the glory which shall be revealed in us.*

—ROMANS 8:18

G od has seen fit to afflict you often and severely. I hope that you
are resigning yourself into the hands of your faithful, covenant God and experiencing the preciousness of the promise, "I will
never leave nor forsake thee." When the Son of God finished the
work of redemption, He conquered all the enemies of our souls (if
we are His) and laid up for us, in Himself, sure and adequate supplies for all our necessities. The cross of Christ is the certain pledge
of the Christian's final victory. Our Lord is Lord and King of death
and the grave. Faint they may; despond they may. Yet, in the mount
of difficulty shall the Lord be seen and command deliverance for
His people. They shall not utterly fall, and even their misgivings
and fears shall abound to the glory of His grace, who giveth power
to the faint, and to them that have no might, increases strength.

Trust yourself then, my sister, with the kind Father, who has
borne you thus far through the wilderness on His faithful arm. Trust
yourself with the dear Redeemer, who loved you unto death and
who has gone to heaven to prepare a place for you. Trust yourself
with that good Spirit, who has been carrying on your sanctification
in order to your preparation for heaven these many years, though
you have grieved Him so often. Trust yourself with Jehovah—
Father, Son, and Holy Ghost—who keeps covenant forever and
ever. Keep hold of the cross of Christ. None ever perished there.
From there draw all your hope of pardon and victory. Though your
sins may look very great and your readiness for heaven very uncertain, yet never forsake the cross. The blood of Christ cleanses from
all sin, and He that has begun a good work in you will perform it
unto the day of Jesus Christ.

&> SUSAN HUNTINGTON

Bread Enough in Our Father's House

And the Lord direct your hearts into the love of God.
—2 THESSALONIANS 3:5

Oh, what an unspeakable mercy, that by the spirit of adoption we can say, "our God" and "our Father." And though He is a consuming fire to those on whom sin is found, yet He has made a "way of escape" by the blood of our elder Brother, having laid upon Him all our iniquities. These briars and thorns were set against Him in battle, and on His sacred person did the fire of divine justice burn them up altogether.

Oh, let us turn aside from creature things and see this great sight, for it is heartwarming and Christ-endearing to see the bush of humanity in that devouring fire, and yet unconsumed; to behold our precious Surety enduring all the bitter anguish till every sin of His chosen was expiated and He could triumphantly say, "It is finished." That was indeed the conqueror's song, and with joy it is reechoed again and again from the believing heart by the power of the blessed Spirit. "It is finished, and finished for me." The personality of it is the sweetness; here is food for faith, here is a feast for love. In such believing views of a crucified Savior, we get raised above the things of a dying world, and, in realizing by faith our union with Him we can say, "I am crucified with Christ"; then He becomes our life, that we which live should henceforth live only for Him. This is a heartwarming subject.

May there be great searchings of heart, causing this inquiry: Why, being a King's child, should there be leanness from day to day? Is there not a cause? Is there not bread enough in the Father's house? Or, rather, has there not been a turning away from His spiritual provision to some beggarly elements of the creature of the world? May the Lord in mercy restore all such to their first love and also lead them on to those more blessed revelations of Him, which are to be enjoyed even in the house of our pilgrimage.

❧ RUTH BRYAN

Sin Hinders the Race

Let us lay aside every weight, and the sin which doth so easily beset us, and let us run with patience the race that is set before us.
—HEBREWS 12:1

Sin hurts believers, in that it hinders them in their spiritual race. And therefore the writer of Hebrews says, "Let us lay aside every weight, and the sin [unbelief] which doth so easily beset us." Every sin is a weight that loads and presses a believer, that he cannot run with swiftness the race that is set before him. A believer is called to run the way of God's commandments, both as to faith and practice, and for his encouragement therein has a crown of righteousness set before him. They that run in a race are called to exert their utmost strength, to make toward the prize, each one striving to outrun his fellow. And this the apostle puts the saints in mind of to excite their diligence in their spiritual race: "Know ye not that they which run in a race run all, but one receiveth the prize? So run, that ye may obtain." And further, he puts them in mind of the wisdom of racers, of that care which they take of their bodies, that no excess may unfit them for running: "And every man that striveth for the mastery is temperate in all things." It is as if he should say, "You saints, learn of racers; they have one great design in view, one great aim, and that is to get the prize. They will deny themselves the delights of sense, all extravagancies of life, that their bodies may not be unfitted thereby, for running their race.

If you keep the crown in view, let this be your great aim, the design in which your hearts are engaged. And knowing you must run for it, be as careful about your souls as racers are about their bodies. Deny yourselves all sinful gratifications, yield not to any of the sinful desires of your corrupt nature, but deny all ungodliness and worldly lusts, that your souls may not be unfitted thereby for running your spiritual race.

☙ ANNE DUTTON

Hope Encouraged in the Contemplation of the Divine Perfections

Why sinks my weak desponding mind?
Why heaves my heart the anxious sigh?
Can sovereign goodness be unkind?
Am I not safe, if God is nigh?

He holds all nature in His hand:
That gracious hand on which I live,
Does life, and time, and death command;
And has immortal joys to give.

'Tis He supports this fainting frame,
On Him alone my hopes recline;
The wond'rous glories of His name,
How wide they spread! how bright they shine!

Infinite wisdom! boundless pow'r,
Unchanging faithfulness and love!
Here let me trust, while I adore,
Nor from thy refuge e'er remove.

My God, if Thou art mine indeed,
Then I have all my heart can crave;
A present help in times of need,
Still kind to hear, and strong to save.

* ANNE STEELE

Walking in Darkness

He that followeth me shall not walk in darkness,
but shall have the light of life.
—JOHN 8:12

My dear sister, though you are sorrowful, yet rejoice in the Lord, in the Lord of light, in the Lord your light. You are a child of light, an heir of light. Light and gladness are sown for you and shall certainly spring up into a glorious crop in the Lord's time. And though at present you may be in some darkness, yet rejoice in tribulation. By this your Lord is to be glorified, your faith tried, and your soul more abundantly made fit for your inheritance in light. You are an heir of light. You shall have light enough ere long—light without darkness, light without an end! Enough to fill all the cravings of your capacious spirit and infinitely to exceed its utmost capacity! You shall dwell in sun: dwell in God, in the light of Jehovah, without the least separation or intervening cloud to the days of eternity.

Wherefore, rejoice in the hope of the glory of God. And when you walk in darkness and have no light of spiritual sense to comfort you, then trust in the Lord and stay yourselves upon your God. And well you may, for Jehovah, in all His infinite fullness, is yours! You have an entire and eternal interest in God. And the darkness and the light are both alike to Him. Darkness, which makes such a change in your spirit, makes no alteration in God's heart toward you. He looks upon you, in all the times that pass over you, with one perpetual, uninterrupted view, as an object of His eternal complacency in His dear Son, and thus forever rests in His love, rejoicing over you with singing! Come then, my dear sister, rest where your God and Father rests. Come, lie down in faith in the bosom of His eternal love! It is a sweet, soft bed that will delight and refresh you exceedingly. Here is a basin of heavenly wine, or, rather, a sea of boundless bliss! Drink your fill, bathe your soul in pleasures, and shout the glories, the fullness, and the praises of the strong Jehovah amid all your felt emptiness, weakness, and imperfections.

ও ANNE DUTTON

The Things That Shall Not Be in Heaven

And God shall wipe away all tears from their eyes; and there
shall be no more death, neither sorrow, nor crying, neither shall there
be any more pain: for the former things are passed away.

—REVELATION 21:4

Our subject today is the things that shall not be in heaven. And first we shall name that there will be no more curse. Very early in man's history, just after Adam's fall, the ground was cursed for Adam's sake. But in the new heavens and new earth there will be no more curse. We shall enjoy a better paradise than the one our first parents lost for us. We come to a very important point when we say there will be no more death. Death came into this world with sin, but "they which shall be accounted worthy to obtain that world and the resurrection from the dead" will not "die anymore," for they shall be "equal unto the angels," and "the children of God," being the children of the resurrection in the most exalted sense of that endearing term "children of God."

Sorrow and tears shall be alike unknown in the glorious place we speak of. "God shall wipe away all tears from their eyes," says John. How perfect the consolation, and how eternal, which the Father of mercies and King of eternity shall Himself give! Pain, too, will never be felt in heaven. The Good Physician, who healed so many on earth and who knew what pain was in its most awful form on the cross, will have none to heal in heaven, for "neither shall there be any pain there." Hunger and thirst and burning heat will be all unknown. None of these earthly troubles shall be in those abodes of bliss, "for the former things are passed away."

And lastly, let me observe how solemn it is to remark that no impenitent sinner will be in heaven. If you hope to go there when you die, remember this now. Many are called, few are chosen! The way to life is narrow, and few find it! These are the sayings of the compassionate Savior Himself, and therefore we ought not to suppress them.

❧ ELIZABETH JULIA HASELL

The Contrast

Behold, his soul which is lifted up is not upright in him:
but the just shall live by his faith.

—HABAKKUK 2:4

Is not godliness gain? Profitable for this life as well as that which is to come? What is the portion of the worldling? Even in this life is "shadowy joy or solid woe," without a balance to the first or consolation in the last; no sure footing in the one nor support in the other. Prosperity encrusts their hearts and increases their carnality; nestling in their worldly comforts, they forget they are the creatures of a day, that an endless eternity lies before them, and only the feeble uncertain thread of life between them and that curse under which they were born.

Not so the child of God; all things work together for his good—all things. His standing is not in himself. His footsteps are directed by infinite wisdom. He is kept by the power of God, through faith, unto salvation. Nothing can separate him from the love of God. His life is hid with Christ in God: there is cause to rejoice always. His privileges are boundless, infinite, for God Himself is become his salvation. Have we then any cause for fear? Yes though nothing can rob us of our charter, there is another side to be beheld. In Christ we have all things richly to enjoy, but we have not all in possession. What we have is by faith; all is secured by our Surety for eternity. We shall overcome by the blood of the Lamb, but we must enter into that rest, that perfect rest, through great tribulation. While our eternal salvation is secured by our Surety, it hath pleased Infinite Wisdom to appoint another connection, which shall exist while we remain on earth—even the connection between our steadfastness, consequently our comfort, and the means of grace which He had appointed, making the first to depend in a great measure on our diligent use of the last. Many exhortations are given in this view: "They that wait on the Lord shall renew their strength." "Seek and ye shall find, ask and ye shall receive, knock and it shall be opened unto you."

ॐ ISABELLA GRAHAM

Listening for the King's Voice

Let my lord the king now speak.
—2 SAMUEL 14:18

Are we not apt to think more of speaking to the King than of the King speaking to us? We come to the throne of grace with the glad and solemn purpose, "I will now speak unto the King." And we pour out our hearts before Him and tell Him all the sins and all the needs, all the joys and all the sorrows, till the very telling seems almost an answer because it brings such a sense of relief. It is very sweet and very comforting to do this. But this is only half communion, and we miss, perhaps, a great deal of unknown blessing by being content with this one-sided audience. We should use another "now," and say, "Let my Lord the King now speak." We expect Him to speak sometime, but not actually and literally "now," while we kneel before Him. And therefore we do not listen, and therefore we do not hear what He has to say to us. What about last time we knelt in prayer? Surely He had more to say to us than we had to say to Him, and yet we never waited a minute to see! We did not give Him opportunity for His gracious response. We rushed away from our King's presence as soon as we had said our say and vaguely expected Him to send His answers after us somehow and sometime, but not there and then.

Not that we should pray less, but listen more. And the more we listen, the more we shall want to say afterward. "Thou shalt call, and I will answer." But we may miss the sweetest whispers of His love by not saying, "Speak, Lord" and not hushing ourselves to "hear what God the Lord will speak." We cannot hear His still, small voice during a torrent of noisy, impatient, and hurried petition. We must let the King now speak—not our own hearts and our wandering thoughts, not the world and not the tempter—we must not let these speak. They must be silenced with holy determination. And we must let the King speak as King, meeting His utterance with implicit submission and faith and obedience; receiving His least hint with total homage, love, and gratitude.

&> FRANCES RIDLEY HAVERGAL

The Acceptable Time

We then, as workers together with him, beseech you
also that ye receive not the grace of God in vain. (For he saith,
I have heard thee in a time accepted, and in the day of salvation
have I succoured thee: behold, now is the accepted time;
behold, now is the day of salvation.)

—2 CORINTHIANS 6:1–2

Nothing but an affectionate regard for you would induce me to write to you on a subject which the world will undoubtedly ridicule, but which engages the attention and constitutes the felicity of the holy inhabitants of heaven. This subject is the religion of the gospel.

If we reflect for a moment, we feel conscious that there is an immortal principle within that will exist when time and nature die. This principle is corrupted by sin, and without the sanctifying grace of God, we should be unhappy, even though admitted to heaven. Do but examine the feelings of your heart one hour, and you cannot for a moment doubt the truth of this assertion.

How important, then, that we should have this work of grace begun in our hearts before it is too late. "Now is the accepted time; behold, now is the day of salvation." Tomorrow our probation may be closed, and we may be irrecoverably lost. My heart is full. What inducements can I offer you to receive Jesus by faith and willingly sacrifice your all for Him? O think of the worth of the soul, the price paid to redeem, the love of Immanuel, your obligations to live to Him, the joys prepared for the righteous. O, think of the torments in reserve for the finally impenitent—and be induced to flee from the wrath to come. May you become a living witness for Him. When our journey through this barren wilderness is ended, may we meet in heaven.

 HARRIET NEWELL

Faint Yet Pursuing (1)

I also will keep thee from the hour of temptation, which shall come upon all the world, to try them that dwell upon the earth.

—REVELATION 3:10

My dear friend, I believe I love you the better for all your mental trials. There is something in beholding your friends suffer in any way that excites sympathy, and sympathy begets love. When all goes on smoothly with our friends, we think they can do well enough without us, and perhaps we do not feel so strong affection where we view ourselves as wholly unimportant. In fain would I write something which may have a quickening influence on us both.

Let us beware of despondency, or a gloomy faithlessness in the covenant of God's grace. It is true, we are all you describe—backsliders, rebellious children, who would, long ago, have wearied out the goodness of our Benefactor if He were not infinite in mercy. We may, on some accounts, be greater sinners than others, if guilt is to be measured by love resisted and grace abused. This should humble us. It should lay us low in the dust with the spirit of filial brokenness of heart before our injured and compassionate God. It should make us sigh and mourn under a sense of our pollution, and labor for sanctification.

But it should not wither our strength and consume our spirits in faithless sorrow. Oh, no. "Faint, yet pursuing," should be our motto. The spiritual sloth that results from indifference and the spiritual debility that arises from unbelief are equally dangerous to the soul. It is no less true in spiritual than in temporal things "that the hand of the diligent maketh rich, but he that dealeth with a slack hand becometh poor."

❧ SUSAN HUNTINGTON

Faint Yet Pursuing (2)

I also will keep thee from the hour of temptation, which shall come upon all the world, to try them that dwell upon the earth.

—REVELATION 3:10

One of the benefits secured to believers by the promises of God's well-ordered covenant is sanctification. This was purchased for them by their great Mediator and Head to bestow upon His people the blessings He has obtained for them. He does not send us on warfare at our own charges. He proffers us all necessary grace. All we need is treasured up in Him in whom we profess to believe and may be obtained by looking to Him in the exercise of a lively faith.

Let us, then, never be contented while our spiritual enemies are not subdued, but fight manfully the good fight of faith. Alas! I know not how it is, but there seems to be something within us that prevents our resolutely determining to give our temptations no quarter. The world holds out her allurements, her flatteries please us; our pride or our selfishness is gratified; and we do not say to the ensnaring tempter, "Get thee behind me, Satan." This is my greatest trouble—the want of singleness of heart toward God, the abiding, practical determination to resist every sin in its first specious advances.

What ingratitude toward Him who loved us unto death; toward Him whom, if we are Christians, we love, after all, far better than we love all other things; toward Him for whom we should be willing to live, labor, suffer, and die!

❧ SUSAN HUNTINGTON

Lament against the Wicked

*And you, being dead in your sins and the uncircumcision
of your flesh, hath he quickened together with him, having forgiven
you all trespasses; blotting out the handwriting of ordinances
that was against us, which was contrary to us, and took it
out of the way, nailing it to his cross.*

—COLOSSIANS 2:13–14

It is much to be lamented: the schisms, varieties, contentions, and disputations that have been, and are, in the world about Christian religion; and no agreement or concord of the same among the learned men. Truly, the devil has been the sower of the seed of sedition and shall be the maintainer of it, even till God's will be fulfilled. There is no war so cruel and evil as this, for the war with the sword kills but the bodies, and this slays many souls. For the poor, unlearned persons remain confused, and almost everyone believes and works after his own way.

And yet there is but one truth of God's Word, by the which we shall be saved. Happy are they that receive it, and most unhappy are they which neglect and persecute the same. For it shall be more easy for Sodom and Gomorrah at the day of judgment than for them (Matt. 11:24). And not without just cause, if we consider the benevolence, goodness, and mercy of God, who had declared His charity toward us, greater and more inestimable, than ever He did to the Hebrews. For they lived under shadows and figures and were bound to the law (Heb. 10:1). And Christ (we being His greatest enemies) has delivered us from the bondage of the law and has fulfilled all that was figured in their law and also in their prophecies, shedding His own precious blood to make us the children of His Father, and His brethren, and has made us free, setting us in a godly liberty. I mean not license to sin, as many are glad to interpret the same, when Christian liberty is godly entreated of.

* KATHERINE PARR

That Ye May Obtain

Therefore, my brethren dearly beloved and longed for,
my joy and crown, so stand fast in the Lord.
—PHILIPPIANS 4:1

And to you that are beloved of the Lord, to you that love the Lord, let me say, "Hate evil." As you have it in your hearts, according to the new nature; put on the new man, and appear to have it in your practice. Watch and oppose all its motions, and especially its outbreaks, which cast such great dishonor upon God and bring such great hurt to your own souls.

Oh, can you love sin, that loathsome, abominable, hurtful thing? Let all the powers of your souls rise up in the fiercest opposition against it. "Crucify the flesh, with the affections and lusts. Let not sin reign in your mortal bodies, that you should obey it in the lusts thereof."

And in order hereto, be frequent in your acts of faith upon Christ, for the pardon of it and strength against it. Be frequent and serious in your meditations on God's Word; keep it in your mind all the day long, and it will be a great means of keeping you from evil. Abide in Christ by faith, and under the influences of His grace, go on in your everyday work, denying ungodliness and worldly lusts, that you may live soberly, righteously, and godly in this present world. We are called to conflict with the powers of darkness. But we have a glorious Captain that has gotten, and will give us, the victory over them. And we have armor of proof provided.

Let us look upon it as our main business, while in this world, to strive against sin all manner of ways, and to stand against the wiles of the devil. And to this end, let us take unto us the "whole armor of God, that we may be able to withstand in the evil day, and having done all, to stand."

☙ ANNE DUTTON

Gracious Calling

Give me thine heart.
—PROVERBS 23:26

If your soul is dissatisfied with the things of the world and tired with disappointment, cast a longing eye to the fountain of happiness. This is the claim of that God whose name is love: "My son, give me thine heart." "Come unto me, all ye that labor and are heavy laden, and I will give you rest." "In the world ye shall have tribulation, but in me ye shall have peace." Be assured, my dear friend, if you could obtain all of this world that your heart could wish for, you would find vanity written on the possession. Nothing short of God Himself can give happiness to the soul, and exactly in proportion as a man becomes weaned from the world, and his affections centered in God, is he in possession of happiness.

But how is this to be attained? By God's own plan, and no other. As many weary themselves in vain, hunting the shadows of time, so many great philosophers, sensible of this great truth that God alone can satisfy the rational soul, also weary themselves in vain because they will not seek the blessing in God's own way. "When the world by wisdom knew not God, it pleased Him, by the foolishness of preaching [what was esteemed so] to save them that believe."

The Savior said, "Ye will not come to me, that ye might have life. No man can come to the Father but by me. I am the way, the truth and the life." "Search the Scriptures, for in them ye think ye have eternal life, and they are they which testify of me." The Scripture testifies what our own hearts must assent to, that human nature is depraved and corrupt; broken off from God; at a distance from Him by sin; enmity against Him in His true character; opposed to His holy law in its extent and spirituality. We are also helpless, dead in trespasses and sins. "O Israel, thou hast destroyed thyself [blessed be God for what follows], but in me is thy help."

ଓ ISABELLA GRAHAM

Adoration

And they sing the song of Moses the servant of God, and the song of the Lamb, saying, Great and marvellous are thy works, Lord God Almighty; just and true are thy ways, thou King of saints.

—REVELATION 15:3

O blessed is he that readeth, and they that hear the words of this prophecy, and keep those things which are written therein; for the time is at hand. It appears, therefore, that a blessing is attached to the devout study of this last book of the Bible, and we will endeavor, with God's help, to meditate on something of the employment of the blessed in glory. One thing is very plain from this and other passages in the same book—praise is a great part of the occupation of the saints in heaven. They seem ever praising God and the Lamb. Salvation through Christ seems to exercise the powers and fill the hearts of saints and angels. Adoration seems the delightful employment of thousands and thousands. These gloried faculties are satisfied and find the theme of redemption ever new. Those enlarged understandings do not tire of the gospel plan of salvation. Nor do angels, who never sinned and never needed a Savior, cease to take their part in the heavenly chorus; but, with all saints, they give thanks to God and the Lamb: "Worthy is the Lamb that was slain, to receive power, and riches, and wisdom, and strength, and honor, and glory, and blessing."

We have a description of rejoicing and triumphant saints praising the Savior. These blessed persons have "the harps of God," and we are admitted to have a glimpse of them and to hear, in imagination, their heavenly music. Many things will not be in heaven, but we rejoice to learn that there will be music there. And if on earth sacred music raises the heart to heaven, what will be the music of heaven itself? No voices there will sing holy words without feeling them, which is—alas—too often the case here below; but all shall feel what they sing, beyond what we can now imagine.

☙ ELIZABETH JULIA HASELL

Winter and Summer Seasons

Be strong and of good courage, and do it: fear not,
nor be dismayed: for the LORD God, even my God, will be
with thee; he will not fail thee, nor forsake thee.

—1 CHRONICLES 28:20

I trust that encouraging promise "I will be with thee withersoever thou goest," which has of late been made very sweet to me, will, if it please Him, be fulfilled also in your experience. He will ever be with you and with everyone whose heart He has touched with His converting grace and redeeming love. But our faith is not always strong and lively enough to realize His heavenly presence.

Like as the natural sun may be obscured from our view by some passing cloud, so may the comforting rays of the Sun of Righteousness be for a time obscured by some mental cloud through which our faith is unable to penetrate. And then we soon begin to fear and say, "My beloved has withdrawn Himself!" To the law and the testimony, therefore, we will turn, rather than to sense and feeling, and, under the darkest cloud, rest upon His blessed word of promise—"I will never leave thee, nor forsake thee." It is in order to produce, or rather to exercise, this stability of faith that we are suffered sometimes to walk in darkness. Every true Christian has his winter and summer seasons. It is only in that blessed country, toward which we are hastening, that there is one unclouded day.

With respect to myself, I have reason to bless the Lord for the storm as well as the calm. That is best for the soul which keeps it low at the foot of the cross, loathing itself and trusting only in Jesus, sinking before Him in order to rise in Him, who is our righteousness and strength.

❧ SARAH HAWKES

Word of Entreaty

Who can tell if God will turn and repent, and turn
away from his fierce anger, that we perish not?
—JONAH 3:9

Unto you that profess faith in Christ and hope to be saved by Him and never felt the efficacy of Christ's blood to make you die unto sin, nor the power of His grace to enable you to live unto God—unto you let me say that your present condition is a Christless state. You make mention of His name but have no interest in His person nor right to His salvation. If any man have not the Spirit of Christ to reveal Christ in him and to work conformity in his heart and life to Him, he is none of His.

Oh, you secure souls that never saw the plague of your own hearts, the necessity of being born again of a better righteousness than your own for your justification in the sight of God, your case is exceeding miserable. You that never saw a necessity of any other faith in Christ than what you had by education nor of any other holiness to God than a little mere morality in an offensive conversation among men—you are yet under the power of unbelief, that sin of sins, and have no true holiness in your souls. You have neither a right to nor are made meet for the inheritance of the saints in light. A terrible day is coming that will strip you of your Christianity and proclaim you workers of iniquity.

You may labor all your days to get the victory over sin, but can never obtain it unless you believe in Jesus. Without Christ, in this respect, without vital union to Him and His living in you, you can do nothing. And faith is the gift of God, a gift bestowed upon poor, unbelieving sinners through the ministry of the blessed gospel. Ask it therefore of the Father of mercies, and seek it in the way of His appointment. For who can tell but the gospel of Christ may be the power of God unto your salvation from unbelief, unto faith, and through faith unto holiness and life forevermore?

&ampersand; ANNE DUTTON

The Whole Heart for Christ

*For I am now ready to be offered, and the time of my
departure is at hand. I have fought a good fight, I have finished
my course, I have kept the faith: henceforth there is laid up for
me a crown of righteousness, which the Lord, the
righteous judge, shall give me at that day.*

—2 TIMOTHY 4:6–8

We live in a dying world, and "we all do fade as a leaf," but this should not distress us, for the sooner the believer departs, the sooner he is with the Lord and his happiness complete. Only let us "make our calling and election sure," and if unbelief invade or Satan tempt us, let us betake ourselves at once to Jesus. We are not in a right position if we are without the sensible presence of the Lord. Concerning this He is very jealous.

If we can make ourselves happy and satisfied with the enjoyment of any earthly good or gift of His, apart from His felt presence, it is not pleasant to Christ. He must have our whole heart. The coldness toward us of one we love would distress us. So is it with the Lord. If, then, we discover coldness in our affections toward Him, let us at once go and tell Him, and He will warm them afresh with His own love—His precious love—that never varies, never chills. And let us not forget, too, that if we ever cherish any idol in our hearts, allowing the creature, however dear, to come between Christ and us, He will remove the idol out of the way or make it a source of trouble and sorrow.

Oh to be ready when the change comes—*quite ready!*

ò MARY WINSLOW

Our Example in Christian Life

But put ye on the Lord Jesus Christ.
—ROMANS 13:14

Charity suffers long and is gentle, envies not, upbraids no man, casts forwardly no faults in men's teeth, but refers all things to God (1 Cor. 13), being angry without sin (Eph. 4:16), reforming others without their slanders, carrying ever a storehouse of mild words to pierce the stonyhearted men. I would that all Christians, like as they have professed Christ, would so endeavor themselves to follow Him in godly living. For we have not put on Christ to live anymore to ourselves in the vanities, delights, and pleasures of the world and the flesh, suffering the concupiscence and carnality of the flesh to have its full swing. For we must walk after the Spirit and not after the flesh, for the Spirit is spiritual, and covets spiritual things, and the flesh carnal (Gal. 5:16), and desires carnal things. Men who are regenerated by Christ despise the world and all the vanities and pleasures thereof.

They are no lovers of themselves, for they feel how evil and infirm they are, not being able to do any good thing without the help of God, from whom they acknowledge all goodness to proceed. They flatter not themselves with thinking everything that shines to the world to be good and holy, for they know all external and outward works, be they ever so glorious and fair to the world, may be done of the evil as well as the good.

They are not also as a reed shaken with every wind (Matt. 11:7), but when they are blasted with the tempests and storms of the world, then remain they most firm, stable, and quiet, feeling in spirit that God, as their best Father, does send and suffer all things for their benefit and commodity. Christ is to them a rule, a line, and example of Christian life.

&ealig; KATHERINE PARR

Flee Foolish Folly

I will hear what God the LORD will speak:
for he will speak peace unto his people, and to his saints:
but let them not turn again to folly.

—PSALM 85:8

Job's confession was, "I abhor myself, and repent in dust and ashes," and justly so. How deceitful is the human heart! How unfaithful the conscience! How little do we know of the sins of our daily walk! We are called to watch and pray, that we enter not into temptation; to walk with God in close intimate communion; "whether we eat or drink, to do all to His glory"; to consult Him in all affairs of life, narrowly observing His providence in connection with our circumstances; weighing all in His presence, requesting Him to determine our wills and direct our steps. We ought not to say, "We will go into such a city," and do this or that, but "if the Lord will." How inconsistent our conduct with these rules! How often do rashness, precipitation, and self-will accompany our determinations and movements! And how often do His goodness and wisdom overrule our folly, save us from our own pits, and prevent the evil that might be expected.

At no time does He deal with us as we sin, though sometimes He stands by and allows us a taste of our folly. Then we are in trouble; we dig our pits and fall into them, but we cannot deliver ourselves. O, what a God, who, even at such a time, says to us, "Call on me in the time of trouble; I will deliver thee, and thou shalt glorify my name"; thou hast destroyed thyself, but in Me is thy help. Blessed help! Mercy to pardon, goodness to restore, wisdom to guide, faithfulness to carry through and perfect what concerns us, overruling our very follies and causing them to teach us to profit. This is God's way, according to many declarations of Himself in His Word, and the experience of all His redeemed. "Blessed then is the man that trusteth in the Lord." They truly are a blessed people whose God Jehovah is.

❧ ISABELLA GRAHAM

The Great White Throne

And I saw a great white throne, and him that sat on it,
from whose face the earth and the heaven fled away; and there
was found no place for them. And I saw the dead, small and great, stand
before God; and the books were opened: and another book was opened,
which is the book of life: and the dead were judged out of those things
which were written in the books, according to their works.

—REVELATION 20:11–12

The Lord Himself shall descend from heaven with a shout, with the voice of the archangel, with the trump of God; and He shall descend as the great Judge of mankind and, thus gloriously attended, take His seat on the great white throne. How grand and how awful is the prophetic description in our text. How solemn and affecting is it to consider that He who shall come in heavenly pomp and dazzling glory is the Lord Jesus, who "was despised and rejected of men, a man of Sorrows and acquainted with grief!" How touching and impressive is it to remember that when we actually see (and we shall most certainly see) that great white throne, and the Judge, and the glorious army of angels round about Him, the day of grace will be over! We ourselves shall be forever with the saved or with the lost, for there will be no change anymore; our state will be fixed for eternity.

Therefore, I do not only ask you to admire and wonder at a solemn and magnificent description; still more do I ask you to lay seriously to heart the importance, the all-importance, of this awesome subject as concerning ourselves. I ask you to remember that if we have not obtained mercy before Christ comes to judgment, it will be too late to cry for it when He does come. Let us remember this, while life and health last, and not put off turning to God through Christ. "Now is the day of salvation." He who will be our Judge presents Himself to us now as our Savior. May we know Him savingly in this character, and then the terrors of the day of judgment shall not overwhelm us when it comes!

≖ ELIZABETH JULIA HASELL

Casting Care upon Christ

Casting all your care upon him; for he careth for you.

—1 PETER 5:7

How is our loving, gracious God dealing with you? In all His dealings, whatever they may be, there is nothing but the tenderest love toward you, all designed to draw you nearer and nearer to Himself. Forget not that it is through much tribulation we are to enter the kingdom, but it is all to prepare us for the fuller enjoyment of it when we arrive there. Wait patiently, looking unto Jesus, trusting Him fully for all things, within and without. Oh, this is sweet living—living upon Christ! It is very nearly like living with Him, even in this vale of tears and in this house of our bondage. For this very cause we are tried, in order to bring us to a better acquaintance with His tenderness, sympathy, and unchanging love. He cares for you. You need not trouble yourself about, or load yourself with earthly cares. Carry them, as they arise, to Him, and do not set yourself about to manage matters, when He, who has sent the cares, will manage better for you than you can for yourself. Trust Him, wholly trust Him. Thus will you honor Him; and they who honor Him, He will honor.

May the Lord comfort and support you; grant you much of His sensible presence, without which we are lonely ones indeed. I must have His presence and His listening ear, too, or I am not happy. How condescending to bow down His ear—to listen to all we have to say to Him! Come with an open heart, and pour all into His own loving heart. This is the confidence He loves. What a mercy to have such a God and Father to deal with us, who pities and loves us too! Oh, let us rejoice together and cast all our cares upon Him and be anxious for nothing.

இ MARY WINSLOW

The Bright Side of Growing Older

And thine age shall be clearer than the noonday; thou
shalt shine forth, thou shalt be as the morning.

—JOB 11:17

I suppose nobody ever did naturally like the idea of getting older.
There is a sense of oppression and depression about it. But how
surely the Bible gives us the bright side of everything! In this case
it gives three bright sides of a fact, which, without it, could not help
being gloomy.

First, it opens the sure prospect of increasing brightness to those
who have begun to walk in the light. Even if the sun of our life
has reached the apparent zenith, and we have known a very noonday of mental and spiritual being, it is not poetic western shadows
that are to lengthen upon our way, but our age is to be clearer than
the noonday.

The second bright side is increasing fruitfulness. Do not let
us confuse between works and fruit. Many a saint in the land of
Beulah is not able to do anything at all and yet is bringing forth
fruit unto God beyond the busiest workers. So that even when we
come to the days when the strong men shall bow themselves, there
may be more pleasant fruits for our Master, riper and fuller and
sweeter, than ever before. Some of the fruits of the Spirit seem to
be especially and peculiarly characteristic of sanctified older years,
and do we not want to bring them all forth? Look at the splendid
ripeness of Abraham's faith in his old age; the grandeur of Moses's
meekness, when he went up the mountain alone to die; the mellow-
ness of Paul's joy in his later epistles; and the wonderful gentleness
of John, wanting to call down God's lightnings of wrath. And the
same Spirit is given to us, that we too may bring forth "fruit that
may abound" and always "more fruit."

The third bright side is brightest of all: "Even to your old age,
I am he"; always the same Jehovah-Jesus with us all the days.
"Even to hoar hairs will I carry you.... Even I will carry and will
deliver you."

› FRANCES RIDLEY HAVERGAL

Our Best Friend

There is a friend that sticketh closer than a brother.
—PROVERBS 18:24

What are earthly friends? How few are steady against all change of circumstances! Of these, fewer still have it in their power to supply every link of friendship's chain; a thousand unforeseen incidents disappoint their wishes and frustrate their hopes, rendering abortive their greatest exertions. But there is a friend everywhere present, thoroughly acquainted with every circumstance of the heart and of the life; all-powerful to relieve; whose love is invariable and ever the most tender when every other friend stands aloof; a friend in adversity; "a friend that sticketh closer than a brother," whose "love surpasseth the love of women." This friend receives sinners—casts out none who come to Him. He was never known to disappoint the hopes of any poor sinner. He receives them in His heart. He takes all their burdens and cares on Himself, pays all their debts, answers all demands against them, and is every way surety for them. They become His own. No one has anything to say to them but Himself. He knows them—how apt to err, to wander, yea, to forget Him and prove ungrateful. All this He knows, but He has made provision for all. He has a rod, and He will subdue their iniquities. He will heal their backslidings. He will bring them back and restore His wanderers. He will in due time perfect what concerns them and present them to His Father purified, without spot or wrinkle.

In the meantime, He requires them to confide in Him; to go up through this wilderness leaning upon Him; to tell Him all their complaints and griefs and to comfort themselves. And He will impress the comfort by means of His great and precious promises, scattered like so many pearls through His sacred Bible, tabled there, on purpose for us to ground our prayers upon and delight ourselves in. This is your friend's Friend, and of ten thousand beside.

☙ ISABELLA GRAHAM

Be of One Mind

Be of the same mind one toward another.
Mind not high things, but condescend to men of low estate.
Be not wise in your own conceits.
—ROMANS 12:16

I beseech the Lord to send the learned and unlearned such abundance of His Holy Spirit, that they may obey and observe the most sincere and holy Word of God and show the fruits thereof, which consist chiefly in charity and godly unity. That as we have professed one God, one faith, and one baptism, so we may be all of one mind and one accord, putting away all biting and gnawing; for in backbiting, slandering, and misreporting our Christian brethren, we show not ourselves the disciples of Christ, whom we profess. In Him was most high charity, humility, and patience, suffering most patiently all ignominy, rebukes, and slanders, praying to His eternal Father for His enemies with most fervent charity; and in all things did remit His will to His Father's, as the Scripture doth witness when He prayed in the mount.

A goodly example and lesson for us to follow at all times and seasons, as well in prosperity as in adversity, to have no will but God's will, committing and leaving to Him all our cares and griefs, and to abandon all our policies and inventions, for they are most vain and foolish and indeed very shadows and dreams. But we are yet so carnal and fleshly that we run headlong, like unbridled colts without snaffle or bit.

If we had the love of God printed in our hearts, it would keep us back from running astray. And until such time as it pleases God to send us this bit to hold us in, we shall never run the right way, although we speak and talk ever so much of God and His Word.

&❧ KATHERINE PARR

Words Contrary to Actions

He that saith he abideth in him ought himself
also so to walk, even as he walked.

—1 JOHN 2:6

When I measure myself by the standard of Christian perfection given by the Lord Jesus in His Word, I feel ashamed to call myself His follower at all, so far do I lag behind in running the race, so destitute do I seem of those traits which would prove me to be the Lord's.

To be Christlike is the duty and privilege of every believer. God's Word distinctly settles that matter when it affirms, "Now if any man have not the Spirit of Christ, he is none of his." I ask myself, oh, will not you do the same? How much of His likeness has been visible in my conduct during this day? How far have I been— that which my Lord expects me to be—His representative in this sinful world? If bearing the cross after Christ is the chief work of the Christian, have I borne it in patience and obedience and full surrender to His will in all things, or have I, as far as I was able, put it aside and thought my own thoughts, walked in my own ways, and done what pleased myself without any reference to Him or recognition of His right to "reign over me"?

There are Christians who think they have liberty to do their own will in a thousand things. They speak very much as they like; they do very much as they like; they use their property and possessions as they like. They are their own masters, and they have never dreamed of saying, "Jesus, we forsake all to follow Thee." May God keep us from the sin and error of thinking that we can accept Christ as our Savior, and yet practically deny Him as our Master!

&» SUSANNAH SPURGEON

The Great Transaction

Then shall the King say unto them on his right hand,
Come, ye blessed of my Father, inherit the kingdom prepared
for you from the foundation of the world.... Then shall he say also
unto them on the left hand, Depart from me, ye cursed, into
everlasting fire, prepared for the devil and his angels.

—MATTHEW 25:34, 41

I am sure no human words can at all bring before our minds, forcibly enough, the solemn scene, the great transaction, in which we must be present! But while we dwell in solemn thought upon the awful grandeur of the Judge of mankind, let us also remember that He who "shall come in his glory, and all the holy angels with him" is the glorified "Son of Man." Before this mighty Judge and heavenly King, "the dead, small and great" shall stand and receive every man his just sentence: "Come, ye blessed" or, "Depart, ye cursed." The books shall be opened, the records of the acts and deeds of those judged shall be read, and they will be judged "according to their works." The wicked king and the wicked beggar alike depart to misery. The godly prince and the holy rich man and the God-fearing laborer will also go together to glory.

The books so solemnly opened and examined at the great day are used as a figure to show us how exactly God remembers our thoughts, words, and deeds. God grant that before these books be opened the bleeding hand of the Savior may have graciously blotted out the record against us!

"Another book" shall be opened at the judgment. This is the Book of Life. In this all the saved are named. Known to God, not always to man, are those who shall be at the Judge's right hand then. In writing to the Philippians, Paul names certain holy women, with others also, "whose names are in the book of life." Are our names in the Book of Life?

&ᴥ ELIZABETH JULIA HASELL

Excuses Foiled

But one thing is needful.

—LUKE 10:42

The "broad road" will "lead to destruction," however carelessly persons may walk therein; and the threatenings of God's Word against sin will be executed, however indifferently persons may hear or read of them. It will not stand as an excuse before Him to say, "I did not feel the force of the threatenings, or did not see any evil in my pursuits." What God has declared to be evil is so, and those who do such things will be judged by Him as evildoers, just as His Word declared: "He will render to every man according to his deeds." Now the pleasures of the world are not only empty and unsatisfactory, but they also destroy the soul and displease God, and all who persist in them are His enemies. They are called "lovers of pleasure more than lovers of God." What a true description!

You say that before anyone can give up the fascinations of the world, he must have a dread of the consequences, and that to this point you are not yet come. But I would now bring before you the certainty of those consequences, even if they are not believed or dreaded. They do not hinge upon the perception or feeling of the creature, but upon the truth of Him who has said, "The end of those things is death." This is a real matter of fact, and, however unfelt, the truth of it will follow you into every party of pleasure, yea, into every one of those streams which are truly called the pleasures of sin; for "whatsoever a man soweth that shall he also reap."

But perhaps you will say, "I have no other sources of pleasure. Would you have me quite miserable?" O beloved, there is not a blood-redeemed sinner before the throne but was miserable once. I should not, therefore, be sorry for you to lose your present poor pleasures and feel "an aching void," for in my Savior's heart there is yet room, and He can fill it all. May the Holy Spirit enable you to pray more earnestly and seek more diligently; it will not be in vain.

ɞ RUTH BRYAN

Thanksgiving Street

Let us offer the sacrifice of praise to God continually, that is,
the fruit of our lips giving thanks to his name.

—HEBREWS 13:15

You have heard of the man who made such a notable change of residence from "Grumble Corner" to "Thanksgiving Street," that the result was his friends scarcely knew him, for "his face had lost the look of care and the ugly frown it used to wear." Without presuming that a need exists for any of my dear readers to remove from their present habitation, it is laid on my heart to remind them of the joy of thanksgiving and to say, "O magnify the Lord with me, and let us exalt his name together!" What a God-honoring employment it is to "offer the sacrifice of praise continually!" We are constantly praying for one thing or another, selfishly spending our breath in a long catalog of our own needs and desires, but our thanks to our gracious God are soon told out, and our praises form but a small part of our devotions.

This is not as it should be—and not as God would have it. To enrobe ourselves daily in the "garment of praise" is not only to secure our own happiness but to fulfill the blessed service of "glorifying God." Prayer is good, but praise is better. Praise is prayer in richest fruitfulness, prayer in highest spirituality, prayer in nearest approach to heaven. Prayer is the language of earth; praise is the native tongue of the angels. Each moment of mercy should strike a note of praise as it passes, and then our days would be one long continued psalm. Praise has power to lift the soul above all care as if on wings.

How many of you, dear readers, will be "chief singers" unto our God and resolve that, henceforth, His praise shall be continually in your mouth?

≈ SUSANNAH SPURGEON

Separation Unto

Seemeth it but a small thing unto you, that the
God of Israel hath separated you from the congregation
of Israel, to bring you near to himself?

—NUMBERS 16:9

There is no true separation from the things which Jesus calls us to leave without a corresponding separation unto things which are incomparably better. One hardly likes to speak of it as compensation, because the "unto" is so infinitely more than the "from"; it is like talking of a royal friendship compensating for dropping a beggar's acquaintance.

First, and chiefly, we are separated unto the Lord Himself. He wants us not only for servants but for friends, and He makes the friendship a splendid and satisfying reality. He wants to bring us near to Himself, that we may be a people near unto Him. He will not have a half-possession in us, and so He says He hath severed you from other people. Why? "That ye should be mine!"—chosen unto Himself, His peculiar treasure, separated from among all the people of the earth to be Thine inheritance. Is it a small thing thus to be the Lord's Nazarite, holy unto the Lord all the days of his separation? Is any earthly crown to be compared to the consecration of his God upon his head? We are separated also to far happier friendships than the world knows. There is no isolation intended. The Lord is able to give you much more than this.

You see your calling. Is it not a high one? Does it seem but a small thing to you? Does it seem too stern a thing? Is it not rather a better thing than fallen man could have dreamed of aspiring to? A brighter life than has entered into the natural heart of man even to imagine? Is it for you? Listen! Be ye separate, and, what then? I will receive you. This is His commandment to you, and this is His promise. Will you obey? Then you shall know a little, but every day more and more, of that unspeakable blessing of being received by the Father, until the day when Jesus shall come again and receive you unto Himself for the grand separation of eternity with Him.

&» FRANCES RIDLEY HAVERGAL

Storing the Word in Our Hearts

Thy word is very pure: therefore thy servant loveth it.
—PSALM 119:140

What I have ever found to be my stay, through every dark and dismal contemplation, is to get my memory stored with Scripture. When thoughts rush in, I do not parley with them, but instantly read, or repeat, some verses of the precious Bible, where I always find an answer for everything. I do indeed, through the help of the blessed Spirit, find the Scripture to be a sacred exorcist that soon puts a legion of fears and miseries to flight, mightily pulling down the strongholds of sin and Satan; casting down imaginations and every rebellious thought; and when mixed with prayer and appropriating faith, effectual to perfect, establish, and settle the soul in peace.

Every passage I read and meditate upon furnishes so many distinct topics for prayer. This I do find to be the secret that obliterates the power and being of second causes. This fills up every aching void in the solitary heart. This turns every wilderness into a pleasant garden—unravels all dark problems—and teaches us to be good arithmeticians, and "reckon, that the present sufferings of this present time are not worthy to be compared with the glory which shall be revealed in us."

How does walking with God, like Enoch, elevate, expand, enrich, enable, compose, and regulate the mind! How much interest does it give to every hour, every moment of the day! There is no aching void, no yawning vacuum in the living Christian's life. All is pursuit, advancement, possession; every object is sublime, animating, filling, eternal. How sweet to begin each day with, "Lord Jesus, into thy hands I commit my spirit," my body, my thoughts, my words, and actions! Peace and communion with God is given, as the apostle says, "at all times, and by all means." Every event and occurrence may be made a means, in the hand of the Holy Spirit, of promoting our peace. May the blessed God, and our Savior, keep you "as the apple of his eye"!

❧ SARAH HAWKES

Why Art Thou Cast Down?

*Why art thou cast down, O my soul? and why art thou
disquieted within me? hope thou in God.*

—PSALM 42:11

There is no doubt that the depression of spirits may be, in most cases, traced immediately to some cause connected with that delicate and subtle part of our constitution called the nervous system; but, primarily, it is from God. I do believe that such a trial of ourselves, such an unsettling of all our strongholds, such a lesson of our extreme weakness and helplessness and poverty is often attended with the most beneficial effects. It is indeed like being laid in the furnace, and we are ready to fear we shall be utterly consumed. Yet our gracious God designs only to consume the dross.

We can grow in grace no farther than we learn to draw all our supplies from the Lord Jesus Christ. It is of His fullness that we must receive grace for grace. And how shall we be made to learn this? Why, by learning that we are poor and weak and blind and naked, dependent on God not only for the bounties of His grace and providence but for every capacity necessary to our enjoyment or improvement of them. And how can we learn this better than by being, for a season, left of God to our own darkness and helplessness? Who can so well know the blessedness of that hope which is an anchor to the soul as the man who has felt himself in eminent hazard of being shipwrecked on the ocean of despair? Who can feel so deeply as he the unfathomable riches of the grace that has redeemed him? Who can so fully understand the force of those infinite obligations that bind him to be wholly the Lord's? It is, I think, a settled point, that whatever promotes our growth in grace is best for us. And I suppose we grow in grace, just in proportion as we live simply on Christ. Therefore, whatever most effectually humbles us and keeps up in our souls a practical conviction of our constant dependence on Him is best for us, though the means may be of such a kind as, in our imperfect apprehension, may threaten us with destruction.

❧ SUSAN HUNTINGTON

The Final Divide

*He shall separate them one from another, as a shepherd
divideth his sheep from the goats: and he shall set the sheep
on his right hand, but the goats on the left.*

—MATTHEW 25:32–33

Truly, if we sought God's glory, as we should do in all things, we should not be ashamed to confess ourselves to digress from God's precepts and ordinances when it is manifest that we have done so, and do so daily. I pray God our own faults and deeds condemn us not, at the last day, when every man shall be rewarded according to his doings. Truly, if we do not redress and amend our living, according to the doctrine of the gospel, we shall receive a terrible sentence of Christ, the Son of God, when He shall come to judge and condemn all transgressors and breakers of His precepts and commandments and to reward all His obedient and loving children.

We shall have no man of law to make our plea for us, neither can we have the day deferred; neither will the just Judge be corrupted with affection, bribes, or reward; neither will He hear any excuse or delay; neither shall this saint or that martyr help us, be they ever so holy; neither shall our ignorance save us from damnation. But, yet, willful blindness and obstinate ignorance shall receive the greater punishment, and not without just cause. Then shall it be known who has walked in the dark, for all things shall appear manifest before Him. No man's deeds shall be hidden, no, neither words nor thoughts. The poor and simple observers of God's commandments shall be rewarded with everlasting life, as obedient children to the heavenly Father. And the transgressors, adders and diminishers of the law of God, shall receive eternal damnation for their just reward. I beseech God we may escape this fearful sentence and be found such faithful servants and loving children, that we may hear the happy, comfortable, and most joyful sentence, ordained for the children of God, which is: "Come, ye blessed of my Father, inherit the kingdom prepared for you from the foundation of the world."

&ctus; KATHERINE PARR

The Voice of Mercy

And therefore will the LORD wait, that he may be gracious
unto you, and therefore will he be exalted, that he may have
mercy upon you: for the LORD is a God of judgment:
blessed are all they that wait for him.

—ISAIAH 30:18

I know not the amount of that over which you mourn with so much agony. We can do nothing in our own strength—no, not so much as think a good thought. You do not know where to look for comfort? To Jesus—not to yourself, not to any creature. "Look unto me and be saved, all the ends of the earth, for I am God and there is none else."

It is the peculiar office of the Spirit to convince of sin. You have sinned in heart, lip, and life. "Thou shalt love the Lord thy God with all thy heart." Oh what prostituted affections! What misspent time, while God says, "Whether you eat or drink, or whatsoever you do, do all to the glory of God." Listen to the voice of convictions, listen to the voice of mercy leading you to Christ, the great propitiatory sacrifice, "the Lamb of God which taketh away the sins of the world."

Go to Christ as a sinner. Tell Him you commit your sinful soul into His hands. Say, "Thou hast bid me look unto thee and be saved. Savior, I do look unto Thee for salvation. Wash me in Thy blood; clothe me in Thy righteousness; sanctify me by Thy grace; accept me.

Rest on Christ. Put your trust in Him. If you do, He will not disappoint you. Now, faith is a saving grace; thereby we receive and rest upon Christ for salvation, as He is offered to us in the gospel. Wait His appointed time, in the use of the means, till He manifests Himself to you.

ও ISABELLA GRAHAM

Eternity

Eternity is just at hand;
And shall I waste my ebbing sand,
And careless view departing day,
And throw my inch of time away?

Eternity! Tremendous sound!
To guilty souls, a dreadful wound;
But, oh! if Christ and heav'n be mine,
How sweet the accents! how divine!

Be this my chief, my only care,
My high pursuit, my ardent prayer,
An int'rest in the Savior's blood,
My pardon sealed, and peace with God.

Search, Lord, O search my inmost heart,
And light and hope, and joy impart;
From guilt and error set me free,
And guide me safe to heav'n and Thee.

⇛ ANNE STEELE

Acknowledging or Returning?

Return, ye backsliding children, and I will heal your backslidings.
—JEREMIAH 3:22

An acknowledgment of wandering is not return; a consciousness of a dry, barren state is not restoration. Perhaps you can hardly conceive of a living soul, convinced of being in the wrong and lingering there without earnestly and diligently seeking after the right—but I can. For this bad, bad heart has experienced what drowsiness and listlessness sometimes follow sleep, when there is not heart to arise and call upon the Lord for deliverance. Seeing the case to be bad, we just shrink from knowing it fully, and fear rather to be thoroughly aroused to reap painfully what has been sown to the flesh than desire at any cost to be brought back to close communion with our God.

O my beloved, did the immaculate Lamb of God so much use retirement and prayer, as we find by many portions of Scripture He did? How much more do we who have sin dwelling in us, often working under the most specious forms, need it! The truth is we cannot thrive without it.

Where the experience has indeed become as a wilderness, what double need there is to withdraw from the cases of others and cry mightily unto God to make that "wilderness rejoice and blossom as the rose." Where there has been much talking about gospel day—but long, long night within—what cause is there to withdraw from all and wrestle with Him, who "turneth the shadow of death into mourning." In so doing the feeling of the wilderness state will probably deepen before the rejoicing returns, and the night will seem to grow darker before the bright shining of the Sun of Righteousness rises again upon the soul. However weak they have become, the Lord does renew His people's youth like the eagles and causes them to sing as in the day when He brought them out of Egypt.

❧ RUTH BRYAN

Heavenly Praise

And after these things I heard a great voice of much
people in heaven, saying, Alleluia; Salvation, and glory,
and honour, and power, unto the Lord our God.

—REVELATION 19:1

When the children of Israel had crossed the Red Sea, led by Moses, they celebrated their great deliverance by a triumphant hymn of praise. When the saints of God, the spiritual Israel, have passed through "the waves of this troublesome world," shall they not adore the Lamb? Shall they not praise "the Captain of their salvation," the greater-than-Moses who triumphed over death and the grave and helped them to triumph also? "Great and marvelous are thy works, Lord God Almighty; just and true are thy ways, thou king of saints." If praise, then, is so delightful to the blessed in heaven, are we learning that sacred art now? Adoration is a principal employment of the inhabitants of heaven. Are we learning it here? We can only learn it if taught by the Spirit. The more our spiritual eyes are opened to see the blessedness of redemption, the more we are enlightened to perceive the wonders of redeeming love, the more our affections are set on heavenly things, the more we shall love and praise God.

Through His mercy, the Christian can never be placed in circumstances where he cannot glorify his God in this manner. Paul and Silas sang praises in their dungeon—saints and martyrs have often done so since. In sickness and in old age, the Christian who has learned adoration will continue to praise and adore. Many a person now reading descriptions of heaven feels honestly that such employments would be very distasteful and dull. May such a reader be led to consider, while he has time, that he requires that change of heart, and that consequent taste for holy employments, that God alone can grant! Not one of the human race ever made himself fit for heaven—but, thanks be to God! The great King of eternity can, and will, give a readiness for heaven, to all who seek it, through a Savior.

❧ ELIZABETH JULIA HASELL

Rooting Out Sin

If a man therefore purge himself from these,
he shall be a vessel unto honour, sanctified, and meet for the
master's use, and prepared unto every good work.

—2 TIMOTHY 2:21

A short space spent in laying open the heart before God and in stretching forth the empty vessel to receive out of His fullness—to abase ourselves at His sacred footstool and to cast ourselves on Christ, by simple and true faith—will do more for us than the longest and strongest efforts of our own.

I trust you find an increasing humility of mind and an increasing victory over every opposing evil principle, together with increasing simplicity of aim and dependence. But remember that the graces of the Spirit, so beautifully enumerated by Paul, will grow only in a soil where there has been much plowing and harrowing and weeding out the roots of bitterness, which are the natural and spontaneous productions of the soil. And the plow, the harrow, and the hoe are instruments we do not love, and they bring out many an ugly reptile, which lay beneath the surface quite undiscovered before.

Bend all your most serious energies to get firmly built on that rock from which no sickness, or loss, or even temptations shall remove you. It is of great importance to get a firm footing, before storms and dangers assail you, for they will come to you, as well as to others. But they do not accomplish their design until they destroy the deep, hidden, and entwining root of self. Now, mark well if you find, in your daily experience, that this root is weakening and withering! It is a gradual work that will never be perfected till death. But still, we should be able to perceive that the crucifixion of self is going on and that the opposite most desirable grace, that of humble dependence and universal submission to Christ, is increasing. You may observe, by marks in themselves very small, how far self is giving way; and in proportion as it does give way, your real peace and comfort will increase.

☙ SARAH HAWKES

The Lord's Fire

Blessed is the man that endureth temptation: for when
he is tried, he shall receive the crown of life.

—JAMES 1:12

Think it not strange, my dear sister, concerning the fiery trials you meet with, as if some strange thing had happened unto you. Remember the Lord has His fire in Zion and His furnace in Jerusalem to refine, not to destroy His people (Isa. 31:9). God sends afflictions upon His children for their good. Sin and Satan indeed aim at our destruction herein, but God bounds their rage and overrules their malice to issue in His own glory and our salvation. The design of sin and Satan is the destruction of our graces as well as of our persons, and therefore they blow up the fire of affliction to the utmost, and would continue it until we are consumed. But "hold," says the Lord. "My children are My gold, precious in My esteem, and they must pass through the fire to be refined, but not lie there till they suffer loss." And therefore, when we are in the furnace, our God sits by to see that the fire be not too hot nor continued too long upon us, as the refiner watches his gold, manages it while in the furnace, and takes it out thence when it is fully purified (Mal. 3:3).

Well, then, my dear sister, since you are one of those who are precious in the sight of the Lord, you must pass through the fire of affliction, but since it is the Lord's fire, which He has appointed, which He manages, and which He will restrain at His pleasure, trust yourself in the hands of your infinitely wise and gracious Refiner, and you will come out of it both with present and eternal advantage. This affliction, as an instrument in the hand of God the almighty agent, is at work upon you and for you to exercise and increase your graces here, and to prepare for your future crown; therefore, endure the trial, for "blessed is the man that endureth temptation: for when he is tried, he shall receive the crown of life, which the Lord hath promised to them that love him."

≈ ANNE DUTTON

Give No Place to the Devil

Resist the devil, and he will flee from you.
—JAMES 4:7

Oh, my dear friend, "give no place to the devil!" "Whom resist steadfast in the faith." "Resist the devil, and he will flee from you." "Taking the shield of faith, wherewith ye shall be able to quench all the fiery darts of the wicked one." He works upon your weak frame, enfeebled mind, and painful circumstances and from or by these leads you to draw wrong conclusions and unjust inferences, and thus tighten the cords of your bondage. But oh, fly for refuge to the hope set before you in the gospel; fly to the shadow of the cross, the shelter of the rock! There is pardon for the guiltiest, cleansing for the filthiest, safety for the weakest, and conquest for the most fainthearted. "Not by might, nor by power, but by my Spirit, saith the Lord of hosts." "For when I am weak, then am I strong," said a captain in Emmanuel's army who, like you, wanted the thorn to be taken out of the flesh; but his King knew better—the proud flesh needed the pricking thorn, and the buffeted soldier was brought to say, "Most gladly therefore will I rather glory in mine infirmities, that the power of Christ may rest upon me."

See what the grace of God can do, and presume not to think your case is beyond its power. When the enemy comes into your soul like a flood, with temptation and insinuations, may the Spirit of God lift up a standard against him. And I must again repeat that striking word, "Give no place to the devil." Parley not, listen not; for, O my beloved, he is insulting your best friend, your pardoning, longsuffering God, who has borne with your manners in the wilderness and who still forbears; to whom still belong forgiveness, though you have so rebelled against Him. Oh, that the Good Shepherd would take you to "the sunny side of the hill," that in His light you might look more at your mercies and less at your miseries!

❧ RUTH BRYAN

The Transferred Burden

If our transgressions and our sins be upon us, and we
pine away in them, how should we then live?

—EZEKIEL 33:10

If they are upon us, how can we live? For "mine iniquities are gone over mine head: as an heavy burden they are too heavy for me." The burden of them is intolerable. It is not the sense, but the burden itself which cannot be borne. No one could bear his own iniquities without being sunk lower and lower, and at last to hell by it.

If! But is it? It is written, "The Lord hath laid on him the iniquity of us all." On Jesus it has been laid. This burden is never divided. He took it all—every item, every detail of it. The scapegoat bore "upon him all their iniquities." Think of every separate sin, each that has weighed down our conscience, every separate transgression of our most careless moments, added to the unknown weight of all the unknown or forgotten sins of our whole life, and all this laid on Jesus instead of upon us! The sins of a day are often a burden indeed, but we are told in another type, "I have laid upon thee the years of their iniquity." Think of the years of our iniquity being upon Jesus! Multiply this by the unknown but equally intolerable sin burdens of all His people, and remember that "the Lord hath laid on him the iniquity of us all," and then think what the strength of enduring love must be which bare the sins of many.

Can we doubt the Father's love to us, when we think what it must have cost Him to lay that crushing weight on His dear Son, sparing Him not, that He might spare us instead? The Son accepted the awful burden, but it was the Father's hand which laid it upon Him. It was death to Him, that there might be life to us. For if our transgressions and sins were upon us, there could be no answer to the question, "How should we then live?" for we could only pine away in them and die. But being laid on Him, how shall we now live? He died for all our sins, that they which live should not henceforth live unto themselves, but unto Him which died for them and rose again.

❧ FRANCES RIDLEY HAVERGAL

Spiritual Conflict

Walk in the Spirit, and ye shall not fulfil the lust of the flesh.
—GALATIANS 5:16

Although the Lord is showing you something of the hidden evil of your own heart, which sometimes puts you at your wit's end, yet He gives you to mourn over and lament it before Him. Remember, too, that He says, "To this man will I look, even to him who is of a broken and a contrite heart, and who trembles at my word." Be not discouraged if you feel the Spirit lusting against the flesh, and the flesh against the Spirit. This is an evidence of your sonship. But aim to walk after the Spirit, and give no allowance to the flesh. Put off the old man, with all his vile affections, and put on the new man, which is created in righteousness and true holiness.

Whenever you feel the conflict, lift up your heart at once to Jesus, and He will give you the victory. It is written, "Sin shall not have dominion over you, for ye are not under the law, but under grace." We are traveling home to God, so be of good courage. The only way to get on comfortably is in casting all our care upon Him, being careful for nothing. The Lord has engaged to provide for body and soul all our journey through and to land us safe at last on that happy shore where there is no more care, sin, or death!

Oh, to walk circumspectly! It is easy to make a Christian profession, but to walk in it is quite another thing. Let us pray for much of the sanctifying influence of the Holy Spirit as well as for His outpouring. Let us aim to grow in grace and to trust in Christ day by day. Never let the cause of Jesus be hindered through us, but let His glory be dearer to our hearts than life itself. We must "watch and pray." These two commands go together.

❧ MARY WINSLOW

Prideful Self

When pride cometh, then cometh shame:
but with the lowly is wisdom.

—PROVERBS 11:2

I have been interested in observing that when I walk with my face toward the sun, my own black shadow is cast behind me; but when my back is toward the sun, this black resemblance of myself marches on before me, full in view. This "I considered and received instruction." So that I was made to cry, "Turn me again, O Lord of hosts; cause thy face to shine, and I shall be saved." Ah, we do indeed want turning by divine power toward the Sun of Righteousness, that self may be out of view; for no precious fruits of humility, love, joy, peace, meekness, long-suffering, faith will flow by looking at our own black self, but the hardness will grow harder, and the darkness more horrible, and pride will fret and grumble, because self can get nothing to glory in. All must be found in Jesus: "In him shall all the seed of Israel be justified, and shall glory."

How many years was I unwittingly going about to establish my own righteousness! I was truly loathing myself and ever seeing "greater abominations," but mourning and fretting daily because I could get no better. I wanted to be spiritual, holy, and humble; to be melted into contrition and repentance, but was looking to the wrong place for it and never thought that the cursed leaven of pride was working in it all, and that I was dishonoring my precious Savior by not being willing to come to Him, empty, needy, naked, and filthy too! But how plainly I see it now, and therefore do I write freely in love to you, thinking you are tainted with the same malady. The Lord hasten the day of power in your soul, when you shall look unto Him and be lightened, and your face no longer be ashamed. "And in that day thou shalt say…, Behold, God is my salvation; I will trust, and not be afraid: for the LORD JEHOVAH is my strength and my song; he also is become my salvation. Therefore with joy shall ye draw water out of the wells of salvation."

☙ RUTH BRYAN

Pleasure in Dependence

*Trust in the LORD with all thine heart; and
lean not unto thine own understanding. In all thy ways
acknowledge him, and he shall direct thy paths. Be not wise
in thine own eyes: fear the LORD, and depart from evil.*

—PROVERBS 3:5–7

I perceive that one design of my long and painful disorder is to bring my spirit not only to submit, but to rest itself in that against which it naturally rises up with a mighty resistance. Nothing has ever been so dreadful, so bitter to my soul, as a state of dependence. I have said, "Ever so little, if it be but in my own keeping; if I may but have it without a suppliant's cry."

I find, by attention to what is passing within, that this old evil principle only gives way, inch by inch, disputing and struggling to the last. If at one time it seems more wounded than at another, it presently, upon some sudden occasion, rises up again like a lion.

O Lord, I am oppressed; undertake for me! Destroy this evil principle of pride and unbelief! Not only do Thou preserve me from repining, because Thou ordainest that I should be (as thousands of Thy children have been before) dependent upon Thee for daily bread, but make me pleased, not only to receive it but to ask it from such hands as are disposed or able to send it me! Enable me to take pleasure in dependence—to say from the bottom of my heart that since Thou doth appoint it, it is the thing I choose. I am ready to hope I do feel some change for the better in this respect. But when my love of independence is utterly destroyed, then indeed I shall have a strong evidence that my affliction has been greatly blessed to my soul.

☙ SARAH HAWKES

The Royal Wine

Thy love is better than wine.
—SONG OF SOLOMON 1:2

Wine is the symbol of earthly joy, and who that has had but one sip of the love of Christ does not know the royal wine, this true wine of the kingdom, to be better than the best joy that the world can give! How much more, then, when deeper and fuller draughts are the daily portion as we follow on to know the love that passes knowledge! It is the privilege not of a favored few, but of all saints, to comprehend something of what is incomprehensible. For whom is this love? Oh how glad we are that it is not for the worthy and the faithful, so that we must be shut out, but for His own, though the chief of sinners! It is the love of the Lord toward the children of Israel, who look to other gods and love flagons of wine. Has it been so with us, that we have been looking away from Jesus to heart-idols and other lords, and loving some earthly flagons of wine—other love, other pleasures, other joys, other things that are not Jesus Christ's? Then only think of the love of the Lord toward us! Well may we say, "Thy love to me was wonderful" and own it to be better than wine, above my chief joy. He proved His love to you and me to be strong as death, and when all God's waves and billows went over Him, the many waters could not quench it.

In His love and in His pity, He redeemed us; in the same love He bears us and carries us all the day long. He "loveth at all times," and that includes this present moment. Now, while your eye is on this page, His eye of love is looking on you, and the folds of His banner of love are overshadowing you. Is there even a feeble pulse of love to Him? He meets it with, "I love them that love me. I will love him, and will manifest myself to him." And so surely as the bride says, "Thy love is better than wine," so surely does the heavenly Bridegroom respond with incomprehensible condescension: "How fair is thy love, my sister, my spouse! How much better is thy love than wine." May this love of Christ constrain us to live unto Him.

❧ FRANCES RIDLEY HAVERGAL

The Pruning Knife

Take away the dross from the silver, and there
shall come forth a vessel for the finer.
—PROVERBS 25:4

The Lord is still trying your faith, and faith must have its perfect work, for it is the grace that most honors the Giver of every good. Oh, the pruning knife! It must be employed, and the earth loosened, and the dead foliage removed, that the roots might strike deeper and the young twigs might have room to shoot forth, and that the Lord might come into His garden and eat His pleasant fruits.

Heaven, dear friend, is peopling fast, and the Lord is calling home His hidden ones. Let us never be satisfied to have this blessed interest obscured. If at any time a cloud should gather over our mind, and unbelief or sin unconfessed come between God and our soul, let us go at once and humble ourselves at His footstool, whose precious blood cleanses from all sin. Let us aim to walk in this holy interaction with a holy Lord God; so shall we keep our Christian evidences bright and pass on our way rejoicing. Prayer—prayer—is the breath of the living soul made alive by the Holy Spirit, and by the same Spirit kept alive.

How great is the mystery of experimental godliness! These things are hid from the worldly wise but are revealed unto babes. I can truly say, advanced in years as I am, I desire to enter into these mysteries of Christ's kingdom more and more in the spirit of a little child—living, hanging upon Him as such. The believer, as he advances in the divine life, sees less and less to boast of, and more and more to humble him.

⇢ MARY WINSLOW

Gospel Wine to Cheer the Warrior

Not by might, nor by power, but by my
spirit, saith the LORD of hosts.

—ZECHARIAH 4:6

It seems to have been the divine will that the children of Israel should learn war, and that those who saw it not at the entering into Canaan should be taught it by the nations that were left unsubdued. Of course these nations would be often striving to invade the possessions and lessen the power of this favored people. Then they must fight for their privileges, and from the records of their battles we plainly see how, while trusting simply in the Lord, a mere handful of them overcame thousands of their foes. Not their own sword or their own bow, but His right hand and His holy arm brought them the victory. Doubtless all was typical of the experience of the spiritual Israel. They have nations of lusts and evils within, headed by that great and fearful captain Unbelief, and nations of snares, allurements, trials, and cares without, while Satan is the great commander of the whole. Yet has he only a limited power, being himself under the control of the mighty Captain of salvation, who always binds him in his attacks with this restriction: "Hitherto shalt thou come, but no further." However, as the spiritual as well as the literal Israel must learn war, you need not wonder that the armies of the aliens often beset you and that the men of your own house rise up against you.

May you, by grace, follow the faith of these ancient worthies, "considering the end of their conversation: Jesus Christ, the same yesterday, and to-day, and for ever." Be in nothing terrified by your adversaries, since your Redeemer is mighty; the Lord of Hosts is His name. What blessed promises are made to the overcomers! But how could these promises belong to us if we knew nothing of foes and fighting? These foes are overcome by the blood of the Lamb, "not by might, nor by power, but by my Spirit, saith the Lord of Hosts."

❧ RUTH BRYAN

The Well in the Wilderness

It shall not seem hard unto thee.
—DEUTERONOMY 15:18

The particular trial, through which I may now be passing, is the very "it" which must not seem hard to me. God's bow is never drawn at a venture; He makes no mistakes, either in telling the number of the stars or in meting out to me the griefs which shall teach me to glorify Him. And, dear reader, if you would find comfort from the words which so comforted me, you must look upon your present trouble, whatever it may be, and say, "Lord, this shall not seem hard to me, for I have received so much bounty and blessing from Thee, I have known so much of Thy pity and pardoning love, that I dare not mistrust Thee or question for a moment the divine wisdom of Thy dealings with me." Ah! Our eyes are so dimmed by earth's fogs and shadows that we cannot see clearly enough to distinguish good from evil, and if left to ourselves, might embrace a curse rather than a blessing. Poor, purblind mortals that we are, it is well for us that our Master should choose our trials for us, even though to our imperfect vision He seems sometimes to have appointed a hard thing.

Yes, it is in absolute and loving surrender to the will of the Lord that the secret of true rest and peace is found. This is the alchemy that turns earth's sorrows into heaven's blessings; here is the antidote to every sting, the cure-all of each care, the unfailing remedy for all disquietude. This comfort cannot apply to troubles which we make for ourselves and which we sometimes glorify into spiritual hardships when they are really selfish sins. These are not God's will for us, but our own perverse way, and they bring nothing better than bitterness and tears. But a God-given burden or sorrow, carried out into the sunshine of His love and laid at His blessed feet, immediately loses all its "hardness" and is transformed into a blessing, for which our soul praises the Lord with tender thanksgiving.

∂ SUSANNAH SPURGEON

Total Trust

Therefore take no thought, saying, What shall we eat?
or, What shall we drink? or, Wherewithal shall we be clothed?
(For after all these things do the Gentiles seek:) for your heavenly
Father knoweth that ye have need of all these things.

—MATTHEW 6:31–32

It is a grief and trouble to me that, after having experienced such a trial so calculated to detach me from this world, I find I have an earthly heart still. I want now to live, feeling as Abraham did when he went out, not knowing whither he went—to be seeking daily grace and daily bread, taking no anxious thought for the morrow.

I have been lamenting before God today, my great guilt in this respect, and feel somewhat relieved. I have been giving myself again entirely to Him, desiring to trust in Him with a simple dependence; to stand ready to go where He shall appoint; to do and to be just what He pleases; to find my future pleasure in doing, with a holy courage and humility and energy, the work which He shall give me to do.

How pleasant will even my widowed life be if I can thus live! No matter where we are or what we are—so long as we can find our happiness in glorifying God and in doing and suffering His will. Oh, blessed, happy life! This was the happiness of the apostles and primitive Christians, who suffered the loss of all things temporal; were persecuted, afflicted, tormented, and slain; and yet sang the song of victory, through Jesus Christ their Lord, on the rack and in the flames. This is the very essence of heavenly felicity. With a capacity to enjoy this happiness, we might well say with the psalmist, "Though the earth be removed, though the mountains be carried into the midst of the sea, we will not fear." Oh my God! I am fully satisfied that here is the only quiet resting place. Help me, oh, help me, thus to stay myself only on Thee! Then shall I be happy.

 SUSAN HUNTINGTON

The Triumphant Security of God's People

Those that thou gavest me I have kept.
—JOHN 17:12

Where are you? On the battlefield, or on the watchtower, or compassed about with songs of deliverance? As we are not our own, we have no right of choice how we shall be led or by what means instructed. "He led them about, he instructed him, he kept him as the apple of his eye"; "kept" by the power of God through faith unto salvation, and "kept" in most wonderful cases and places; "kept" in the flood and in the flame; "kept" in the light and in the dark; "kept" in plenty and in poverty; "kept" in the seven-times heated furnace and in the den of lions; and "kept" safely through all; "kept" also when the Divine Keeper seems to give advantage to our enemies. "Thou broughtest us into the net; thou laidst affliction upon our loins. Thou hast caused men to ride over our heads; we went through fire and through water: but thou broughtest us out into a wealthy place."

Oh! This is precious leading and keeping, to bring us out from self and creatures into Christ our wealthy place, for in Him we shall be safe from fear of evil, shall be satisfied in the days of famine, and shall not be afraid in the year of drought. Abiding in Him, all the schemes of our foes shall be disappointed.

Oh, my dear, happy are they that have the God of Jacob for their refuge, and whose hope the Lord is. "He is the Rock; His work is perfect." "Let the inhabitants of the rock sing; let them shout from the top of the mountains," for there is both protection and supply. "His place of defense shall be the munitions of rocks; bread shall be given him; his waters shall be sure"—sure indeed, for they drink of that spiritual rock which follows them, which rock is Christ. "Thou wilt keep him in perfect peace whose mind is stayed on thee, because he hath trusteth in thee."

→ RUTH BRYAN

Words of Love

Return unto me, and I will return unto
you, saith the LORD of hosts.

—MALACHI 3:7

You cannot resolve upon a happier life than the life of a Christian. This is the end for which we were created; consequently, this alone can make us happy. Are not all the pursuits which engage our attention, except religion and those which are consistent with it, vanity?

Do we not follow a phantom, which shines but to deceive, which blazes but to ensnare us? We are all in pursuit of happiness. "Who will show us any good?" is the universal question. And how can it be better answered than by pointing to that religion which heals every wound—than by directing the inquirer to the balm in Gilead and the Great Physician there? Real happiness cannot exist in an unrenewed heart. We have lost our felicity by renouncing the God who is the glorious fountain of everlasting consolation. Yet He has said, "Return unto me, and I will return unto you." Self-deceived mortals! How can we slight the words of love which flow from the Judge of all the earth toward His offending, guilty creatures?

Christianity alone can make us happy. The cold apathy and insensibility, or suppression of feeling, that was inculcated by some of the ancient philosophers, might dignify a heathen. But their erroneous system of theology was not capable of affording to its disciples that holy peace and heavenly pleasure which are the blessed effect of real conversion to the religion of Jesus. His voice alone can speak peace to a troubled spirit. "Thou hast destroyed thyself; but in me is thy help." "Return ye backsliding children, and I will heal your backslidings." "Ho, every one that thirsteth, come ye to the waters; and he that hath no money, come ye, buy and eat; yea, come buy wine and milk, without money and without price." Blessed be our God that He has not left us without hope!

≈ SUSAN HUNTINGTON

A Call to Repentance

If my people, which are called by my name, shall humble
themselves, and pray, and seek my face, and turn from their
wicked ways; then will I hear from heaven, and will
forgive their sin, and will heal their land.

—2 CHRONICLES 7:14

Let us most earnestly seek for the Spirit of grace and of supplications to be poured down upon us, that we may look afresh
upon Him whom we have pierced, and mourn, and be in bitterness
for Him and for all that we have done against Him by our carnal
walk, even since we were spiritual people. Let us mourn and be
deeply humbled before the Lord for our own sins and for the sins
of our brethren. For the sins of persons, families, and churches. For
the sins of church and state, court and country, all men of high and
low degree.

At such a time as this, when iniquity runs down our streets
like a mighty torrent and sweeps down all before it, as it were: God
expects that His own people should mourn for the dishonor cast
upon His great name and the injury done to His glorious cause in
the earth. And in particular, He expects that every one of His children should mourn for his own part in the general guilt for what
he himself has done to advance iniquity, instead of attending to
his duty, with might and main, to stop the tide of it. Oh my dear
brethren, let us begin in good earnest to be Christians indeed—to
answer the name. Let us labor in the whole of our carriage to behave
so, that it may appear we are such that are anointed with the Holy
Ghost, that we are under the same Holy Spirit, in our measure, that
was immeasurably poured out upon Christ, our glorious head. Oh
what an incongruous thing it is for a Christian to be unlike Christ,
unlike Him in faith, love, zeal, humility, patience, meekness, gentleness, and goodness toward all! And if we would be like Christ, let
us make this our main business, which is the great end of our calling, "to show the virtues, the praises of him who hath called us out
of darkness into his marvelous light."

&❧ ANNE DUTTON

A Beautiful Bride

Thou art all fair, my love.
—SONG OF SOLOMON 4:7

I hear some timid, trembling believer say, "Such a text can have nothing to do with me. I am the very opposite of all that is fair and spotless. The eyes of my soul have seen hideous sights, within which I can never forget, and I loathe myself and my sin so much that, though I believe God has forgiven me for Christ's sake, I feel it impossible to take those precious words as addressed to one so erring and imperfect."

Yet, trembling soul, I would bid you take courage and look up! Christ's love for His church is marvelously set forth in this Song of Songs, and if you are a believer in Him, you must be part of that church—as much His bride and spouse as the greatest saint or most renowned disciple. Come, then, timid one, fear not to grasp the truth now put before you; delay not to rejoice in the blessed fact that you are indeed dear to the Lord. And when He says, "Thou art all fair, my love," do not contradict Him by lamenting your blackness, but rather, adoringly bow before Him in wonder at the miracle His love has wrought in you. It ill becomes the bride of Christ to ignore His comeliness which He has put upon her and go about bemoaning the scars and blemishes which His great love overlooks and forgets.

It is quite true that, in themselves, believers are sorrowfully imperfect and sinful, but if the Lord Jesus, in His marvelous mercy, unrobes Himself to cover over their unrighteousness, they may well be content to be thus made "fair" in His sight. Do you ask, "Why should He do this?" Look at the succeeding words, "my love." We cannot comprehend the mystery and sublimity of divine love, but it is the sole and all-sufficient reason for the dear Lord's estimate of us. And when He uses such endearing language, our hearts melt and are ravished by His condescension.

❧ SUSANNAH SPURGEON

Suffering as a Christian

Choosing rather to suffer affliction.
—HEBREWS 11:25

Whenever you are afflicted in body and meet with unkindness from creatures, care not much of it, but haste away by faith to Christ, whose open heart and arms are ready to embrace you, who is afflicted with you in all your afflictions, as by love-sympathy He makes them His own. If you can't find a drop of pity flow in the creature-stream, haste away to the full fountain, the immense ocean of all compassion, the bowels of God in Christ. And there bathe your soul in new and ever-springing pleasures, and rest at ease when in the midst of pain.

And as to your afflictions of mind, when thwarted about serious things and they are made a jest of: look unto Jesus, the meek and lowly Jesus, who endured such contradictions of sinners against Himself, lest you be weary and faint in your mind. The followers of Christ, who was meek and lowly in heart and has bid us learn of Him, should be likeminded. And He, though He were a son, learned obedience by the things which He suffered. Labor to do likewise and to show forth the same graces in your measure, under your sufferings, which conspicuously shone in Christ under His.

And think it not strange, if you seek Jesus and desire to follow Him, that you meet with opposition from nearest relatives. In no wise let the opposition you meet with deter you from a meek and humble testimony for Christ and His things. For you know the Lord of Christians has said, "Whosoever therefore shall confess me before men, him will I confess also before my Father which is in heaven. But whosoever shall deny me before men, him will I also deny before my Father which is in heaven." If you suffer as a Christian, be not troubled, but rather rejoice that you are made partaker of the sufferings of Christ, that when His glory shall be revealed, you also may be glad with exceeding joy; that having suffered with Christ, you may be glorified together.

☙ ANNE DUTTON

The Prayers of the Saints

And take the helmet of salvation, and the sword of the Spirit,
which is the word of God: praying always with all prayer and
supplication in the Spirit, and watching thereunto with
all perseverance and supplication for all saints.

—EPHESIANS 6:17–18

What, my dear friend, shall be the subject of our letters? Shall the common occurrences of life and the flattering compliments of the polite world fill our papers, or that religion, which is the glory of the bright intelligences of heaven and the consolations of trembling believers on earth? I think I can confidently affirm that the latter will be your choice.

It is a duty incumbent on the children of God to reprove, encourage, and animate each other on their journey to the upper world. Every Christian has difficulties to overcome, temptations to encounter, and warfare to accomplish which the world is a stranger to. If pilgrims in the same country can in the least console each other and sweeten the thorny journey by familiar interaction, they ought not to neglect it.

Our home is professedly in heaven; we have temptations, difficulties, trials, and doubts which, if we are believers, are in unison. I feel that I need the prayers and the advice of all the followers of the Lamb. "I have an evil heart of unbelief," prone to "depart from the living God." If the Friend of sinners will lend a listening ear to our feeble cries, we shall be strengthened and blessed. May you enjoy the influences of the Holy Spirit in life, consolation in death, and a seat in the mansions of blessedness.

❧ HARRIET NEWELL

The Blessed House of God

I was glad when they said unto me,
Let us go into the house of the LORD.
—PSALM 122:1

The house of the Lord—whither the tribes go up, the tribes of the Lord unto the testimony of Israel, to give thanks unto the name of the Lord, to seek His face, to learn His will, to taste His love, to behold His glory, to enjoy God as their own God and reconciled Father.

Lord, let my heart be warmed more toward Thy house! I have sought and found Thee in Thy sanctuary, read Thy providences, and been taught Thy will. I have tasted Thy love and beheld Thy glory. I have enjoyed Thy presence as my own reconciled Father in Christ Jesus. I have been satisfied with Thy goodness, as with marrow and fatness, and yet how cold and languid at times, how little desire to return, how small my expectations, how wandering my imagination! Lord, I should blush and be ashamed were a fellow mortal to see my heart at times. After all I have heard, seen, tasted, and handled of the word of life, I am still of myself an empty vessel.

The house of God—the owner, the builder, and maker is God, and it is His peculiar treasure. Christ is the foundation and chief cornerstone, and His house are we, built upon Him, cemented together, a spiritual building; the foundation cannot fail, the cornerstone can never give way; neither can we fall to pieces or be separated from Him.

The house of God—Jerusalem, Zion, the rest of God, where He delights to dwell, where He will forever stay; the house of God, the church, yea the body of Christ: Christ is the head, His people the church, His members whose life is in Him and derived from Him. And because He lives, we shall live also. Lord, enlarge my understanding to comprehend more and more of "the height and depth, length and breadth of the love of Christ, which passeth all understanding."

❧ ISABELLA GRAHAM

Fear Not to Follow the Lamb

In thee, O LORD, do I put my trust.
—PSALM 31:1

May the Lord strengthen your faith so that you may be reconciled to all His ways and dealings. When fully reconciled, we can walk lovingly with Him, even while He walks contrary to our flesh and its idols. Oh to follow Him fully, as Joshua and Caleb did, who held fast to His faithfulness amid all the caviling and improbabilities of flesh and blood, and even though the people talked of stoning them. They were quite sensible of their own weakness and the strength of their enemies, but what of all this? Faith did not look to the creature arms of might, but stood on firmer ground. "If the Lord delight in us, then he will bring us into this land, and give it us; a land which floweth with milk and honey."

Surely Christ is our good land, and though unbelief and Satan rage and carnal reason cavil, the children of promise shall possess their possessions. "I am thine inheritance," says the Lord. In Him all things are ours, not to glory in or rest in but to seek the things of Christ in them, and His glory by them. Oh, this precious grace of faith, may the Lord nourish and cherish it. Yea, faith is strong in old age to claim the fulfillment of the promise; and, having seen many wars and wonders of the Lord, it puts in the plea for every inch of ground for which the word has gone forth.

Oh, for more Joshuas and Calebs! For truly "no good thing will he withhold from them that walk uprightly," which is to walk in Him, not in the flesh. His yoke is easy, and His burden light; it is the endeavor to evade it which is the misery. His cross is lined with love, however rugged and unsightly the outside may appear to carnal reason. Praise Him, O my soul, and praise Him, O ye cross-bearing companions. See what your forerunner did. He, bearing His cross, went forth. Fear not to follow the Lamb, wherever and however He leads. In each footprint He has left a blessing. "The Lord is with you while ye be with him," and if He be for us we need not fear what flesh can do unto us.

☙ RUTH BRYAN

Unsteady Seasons

*Why art thou cast down, O my soul? and why art
thou disquieted in me? hope thou in God.*

—PSALM 42:5

What ails you? Oh, what a God of mercy is our God! Often has He hailed me in some such language: "What ails you? Why is your countenance sad? Am I not better to you than ten friends?" Then has He turned my heart to Him, made me feel myself close to Him; He has suffered me to lean on His bosom, hang on His arm, and lisp out, "Abba." At such blessed moments I have thought the whole earth but one point, and from that to heaven but one step, and the time between but as one moment; and my company here sufficient to satisfy me by the way. At such blessed moments I felt perfect, full, entire satisfaction with all that God is, all that He does, and could trust Him fully with all my concerns—spiritual, temporal, and eternal.

Oh, what a God of patience and longsuffering! And Oh, how rich that well-ordered covenant that provides suitable grace for all these unsteady seasons! It is my greatest consolation that the Lord knows it all. There are times when I cannot see Him, but every moment He sees me. I should fall off and leave Him, but He holds me fast and never leaves me. Oh, blessed plan, where God secures us in safety, even from ourselves! We have not only destroyed ourselves, and He has been our help, but we are ever destroying ourselves, and still He renews this help.

Well, what shall we say? Father, glorify Thy name, and let us lie in Thy hand as clay in the potter's, till Thou finish Thy workmanship and fit us vessels of mercy, to be filled with happiness, when Thou shalt have done Thy good pleasure in us and by us, in this world, through the grace that is in Christ Jesus.

ॐ ISABELLA GRAHAM

What Think Ye of Christ?

What think ye of Christ?
—MATTHEW 22:42

This is a question which concerns all of us. There is not a man or woman upon earth to whom it is not of importance to know about the Lord Jesus Christ. I would again ask the question—"What think ye of Christ?"—and try to show what we ought to think of Him.

And first, as to His divinity. What think ye of Christ? Do we indeed know that He is the almighty God, the Second Person of the Trinity, equal to the Father, though the well-beloved Son of the Father?

What think ye of Christ touching His human nature? Do we believe in Him as "perfect God and perfect man"? As truly as we believe Him to be the mighty God, so do we believe Him to be the compassionate Son of Man?

What think ye of Christ Jesus as your Savior? Are you fully persuaded that beside Him there is no Savior; that He came to save His people from their sins; that in His blood and righteousness is all your hope?

What think ye of Christ, the anointed of God, as prophet, priest, and king? Do you take Him as your divine prophet or teacher, beseeching Him to make known, by His Spirit, unto you all the will of God? In Christ are hid "treasures of wisdom and knowledge." Do you ask Him to impart them unto you?

Has the Holy Spirit indeed shown you the preciousness of Christ and led you to see that you can only be saved through Him? It is to those who believe that Christ is precious, the "chiefest among ten thousand." Do you "believe on the Lord Jesus Christ"?

⮞ ELIZABETH JULIA HASELL

Jesus the Savior

For unto you is born this day in the city of David
a Saviour, which is Christ the Lord.

—LUKE 2:11

Praise! The well of Bethlehem opened.

A debtor to mercy alone,
Of covenant mercy I sing.

Through a covenant Savior, yes, through His very heart and veins so precious, which were pierced that there might be an outflow of the living stream to the covenant family and that we might know how deep was His love, which thought not such a cost too much for His bride, the church. And am I a covenant child? Am I one of that happy number? Can such a vile worm be of the royal family? Even so: all praise to my covenant God.

How I am thinking of the shepherds and the angel's message: "Unto you is born this day in the city of David a Savior, which is Christ" Jehovah. And now we can take up the song in nearer interest, "Unto us a child is born; unto us a Son is given." Oh, it is "an unspeakable gift," a precious gift. I feel it to be so, and long ardently that all my loved ones might share my full cup of joy and gladness. Precious, precious Jesus, visit them all, and then they will, they must, sing unto Thee and will not condemn me for being too happy in Thee. O Father, do pour out Thy Spirit more copiously upon Thy redeemed, to raise them more above flesh and sense, that they may sit in heavenly places. Oh, that they sought it more, for Thou art a liberal giver. "Yet for all these things will I be inquired of by the house of Israel," saith the Lord. That was a blissful day when, in the stable, the Lord of glory came forth in the prepared body—an Infant of days, and yet the Father of eternity. Profound mystery, and in His praise would join that most wonderful concert, when a multitude of the heavenly host sang His entrance into the church by the door; for He was the Good Shepherd.

❧ RUTH BRYAN

Running the Christian Race

Know ye not that they which run in a race run all, but one receiveth the prize? So run, that ye may obtain.

—1 CORINTHIANS 9:24

My hope abides that you have really and truly set out on your journey heavenward. May the Lord speed you on your way! May He keep you, moment by moment, looking unto Him who is your life! May you be led to see unceasingly that this world is not worthy of one anxious thought. It is all passing away, and we shall soon stand before the great white throne. As you have commenced your journey, so go forward. Do not rest where you are. We are on a racecourse. The point from which we start is conversion; the goal to which we run is heaven; the prize for which we contend is a crown of glory, which the righteous Judge will give us at that great day.

If, dear friend, you have started in this race, "so run, that you may obtain." How few lay these great things to heart! The world and its trifles so engross the thoughts that God, Christ, and eternity, with our vast responsibility, are shut out of sight; and Satan, the great foe of mankind, gains his point unless sovereign grace interferes and opens the blind eye to see the danger, and Jesus the refuge. Oh, what a mercy of mercies to know all this and to act upon it!

Oh, it is with a holy, heart-searching God that we have to do. And the soul is of more value than ten million worlds. "What shall it profit a man if he gain the whole world and lose his own soul?" These are solemn, awful truths, but only by a few are they laid to heart. May the Lord enable you to bring your heart to Him, who alone can heal it thoroughly; and may He lead you in the right way.

&» MARY WINSLOW

Time Flies

He that saith, I know him, and
keepeth not his commandments, is a liar,
and the truth is not in him.

—1 JOHN 2:4

How can we love God if we are careless of offending Him? How can we, for a moment, think we love Him if we allow ourselves in anything He hates? "This is the love of God, that we keep His commandments. He that saith, I know him, and keepeth not his commandments, is a liar, and the truth is not in him." My dear sisters, can we, with these passages of Scripture before us, appeal to our master and future judge, as Peter did, and say, "Lord, Thou knowest all things; thou knowest that I love thee"? If so, then are we the children of God, heirs of God and joint heirs with Christ; then are we preparing for heaven; then our God will lead us in a right way to the city of habitation. He will smooth the path of life or give us strength to surmount every difficulty on the way, accompanying every cross with His blessing, and ultimately bring us to the heavenly Jerusalem, the inner temple of His glory, to the full and endless enjoyment of Himself in heaven.

Is it so, my beloved sisters? Dust and ashes, pollution and guilt as we are—does the infinite Jehovah allow us to indulge such a hope as this? And can we live in sin? Can we live without panting after grace to glorify Him much, from whom we have received all? Can we go on day after day and month after month, doing nothing for His glory, for His cause, for His people? Time flies. We are drawing near to eternity. Our friends are, in rapid succession, called away. Our turn must soon come. What are we doing that evinces our hope to be that which makes not ashamed and will receive the Master's gracious reward? These are inquiries in which we are all deeply concerned. Alas! What bitter self-reproaches do they cause me to feel. Oh for grace to have our lamps trimmed and burning, and to be waiting for the coming of our Lord.

&. SUSAN HUNTINGTON

The Book of Life

And there shall in no wise enter into it any thing that defileth,
neither whatsoever worketh abomination, or maketh a lie:
but they which are written in the Lamb's book of life.

—REVELATION 21:27

The book in heaven I would speak of today is the Book of Life, that book in which are inscribed the names of "all the elect people of God," from the earliest till the latest time. Known to God are all the names of the saved: "The Lord knoweth them that are his." How blessed are they who are "written among the living in Jerusalem," even in the heavenly Jerusalem! How terrible to be blotted out of the Book of Life! This shall not be the end of any real believer: "I will not blot out his name out of the book of life; but I will confess his name before my Father and before his angels." It is of holy women and others of his fellow laborers that Paul writes, "whose names are in the book of life."

Those who are in the Lamb's Book of Life are not only called, but chosen—chosen of God in Christ, "before the foundation of the world." How weighty is it for each of us to inquire, "Is my name in that important book? I cannot expect an angel to come from heaven to tell me this; I can only search the Bible to find who the people are whom God undertakes to save. I find they are devout believers in His Son, becoming gradually sanctified by His Spirit. To such God promises salvation. Am I then one of them?"

Two sorts of people are described in the Bible—those who will be at Christ's right hand and those on His left. Men madly act as if there were a middle class, so to speak, between the two. No such class of persons is recognized by God. Let us earnestly pray that our names may never be blotted out of that solemn and holy record. May we belong to Christ now, and all the days of our life, being kept by Him in the midst of an evil world! Then, at the last day, He will not be ashamed to own us before men and angels and before the Lord God Almighty, His Father and our Father.

❧ ELIZABETH JULIA HASELL

Forever and Ever

And as it is appointed unto men once to die,
but after this the judgment.
—HEBREWS 9:27

There is no medium state. With every soul of man it must be joy inconceivable or woe unutterable, and whichever of these be our portion, it will be forever and ever and ever. There will be no fear of the happiness ending and no hope of the suffering terminating or even abating, for in that darksome prison, never, never will be heard those precious words, "It is finished!" Sin will never be made an end of, and therefore the consequences of sin can never cease; but while eternal ages roll, it will be "wrath to come," "wrath to come."

I have eternity in near prospect, and solemnly feel it will profit a man nothing if he should gain the whole world and lose his own soul. My heart says with Moses, "Oh that they were wise, that they understood this, that they would consider their latter end." The fact is, it will come whether it is considered or not. For the Scriptures say, "It is appointed unto men once to die: but after this the judgment," and Jesus has declared of those that die in their sins, "Whither I go ye cannot come"; "Cast ye the unprofitable servant into outer darkness: there shall be weeping and gnashing of teeth."

How is it that while under the sentence of death and with the wrath of God already on us, we can be merry and sportive and care for none of these things? It is because we are not only "shapen in iniquity and conceived in sin," but "we are dead in trespasses and sins"; that is, spiritually dead, so that we cannot know God or love Him or feel our real state before Him. May you, by the Spirit, be wounded under a sense of sin. Then will you, with like earnestness, seek to be led to Jesus the Savior, for you must die, and oh, what will you do if you die without finding salvation?

❧ RUTH BRYAN

Readiness to Die

Prepare to meet thy God.
—AMOS 4:12

Truly we live in a dying world. Death is stalking about, cutting off those appointed to die, and the eternal world is peopling both with the saints and sinners. Oh, to be quite sure where we are to go when summoned by the pale messenger to part with earth! May this be to you and to me the one thing: to be quite sure, to have no misgivings, to have the witness within us that we are in Christ, and Christ in us the hope of glory.

The one business of our short and uncertain life should be to secure the inheritance that is to last through the countless ages of a vast eternity. If we knew that we were going to a distant land to take up our abode for life and that an inheritance awaited us there, how anxious we should be to make all possible inquiry about the place, the manners of the people among whom we expected to dwell, and how little we should care about the place we were shortly to leave altogether.

And yet how contrary to this is the case with many who profess to be going to a better and eternal world! How seldom is it thought of, when in a moment we may be ushered into the immediate presence of Him who is to be our judge. Oh, let us strive and pray that we might be helped to give up our whole minds to the things that make for our everlasting peace: a close walk with Jesus—constant communion with Him who is our life and from whom we have even now, if we are truly His, eternal life.

☙ MARY WINSLOW

The Free Invitation

And the Spirit and the bride say, Come. And let him
that heareth say, Come. And let him that is athirst come. And
whosoever will, let him take the water of life freely.

—REVELATION 22:17

The Spirit often speaks directly to the human heart, without making use of any human instrument. The bride speaks with the Spirit by the word and sacraments. She speaks every time there is a service in church, every time God's Word is read and preached. She speaks by all the agencies used in faith to make Christ known to the ignorant and sinful. She speaks by her missionaries, sent to foreign lands in obedience to the Savior's precept. And what do "the Spirit and the bride" say to us in this beautiful passage? They say, "Come!" They give us a plain, simple invitation without one condition: it is an invitation free and unlimited. Then says the verse, "Let him that is athirst come,"—let everyone come who in any degree wishes to do so.

And at last we find, "Whosoever will, let him take the water of life freely," intending, as I cannot doubt, by these strong expressions, a full, free offer of salvation to whosoever will accept the same. This is the free invitation, this is the offer made by "the Spirit and the bride." God be thanked for such an unlimited offer, and may He give us grace to accept it! This offer is made to sinners. This salvation was purchased by the Lord Jesus Christ.

Reader, have "the Spirit and the bride" made their solemn appeal to you year after year, and have you turned a deaf ear to the invitation? How solemn is the thought that a free salvation is offered to all who will accept it, and that many will never close with the offer at all! Pray, I beseech you, for the Holy Spirit to make in you clean hearts and right spirits. Neglect not the salvation offered so graciously by God.

ᘏ ELIZABETH JULIA HASELL

Biographical
Sketches

Ruth Bryan (1805–1860)

An only child, Ruth Bryan was born in London; her father was a preacher of the gospel. Her biographer writes that her life was composed of "scenes of trial and deep soul-exercise," yet in her writings she displayed great trust in her Lord to provide all she needed. Ruth's parents taught her to discipline herself and to minimize pain and inconvenience. Although this training seemed difficult at the time, Ruth saw the Lord's hand in it, training her for the sevenfold-heated furnace of affliction through which she was called to pass.

Ruth had a close, loving relationship with her parents, especially her mother, whom she considered her dearest earthly friend. Her parents' deaths, the greatest trials she faced in a lifetime of struggles, brought her deep sorrow. She never married, but she was comforted by the words "Thy maker is thine husband." "It is so sweet," she said, "to think, who is to manage the house? Surely the Husband. Who is to pay the debts? The Husband. Who is to order everything? The Husband. And who has a right to remove anything from the house that has taken too much of the Bride's heart away from Himself? Why, surely the Husband. And that is what He has done in removing my dear mother, for since then, He Himself has been more precious to my soul. I see Him in it all, and that stops repining and murmurings."

For many years, Ruth experienced poor health, but she viewed this difficult providence as God's love toward her, bringing her into conformity with His will. She wrote, "I have been led to see this fever my Father's servant.... And it comes, but all is in covenant love." Only a few days before her death she testified, "I can never fully record Thy goodness and mercy." Through her letters, visits, and prayers, she spent her life serving others. Her letters have been compiled in *The Marvelous Riches of Savoring Christ* (Grand Rapids: Reformation Heritage Books, 2005), and her diary has been published as *Handfuls of Purpose: Gleanings from the Life of Ruth Bryan* (Grand Rapids: Reformation Heritage Books, 2006).

Anne Dutton (1692–1765)

Anne Williams was born in Northampton, England, into a loving, devout family. "From a child," she says, "I was under convictions at times; and my conscience was kept so tender, that it was easily touched with the guilt of sin, when I thought I had done any thing amiss." She did not come to faith until her teen years. Married sometime in her twenties, Anne was widowed after five years, and a year later she married Benjamin Dutton, a Baptist preacher.

At a time when women theologians were rare, Anne was unique for her theological insight and her personally edifying ministry of letter and hymn writing. She read extensively and had a great interest in Calvinism. She corresponded with many prominent religious leaders of her day, including John Wesley and George Whitefield. She became well known for her letters and spiritual writings, and her gravestone says that she wrote twenty-five volumes of letters and thirty-eight published works during her lifetime. In her letters, she encouraged her readers to guard their thoughts from sin and desire to do good works. Anne often wrote about God's sovereignty in salvation and other prominent Reformation doctrines.

After twenty years of marriage, Anne again became a widow when her husband was lost at sea on a return from America. After her husband's death, in the remaining two decades of her life, she devoted many hours each day to writing. In 1764 Anne became ill with a throat condition, possibly cancer, and could no longer eat. With impending death and many writing projects to complete, she spent sixteen to eighteen hours a day during the following months writing and finished eight volumes of unpublished letters.

Anne's writings impacted evangelical revival both in England and America. JoAnn Ford Watson has recently compiled many of her writings into six volumes titled *Selected Spiritual Writings of Anne Dutton: Eighteenth-Century, British-Baptist, Woman Theologian* (Macon, Ga.: Mercer University Press, 2003–2009).

Isabella Graham (1742–1814)

Isabella Marshall was born in Lanarkshire, Scotland, to godly parents. As long as she could remember, she "took delight in pouring out her soul to God." In the woods near her home was a small bush that became her favorite spot for retreat from troubles. One biographer writes, "Under this bush she believed she was enabled to devote herself to God, through faith in her Redeemer, before she had entered on her tenth year."

At age twenty she married John Graham, an army surgeon, and they moved to Canada. In 1774, John died, leaving her with three young children; the couple's fourth was soon to be born. She returned to Scotland to her family and began a girls' school. In 1789 she immigrated to America, where she opened a girls' school in New York.

One of the greatest trials of Isabella's life was her rebellious son, her youngest child. She shed many tears for the soul of this young man. He became a sailor and was shipwrecked three times, taken captive once, became very ill, and was ultimately lost at sea. In this affliction Isabella pleaded with the Lord to have covenant mercy on her son before he died. Shortly after her son's death, her oldest daughter died.

Despite her difficulties, Isabella devoted her life to serving others. She is remembered for her charitable work, which was inspired by her faith in God. In 1798 she became the director of a society to assist the widows and orphans of a yellow fever epidemic in New York. Not only did she seek to offer physical relief, but she brought spiritual comfort as well. Her daughter, Joanna Bethune, wrote *The Life of Mrs. Isabella Graham* and edited *The Unpublished Letters and Correspondence of Mrs. Isabella Graham*.

Elizabeth Julia Hasell (1830–1887)

Elizabeth Julia Hasell was born to a wealthy family near Penrith, England. She was educated at home and taught herself Latin, Greek, Spanish, and Portuguese. She was an expert in classic and contemporary literature and published numerous essays and reviews, but she also studied theology extensively and wrote a number of theological works.

Along with studying and writing, Elizabeth promoted education and the general welfare of the district in which she lived, often walking long distances across the hills to teach in village schools or deliver addresses. Her exertions probably hastened her death; in her desire to do good to a scattered population, she ignored fatigue and suffered frequent exposure to rain and cold.

She wrote a number of devotional works including *The Rock: And Other Short Lectures on Passages of Holy Scripture* (1867), from which the devotionals in this book are taken; *Short Family Prayers* (1884); and *Bible Partings* (1883). In *The Rock* she expressed her desire for her writing: "The following papers, on sacred subjects, were written for my own class of young women. May this volume be permitted to speak to the poor, to the sick, and to the sorrowful and those who have not much time for devout reading."

Frances Ridley Havergal (1836–1879)

Frances Havergal, well-known writer of hymns, devotional materials, and poetry, was born in Worcestershire, England, the youngest of six children. Her father was a minister, composer, and hymn writer. An exceptionally intelligent child, by the age of four she was able to read her Bible and was also beginning to write poetry. Although the young girl was filled with energy and charm, she often struggled with her sins and need for conversion, but she felt unable to talk to anyone. Her mother's unexpected death impressed upon her even more the need for conversion, and her struggles intensified, but it was not until she was fourteen that the Lord powerfully worked in her heart.

Frances mastered several languages and had training in linguistics and music; she was a pianist and singer. She also memorized the Psalms, Isaiah, and most of the New Testament. Frances never married, and her life was devoted to the service of the church. Being equipped with the Word of God and her desire for others' conversion, Frances spoke often to all she met, especially her peers. One time while she visited with ten young girls, her prayer for several of them (some saved and some not) had been that they would come to see Christ and His beauty; before she left the Lord answered her prayer. The night before her visit ended her joy was so great that she spent most of the night awake in prayer and thankfulness to the Lord and penned "Take My Life, and Let It Be," her most famous hymn.

Frances died in Wales at the age of forty-two of peritonitis. After suffering illness and intense pain, she folded her hands and exclaimed, "There, now it is all over! Blessed rest!" After gazing up for ten minutes, she tried to sing; after one high note, "He...," her voice failed, and she was taken home to be with her Savior.

Her writings include *The Ministry of Song; My King, or Daily Thoughts for the King's Children; Kept for the Master's Use;* and *Little Pillows, or Goodnight Thoughts for the Little Ones.*

Sarah Hawkes (1759–1832)

Sarah (Eden) Hawkes was born in Gloucestershire, England. Although she was raised in a pious home, her youth was marked by a love of "gaiety and amusement," her biographer says. Her marriage brought her worldly prosperity, but not happiness. When Sarah was about thirty, God touched her heart, and of that encounter she wrote: "I have literally 'roared with anguish of spirit' during the last two years, the arrows of the Almighty have stuck so fast in me. I have been mad with vanity and folly; but I trust, that, now the Lord is bringing me to a right mind."

Although Sarah was not well known outside her circle of acquaintances, her diary and letters have been food for many souls. Her correspondence demonstrates beautifully the communion of saints. She was filled with sympathy for others, and her own experience with affliction drew mourners to her in friendship. She wrote her letters in a most caring and affectionate manner, as one who had been taught by the Lord.

Sarah suffered from bodily afflictions for many years, and in her final years she suffered great pain and died a painful death from several diseases. Among her final recorded words were these: "I look back on my long life, and see much self-righteousness. I have thought better of myself than I ought to think, but now I think only of my Savior."

Sarah's diaries and letters were preserved by Catherine Cecil, a close friend, in *Memoirs of Mrs. Hawkes, Late of Islington; Including, Remarks in Conversation and Extracts from Sermons and Letters of the Late Rev. Richard Cecil.*

Susan Huntington (1791–1823)

Susan Mansfield was born in Killington, Connecticut, where her father was a pastor. From her childhood, Susan suffered from bodily afflictions and spent most of her time reading and cultivating her mind. She had a tender conscience, which was evidenced in her actions and speech, and she believed that between the ages of five and ten she experienced the beginnings of holiness in her heart.

In 1809, Susan married Joshua Huntington, pastor of the Old South Church in Boston. She felt inadequate to serve as a minister's wife but was comforted in knowing that this was the Lord's will for her and He would uphold her. She endured bodily afflictions and trials that tested her faith and deepened her love for and dependence on her Lord and Maker. In 1817 she lost both of her parents only months apart; in 1819 her husband died when she was eight months pregnant; and in the fall of 1821, two of her children died. In all these afflictions her suffering was intense, and she felt as if her feeble frame could not sustain her. But her merciful Father, who taught her that her strength was made perfect in weakness, upheld her, and she looked to Him as her only portion in life.

Although Susan died at the age of thirty-three of a painful illness, her impact was profound and far-reaching. Reflecting on her life she said, "My path has been rough; but I have not had one trial which my heavenly Father could, in faithfulness, have spared me. He has dealt with me only in loving-kindness and tender mercy. I have not a doubt now, I shall see hereafter, that all His dealings with me have been for my good."

Upon Susan's death, her husband's successor, Rev. Benjamin Wisner, wrote *Memoirs of the Late Mrs. Susan Huntington*, which includes many of Susan's letters to various acquaintances.

Harriet Newell (1793–1812)

Harriet Atwood was born in Haverhill, Massachusetts, to a family of nine children. Her parents were deeply pious and taught their children godliness, holiness, and virtue. Recognizing the brevity of life, Harriet's mother willingly consecrated her children to the Lord.

The Lord began to work in Harriet's heart when she was twelve. Even though she experienced a time of deep conviction, she wished that she was even more distressed about her sin. As her convictions were deep, her deliverance was great. After she publicly professed her faith in the Lord to free her from her sin at age sixteen, Harriet's desire was to see others, especially the heathen, find her Savior. In one of her journal entries she exclaimed, "O who would not sacrifice all that is dear in life to carry the glad tidings of salvation to heathen lands!"

Soon her desire would be fulfilled. In 1811, missionary Samuel Newell asked for her hand in marriage. Harriet struggled with her emotions, realizing that she would most likely be leaving her homeland and family to die among the heathen. She wrote, "Providence now gives me an opportunity to go myself to the heathen. Shall I refuse the offer? Shall I love the glittering toys of this dying world so well that I cannot relinquish them for God? Forbid it heaven! Yes, I will go. However weak and unqualified I am, there is an all-sufficient Savior ready to support me."

The Newells and another well-known couple, Adoniram and Ann Judson, the first American missionaries to serve under the American Foreign Mission Board, set sail for India in 1812. Expelled from Calcutta by the East India Company, the Newells journeyed to Mauritius. During the voyage, Harriet gave birth to a daughter who died five days later. About a month later, after the ship arrived in port, Harriet died of tuberculosis at the age of twenty—the first American to give her life for the cause of Christ as a missionary. *Memoirs of Mrs. Harriet Newell* contains some of her letters and journals.

Katherine Parr (1512–1548)

Katherine Parr was born in London, and her parents served in the court of King Henry VIII of England. Interestingly, Katherine was named after Katherine of Aragon, Henry's first wife, whom her mother served; she eventually became his sixth and last wife. She had been widowed twice when she married the king in 1543.

As queen, Katherine chose the motto "to be useful in all I do." She was known as a dutiful and kind person as well as a devoted scholar. She was well educated and fluent in French, Latin, and Italian, and she published two books. She was passionate about the theology of the Reformation, and her rooms became forums for theological debates over the ideas of this "new faith." She showed great courage in promoting the ideas of the Reformation in her writings and in urging her husband to accept them, which, at times, put her life at risk. She had enemies among members of Henry's court who despised her interest in the Reformed faith and plotted against her, nearly succeeding in having her executed for heresy at one point. By her cleverness, she persuaded the king to spare her. She influenced Henry and his children with Protestant ideas and gave her royal stepchildren instruction, guidance, and motherly love.

Katherine wrote *Prayers or Meditations* and *The Lamentation or Complaint of a Sinner*. She urged her readers to trust in Christ and put Him first, forsake sin, and find forgiveness. After Henry died in 1547, Katherine married Thomas Seymour. In August 1548, at age thirty-six, she died shortly after the birth of her only child.

Susannah Spurgeon (1832–1903)

Susannah Thompson was born to godly parents in London. She came to understand her need for salvation when she heard a sermon on Romans 10:8: "The word is nigh thee, even in thy mouth, and in thy heart." "From that service," she says, "I date the dawning of the true light in my soul.... That night witnessed my solemn resolution of entire surrender to Himself."

Susannah first met her husband, the great preacher C. H. Spurgeon, when he was preaching at a worship service. They were married in 1856. Susannah struggled with Charles's demanding ministerial duties, which often took him away from her. Her struggles culminated one evening at church when Charles was called away from her side and did not return. She ran home to her mother, who reminded her that "my chosen husband was no ordinary man, that his whole life was absolutely dedicated to God and His service, and that I must *never*, never hinder him by trying to put myself first in his heart." From that point on, Susannah faithfully supported her husband and labored alongside him.

After the birth of twin boys, Susannah suffered from physical ailments that often kept her bedridden. Yet she continued to serve faithfully, supporting her husband in his work and establishing the Book Fund, a ministry that supplied theological books to ministers who were too poor to buy them. After her husband died, she also gave a great deal of time to the ministry of writing and published a biography of her husband, as well as *Ten Years of My Life in the Service of the Book Fund, Ten Years After,* and several devotional books.

Anne Steele (1717–1778)

Anne Steele was born into a pastor's family in Broughton, Hampshire, in the English countryside. Her mother died when she was only three years old. Anne loved literature and began writing poetry when she was a child. She became an invalid at the age of nineteen when she severely injured her hip and suffered pain from the injury the rest of her life. At age twenty-one, Anne was engaged to be married, but her fiancé drowned the day before their wedding. His death was a severe trial for Anne, and she remained single the rest of her life.

Anne devoted herself to helping her father in his ministry and to writing. She wrote 144 hymns, 34 psalms in verse, and about 50 poems. She published two volumes of her poetry in 1760 under the pen name Theodosia. She resisted having her poetry published but finally agreed and gave the profits from her publications to charities. Eventually, a third volume of her poetry was published.

Anne spent the last nine years of her life bedridden and in much pain. When her departure from this world finally arrived, she exclaimed, "I know that my Redeemer liveth" and gently fell asleep in Jesus. Her writings are preserved in *Hymns by Anne Steele*; *Hymns, Psalms and Poems, by Anne Steele, with Memoir by John Sheppard*; *Miscellaneous Pieces, in Verse and Prose, by Theodosia*; and *The Works of Mrs. Anne Steele: Complete in Two Volumes*.

Mary Winslow (1774–1854)

An only child, Mary Forbes was born and raised in Bermuda and later moved to England with her husband, Thomas, an army lieutenant. When the family fell on hard times financially, she emigrated from England to New York in 1815 with her ten children; Thomas was to follow after they were settled. Shortly after arriving, Mary's only daughter, an infant, died; before the child could be buried, she received word that her husband had also died back in England.

For several months Mary was despondent, wrestling with a sense of loneliness and anxiety, feeling overwhelmed as a widow with nine sons dependent on her. After an especially trying day, she felt she was sinking beneath her weakness and insufficiency and could not sleep. She spent the night in prayer, and at dawn, she writes, "These words were spoken to my ear and heart, as if an audible voice had uttered them: 'I will be a Father to thy fatherless children.' I knew this voice, and could make no mistake. So powerful was it, I instantly replied aloud, 'O Lord, *be* Thou the Father of my fatherless, O my God!' Oh, the solemnity of that hour. I felt God was with me, and my soul was filled with joy and holy reverence."

Recognizing that her affliction was for her good, she confessed, "I think I have learned more of my dreadfully wicked heart, and the preciousness of Jesus during this trial than I ever learnt before." She believed that the Lord was promising to be her sons' Father for eternity and that she would see all her children in heaven.

Throughout her life, Mary depended solely on her Savior to meet her needs, and the Lord did bless her with the conversion of all her sons. Three became ministers, and Octavius, the most famous, became one of the most valued nonconformist ministers in nineteenth-century England. On her deathbed, in 1854, Mary's last words, repeated over and over, were, "I see Thee, I see Thee, I see Thee." Octavius Winslow compiled his mother's letters into a volume titled *Heaven Opened* (Grand Rapids: Reformation Heritage Books, 2001), and he wrote a memoir of her, drawn from her letters and journal entries, titled *Life in Jesus* (Grand Rapids: Reformation Heritage Books, 2013).

Scripture Index

64:1	June 1	12:36	February 23
		13:58	July 28
Jeremiah		14:28, 29	March 8
3:22	December 1	14:31	May 16 & 17
9:24	July 4	15:32	April 28 & 29
17:9, 10	March 3	16:18	June 21
32:17	January 5	16:24	March 25
49:11	September 29	17:20	June 17
50:5	September 24	18:11	July 9
		18:21, 22	June 14
Ezekiel		21:22	February 5
33:10	December 6	22:42	December 24
		25:32, 33	November 29
Hosea		25:34, 41	November 23
6:1	January 20	25:40	June 19
14:1	August 31	26:42	March 31
		28:20	January 19
Amos			
4:12	December 30	**Mark**	
		8:34	August 18
Jonah		8:36	February 20
3:9	November 13	9:41	October 15
Habakkuk		**Luke**	
2:1	September 21	2:11	December 25
2:4	November 3	3:5	March 6
		6:46	April 14
Micah		7:12	October 10
7:7	January 8	8:25	September 8
		9:23	April 13
Zechariah		10:19	February 10
4:6	December 12	10:42	November 24
9:12	February 16	12:19–21	April 17
		12:32	October 6
Malachi		17:4	May 27
3:7	December 16	17:5	June 6
3:16	October 2	17:17, 18	August 4
		18:13	March 9
		24:40	April 3
NEW TESTAMENT		19:10	February 25
Matthew		**John**	
6:10	June 11	1:16	July 12
6:31, 32	December 14	3:7	October 5
6:33, 34	August 17	3:16	October 22
7:7	July 27	4:4	February 17
7:17	October 1		
11:28	January 21		

(*John continued*)

4:29	June 12 & 13
5:24	August 9
5:39	January 3
5:40	May 31
6:17	August 29
6:37	January 20, July 24
6:65	July 1
8:12	November 1
10:4	February 21
14:18	May 7
14:26	July 19
14:27	May 11
15:2	May 9
15:9	October 14
15:11	January 11
15:12	April 23
16:13	March 14
16:13–15	June 2
16:23	January 23
16:27	September 22
16:32	March 28
17:12	December 15
17:21	March 16
19:30	April 1

Acts

3:19	April 25
27:25	May 8

Romans

1:16	June 15
5:7, 8	April 5
5:19	August 13
6:9–12	September 6
7:18	August 1
8:9	June 20
8:13	September 11
8:16	May 13
8:18	October 29
8:28	September 18
8:37	August 30
10:17	June 26
12:2	July 2
12:15a	August 2

12:16	November 21
13:14	November 15
14:23	October 8

1 Corinthians

2:9	July 26
3:11	July 10
3:18	October 27
7:29	January 2
8:11, 12	October 24
9:24	December 26
10:4	April 15
10:13	August 24
14:12	June 27
16:13	January 26

2 Corinthians

1:5	March 2
4:11	April 12
4:16	August 11
4:17	July 3
4:18	September 17
5:9	May 21
6:1, 2	November 5
7:1	June 10
9:8	February 26
10:5	July 30
12:9	August 8
13:5	June 9

Galatians

3:8	March 10
4:20	June 22
5:16	December 7
5:25	October 18
6:9	September 23

Ephesians

1:15,16	January 12
1:19	May 5
3:19	August 19
4:29	January 7
4:30	February 22
5:15	February 27
6:17, 18	December 20

Philippians

1:6	January 4
2:1, 2	February 14
2:8	March 30
2:12	October 13
4:1	November 9
4:11	June 3
4:13	March 23

Colossians

2:2,3	February 7
2:13, 14	November 8
3:5	May 20

1 Thessalonians

5:17	June 28

2 Thessalonians

3:5	October 30

1 Timothy

6:6	February 3
6:12	August 26

2 Timothy

2:12	September 2
2:21	December 3
3:5	January 16
3:16, 17	October 28
4:6–8	November 14
4:7	September 13

Hebrews

2:3	August 5
2:18	August 15
3:13, 14	February 9
4:7	March 22
4:16	March 27
6:17	February 8
7:25	August 27
9:26	September 28
9:27	December 29
10:10	October 17
10:23	August 10
11:4	August 22
11:34	May 12

12:1	October 31
12:11	January 24 & 25
11:25	December 19
13:3	July 8
13:5	May 29
13:15	November 25

James

1:5	February 19
1:12	December 4
4:7	December 5
4:11	June 16
5:16b	September 12
5:16a	February 12
5:8	October 25
5:11	September 16

1 Peter

1:5	May 30
1:7	January 29
1:22	June 25
2:7	June 7
2:21, 24	April 2
3:8	July 21
4:12	January 17
4:16	July 29
5:7	November 18
5:8	March 7
5:10	May 28

2 Peter

2:9	May 18
3:17	February 13
3:18	March 13
3:18	October 21

1 John

1:9	March 20 & 21
2:4	December 27
2:6	November 22
2:16	March 12
2:28	July 18
3:9	January 18
3:23	February 29
4:4	February 17
5:1	May 4